Using Illustrator 8

Using Illustrator 8

Suzanne Sayegh Thomas

I(T)P™ **Delmar Publishers**™

An International Thomson Publishing Company

Albany • Bonn • Boston • Cincinnati • Detroit • London • Madrid •
Melbourne • Mexico City • New York • Pacific Grove • Paris •
San Francisco • Singapore • Tokyo • Toronto • Washington

NOTICE TO THE READER

Cover design: Mick Brady

Delmar Staff:

Publisher, Alar Elken

Acquisitions Editor, Thomas Schin

Production Manager, Larry Main

Art/Design Coordinator, Nicole Reamer

Editorial Assistant, Fionnuala McAvey

COPYRIGHT © 1999

By Delmar Publishers

a division of International Thomson Publishing Inc. • The ITP logo is a trademark used under license
Printed in the United States of America

For more information, contact:
Delmar Publishers
3 Columbia Circle, Box 15015
Albany, New York 12212-5015

International Thomson Publishing Europe
Berkshire House 168-173 • High Holborn
London, WC1V7AA

International Thomson Editores
Campos Eliseos 385, Piso 7 • Col Polanco 11560 Mexico
D F Mexico

International Thomson Publishing GmbH
Königswinterer Strasse 418 • 53227
Bonn • Germany

Thomas Nelson Australia
102 Dodds Street • 221 Henderson Road
South Melbourne, 3205 • Victoria, Australia

International Thomson Publishing Asia
#05-10 Henderson Building • Singapore 0315

Nelson Canada
1120 Birchmont Road • Scarborough, Ontario
Canada M1K 5G4

International Thomson Publishing - Japan
Hirakawacho Kyowa Building, 3F
2-2-1 Hirakawacho
Chiyoda-ku, Tokyo 102 • Japan

4 5 6 7 8 9 10 XXX 00

Library of Congress Cataloging-in-Publication Data
Thomas, Suzanne Sayegh.
     Using Illustrator 8 / Suzanne Sayegh
          p.   cm.
     Includes index.
     ISBN: 0-7668-1226-X
     1. Computer graphics.   2. Adobe Illustrator (Computer file)
I.   Title
T385.T495395   1999   99–11920
006.6' 869--dc21   CIP

Printed in Canada

Dedication

For my first quilting instructor, Lynn Kough, who let me play with all her colors and showed me how to make quilts that dance. And for all the quilters at West End Fabrics, especially Alison, Barbara, Joy, Lynn, and Nancy, who taught me the steps to all the dances, while sharing their wisdom with me over scraps that became works of beauty and delight. ❋

Unit 2   Drawing Paths   21

Unit 3   Drawing with Basic Shapes   39

Unit 4   Painting Objects   51

Unit 5	**Painting Tools**	**69**

Unit 10 Tracing, Measuring, and Moving Objects   161

Unit 11   Transformation Tools   179

Unit 17   Automating with Actions   275

PREFACE

This book is written primarily for teachers, trainers, and students of Adobe Illustrator, especially those who are new to a PostScript drawing program. Although it is helpful to have some drawing expertise when working with Illustrator, you really don't need it to use this electronic art box effectively. So powerful are its tools and so intuitive its interface that, with practice, you will soon find yourself comfortable with this remarkable program. Once you become familiar with the Pen tool, for example, you can trace scanned images to generate any kind of illustration, as well as create complex artwork by modifying objects created with the basic shape tools.

With the release of version 8, Adobe has transformed Illustrator into an application capable of producing truly glorious images for print and Internet distribution. New tools and expanded versions of several original tools give artists and designers enormous control, while Illustrator's seamless interface with Adobe Photoshop makes it possible for the artist and designer to translate even their most visionary ideas into digital masterpieces.

This text covers all the major functions of Illustrator 8, which include those in version 7. When those commands differ from the earlier version, an explanation has been provided in the text and commands and tools specific to version 7 are listed in the index. Users still on version 7 will be able to use this book easily, although they will not be able to do the exercises that use the new tools and functions in version 8.

The author wishes to express her gratitude to a number of people who were helpful in putting this material together:

✳ Adobe Systems Incorporated, which actively encourages and supports the development of ancillary materials for its applications.

✳ Ralph Warwick, for his delightful illustrations created in our Illustrator class at Ocean County College.

✳ Joon Y Lee and Michael Zielinski, for their illustrations created in our Illustrator class at Brookdale Community College.

✳ Marilyn Cohen, Joseph Dai, and Tracey Attlee, for gracious permission to reproduce their photographs.

✳ Meg Makofsky, who reviewed the manuscript for Macintosh and Windows issues and who let me know when I wasn't making sense.

✳ And to Tom Schin, my editor at Delmar, who had enough sense to let me do it the right way.

HOW IT WORKS

Adobe's Critter Type from the Wild Type series was applied to a circular path using the Path Type tool. The path has no stroke and no fill colors.

WELCOME TO ADOBE ILLUSTRATOR

If your computer drawing experience has been limited to bitmap programs like Fractal Design Painter and Adobe Photoshop, your study of Adobe Illustrator will take you into a world where lines are perfectly straight and curves are beautifully smooth—even if you move or resize them. In the world of vector art, image size and resolution are never an issue, unless your vector file is dancing with a bitmap image.

Because Adobe Illustrator is a PostScript-based drawing program, the mathematically precise definitions of lines and curves are maintained in the drawing and printing process. This allows you not only to draw precise lines and shapes, but also to draw them at any size with any stroke weight, to fill them with colors and patterns, and to use PostScript type as an illustration element. There is no limit to what you can produce with Adobe Illustrator once you learn how to use its tools and functions.

VECTOR VS. BITMAP ART

Vector art is created using mathematical algorithms executed by the PostScript page description language. When you draw a circle in Illustrator, the PostScript language built into Illustrator scurries around for the math to create a perfect 360° circle with the diameter you specify, and sends that information to the PostScript printer. Likewise, when you specify PostScript type in Illustrator, the PostScript language creates every nuance of the type—slope, serifs, and dark and light strokes—with mathematical precision.

Bitmap art, however, is created from pixels on a grid, as in Photoshop, and is device dependent. The more pixels per inch the printer is able to produce, the more pixels per inch in the document, and the more detailed the printed artwork. You can never get the smooth lines and curves for shapes and type in Photoshop that you have in Illustrator. And, unlike vector art, bitmap art loses detail when it is scaled to a larger size.

WHY USE ADOBE ILLUSTRATOR?

Adobe Illustrator is an art production tool used by graphic designers, production artists, typesetters, and service bureaus. Artwork created in Illustrator can be imported into programs such as Page-Maker, Photoshop, PageMill, and QuarkXPress, where it can be further manipulated for press or Web. Because Illustrator files are Encapsulated PostScript (EPS) files, they move easily and without loss of color or detail to and from other applications, especially PostScript applications.

The PostScript circle and type created in Illustrator (top) keep their shapes, especially when enlarged, unlike the bitmap circle and type created in Photoshop (bottom).

WHAT THIS BOOK COVERS

Lessons in this book are organized in twenty-one units and are designed to cover the main functions and features of Adobe Illustrator 8.0. The first unit introduces you to Illustrator's interface and Toolbox. Units 2 and 3 cover drawing paths with the basic shape tools. Applying color attributes is covered in Units 4 and 5, and using patterns and gradients is discussed in Units 6 and 7.

Unit 8 is devoted to the Pen tool, Illustrator's most powerful drawing tool. Organizing files in layers is the subject of Unit 9, while tracing, measuring, and moving objects are covered in Unit 10.

Transforming objects and the transformation filters are the subjects of Units 11 and 12, along with lessons on aligning and arranging objects in a file. Illustrator's new blending features are covered in Unit 13.

Units 14 and 15 treat the program's extraordinary type functions, dealing with them as illustration tools, especially in reference to paths. Unit 16 covers text as a word-processing function, including Illustrator's typesetting abilities.

The new Actions palette is the subject of Unit 17 with information on automating illustrations using the Actions palette. Unit 18 covers masks and compound paths, including the Pathfinder palette.

Raster images and filters appear in Unit 19, and Unit 20 deals with how Illustrator interfaces with other graphics applications such as Photoshop. The final unit, Unit 21, covers printing Illustrator files. A comprehensive glossary of all the terms listed at the beginning of each unit and a cross-referenced index complete the book.

HOW TO USE THIS TEXT

This cross-platform text has been designed so you can easily lay it flat next to your computer and work directly from it. Each unit contains lessons on a particular topic and ends with a Review that will help you to pull together the different kinds of material covered in the lesson. An instructor's folder on the CD-ROM contains review questions and review projects to reinforce what you learned in the units.

Although different functions are presented in each unit, you can move sequentially from one unit to another or skip a unit if you like. For example, if you want to work with type before learning how to blend objects, you can easily do so, because every lesson in every unit contains all the information necessary to complete the exercises. This repetition of information is critical to learning such a complex application.

Version 7.0

With very few exceptions, such as the new tools and features, version 7 and version 8 share the same tools, functions, and interface. Where these are different, an explanation appears in the minor column of the text.

FYI

The Adobe Illustrator *application* is another name for the Adobe Illustrator *program*. An Adobe Illustrator *document* is another name for an Adobe Illustrator *file*. Documents/files are created with the Illustrator application/program.

Macintosh Keystrokes
⌘-K File/Preferences/ General

Windows Keystrokes
Ctrl-K File/Preferences/ General

Look for these keyboard shortcuts on pages where their commands are given in the exercises.

ANCILLARY INFORMATION

To help you keep track of the various kinds of information you are working with, the narrow column on each page is where you will find much helpful information on using the features in Adobe Illustrator. Tips, warnings, and examples are provided without intruding on the work in the exercises.

MENU COMMANDS

In this book, menu commands for Macintosh and Windows appear followed by the keyboard command where they appear on the menu. When, for example, you are told to choose View/Actual Size, click on the View menu and drag down to select (highlight) Actual Size.

KEYBOARD SHORTCUTS

If a keyboard shortcut or Function key exists for a command, it will be given in the text and will also appear in the minor column. For example, the keyboard shortcut for viewing artwork at actual size is Command-1 (Macintosh) or Ctrl-1 (Windows). The text will read, "Press Command/Ctrl-1 to view the artwork at actual size." Macintosh users should press Command-1; Windows users, Ctrl-1. These modifier keys (the Command and Ctrl keys) must be pressed simultaneously with the other key and released only *after* the mouse button is released. Learning to use these keyboard shortcuts will make your work in Illustrator faster and more efficient.

UNDOING ACTIONS

Illustrator allows multiple undos. If you perform a function or execute a command, then change your mind, choose Edit/Undo (Command/Ctrl-Z) to undo the most recently completed action. Selecting Edit/Undo again and again will undo the previous actions and commands.

LAUNCHING THE PROGRAM

Launch (run) Adobe Illustrator either by double-clicking on the Adobe Illustrator icon or by double-clicking on an Adobe Illustrator document icon.

An Adobe Illustrator document can be a new document or a previously created Illustrator file. When you launch Adobe Illustrator, a document labeled *Untitled art 1* is created, the Menu Bar appears at the top of the screen, and the Toolbox and other palettes appear on the screen (Figure 0.1).

Good news for cross-platform users!

Where Illustrator for Mac OS uses the Command (⌘) key, Windows uses the Ctrl key. Where the Mac OS uses the Option key, Windows uses the Alt key. Even the Function keys at the top of the keyboard are the same on both platforms.

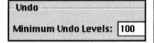

Select a menu item by clicking on the Menu Bar item and dragging down to highlight an option.

The Units & Undo Preferences dialog box under the File menu lets you specify the number of undos. However, the more undos you specify, the more RAM you need.

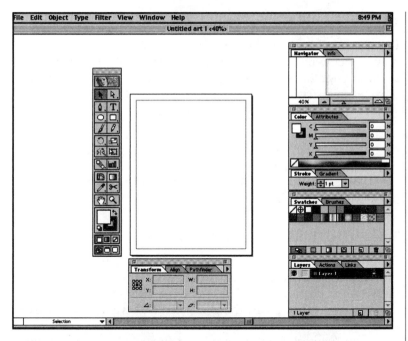

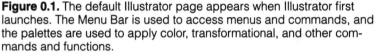

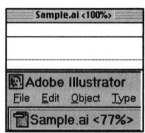

The title bar (Macintosh, top; Windows, bottom) for this Illustrator document displays its name (Sample.ai) and its view percentage (100%). The .ai suffix stands for Adobe Illustrator and identifies the file as an Illustrator file as opposed to an EPS or Photoshop file.

Figure 0.1. The default Illustrator page appears when Illustrator first launches. The Menu Bar is used to access menus and commands, and the palettes are used to apply color, transformational, and other commands and functions.

THE DRAWING AREA

The drawing area is the large area in the center of the page surrounded by a dotted line and called the *imageable area*. Only artwork inside this dotted line will print. The imageable area is actually defined by the selected printer, as most printers cannot print to the edge of the page.

The outside lines (drop shadow box) indicate the page size. To adjust a page using the Page tool, select the Page (behind the Hand tool) and drag the page to a new location. The two gray rectangles are displayed and anything inside the inner rectangle will print.

Once you save a document, the title bar displays the name of the document and the view percentage. If you're viewing a page at actual size, then the document's name followed by <100%> appears.

The Status Bar in the lower left corner of the page displays information about the tools and their current function. Clicking on the black triangle in the Status Bar window displays four categories of information you may find useful.

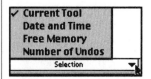

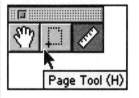

The Status Bar in the lower left corner of the document page can display different kinds of information. It indicates that the Selection tool is the currently selected tool.

NAVIGATING A DOCUMENT

Use the scroll bars on the right and bottom sides of the page to move quickly through the window, or click on the scroll arrow to scroll through the window a little at a time. Drag the scroll bars to move even faster up, down, or from right to left.

You can also select the Hand tool, press the mouse button (keep it pressed), and drag the Hand cursor around the screen to move to different areas of the document. If you're using any tool *except a type tool*, press the spacebar to change that tool into a temporary Hand tool. Then click and drag with the mouse to move around the page without moving or changing the artwork.

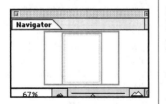

The Navigator palette is the easiest way to move around a file. Drag the red frame around the document to display the artwork within the frame at the current view percentage specified in the Percentage field in the lower left corner of the palette. Click on the Zoom Out and Zoom In triangles or drag the Zoom Slider at the bottom of the palette to increase or decrease the view percentage.

VIEWING MODES (VIEWS)

Illustrator has three viewing modes: Preview, Artwork, and Preview Selection. In Preview view, all the fills, strokes, gradients, and patterns are displayed. In Artwork view, only an object's outline appears. If you have something selected and want to see what it looks like with its fill and stroke attributes while leaving the rest of the art in Artwork view, choose Preview Selection from the View menu (Figure 0.2).

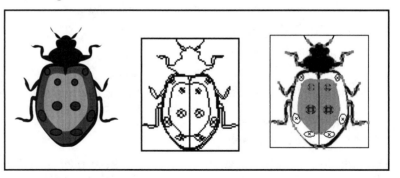

Figure 0.2. The bug on the left is in Preview view with all the colors and fills displayed. The center bug is in Artwork view with only the path outlines displayed. The bug on the right is in Preview Selection view with only the selected paths displaying their fill and stroke colors.

ZOOM TOOL

To magnify an area of the page, click on that area with the Zoom tool. To reduce magnification, Option/Alt-click with the Zoom tool. Or, press Command-+/- (Macintosh) or Ctrl-+/- (Windows) to increase or decrease magnification. Double-click the Zoom tool to return to a 100% view.

Version 7

There is no Navigator palette in version 7.

CUSTOM VIEWS

When working on a specific area of a document, you may find yourself constantly magnifying that area, then going back to actual size to view the whole document. By creating a custom view, you can display the artwork at that custom magnification with a key-stroke or by selecting the custom view from the View menu.

ILLUSTRATION WINDOWS

The three buttons at the bottom of the Toolbox are used to change the display screen mode. The left window button displays artwork in the standard default window with the Menu Bar and scroll bars. Click the center button to display artwork in a full-screen window with only the Menu Bar. Select the right button to display artwork in a full-screen window with no document title bar and with no Menu Bar or scroll bars.

SELECTING TOOLS

The Illustrator 8.0 Toolbox is a floating palette that you can move anywhere on the page. To select a tool, click once on that tool. If a tool displays an arrow, that indicates that there are more tools behind the primary tool. Click on the arrow to display and select another tool.

Press the Option/Alt key and click a tool in the Toolbox. Each click displays and selects the next hidden tool in a sequence of multiple tools.

To change any tool's icon to a crosshair, press the Caps Lock key on the keyboard. You can also specify Precise Cursors in the General Preferences dialog box. The center of the crosshair is the cursor's "hot spot."

TEAROFF PALETTES

Multiple tools can be "torn off" the Toolbox by clicking on the Tearoff Tab; thereafter they become separate floating palettes. This lets you keep frequently used tools handy wherever you're working (Figure 0.3). Each floating tool palette has a close box. Click the close box to close just the floating tool palette.

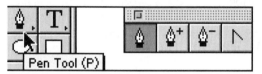

Figure 0.3. Click on the Pen tool's arrow to display the Add Anchor Point, Delete Anchor Point, and Convert Anchor Point tools.

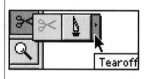

Click on the Tearoff Tab to create a floating palette of multiple tools.

The three buttons at the bottom of the Toolbox are used to change the screen display.

Version 7

There are no tearoff palettes in version 7.

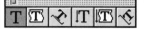

The type tools tearoff palette displays all the type tools on a floating palette.

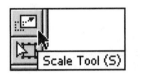

Scale Tool (S)

Sliding—not clicking—the cursor over a tool displays its name and keyboard shortcut.

FYI

Saving a file in 1-bit format saves it as a black-and-white preview.

Art.ai   Art.eps

Illustrator saves an Illustrator file with the AI 8 tag and an EPS file with the EPS 8 tag. Always add the .ai or .eps suffix to your files to identify them.

TOOL TIPS

If you drag the cursor over a tool—don't click, just drag—the name of the tool and its keyboard shortcut are displayed. When one tool is selected, pressing the keyboard shortcut (one letter) for a tool selects that tool. For example, if you have the Rectangle tool selected, pressing *b* selects the Paintbrush tool. Pressing *v* when any tool is active selects the Selection tool. If a tool has multiple tools attached to it, such as the Pen tool, pressing Shift-p, for example, cycles through all the Pen tools.

OPENING AND CLOSING FILES

To open a previously created Illustrator file, you must be in the Adobe Illustrator application. Choose File/Open (Command/Ctrl-O) and scroll through the drives and folders to locate the file. When the file appears in the scroll box, double-click on it or click once on the file and once on the Open button. The document will appear on the screen.

Files can be closed without quitting the program. When you have finished working on a document, choose File/Close (Command/Ctrl-W). If you haven't saved the file, you will be prompted to save any changes you made since you last saved that file.

SAVING FILES

Once you have created a file, you can save it, then open it and modify the artwork again. To save a file, choose File/Save (Command/Ctrl-S). The first time you save a file, you will be asked to type a name for the file and select a preview format for viewing the file You will usually choose 8-bit Macintosh or 8-bit PC, which saves not only the file but also a preview color image of the file. Once a file has been named and saved, choosing File/Save overwrites the original file with the new information without prompting you to name it or choose a format.

PROJECTS FOLDER

You should create a folder on your hard drive named *Projects Folder* where you can save the exercises you're working on. It's also a good idea to move the unit folders from the CD-ROM to the Projects folder so you can access them more easily. Otherwise, open the files directly from the CD-ROM.

HELP!

The complete *Adobe Illustrator User Guide,* along with keyboard shortcuts and other information is, available online from easily accessible menus. Macintosh users can choose Help from the Menu Bar and drag to select Contents. Window users press F1 to display the Help Contents menu or choose Help/Contents.

By typing or selecting a keyword, you can display all the information in the *User Guide* on the screen. Even better, you can copy the information you need using the Edit/Copy command and paste it into an Illustrator or word-processing document using the Edit/Paste command. There it will be available (if you save it or print it) for future reference.

If you have Internet access, clicking on the Adobe Illustrator logo at the top of the Toolbox will connect you to the Adobe site on the Internet, where you can follow the links to even more help.

Because this book is designed as a training tool for artists and designers and is not intended for business use, the Graph tool—really a separate application within Illustrator—is not covered.

Click here to connect to Adobe's Internet site.

WHAT'S ON THE CD-ROM

The CD-ROM accompanying this book contains tutorial files that you will use to do the exercises. All the files are locked, so it might be helpful to first move them to your Projects folder on the hard drive or to an external drive such as a Zip drive. Then when you make changes to a file, save it under a new name. This lets you manipulate the document without losing the original file. When you are told to open a file from the CD, open it from your Projects folder instead.

The CD also contains tryout versions of Adobe Illustrator 8.0 for Macintosh and Windows. Although you can't save files created with this version and printing functions are limited, you will be able to work with all of Illustrator's features and commands.

The demo TransparencyFX plug-in and its manual, from Lucid Dream Technologies for the Macintosh platform, are also included. Just drag the plug-in to the Plug-ins folder in the Illustrator folder and relaunch Illustrator.

ILLUSTRATOR 8.0 TOOLBOX

The entire suite of tools in Illustrator 8.0 is listed on the next page. Although tools are pictured in the minor column whenever they are referenced in the text, you may find it helpful to refer to the Toolbox when you're not sure which tool to use when creating your next digital masterpiece.

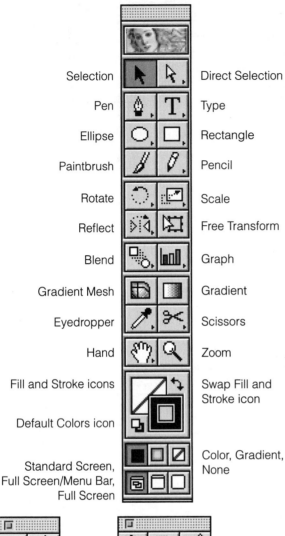

Selection   Direct Selection

Pen   Type

Ellipse   Rectangle

Paintbrush   Pencil

Rotate   Scale

Reflect   Free Transform

Blend   Graph

Gradient Mesh   Gradient

Eyedropper   Scissors

Hand   Zoom

Fill and Stroke icons   Swap Fill and Stroke icon

Default Colors icon

Standard Screen, Full Screen/Menu Bar, Full Screen   Color, Gradient, None

Selection Tools

Selection, Direct Selection, Group Selection

Type Tools

Type, Area Type, Path Type, Vertical Type, Vertical Area Type, Vertical Path Type

Pen Tools

Pen, Add Anchor Point, Delete Anchor Point, Convert Anchor Point

Basic Shape Tools

Ellipse, Polygon, Star, Spiral Rectangle, Rounded Rectangle

Rotate, Twirl

Hand, Page, Measure

Pencil Tools

Pencil, Smooth, Eraser

Cutting Tools

Scissors, Knife

Blend, Auto Trace

Transformation Tools

Scale, Reshape; Reflect, Shear

Painting Tools

Eyedropper, Paint Bucket

UNIT 1
How Illustrator Works

OVERVIEW

In this unit you will learn how:
to work with objects
to use the bounding box and
    Smart Guides for precise
    alignment
palettes are displayed and
    organized
to set Preferences

TERMS

anchor point
bounding box
default settings
Direct Selection tool
Group Selection tool
line

object
open path
path
segment
Selection tool
shape
Smart Guides
vector art

HOW IT WORKS

Draw a circle, stroke it, and apply the Zig Zag filter. Select the Scale Stroke Weight
option in the General Preferences dialog box. Scale the circle 80%, selecting Copy in
the Scale dialog box. Choose Object/Transform/Transform Again several times to
create the wavy effect.

11

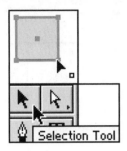

Selection Tool

The Selection tool displays a white square when you click on an anchor point. Selecting an object with this tool selects the entire object.

Deleting objects

To delete an object, select it with the Selection tool and press the Delete/Del key. To delete a path segment, select it with the Direct Selection tool.

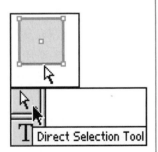

Direct Selection Tool

Clicking with the Direct Selection tool selects only segments and anchor points, not the entire object.

Group Selection Tool

ILLUSTRATOR ARTWORK

Creating Illustrator artwork means creating vector art using tools in the Toolbox, selecting options from the pull-down menus in the Menu Bar, making selections in a dialog box, and accessing functions from the many floating palettes. Whether you are painting an object or transforming it, you need to access a tool, a menu item, or a palette—sometimes all of these! For example, you can select a tool such as the Rotate tool in the Toolbox, but unless you have an object selected, you can't use the tool. If you have an object selected, you can click on it and rotate it, or you can Option/Alt-click on an anchor point to display a dialog box where you enter a degree of rotation and specify the rotation for either the selected object or for a copy of the object. Or, you could select the object and choose Rotate from the Transform menu under the Object menu in the Menu Bar. The important thing to remember is that functions and commands can be accessed from different places in Illustrator. Once you have some practice navigating the Toolbox and menu commands, you'll instinctively know what you need to do to accomplish a specific task.

SELECTING OBJECTS

Whenever you draw something with the drawing tools, you create an *object*. Before you can do anything to that object—color it, resize it, move it, etc.—you must select it. When you click and drag to draw an object with any of the basic shape tools, such as the rectangle, star, polygon, or ellipse tools, that object is selected once you release the mouse button. It displays anchor points around its sides and those anchor points are solid, indicating that the entire object is selected and that any actions performed on it will affect the entire object, not just segments of the object. To deselect the object, choose Edit/Deselect All or Command/Ctrl-click on an empty area of the page.

SELECTION TOOLS

If you want to select an object, you must use one of the selection tools. The three selection tools in the Toolbox are the Selection tool (black arrow), the Direct Selection tool (white arrow), and the Group Selection tool (white arrow with + sign). The Selection tool selects the entire object. The Direct Selection tool selects paths, segments, and anchor points depending on which area of the object you click. If you click on the center point of an object with the Direct Selection tool, the entire object is selected, just as if you had used the Selection tool. But if you click on a segment of the object or on one of its anchor points, only that segment or anchor point is selected, and any changes you make to the object will affect only the selected areas.

The Group Selection tool selects individual objects in a group and the group itself. Click once on any object in a group to select just that object; click again to select the group of which that object is a part.

AREA SELECT

Area Select is an option in the General Preferences dialog box. When it is selected (the default setting), and you are in Preview view, you can click with any of the selection tools on an object's fill to select the whole object.

BOUNDING BOX

When you select one or more objects with the Selection tool, a rectangular bounding box appears around the object or objects. This bounding box displays as a solid line with eight handles around it. These handles, or outlined squares, are filled with white and are used to transform the object. Click on any handle to resize (scale) the object or objects within the bounding box.

To move objects inside a bounding box, use the Selection tool and drag any part of the selection—but not a handle—to move but not resize the bounding box contents. Or, click inside the bounding box with the Free Transform tool and drag to move the bounding box contents (Figure 1.1).

Figure 1.1. The box on the left is selected as soon as it is drawn. When it is selected with the Selection tool, it displays eight handles around its bounding box (center). A deselected object displays no anchor points or bounding box.

EXERCISE A

1. In a new file (File/New), choose File/Preferences/General (Command/Ctrl-K). In the General Options area, select Use Bounding Box and Use Area Select. Click on OK. Choose Window/Show Swatches to display the Swatches palette.

Macintosh Keystrokes

⌘-K File/Preferences/
   General

Windows Keystrokes

Ctrl-K File/Preferences/
   General

┌── **General Options** ──┐
☑ **Use Bounding Box**
☑ **Use Area Select**

Choose Use Area Select to select the entire object with any selection tool when in Preview view.

When any function is selected, a check mark appears next to it. Highlight the function and release the mouse to deselect (turn off) the function.

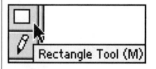

Version 7

There is no Bounding Box option in version 7.

⌘-U View/Show Hide
   Smart Guides
⌘-W File/Close

Windows Keystrokes

Ctrl-U View/Show Hide
   Smart Guides
Ctrl-W File/Close

Click the Fill icon to make it the active icon or press x to toggle between the Fill and Stroke icons.

2. Pull down the View menu and deselect Smart Guides. If it is checked, highlight it and release the mouse to toggle the function on and off.

3. Click on the Rectangle tool to select it and then click and drag on the page to draw a rectangle. When you release the mouse, the rectangle displays four anchor points and a center point. It is filled and stroked with the current paint selections.

4. Because the rectangle is selected, it can be edited. Click on the Fill icon in the Toolbox to make it active. Click on the Yellow & Orange Radial swatch in the Swatches palette to fill the selected rectangle with the radial fill (Figure 1.2).

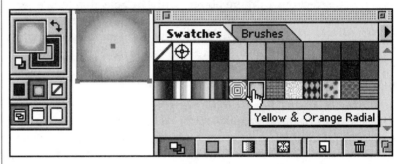

Figure 1.2. Clicking the Fill icon in the Toolbox (left) makes the fill function active. Clicking a swatch in the Swatches palette (right) fills the selected object with that color (center).

5. The rectangle fills and remains selected. Click on another swatch in the Swatches palette to fill it with another color.

6. Click on the Selection tool in the Toolbox. As soon as you do this, the bounding box appears around the rectangle, displaying eight resizing handles. Click on the right center handle and drag to the right to widen the rectangle. Click on the lower right corner handle and drag down and to the right to lengthen and widen the rectangle. The corner handles can scale an object in both directions (Figure 1.3).

7. When you drag a side handle, the object resizes from the opposite edge. Click on any side handle and press the Option/Alt key as you drag to resize the object from the center.

8. Continue to draw, select, and resize objects until you are comfortable with the process. Close this file (File/Close). Don't save your changes.

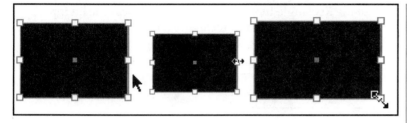

Figure 1.3. When an object is selected with the Selection tool (black arrow), it displays a bounding box with eight transforming handles (left). Drag a right side handle to widen the object from the left edge of the object (center). Drag on a corner handle to scale both the height and width of the object (right).

SMART GUIDES

Smart Guides are nonprinting lines that help you create, align, and edit objects in relation to other objects on the drawing page. Use them to quickly align a point or segment on an object to a point or segment on another object. They are also temporary "snap to" guides, originating from a selected object, that let you properly align that object with another object on the page at a specific angle. Smart Guides are configured in the Smart Guides Preferences dialog box and toggled on and off from the View Menu.

EXERCISE B

1. In a new document (File/New) use the Rectangle tool to draw two rectangles, one above the other. Choose File/Preferences/Smart Guides to display the Smart Guides Preferences dialog box (Figure 1.4). Select Text Label Hints to display text labels for anchor points, center points, and direction angles. Select Construction Guides to display guidelines when you use the Smart Guides. Select Transform Tools to let Smart Guides help you when you scale, rotate, or shear an object. Select Object Highlighting to highlight the object below the pointer as you drag around it.

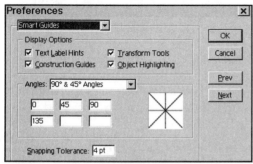

Figure 1.4. The Smart Guides Preferences dialog box.

FYI

You can draw happily ever after without Smart Guides if you find them too distracting. Just remember to turn them off from the View menu.

Sorry

Smart Guides won't work when Snap to Grid is selected from the View menu.

Select the Smart Guides Preferences dialog box from the File menu.

Rectangle Tool (M)

Version 7

Version 7 does not have Smart Guides.

Macintosh Keystrokes

⌘-Y View/Preview/Artwork
⌘-A Edit/Select All
⌘-W File/Close

Windows Keystrokes

Ctrl-Y View/Preview/
    Artwork
Ctrl-A Edit/Select All
Ctrl-W File/Close

FYI

Clicking with the Direct Selection tool on the center point of a basic shape closed path like a rectangle or circle selects the entire path, just as if you had used the Selection tool.

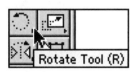

2. Use the Rectangle tool to draw two rectangles, one on top of the other. Click on the top rectangle with the Selection tool (black arrow) and drag it down at an angle. Notice how the Smart Guides appear, indicating the angle of movement, and how the anchor points and center points are labeled as you cross over them (Figure 1.5).

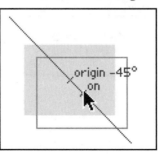

Figure 1.5. A rectangle is selected with the Selection tool and Smart Guides specify the angle of movement.

3. Choose Edit/Select All and press the Delete key to delete both objects. Use the Ellipse tool and press the Shift key while dragging to create a circle. Use the Rectangle tool to draw a long rectangle to the right of the circle. Choose View/Artwork (Command/Ctrl-Y) to display only the outlines of the filled objects.

4. Click on the rectangle's center point with the Selection tool and drag to the left, passing over the circle's right anchor point to the circle's center point. When *center* appears—because you have Text Label Hints turned on in the Smart Guide Preferences—release the mouse button. You have aligned the rectangle's center point with the circle's center point (Figure 1.6).

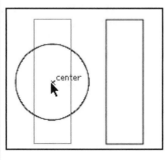

Figure 1.6. The Text Label Hints option tells you when you have moved onto the center of an object.

5. With the rectangle still selected, click on the Rotate tool in the Toolbox and click on the lower right anchor point on the rectangle. Drag to the right and notice the guidelines that appear; they show because the Transform Tools option is selected in the Smart Guide Preferences (Figure 1.7).

6. Close this file (Command/Ctrl-W). Don't save your changes.

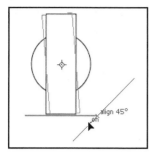

Figure 1.7. If the Transform Tools option is selected in the Smart Guides Preferences dialog box, guide lines appear when you use a transformation tool such as the Rotate tool.

PALETTES

Many of Illustrator's functions are accessed from floating palettes that can be docked together, separated, hidden, and displayed. If a palette is displayed, for example, the Swatches palette, the Window menu displays "Hide Swatches Palette." To display that palette, highlight "Hide Swatches Palette" and release the mouse button. This toggles the hide/display function for every palette. If you select the Show palette command from the Window menu and that palette is part of a group of palettes, the selected palette appears at the front of the group and becomes the active palette. To activate a palette, just click on its Name Tab.

Palettes do not display check marks under the Window menu. Selecting the Hide command hides the palette; selecting Show displays it.

PALETTE DISPLAY OPTIONS

To move a palette group, click and drag on its title bar. To undock a palette from a palette group, drag its Name Tab off of the group. To add a palette to another palette group—even if that group consists of only one palette—drag the palette's Name Tab into the new group. As you drag the palette over the new group, the group is outlined in black. Once you release the mouse button, the palette is docked to the group and becomes the active palette in the group (Figure 1.8).

Clicking on a palette's Name Tab brings it to the front and makes it active.

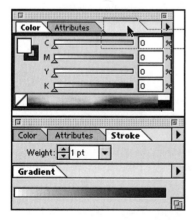

Figure 1.8. The Stroke palette is dragged out of the lower palette group (below) and onto the upper palette group (above), displaying the black outline around the target group. Once the mouse button is released, the Stroke palette becomes the active palette in the new palette group (below).

Dock as many palettes as you like to create a "super palette." Click on the palette's Name Tab to bring it to the front.

Double-click on a palette's title bar to collapse the palette while keeping it displayed.

Windows users click the - button to minimize the palette and ✗ to close it.

Select Hide Options or Show Options from a palette's pull-down menu on the right side of the palette. Some palettes also have other selections besides hiding and displaying options.

Many palettes can be resized using the Resize box in the lower right corner of the palette. To return a palette to its default size, click the Zoom box (Macintosh) on the right side of the title bar or the Minimize/Maximize box (Windows). You can also collapse a palette by double-clicking on its title bar (Figure 1.9).

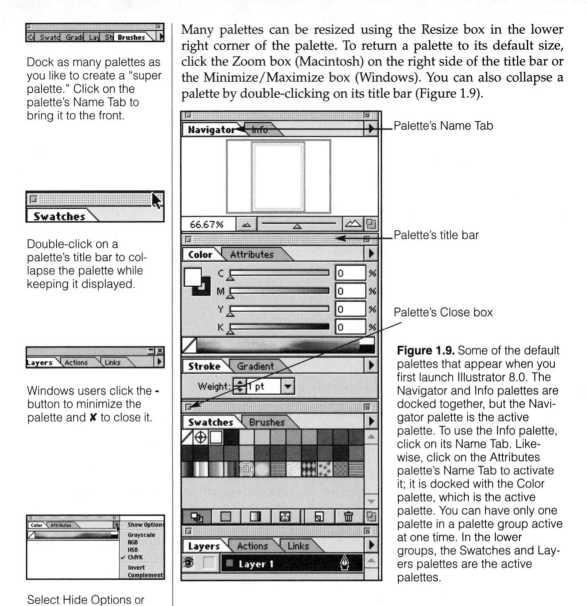

Palette's Name Tab

Palette's title bar

Palette's Close box

Figure 1.9. Some of the default palettes that appear when you first launch Illustrator 8.0. The Navigator and Info palettes are docked together, but the Navigator palette is the active palette. To use the Info palette, click on its Name Tab. Likewise, click on the Attributes palette's Name Tab to activate it; it is docked with the Color palette, which is the active palette. You can have only one palette in a palette group active at one time. In the lower groups, the Swatches and Layers palettes are the active palettes.

PALETTE MENUS

All palettes have a pull-down menu at the right side of the palette where you can select Hide or Show Options to hide or display other options for that palette. Many palettes also have options for color mode and display options that you can select from the pull-down menu. To select an option, click on the palette's black triangle and highlight another option.

Unit 1 ★ How Illustrator Works

ILLUSTRATOR PREFERENCES

Adobe Illustrator stores its default or "factory settings" in the Adobe Illustrator 8 Preferences file. This file is located in the System folder (Mac OS) or in the AIPrefs folder (Windows). It contains all the information about choices you made in the General Preferences dialog box and affects the way palettes are displayed, how tools behave, and many other functions in Illustrator.

DEFAULT PREFERENCES

When learning Adobe Illustrator, it is best to start with the program's default settings, especially as they apply to the colors and patterns that ship with the program and appear in the Swatches palette. To ensure that you are working with Illustrator's default settings, first quit Adobe Illustrator if you have already launched the program. In Mac OS, open the System folder and scroll to locate the Preferences folder. Open the Preferences folder and drag the Adobe Illustrator Prefs file out of the folder onto the Trash icon. Be sure to empty the Trash. Now launch Adobe Illustrator, which will create a new Preferences file that includes all of the program's default settings. In Windows, go to the AIPrefs file in the Adobe Illustrator folder. Delete the Adobe Illustrator 8 Preferences file and relaunch Illustrator.

GENERAL PREFERENCES

The General Preferences dialog box (File/Preferences/General) is where you make choices about how tools behave; for example, how accurately the Auto Trace tool draws over a template. Other options (Figure 1.10) affect the way objects relate to one another. For example, if you select (check) the Transform Pattern Tiles option, when you transform (rotate, scale, etc.) an object filled with pattern tiles, those tiles will also be transformed (rotated, scaled, etc.). Likewise, if you select Scale Stroke Weight, when you scale (enlarge or reduce) a stroked object, that stroke's weight will be proportionally increased or decreased.

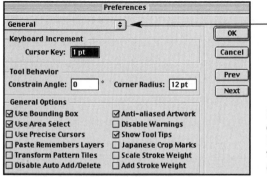

Access more Preferences from the General menu.

Figure 1.10. Select options for the way Illustrator works in the various Preferences dialog boxes.

Defaults

When Illustrator creates a new Preferences file, that file contains the settings Adobe specified for that file. For example, Use Bounding Box is selected in the default file. Once you deselect it, that option becomes the new default until you trash that Preferences file.

Setting Preferences

Because options selected in the Preferences dialog boxes affect the way Illustrator behaves, especially the way tools function, it's always a good idea to take a look at the way Preferences let you customize the program for the way you want to work.

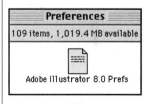

Trash the Adobe Illustrator 8.0 Prefs file (Macintosh) to launch Illustrator with the default settings. In Windows, rename the AIPrefs file located in the Illustrator directory.

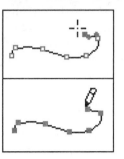

Another option, Use Precise Cursors, changes the normal tool icon to a crosshair when you select the tool (Figure 1.11).

Figure 1.11. When Use Precise Cursors is selected, the graphic tool cursor, such as the Pencil cursor that appears when the Pencil tool is used, is replaced by a crosshair cursor. The center of the crosshair is the "hot spot" or activation point.

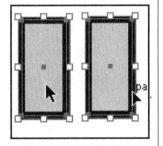

☑ **Use Precise Cursors**

Select this option in the General Preferences dialog box to display cursors as crosshairs.

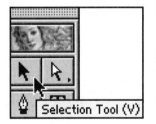

When Use Area Select is checked, click anywhere in the object to select it (left). Without that option, you must click on an anchor point or on a path.

The Area Select option is one you should select if you want to click on an object's fill to select it. Unless Area Select is checked, you must click on an object's path or anchor point to select it. You can't click inside the object to select it. With this option checked, clicking anywhere inside the object, as well as on a path or anchor point selects the object.

Until you are familiar with the tools, keep the Show Tool Tips option selected. This way, when you place your cursor on a tool in the Toolbox, its name appears along with its keyboard shortcut. You have to wait a second or two for the tool name to pop up.

REVIEW

In this unit you learned that:

1. Illustrator is a PostScript vector program which creates art that can be edited without losing detail.

2. Palettes, menus, commands, and dialog boxes are all used to create artwork.

3. Most palettes contain menus that display more options for using those palettes.

4. Before an object can be edited, it must first be selected with one of three selection tools.

5. Using the Bounding Box and Smart Guides options helps you transform and align objects accurately.

6. Several Preferences files let you customize Illustrator for the way you want to work.

Slide the cursor over a tool—don't click—to display its name and keyboard shortcut.

Selection Tool (V)

Jesters do often prove prophets.
William Shakespeare

Ralph Warwick

Fools by Ralph Warwick

UNIT 2
Drawing
Paths

OVERVIEW

In this unit you will learn how:
to draw open and closed
   paths
to select objects using the
   Selection tools
to select points and paths
to use the Join and Average
   commands
to cut paths
the difference between corner
   points and smooth points

TERMS

Artwork view
Average command
center point
closed path
corner point
direction handles
endpoints
Join command
line

Miter Join
open path
path
Preview view
segment
shape
slice
smooth point
transform

HOW IT WORKS

Use the Pen tool and basic shape tools to draw the paths. Create and apply gradients and patterns to selected paths. Use the transformation tools and commands with the Copy option to create multiple objects

PATHS

Before you can manipulate shapes in Illustrator, you have to understand how Illustrator creates those shapes. All lines and curves in a drawing exist between anchor points. This line or curve between those two anchor points is called a *segment*, and all of the connecting segments are called a *path* (Figure 2.1).

Peek-a-boo!

Hide or display a selected object's anchor points by choosing Hide Edges or Show Edges from the View menu.

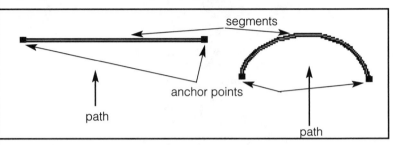

Figure 2.1. Displays two selected open paths with their anchor points visible. The line and curve between the anchor points are the segments. The line and curve are also paths.

CLOSED AND OPEN PATHS

If the last segment is connected to the first segment, the path is a closed path. A closed path is called a *shape*. A path is the entire group of connected segments. In a rectangle, the four segments form a path and, because the last segment is connected by an anchor point to the first segment, a closed path is created. When you move a rectangle with the Selection tool, you move the whole path.

If the last segment is not connected to the first segment, the path is an open path. An open path is called a *line* (Figure 2.2).

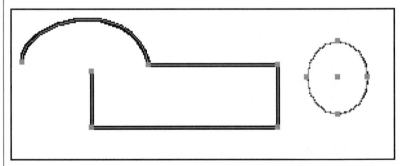

Figure 2.2. The path on the left is an open path because no segment connects the first and last segments. The path on the right is a closed path because the first and last segments are connected.

DRAWING AN OPEN PATH

An open path is a segment or connected segments in which the last segment is not connected to the first segment. For example, a rectangle is a closed path because the last segment, the fourth segment in the object, shares the same anchor point as the first segment in the object. With an open path, however, the last segment does not share the same anchor point as the first segment. A line, for example, is an open path because the first anchor point is not connected to the last anchor point (Figure 2.1). In Illustrator an open path is called a *line*, whereas a closed path is called a *shape*.

EXERCISE A

1. In a new document, click on the Default Colors icon in the Toolbox to specify the default white fill and default black stroke. Choose View/Artwork (Command/Ctrl-Y). You will not be able to see fills and strokes in Artwork view, but Illustrator works much faster in this mode, because it doesn't have to generate fills and strokes, only path outlines. Click on the Pencil tool and click and drag to draw a line. It doesn't have to be straight.

2. When you release the mouse button, the line (path) displays all the anchor points between the segments as filled (selected). This means that anything you do to this path affects every segment on the path.

3. Click on the Selection tool to select it and then move it over the path. Notice that when you are on a path segment, the black arrow becomes an arrowhead. Drag the black arrow over an anchor point and notice how the arrowhead displays a white square, indicating that if you click now you will select an anchor point (Figure 2.3). Click on a path segment and drag the entire path around the page.

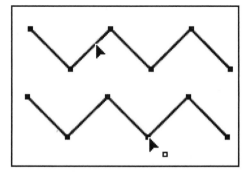

Figure 2.3. When the Selection tool is on a selected path segment, the black arrow becomes an arrowhead. When it is on a selected anchor point, the arrowhead displays a white square.

Macintosh Keystrokes

⌘-Y View/Artwork/Preview

Windows Keystrokes

Ctrl-Y View/Artwork/ Preview

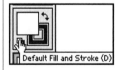

Clicking the Default Fill and Stroke icon makes the default fill white and default stroke 1-pt. black.

Tip

You may find it easier to turn off the Bounding Box option in the General Preferences dialog box. Choose File/Preferences/ General and deselect the Bounding Box check box.

Macintosh Keystrokes

⌘-Shift-A Edit/Deselect All
⌘-Z Edit/Undo

Windows Keystrokes

Ctrl-Shift-A Edit/Deselect
All
Ctrl-Z Edit/Undo

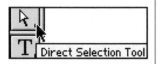

When the Direct Selection tool is on a non-selected path segment, it displays a black square. When it is on an anchor point, it displays a white square.

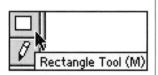

4. Switch to Preview view (View/Preview). Click away from the path to deselect it or choose Edit/Deselect All (Command/Ctrl-Shift-A).

5. Click on the Direct Selection tool and click on the path to select just the path segment you click on (Figure 2.4). If you drag that path segment, you will reshape only that segment, not the entire path, because none of the anchor points are selected and only one segment is selected.

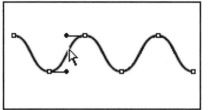

Figure 2.4. Clicking on a path with the Direct Selection tool selects only that segment, not the entire path.

6. Drag the segment and notice how only the segment between the anchor points moves. Choose Edit/Undo (Command/Ctrl-Z) to restore the path.

7. Click on a hollow anchor point with the Direct Selection tool. It turns black, indicating that it is selected and available for editing. Drag the selected anchor point to reshape the path.

8. With the Direct Selection tool still active, Option/Alt-click on the path to select the entire path—all its points and segments. Choose Edit/Clear to delete the path without placing it on the Clipboard and clogging up your computer's memory.

9. Switch to Artwork view (Command/Ctrl-Y) and click on the Rectangle tool to select it. Move onto the drawing area, then press the mouse button and drag to draw a rectangle. A rectangle with 5 points appears, one at each corner and one in the center. The corner points are called anchor points; the straight lines between these anchor points are called segments; and the center point is called the center point. The rectangle comprised of the four segments joined by the four points is called a path (Figure 2.5).

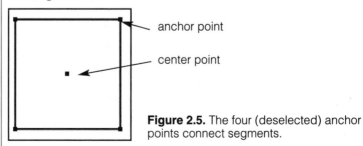

anchor point

center point

Figure 2.5. The four (deselected) anchor points connect segments.

10. The solid anchor points indicate that they are selected and therefore available for editing. Choose Edit/Deselect All [Command-Shift-A (Macintosh); Ctrl-Shift-A (Windows)] to deselect the rectangle. Only the path comprised of the four segments and a center point appear.

11. Click on the Selection tool (black arrow) and click on any segment of the rectangle. All five points appear solid, indicating that the object is selected and can be moved.

12. Click and drag on a segment to move the entire rectangle. Because every point is selected (solid), every segment moves. Because all the segments are connected to form one object, the rectangle (the entire object or path) moves.

13. Click anywhere on the empty page to deselect the rectangle or choose Edit/Deselect All. Click with the Selection tool on another segment and drag the rectangle around the screen. Repeat deselecting, selecting, and moving until you get bored.

14. Close this file (File/Close). Don't save your changes.

SELECTION TOOLS

Before you can edit a path in Illustrator—move it, color it, resize, it, etc.—you must first select it. You do this by clicking on a path, segment, or anchor point with one of the selection tools. The three selection tools in Adobe Illustrator are the Selection tool (black arrow), Direct Selection tool (white arrow), and Group Selection tool (white arrow with plus sign).

SELECTING OBJECTS

In most cases, selecting an object with one selection tool applies that tool's selection attributes until you deselect the object. Just because you select a tool by clicking on it does not mean that every path is selected with that tool. For example, if you first select a path with the Selection tool, every path and point on the object is selected. Clicking on the Direct Selection tool and clicking on the object first selected with the Selection tool does absolutely nothing. The object remains totally selected. To select segments with the Direct Selection tool, first *deselect* the object (Command/Ctrl-Shift-A), *then* click on it with the Direct Selection tool.

There are two exceptions to this rule: When a shape or path is first selected with the Direct Selection tool, selecting the object with either the Selection tool or the Group Selection tool overrides the direct selection and selects the whole path or shape.

Macintosh Keystrokes

⌘-Y View/Artwork/Preview
⌘-Shift-A Edit/Deselect All

Windows Keystrokes

Ctrl-Y View/Artwork/
    Preview
Ctrl-Shift-A Edit/Deselect
    All

A path by any other name...

A path in Illustrator is also called an *object*.

Macintosh Keystrokes

⌘-K File/Preferences/
General
⌘-Y View/Artwork/Preview
⌘-Shift-A Edit/Deselect All

Windows Keystrokes

Ctrl-K File/Preferences/
General
Ctrl-Y View/Artwork/
Preview
Ctrl-Shift-A Edit/Deselect
All

Important info

Clicking with the Direct Selection tool on the center point of a basic shape closed path like a rectangle or circle selects the entire path, just as if you had used the Selection tool.

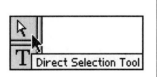

SELECTION TOOL

The Selection tool selects an entire path, shape, or object. Any segments connected by anchor points are selected with the Selection tool. If you edit the object in any way—drag, rotate, scale it, whatever—everything moves.

DIRECT SELECTION TOOL

In the last exercise, when you used the Selection tool (black arrow) to select the rectangle, it selected every anchor point and therefore every segment in the object. So, when you clicked and dragged to move the object, every segment moved simultaneously and the rectangle moved without becoming distorted. However, you can also choose to move only certain segments in an object. To do this, use the Direct Selection tool, the white arrow. Selecting a segment with the Direct Selection tool allows you to move only the segment or segments attached to the anchor points; or selecting an anchor point or points lets you move only those points.

EXERCISE B

1. Turn off the Bounding Box option in the General Preferences dialog box (Command/Ctrl-K). Choose View/Artwork (Command/Ctrl-Y). Click the Default Fill and Stroke icon in the Toolbox to set the fill at white and the stroke at black.

2. Use the Rectangle tool to draw a rectangle, longer than it is wide. When you release the mouse button, the entire object is selected, as indicated by the filled anchor points. Click on any empty area of the page or choose Edit/Deselect All (Command/Ctrl-Shift-A) to deselect the rectangle.

3. Click on the Direct Selection tool, the white arrow to the right of the Selection tool, and click on any of the four segments of the rectangle. The rectangle is selected, but notice that now the anchor points are hollow (Figure 2.6). This means that you cannot move (edit) the anchor points, although you can edit (move) the segments between those anchor points.

Clicking on the center point with the Direct Selection tool selects the entire object.

Figure 2.6. A rectangle selected with the Direct Selection tool. The anchor points are hollow, indicating that segments can't be moved without the object becoming distorted.

4. Click on the top segment of the rectangle and move it up and down and right and left. Notice that only the segments connected to the anchor points that anchor the top segment move. Those three segments are the top segment, the left segment, and the right segment. The bottom segment doesn't move, because its anchor points are used to anchor only the bottom segment (Figure 2.7).

Macintosh Keystrokes

⌘-Z Edit/Undo
⌘-Shift-A Edit/Deselect All
⌘-W File/Close

Windows Keystrokes

Ctrl-Z Edit/Undo
Ctrl-Shift-A Edit/Deselect
     All
Ctrl-W File/Close

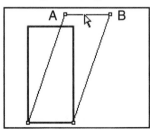

Figure 2.7. The rectangle was reshaped when the top segment between anchor points A and B was moved to the right.

5. Choose Edit/Undo (Command/Ctrl-Z) to return the rectangle to its original shape.

6. Click on the bottom segment and move it to the right and left. Notice that only the bottom segment, the left segment, and the right segment move. The top segment doesn't move this time because you didn't drag it, and its two anchor points are not connected to the bottom segment.

7. Click on the left segment of your distorted rectangle and move it around. Notice that only the left, top, and bottom segments move. The right segment doesn't move because its anchor points are not connected to the left segment which you are moving.

8. Continue to click and drag on each of the four segments and notice how the only segments that move are those whose anchor points are connected to the segment you are currently moving.

9. Close this file (Command/Ctrl-W). Don't save your changes.

Rectangle Tool

SELECTING ANCHOR POINTS

When you select an object with the Direct Selection tool and Use Area Select is deselected in the General Preferences dialog box, unless you click on the center point, none of the anchor points is selected. This means that unless you select anchor points, you can't move them. In the last exercise you clicked on a segment and dragged to move the segment. The segments between the anchor points moved and the anchor points moved with the segment, but only in relation to the way the segment moved. The anchor points did not move independently of the segment.

Use Area Select

If Use Area Select is selected in the General Preferences dialog box, clicking anywhere in or on the object with the Direct Selection tool will select the whole object, just as if you had selected it with the Selection tool.

Macintosh Keystrokes

⌘-Y View/Preview/Artwork
⌘-Shift-A Edit/Deselect All

Windows Keystrokes

Ctrl-Y View/Preview/
Artwork
Ctrl-Shift-A Edit/Deselect
All

Rectangle Tool

Selection Tool

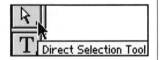

Direct Selection Tool

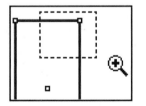

Drag the Zoom tool around an area to magnify that area.

Version 7

You'll know you've reached the center point when the black cursor becomes hollow

When you select an anchor point with the Direct Selection tool, you can move that anchor point and force the segments connected to that anchor point to move with it. In other words, when you move a segment, the position of the segment determines the location of the anchor points. When you move an anchor point, the anchor point determines the position of the segment.

EXERCISE C

1. Choose View/Artwork (Command/Ctrl-Y). Use the Rectangle tool to draw a rectangle. Choose Edit/Select None (Command/Ctrl-Shift-A) to deselect it.

2. Click on the Selection tool (black arrow) and click on the rectangle. Notice that the entire shape is selected. Click and drag on the selected shape to move it around the screen.

3. Keeping the rectangle selected, click on the Direct Selection tool (white arrow) and click on the selected rectangle. Nothing happens. That's because the rectangle is still selected by the Selection tool, which selects the whole object.

4. Choose Edit/Deselect All (Command/Ctrl-Shift-A) or click on an empty area of the page to deselect everything.

5. Click on the Direct Selection tool (white arrow) and click on the rectangle. It appears with its segments deselected, as indicated by the hollow anchor points. Click on any *segment*—not on an anchor point—and drag to reshape the rectangle.

6. Click on an empty area of the page or choose Edit/Deselect All (Command/Ctrl-Shift-A) to deselect the reshaped rectangle. Then click on any segment of the rectangle to display its anchor points. The anchor points are hollow, indicating that they are not selected and that they will move only in relation to a segment.

7. Use the Zoom tool to draw a marquee around the upper left point to magnify it.

8. Make sure you are in Artwork view (View/Artwork), so the center point of the rectangle is displayed when you select the rectangle. Use the Direct Selection tool, click on any segment of the rectangle, and click once on the upper left point to select it. Release the mouse button. The point becomes solid, indicating that it is selected and therefore can be edited (moved).

9. Click on the selected point and move it down and to the right until it meets the center point of the rectangle (Figure 2.8). You'll know you've reached the center point when the points snap together.

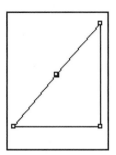

Figure 2.8. When you move the top right point down toward the center point, the cursor snaps to the center point as soon as the anchor point moves over it.

Macintosh Keystrokes

⌘-Y View/Artwork/Preview
⌘-Z Edit/Undo
⌘-W File/Close

Windows Keystrokes

Ctrl-Y View/Artwork/
        Preview
Ctrl-Z Edit/Undo
Ctrl-W File/Close

10. Release the mouse button. Notice that by moving the point, you've also moved the segments related to that point and reshaped the rectangle into a triangle. However, the four segments of the original rectangle still exist. What happened is that when you moved the anchor point connecting those two segments, you positioned the segments so that they became tangential.

11. Choose Edit/Undo Move (Command/Ctrl-Z) to restore the rectangle to its original shape. Then use the Direct Selection tool (white arrow) to drag the center point in the rectangle. Notice that once you clicked and dragged that center point, all of the points became selected and the entire object moved.

12. Deselect the rectangle by clicking on any blank area of the page. Click on another anchor point with the Direct Selection tool and move it to reshape the rectangle. Continue to select and move anchor points and segments until you are comfortable with the process.

13. Shift-click on two anchor points to select them and drag to reshape the rectangle. You can also Shift-select nonadjacent anchor points.

14. Close this file (Command/Ctrl-W). Don't save your changes.

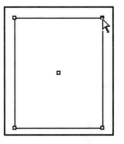

Clicking on an anchor point with the Direct Selection tool selects just that anchor point, not the whole object. To select the object, click on its center point.

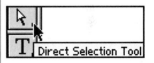

ENDPOINTS

An open path, or line, has two endpoints. When you have two open paths and want to create a single open or single closed path, you can either move the endpoints with the Direct Selection tool or use the Join command to create a new line segment between the two selected anchor points. If you want to move the endpoints close together without joining the paths, use the Average command. Of course, if you join two endpoints, you will create a closed path, or shape.

FYI

The first and last anchor points of an open path are called *endpoints*.

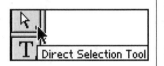

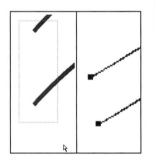

Dragging a selection marquee with the Direct Selection tool (left) selects only those anchor points (right).

Fill icon in the Toolbox

JOIN COMMAND

The Join command joins two selected endpoints into one anchor point. It does this by drawing a new line segment between the two selected anchor points if the points are some distance apart. If the points overlap, the Join command creates a single anchor point from the two points.

AVERAGE COMMAND

The Average command is used to reshape paths by realigning their endpoints or any of their anchor points. The Horizontal Average option aligns the selected points along the horizontal axis; the Vertical Average option aligns points along the vertical axis. Points can also be aligned along both the horizontal and vertical axes so that they overlap. The Average command does not join endpoints; it only realigns them or overlaps them.

EXERCISE D

1. Open the *Endpoints.ai* file in the Unit 02 folder on the CD-ROM (File/Open). This file displays several sets of wavy lines, or open paths. It also displays the Swatches palette where you can select fill and stroke colors.

2. Choose View/View #1 to magnify the left endpoints of the first set of lines (Paths #1). Use the Direct Selection tool to drag a selection marquee around those endpoints.

3. Choose Object/Path/Join (Command/Ctrl-J) to create a new line segment between the selected anchor points.

4. Choose View/Endpoints #2. Use the Direct Selection tool to select the two right endpoints in Paths #1 and press Command/ Ctrl-J to create a new segment between those two endpoints. You have now created a closed path. Click on the Fill icon in the Toolbox and click on any color in the Swatches palette to fill the new closed object (Figure 2.9).

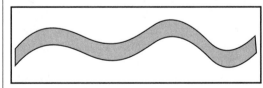

Figure 2.9. When the two endpoints at each end of the open paths are joined, a closed path results.

5. Choose View/Endpoints #3 to magnify the left endpoints of the second set of lines (Paths #2). Choose Object/Path/Average [Command-Option-J (Macintosh) or Ctrl-Alt-J (Windows)]. Select Both in the Average dialog box to overlap the selected points along both the horizontal and vertical axes. Click on OK. The two endpoints are overlapping, not joined.

6. Choose View/Endpoints #4 to magnify the right endpoints of the second set of lines (Paths #2). Select both endpoints with the Direct Selection tool and choose the Average command again. Select Both and click OK. Although the two lines appear to be a closed path, because the Average command overlaps but does not join endpoints, you still have two open paths or lines. Use the Selection tool to Shift-select both paths, select the Fill icon on the Toolbox, and click on a color in the Swatches palette. Notice that although the lines are filled, they still do not form a closed path (Figure 2.10).

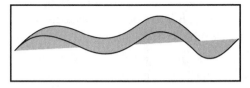

Figure 2.10. When the two endpoints at each end of the open paths are averaged, the points are overlapped, not joined.

7. Use the Direct Selection tool to select the left endpoint of the top path in Path #3. Press the Shift key and select the right endpoint of the top path also in Path #3. Choose Object/Path Join. A new segment connects the two endpoints in the same path. When joining endpoints, the selected endpoints can be on the same or on different paths.

8. Close this file (File/Close). Don't save your changes.

CUTTING PATHS

Frequently, it's easier to split a path and use only part of it for an illustration. You can cut a path in a freehand motion, you can cut it using a pattern guide, or you can just snip the path. Illustrator provides three ways of cutting paths: the Scissors tool, the Knife tool, and the Slice command.

SCISSORS TOOL

Use the Scissors tool on an open path to split it into two paths. Use the Scissors tool on a closed path to split it into an open path. You can use the Scissors tool on an anchor point or on any part of a segment.

Macintosh Keystrokes

⌘-Option-J Object/Path/
   Average
⌘-J Object/Path/Join
⌘-W File/Close

Windows Keystrokes

Ctrl-Alt-J Object/Path/
   Average
Ctrl-J Object/Path/Join
Ctrl-W File/Close

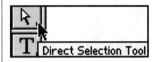

Direct Selection Tool

Default Fill and Stroke (D)

Clicking the Default Fill and Stroke icon makes the default fill white and default stroke 1-pt. black.

Macintosh Keystrokes

⌘-N File/New
⌘-A Edit/Select All
⌘-W File/Close

Windows Keystrokes

Ctrl-N File/New
Ctrl-A Edit/Select All
Ctrl-W File/Close

Transform Again

The Transform Again command creates a copy of the last copy made.

KNIFE TOOL

The Knife tool works like any knife, carving paths into separate shapes. Press the Shift key while slicing to constrain the cut to a straight line.

SLICE COMMAND

This command (Object/Path/Slice) works like a cookie cutter. Position one object over another and choose the Slice command. The topmost object will cut the underlying objects beneath it, just as if you had pressed a cookie cutter down on (naturally!) chocolate chip cookie dough.

EXERCISE E

1. Create a new document (File/New) and click the Default Fill and Stroke icon in the Toolbox to set the fill color to white and the stroke to 1-pt. black. Use the Ellipse tool to draw a circle. Press the Shift key as you draw to create the circle.

2. Use the Selection tool and click on the left edge of the circle. Drag it down and once you start to drag, press the Option/Alt-Shift keys to create a duplicate circle directly below the original circle.

3. Choose Object/Transform/Transform Again (Command/Ctrl-D) to create a third circle below the second circle. You should have three circles on the page.

4. Use the Selection tool to select the top circle and display its four anchor points and center point. Select the Scissors tool and click on the right anchor point, then on the left anchor point. Nothing appears to happen, but the circle is split. Use the Selection tool to click on the top of the split circle and drag it away, leaving only the bottom half of the circle (Figure 2.11).

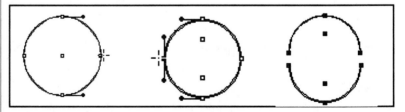

Figure 2.11. Selecting the Scissors tool turns the cursor into a crosshair. Click on an anchor point to split the path at that point. Clicking with the Scissors on the other anchor point displays the direction handles (center) and splits the circle's path into two paths, each with their own center points (right).

5. Select the second circle with the Selection tool. Select the Knife tool—it lives behind the Scissors tool. Drag the Knife tool from the top anchor point to the bottom anchor point, pressing the Shift key as you drag. Deselect everything. Use the Selection tool to move the right half away from the left half.

6. Drag the Knife tool around the right half of the circle, cutting it as you would a piece of cloth. When you release the mouse button, use the Selection tool to drag the separate pieces away from each other (Figure 2.12).

Selection Tool

Scissors Tool

Knife Tool

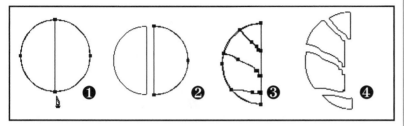

Figure 2.12. Use the Knife tool with the Shift key pressed to slice the circle from the top to the bottom through the anchor points (1). Drag the circle half away from the original circle (2). Use the Knife tool in one motion to slice through the circle half (3). Use the Selection tool to drag the separate pieces (paths) apart (4).

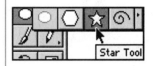
Star Tool

Click and drag the Ellipse tool to select the Star tool.

7. Choose Edit/Select All and press the Delete key to delete all the objects. Use the Rectangle tool to draw a rectangle. Fill it with a color.

8. Select the Star tool—behind the Ellipse tool—and drag to draw a star on top of the rectangle. Let some of the points overlap the rectangle. Fill the selected star with a contrasting color.

9. With the star still selected, choose Object/Path/Slice. Deselect everything by clicking on a blank area of the page. Use the Selection tool to select the rectangle and notice the path outline of the cutout. Click on the cutout and drag it away from the rectangle (Figure 2.13).

10. Close this file (File/Close). Don't save your changes.

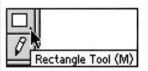
Rectangle Tool (M)

Figure 2.13. The star is selected, making it the cutting object (left). When the Slice command is applied, the star is deleted, leaving only the outline of any overlapping paths (center). The outline can then be moved away from the rectangle, leaving only its outline (right).

Macintosh Keystrokes

⌘-N File/New
⌘-Y View/Artwork/Preview
⌘-Shift-A Edit/Deselect All

Windows Keystrokes

Ctrl-N File/New
Ctrl-Y View/Artwork/
    Preview
Ctrl-Shift-A Edit/Deselect
    All

CORNER POINTS AND SMOOTH POINTS

Points in Illustrator can be either corner points or smooth points. Corner points connect line segments such as the four line segments in a rectangle. Corner points also connect noncontinuous curve segments such as those in a wavy line. Smooth points connect the segments of continuous curve paths, those paths that follow a continuous wavy shape (Figure 2.14).

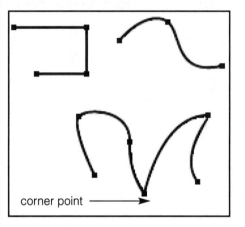

corner point

Figure 2.14. The path on the top left is comprised of four corner points connecting the three line segments. The path on the right is comprised of three curve points connecting two curved segments. The path at the bottom displays a corner point where the two curves meet.

When you click with the Direct Selection tool (white arrow) on a segment connected to a smooth point, direction handles appear which allow you to manipulate the segments on either side of the anchor point. When you click on a corner point and move its direction handle, only the curve segment on the same side of the point as the direction handle is adjusted (Figure 2.15).

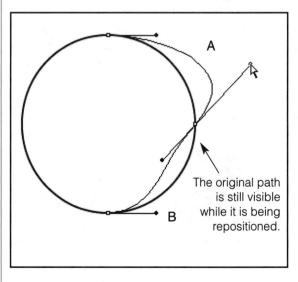

A

B

The original path
is still visible
while it is being
repositioned.

Figure 2.15. Moving the direction handle on a smooth point moves both segments (A and B) on either side of the point simultaneously. The anchor point does not move while the segments are being repositioned.

EXERCISE F

1. Create a new file (File/New). Choose View/Artwork (Command/Ctrl-Y). Click on the Ellipse tool and press the Shift key before dragging to create a circle. It appears with all five of its points selected.

2. Click on the Selection tool (black arrow) and click on any segment of the circle. Drag the entire circle around the page.

3. Choose Edit/Deselect All (Command/Ctrl-Shift-A) to deselect the circle. Click on the Direct Selection tool (white arrow) and click on the upper right segment of the circle. It appears selected, with all of its points hollow. Notice, however, that the segment you clicked also displays two direction handles poking out from the two anchor points (Figure 2.15). This is because a circle is comprised of smooth points, whereas a rectangle is comprised of corner points. Corner points don't have direction handles (unless they're connected to a smooth point), whereas smooth points have two direction handles. A direction handle is used to adjust the segments on either side of the anchor point. When you move these levers, only the segments move, not the anchor point (Figure 2.15).

4. With the Direct Selection tool still active, click on the tip of the lower direction handle and move the handle to the right and left. Notice that the anchor point doesn't move; only the segments on either side of the anchor point move.

5. Choose Edit/Undo Move (Command/Ctrl-Z) to restore the circle to its original shape.

6. Click on the upper direction handle and move it up and down and right and left. Notice again how only the segments connected to the anchor point move; the anchor point itself does not move.

7. If you click on the center point, you will select the entire object, just as if you had used the Selection tool. If that happens, click on any blank area of the page, then click on a segment with the Direct Selection tool.

8. Close this file (File/Close). Don't save your changes.

Macintosh Keystrokes

⌘-N File/New
⌘-J Object/Path/Join
⌘-Y View/Artwork/Preview
⌘-Shift-A Edit/Deselect All
⌘-W File/Close

Windows Keystrokes

Ctrl-N File/New
Ctrl-J Object/Path/Join
Ctrl-Y View/Artwork/
　　　Preview
Ctrl-Shift-A Edit/Deselect
　　　All
Ctrl-W File/Close

Ellipse Tool

Selection Tool

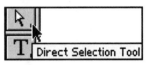
Direct Selection Tool

FYI

Center points are not anchor points. They cannot be edited, and they do not display any direction handles.

Pencil Tool

Options

☑ **Keep selected**

The Keep selected option displays drawn objects with their anchor points selected. You must deselect and then select with the Direct Selection tool to edit individual segments.

Pencil Tool (N)

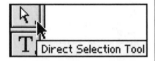
Direct Selection Tool

Selection Tool

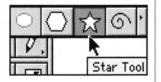
Star Tool

Knife Tool

1. Create a new document (File/New). Make sure the Toolbox is displayed (Window/Show Tools). Choose View/Artwork (Command/Ctrl-Y). Double-click on the Pencil tool and click the Keep selected check box in the Pencil Tool Preferences dialog box.

2. Click on the Pencil tool to select it and then move the cursor onto the page, where it changes into a pencil.

3. Click and drag to draw a heart, just as if you were drawing with a real pencil. Don't worry if your heart looks like a coronary disaster; you'll fix it later.

4. When you release the mouse button, the heart appears with all its points selected (filled). Deselect. Click on the Direct Selection tool (white arrow) and click and drag on a segment to reposition just that segment.

5. Click on a hollow point to select that point and move the point. Continue to move segments and points to reshape the heart until it resembles an organ in the human body.

6. Select the heart with the Selection tool by clicking on any segment and drag it away. If all the segments are not connected, use the Average command to overlap the endpoints of the open paths and the Join command to join the endpoints. The heart should be one complete path.

7. Choose File/Save (Command/Ctrl-S) and type *Heart.ai* in the Save this document as field. Select Illustrator from the Format menu (Macintosh) or Save as type menu (Windows). Navigate to your Projects folder. Choose 8.0 in the Compatibility field in the Illustrator format dialog box and click on Save. You will now be able to open the file again in Illustrator and edit it.

8. Click on the Default Colors icon in the Toolbox to set the fill to white and the stroke to 1-pt. black.

9. Use the Star tool (behind the Ellipse tool) and drag to create a star.

10. Click on the Knife tool and then drag it across the star from the left star point to the right star point. The star does not have to be selected.

11. Deselect and use the Selection tool to drag one of the pieces away from the whole object (Figure 2.16).

Figure 2.16. The star (left) is sliced with the Knife tool (center). It is then deselected. The top part is then selected with the Selection tool and moved away from the lower part (right).

12. Draw two objects with the Ellipse tool. Draw a third object over the first two with the Rectangle tool and keep it selected. Choose Object/Path/Slice. Deselect and use the Selection tool to move each separate object around the page (Figure 2.17).

13. Close this path (File/Close). Don't save your changes.

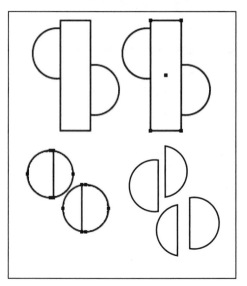

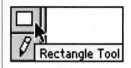

Figure 2.17. The original two objects are cut by the rectangle (top). This results in separate objects with long vertical edges reflecting the outline of the rectangle (bottom).

REVIEW

In this unit you learned that:

1. Paths are comprised of segments and segments are connected by anchor points.

2. Paths can be open (lines) or closed (shapes).

3. Open paths are called *lines*.

4. Closed paths are called *shapes*.

5. The Selection tool is used to select an entire path with all its segments and anchor points.

6. The Direct Selection tool is used to select path segments and anchor points.

7. An object must first be deselected before it can be selected with the Direct Selection tool.

8. Open paths have an endpoint at each end.

9. Endpoints on different lines can be averaged and joined.

10. Paths can be cut with the Scissors tool, Knife tool, and Slice command.

11. Corner points connect straight line segments; smooth points connect curve segments.

12. Smooth points display direction handles that can be used to reshape the curve.

Drawing with Basic Shapes

OVERVIEW

In this unit you will learn how to:
draw objects using the basic shape tools
duplicate (clone) objects
specify dimensions for drawn objects

TERMS

constrain
Default Colors icon
Encapsulated PostScript
modifier keys

HOW IT WORKS

Create the type and convert to outlines. Use the basic shape tools to create a cluster of small basic shapes. Apply a white fill and black stroke. Select the cluster and define a pattern. Select the path outlines and fill with the new pattern. Use the Selection tool and tilde key (~) to move the pattern around in the paths. To work with the individual paths, select the path with the Direct Selection tool, press (and keep depressed) the tilde key to reposition the pattern in just that path.

The basic shape tools are the Ellipse tool and the three tools accessed by clicking on its triangle, and the Rectangle tool and the two tools accessed via its triangle.

Version 7

There are nine basic shape tools in version 7, which includes Centered Ellipse, Rectangle, and Rounded Rectangle tools.

FYI

The center point cannot be moved or deleted. If Snap to Point is selected under the View menu, you will feel the center of one object snap to the center point of the object below it.

Click on the Tearoff Tab at the end of the any multiple tool to create a separate palette of just those tools.

BASIC SHAPE TOOLS

Because Adobe Illustrator is an illustration tool, those who can draw are ahead of the game before they even launch the application. However, Illustrator is also designed for the drawing-impaired, those who need to create illustrations but whose background is in anything else but fine art. If you can't just pick up a pencil and a paper napkin and create a masterpiece that will eventually be displayed in a major museum, the basic shape tools in Illustrator are made just for you.

DEFAULT TOOL VALUES

Whenever you draw with the basic shape tools, the values last input in that tool's dialog box prevail. You can either change those values before drawing an object or draw the object and then manually resize it.

ACCESSING BASIC SHAPE TOOLS

There are six basic shape tools in the Illustrator 8 Toolbox. To access the ones that are not visible, click and drag on the triangle in the lower right corner of the tools (Figure 3.1).

 ⟵ Tearoff Tab

Figure 3.1. All of the basic shape tools are accessed from the Ellipse tool and the Rectangle tool. Click on the black triangle in the lower right corner of the tool and drag to select another basic shape tool. Use the Tearoff Tab to drag the tools anywhere on the page.

ELLIPSE TOOL

The Ellipse tool draws ovals and circles. When you drag to draw with the Ellipse tool, the oval or circle grows from the point where you started to draw. If you press the Option/Alt key before releasing the mouse button, however, the circle grows from the center outward from where you began to draw (Figure 3.2).

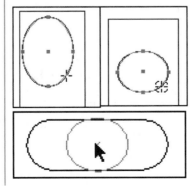

Figure 3.2. Drawing with a basic shape tool draws from the top to the bottom. With this tool, the center point moves in relation to the sides of the drawing. Pressing the Option/Alt key while drawing draws from the center outward. The center point remains stationary while the circle is drawn around it (above). Use the center point to align objects (below).

RECTANGLE TOOLS

The Rectangle tool has another tool associated with it: the Rounded Rectangle tool, which draws rectangles with round corners. To draw rectangles from the center outward, press the Option/Alt key when drawing with any Rectangle tool.

DRAWING CIRCLES AND SQUARES

To draw a perfect circle, press the Shift key before you begin to draw with any of the Ellipse tools. If you don't press the Shift key while drawing, you will create an oval. However, you can press the Shift key anytime *before* releasing the mouse button to create a circle. Likewise, to create a square with any of the Rectangle tools, press the Shift key before drawing or before you release the mouse button. Pressing the Shift key when drawing with the Ellipse and Rectangle tools constrains the object to a circle or to a square.

DUPLICATING OBJECTS

You may be surprised to learn that there is no duplicate command in Illustrator. To create a duplicate of any object, Option/Alt-drag the object with the Selection tool. As you copy-drag, the pointer turns into a double arrowhead. You must press the Option/Alt key after you begin dragging and *before* releasing the mouse button. Always release the mouse button before releasing the Option/Alt key.

EXERCISE A

1. Create a new document (File/New). Command/Ctrl-Shift-double-click on any tool to restore the Toolbox to its default tools. Display the Swatches palette (Window/Show Swatches).

2. Click on the Default Fill and Stroke icon in the Toolbox to set the fill to white and the stroke to black.

3. Select the Ellipse tool and drag to draw an oval. Release the mouse button, then the modifier key. Press the Shift key and drag again to draw a circle.

4. Select the circle with the Selection tool, start dragging, and press the Option/Alt key to create a duplicate circle.

5 Select the Ellipse tool, press the Option/Alt key, and drag to create an oval from the center outward.

6. Press the Option/Alt-Shift keys and drag with the Ellipse tool to create a circle from the center outward.

Macintosh Keystrokes

⌘-N File/New

Windows Keystrokes

Ctrl-N File/New

Selection Tool

Ellipse Tool

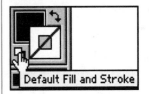

Default Fill and Stroke

Version 7

Illustrator 8.0 does not have a Centered Ellipse or Centered Rectangle tool as does version 7. In version 7, drawing with the Centered Ellipse tool creates the ellipse from the center outward.

In version 8, press the Option/Alt key before dragging with the Ellipse or Rectangle tool to draw the ellipse or rectangle from the center outward.

FYI

Pressing the Shift key while dragging with the Ellipse or Rectangle tool creates a circle or a square.

Ellipse Tool

Selection Tool

Color problem?

Remember that an object must be selected before it can be filled or stroked.

7. Use the Ellipse tool to draw a large oval to create a face. Press the Shift key and drag with the Ellipse tool to create a circular eye on the left side of the circle. Select the smaller circle with the Selection tool, start dragging, and press the Option/Alt key to create a duplicate eye on the right side of the face.

8. Choose View/Artwork (Command/Ctrl-Y) to display the center points of the objects. Select the Ellipse tool, click on the center point of each eye, press the Shift key, and drag to create a smaller circle for the eyeball.

9. Shift-Select both eyeballs with the Selection tool, click on the Fill icon in the Toolbox, and click on a color in the Swatches palette to color both eyeballs. Choose View/Preview to display the colors.

10. Use the Ellipse tool to draw a mouth. Click on the Default fill and stroke icon and use the Rectangle tool to draw teeth inside the mouth.

11. Switch to Artwork mode (Command/Ctrl-Y), select the Rectangle tool, press the Option/Alt key, and click on the center of the large circle (the face). Drag to create a rectangle that extends beyond the face. Switch to Preview mode (Command/Ctrl-Y), and with the rectangle still selected, click on a color in the Swatches palette. The rectangle is the topmost object and covers the face. Choose Arrange/Send to Back to move the selected rectangle behind the other artwork. Your screen should resemble Figure 3.3.

Figure 3.3. Use the different Ellipse and Rectangle tools to create a drawing made from basic shapes.

12. Choose File/Save. You could save this file in native Illustrator format, which allows you to open and edit it in Illustrator or in Photoshop at a later date. However, to import the illustration into another application like QuarkXPress or Pagemaker, which does not read the native Illustrator format, you must save it as an Encapsulated PostScript file (EPS). Choose Illustrator EPS from the Format menu (Macintosh) or from the Save as type menu (Windows). Type *Face.eps* in the Save this document as field, navigate to your Projects folder, and click on Save.

13. Close the file (File/Close).

STAR TOOL

To access the Star tool, click on the Ellipse tool and drag to select the Star tool. When you click and drag to draw with the Star tool, the object defaults to a five-pointed star. Dragging in toward the star makes it smaller; dragging away from the star makes it bigger. Rotate the star by dragging it in a circular motion.

STAR TOOL MODIFIER KEYS

If you press the **Shift** key while dragging with the Star tool, you constrain one or two points of the star to the horizontal axis. Press the **spacebar** while dragging to move the star on the page. Press the **Option/Alt** key while dragging to make the opposite segments of the star parallel to one another. Press the **Up Arrow** while dragging to increase the number of star points; press the **Down Arrow** to decrease the number of star points. You can decrease to three points, creating a triangle instead of a star. Press the **tilde** key (~) while dragging with the Star tool to create progressively larger copies of the current star shape.

EXERCISE B

1. In a new document (File/New), drag the triangle on the Ellipse tool to access the Star tool. Click and drag on the page to draw a star. Drag into the star to make it smaller; drag away from the star to make it bigger. Release the mouse button.

2. Drag to create another star, but press the Up Arrow and Down Arrow keys to add and delete points from the star. Release the mouse button.

3. Continue to draw stars using the modifier keys to alter the size, shape, and number of stars. Figure 3.4 displays some of the effects you can achieve with this tool.

4. Close this file (File/Close). Don't save your changes.

Figure 3.4. The original star (top left) with increased points using the Up Arrow key (center) and with parallel opposite segments (right). The lower star was created by dragging while pressing the tilde (~) key. In Artwork mode, all the progressively larger stars were selected and given a fill of None and 1-pt. black stroke.

Macintosh Keystrokes

⌘-N File/New
⌘-W File/Close

Windows Keystrokes

Ctrl-N File/New
Ctrl-W File/Close

Default values

The basic shape tools display the values last typed in their dialog boxes. To return to the default values, trash the Illustrator Preferences file.

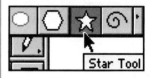

Modifier keys

You can use the same arrow modifier keys to adjust the rounded rectangle as you draw it.

Sorry!

Even if you restore the Toolbox to its default tools, when you use the Star tool it reverts to the last star you created. The only way to get back to the default Star tool is to trash the Adobe Illustrator Preferences file.

Tip

To restore the Toolbox to its default tools, Command-Shift-double-click on any tool (Macintosh) or Ctrl-Shift-double-click on any tool (Windows).

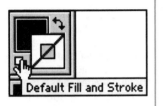

Fill icon in the Toolbox

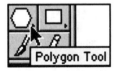

POLYGON TOOL

The Polygon tool is used to draw objects with sides of equal length. As with the Star tool, using the modifier keys increases, decreases, rotates, and copies the polygon. The Polygon tool creates an object with a minimum of three sides; like the Star and Spiral tools, the Polygon tool always draws from the center outward.

SPIRAL TOOL

The Spiral tool was added to the program only after many Illustrator gurus made a fortune explaining exactly how to use the Ellipse tool to create a spiral. What used to be a complicated task is now a matter of a single keystroke. While dragging, drag away from or toward the center of the spiral to increase or decrease its size, just as you do with the Star and Polygon tools. Press the **Option/Alt** key while dragging to add or delete segments from the center of the spiral while changing its size. This modifier increases the size of the spiral by adding spaces between the swirls. To tighten the spiral winds, press the **Command/Ctrl** key while dragging away from or toward the center of the spiral. Press the **Up Arrow** or **Down Arrow** key without dragging (keep the mouse button pressed) to add or delete segments from the center of the spiral.

EXERCISE C

1. Click the Default Fill and Stroke icon in the Toolbox to set the default color values. Click on the Polygon tool to select it. Drag and press the Shift key to constrain the bottom segment to the horizontal axis. Release the mouse button.

2. Move to an empty area of the page. Press the tilde key (~) and drag quickly to create a spider-web effect. Release the mouse button.

3. Move to an empty area of the page and drag, pressing the Up Arrow key (keep it pressed) to add segments as you drag. Press (and keep pressed) the Down Arrow key to add and delete segments. Release the mouse button. If you don't drag while pressing the arrows, segments will be added to or deleted from the currently sized polygon.

4. Select the Spiral tool and click and drag, pressing the Up Arrow to add swirls to the spiral. Press the Down Arrow to remove spirals. Eventually you will end up with only a curved segment. Figure 3.5 displays some of the effects you can achieve.

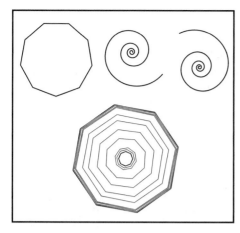

Figure 3.5. The center spiral was created by dragging down; the one on the left by dragging up. The spider web polygon was created by pressing the tilde (~) key and dragging quickly. The new polygons were given a fill of None and a black stroke.

SPECIFYING DIMENSIONS

Thus far you have created geometric objects with the basic shape tools by clicking and dragging. Illustrator also provides a dialog box for each of these tools where you can enter the precise values for the object's segments and spacing. When you first display any basic shape tool's dialog box, it contains the values last used to create that basic shape, unless you first delete the Adobe Illustrator Preferences file before launching Illustrator.

The values entered in these dialog boxes are based on the unit of measure selected for objects in the Units & Undo Preferences dialog box (Figure 3.6).

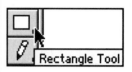

Figure 3.6. The Units & Undo Preferences dialog box is where you specify the unit of measure for objects from the General menu. It's best to leave the value for Type set to points. (The Macintosh dialog box does not have a Stroke option.)

Select Units & Undo from the Preferences submenu (File/Preferences) to select a unit of measure for objects and for type.

Version 7

Clicking on the page with the Centered Ellipse tool displays the Ellipse dialog box, but creates the ellipse or circle using the point where you clicked as the object's center point.

ELLIPSE TOOL OPTIONS

If you click but don't drag with the Ellipse tool, the Ellipse dialog box appears, where you can specify the width and height of the ellipse. If the width and height have the same value, you will create a circle. Option/Alt-click with the Ellipse tool to create an ellipse with its center point at the spot where you clicked.

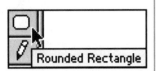

RECTANGLE TOOLS OPTIONS

Clicking on the page with either the Rectangle or Rounded Rectangle tool displays the appropriate dialog box. Here you enter the height and width of the rectangle. In the Rounded Rectangle dialog box you can also specify a value for the corner radius, which determines how curved the corners of the rectangle will be (Figure 3.7).

Figure 3.7. The Rectangle dialog box creates rectangles (or squares) with sharp corners. The Rounded Rectangle dialog box creates a rounded rectangle with a half-inch Corner Radius value.

POLYGON TOOL OPTIONS

The Polygon tool is used to draw objects with a specific number of sides, all of equal length, with each side being the same distance from the center of the object.

EXERCISE D

1. In a new file (File/New), choose File/Preferences/Units & Undo. Select Inches from the General pull-down menu and click on OK.

2. Click on the Polygon tool in the Toolbox to select it. Click once on the page to display the Polygon dialog box.

3. Type 2 in the Radius field to create a polygon with all sides two inches long. Type 3 in the sides field or use the arrows to specify three sides for the polygon. With these dimensions, you will create an equilateral triangle. Click on OK. Your screen should resemble Figure 3.8.

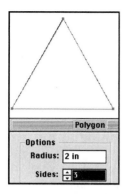

Figure 3.8. Specify a length for the polygon's segments in the Radius field and the number of segments in the Sides field.

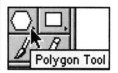

4. Select the Polygon tool again and click on the page. Change the Radius and Sides values and click on OK. Click and drag to create a new polygon. Press the Up or Down Arrow keys to increase or decrease the number of sides in the polygon. Press the spacebar to move the polygon around the page.

5. Click on the page with the Polygon tool and notice that the Polygon dialog box now displays the values last used when you created the polygon by dragging it.

6. Close this file (Command/Ctrl-W). Don't save your changes.

STAR TOOL OPTIONS

Use the Star dialog box to create a star-shaped object with a specified number of points and of a specific size.

EXERCISE E

1. Make sure the Ruler Units field in the General Preferences dialog box is set to inches. Click on the Star tool and click once on the page to display the Star dialog box (Figure 3.9).

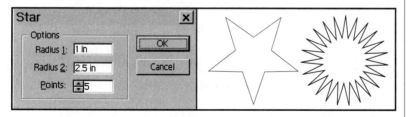

Figure 3.9. These values in the Star dialog box create the five-pointed star. Pressing the Up Arrow key adds star points and creates the other star.

Macintosh Keystrokes

⌘-N File/New
⌘-W File/Close

Windows Keystrokes

Ctrl-N File/New
Ctrl-W File/Close

Relax!

The terminology for the Spiral tool gets a bit dense. It's usually easier just to drag with the tool until you get the spiral you want.

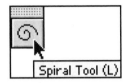

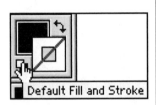

2. The Radius 1 value specifies the distance from the center of the star to its *inner* point. Type 1 in the Radius 1 field.

3. The Radius 2 value specifies the distance from the center of the star to its *outermost* point. Type 2.5 in the Radius 2 field to create a star that is two and a half inches from its center to the top point.

4. Use the arrows or type 5 in the Points field. Click on OK to create the star shaped like the one in Figure 3.9.

5. Click on the Star tool again and drag to create a five-pointed star. While dragging, press the Up Arrow key or the Down Arrow key to add or delete sides to the star.

6. Click with the Star tool and change the number of points in the Star dialog box to 10. Drag to create another star and hold down the Option/Alt key to makes the slopes of alternate sides of the star run parallel to each other. You can hold down the spacebar to move the star around the page as you are drawing it.

7. Close this file (File/Close). Don't save your changes.

SPIRAL TOOL OPTIONS

The Spiral tool creates a spiral-shaped object with a specified radius and number of winds (complete turns) that the spiral will complete from start to finish. The Spiral dialog box lets you specify the radius and the number of winds between turns as well as the direction of the spiral.

EXERCISE F

1. In a new file (File/New), make sure that Inches is the unit of measure (File/Preferences/Units & Undo). Click the Default Colors icon in the Toolbox. Click on the Spiral tool in the Toolbox and click on the page to display the Spiral dialog box.

2. The values in the Spiral dialog box reflect the last set of values typed in that box, as well as the Ruler Units option selected in the General Preferences dialog box. Type 150 in the Radius field to specify 150 points as the distance from the center of the spiral to its outermost point.

3. Type 80 in the Decay field to specify the amount by which each wind (turn) will decrease relative to the previous wind in the Decay field. Increasing the Decay value closer to 100 creates tighter winds.

Unit 3 ★ Drawing with Basic Shapes

4. Type 12 in the Segments field or use the arrows to create twelve segments. Because each full wind contains four segments, the more segments you specify, the more winds you will get (Figure 3.10). However, you may not be able to view all the winds if your Radius value is not great enough.

Figure 3.10. Spirals composed of 4, 8, 12, and 16 segments.

5. Click on either the clockwise (left) or counterclockwise icon (right) to specify the direction of the spiral. Click on OK. Experiment with this tool to create different effects (Figure 3.11).

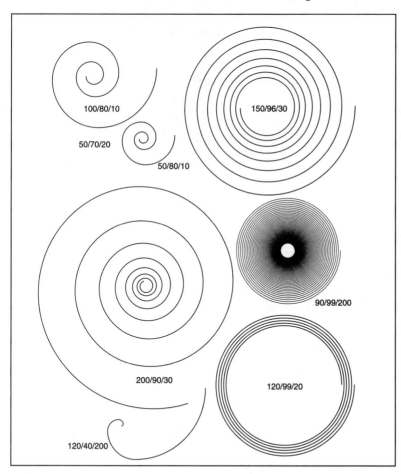

Figure 3.11. Spirals created by using different values in the Spiral dialog box.

REVIEW

In this unit you learned that:

1. The basic shape tools create open and closed paths.

2. Basic shapes can be edited by manipulating their anchor points and path segments.

3. Basic shapes are created both by dragging with the tool and by making selections in the tool's dialog box.

4. Basic shape objects can be modified as they are being drawn by using modifier keys.

5. Objects can be duplicated by Option/Alt-dragging.

6. The basic shape tools appear on a palette with a Tearoff Tab.

UNIT 4
Painting Objects

OVERVIEW

In this unit you will learn:
how to create and apply fill and stroke colors to objects
the difference between spot color and process color
how to use the Swatches and Color palettes
how to convert colors to and from spot and process color
how to apply different kinds of strokes to objects
how to use swatch and custom libraries
how to replace colors globally

TERMS

Bevel Join
cap
CMYK sliders
custom colors
Dash/Gap fields
fill
Miter Join
Miter Limit
None button
process color
Round Join
Shift-select
Spectrum Bar
spot color
stroke
Swap Colors icon
Tint Ramp
Tint Slider

HOW IT WORKS

Create the type and convert to outlines. Select the first character (now a path) and drag it away from the others. Use the Pen tool with no fill and a contrasting stroke to draw zig-zag lines through the path. Select the character path and the lines and apply the Divide filter (Object/Pathfinder/Divide). Use the Direct Selection tool to select the individual paths created by the Divide filter and apply a different color to each path.

51

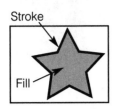

Stroke

Fill

FYI

Unless you fill or stroke an object, you won't see its outline in Preview view, only in Artwork view.

FYI

Drag a color from the Fill or Stroke buttons in the Toolbox, Color, or Gradient palettes onto an object to apply the color without first selecting the object.

Version 7

The Color and Swatches palettes in version 7 do not display a None icon.

Clicking the None button causes the Fill or Stroke icons to display the None symbol, depending on which one is selected. If an object is selected on the page when you click this button, its fill and/or stroke colors will be removed, and you will only be able to see its outline in Artwork mode unless it is selected.

APPLYING COLORS

Creating, editing, and applying colors in Illustrator is a cumbersome task involving the use of four palettes. A color is mixed and edited in the Color palette, stored in the Swatches palette, identified as a fill or stroke color in the Toolbox and/or Color palette, and applied as a stroke weight in the Stroke palette.

FILL AND STROKE

Every object is enclosed by a path outline. When a fill color is applied to the object (path), that outline is filled with color. Stroking an object applies a color to the outline of that path. Paths can be filled or stroked or filled and stroked. When None is applied to an object for either its fill and/or stroke, the object displays no color in its enclosed area or along its path outlines (Figure 4.1).

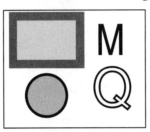

Figure 4.1. The box at the top has a fill and wide stroke. The circle has a fill and narrow stroke. The letter M has a fill and no stroke. The letter Q has a stroke but no fill.

FILL AND STROKE ICONS

Before you can apply a fill or stroke to a path, you must specify which it is you're applying. You do this by selecting the appropriate icon in the Toolbox (Figure 4.2) or in the Color palette. Click on the Fill or Stroke icon before applying the color to a selection. Toggle between the Fill and Stroke icons by pressing x.

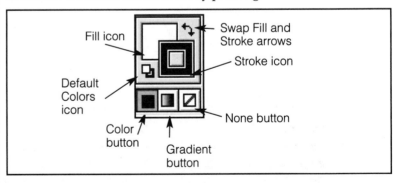

Fill icon

Swap Fill and Stroke arrows

Stroke icon

Default Colors icon

None button

Color button

Gradient button

Figure 4.2. The Fill and Stroke icons in the Toolbox determine where color is applied. Click on the Fill icon to apply a fill; click on the Stroke icon to apply a stroke. When you click on an icon, it comes forward. Here, the Stroke icon is selected and any color applied to a selection will be applied as a stroke.

DEFAULT COLORS AND SWAP COLORS ICONS

Click the Default Fill and Stroke icon in the Toolbox to display the default white fill and black stroke in the Toolbox and in the Fill and Stroke icons on the Color palette. Click the Swap Fill and Stroke arrows to swap the current fill and stroke colors, or press x to swap the fill and stroke colors.

COLOR, GRADIENT, AND NONE BUTTONS

Click the Color button to apply the current fill or stroke to a selection—depending on which icon is frontmost in the Toolbox and Color palette. When you click this button, the Color palette is automatically displayed. Clicking the Gradient button displays the Gradient palette and fills the selected paths with the default gradient. Click the None button to fill and stroke with none—no color at all.

The Color button displays the selected color for the selected icon, fill or stroke. Click this button to display the Color palette. The Gradient and None buttons are to its right.

APPLYING A FILL

You can apply a fill to both open and closed paths. The first time you create a path, that path is automatically painted with the current fill and stroke colors displayed in the Toolbox. Before a path can be filled, however, it must be selected with any of the selection tools and the Fill icon must be selected in the Toolbox. If you're applying a fill and nothing happens, it's probably because (1) you've forgotten to select the object, or (2) you didn't click the Fill icon in the Toolbox.

To fill more than one object with the same fill, use any selection tool to select the first object, press the Shift key, and select the other objects you wish to fill. When you select a color from either the Swatches or the Color palette, all the selected objects will display that one fill.

Filling open paths

Illustrator fills an open path as if the endpoints were connected by a straight line.

APPLYING A STROKE

To outline a path with any color, click the Stroke icon in the Toolbox, click on a color in the Swatches palette, and use the Stroke palette to specify a stroke width (Figure 4.3). Until you change the Weight value, everything you draw will be stroked with that weight and in the current stroke color.

Click the Fill or Stroke icon on the Color palette to specify where the new color is to be applied. Click the None icon to apply no color to the fill or stroke.

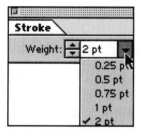

Figure 4.3. Specify a stroke width from the Weight menu on the Stroke palette or by typing a value in the Weight field. Using the up and down arrows increases or decreases the stroke weight without using the pull-down menu.

FYI

Type *in* after a stroke weight and Illustrator converts the points value to inches.

Macintosh Keystrokes

⌘-N File/New
F6 Window/Show Color
F10 Window/Show Stroke
⌘-K File/Preferences/
    General
⌘-W File/Close

Windows Keystrokes

Ctrl-N File/New
F6 Window/Show Color
F10 Window/Show Stroke
Ctrl-K File/Preferences/
    General
Ctrl-W File/Close

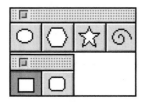

Many of the basic shape tools are pulled out from the Ellipse and Rectangle tools.

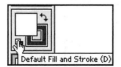

FYI

Press x on the keyboard to switch from the Fill to the Stroke icon in the Toolbox and in the Color palette.

EXERCISE A

1. Create a new document (File/New). Display the Swatches palette (Window/Show Swatches), Color palette (F6), and Stroke palette (F10).

2. Click the Default Colors icon in the Toolbox. Use any of the basic shape tools to draw a few objects on the page. They appear displaying the default white fill and black stroke (Figure 4.4).

Figure 4.4. The basic shape objects display the default black stroke and white fill.

3. Choose File/Preferences/General (Command/Ctrl-K) and turn off the Bounding Box option, unless you really like working with it. Click on OK.

4. Click on the Selection tool (black arrow) and click on one of the objects. The Fill icon should be the selected icon in the Toolbox. Click on any swatch in the Swatches palette to fill the object with that color. Click on the Stroke icon in the Toolbox or press x and click on another color in the Swatches palette The object keeps its fill color, but the new color is applied to the stroke. Notice that the current fill and stroke colors appear in the appropriate icons in the Toolbox and in the Color palette.

5. With the object still selected, use the pull-down menu on the Stroke palette to increase the stroke weight. Use the up and down arrows to increase and decrease the stroke weight. Drag to select the value in the Weight field and type another value. Press Return/Enter to execute the change. You must always press Return or Enter to execute any command typed in a palette's text field.

6. Continue to fill and stroke the objects until you are comfortable with selecting the icons and applying different weight strokes.

7. Close this file (Command/Ctrl-W). Don't save your changes.

SPOT COLOR AND PROCESS COLOR

Color comes in two flavors, spot color and process color. Spot colors, also called *custom colors*, are premixed colors that print on separate plates on press. If you apply a single spot color to an illustration, two plates will print: the black plate and the spot color plate.

Process colors, however, are mixed from percentages of the four process colors, cyan, magenta, yellow, and black. When you apply a process color to an illustration, four plates will print, one for each process color. It's cheaper, therefore, if you are applying more than three colors to an illustration, to specify those colors as process colors, because you can separate an unlimited number of process colors on only four plates.

SWATCHES PALETTE

The default Swatches palette (Figure 4.5) displays process colors, gradients, and patterns. The None swatch strips the selected object of any fill or stroke color, depending on which icon is selected in the Toolbox or Color palette.

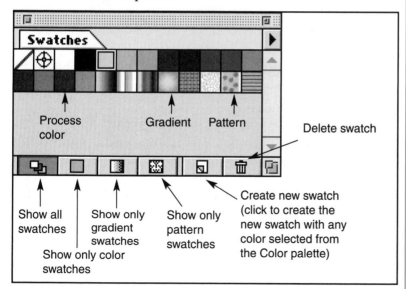

Process color

Gradient Pattern

Delete swatch

Show all swatches

Show only gradient swatches

Show only pattern swatches

Create new swatch (click to create the new swatch with any color selected from the Color palette)

Show only color swatches

Figure 4.5. The default Swatches palette displays thumbnails of color swatches and icons for displaying, creating, and deleting swatches.

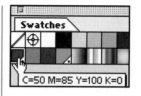

C=50 M=85 Y=100 K=0

A spot color displays a dot in the lower corner of its swatch on the Swatches palette. Click on the corner of any color swatch to see its CMYK percentages.

[Registration]

The Registration color is applied to objects that you want printed on all plates when printing on press, including any spot color plates. Registration color is usually used for crop marks and trim marks.

The currently active color is displayed in the Color button in the Toolbox.

As long as an object is selected, you can change its stroke weight from the Stroke palette without selecting the Stroke icon in the Toolbox, because the palette affects only the object's weight, not its color.

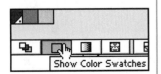

Clicking the Show Color Swatches button on the Swatches palette displays only the color swatches, not patterns or gradients.

Even as we speak...

The Color palette works in the background even if you don't display it. Once you display it, you'll see the current fill and stroke colors reflected in the icons.

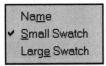

Use the Swatches palette menu to select a display option for the swatches.

Spot colors have a dot in the lower right corner of the swatch; process colors do not. Gradient swatches appear as bands of color, and pattern swatches display thumbnail views of the pattern. There are no spot colors in the default Swatches palette. You create your own spot colors or import them from a Swatches library.

SELECTING COLORS FROM THE SWATCHES PALETTE

Click on any color swatch in the Swatches palette to select it and apply it as a fill or stroke to a selected object. You can select process colors, spot colors, gradients, and patterns from the Swatches palette. Remember to select the Fill icon or Stroke icon in the Toolbox before selecting a color from the Swatches palette.

ADDING COLORS TO THE SWATCHES PALETTE

Once you mix a color in the Color palette, it appears in the Fill or Stroke icon in the Toolbox and on the Color palette. If you have objects selected, the new color is applied to the objects' fill or stroke, depending on which icon is selected in the Toolbox or Color palette. To save that color for later use in the same document, *select the object* to display its fill or stroke color in the Toolbox and Color palette and do one of the following:

▲ Drag the icon from the Toolbox or Color palette into the Swatches palette to add it to the swatch library;

▲ Click the New Swatch icon at the bottom of the Swatches palette to add the current color to the swatches;

▲ Choose New Swatch from the Swatches palette menu and enter a name and color mode for the new color;

▲ Select Add All Unused from the Swatches palette menu.

DUPLICATING COLORS

To duplicate a color swatch, drag the swatch over the New Swatch icon in the Swatches palette. Double-click on the duplicate and make any changes to the color in the Swatch Options dialog box. You can also select the color swatch and choose Duplicate Swatch from the Swatches palette menu.

DELETING COLORS

To delete a swatch, select it and click the Trash icon in the Swatches palette. Delete only those swatches that are not currently applied to objects in the document. If you delete a color you have used in the file, the only way to get the swatch back is to choose Undo Delete Swatches or to select the object with the deleted color and drag the fill or stroke icon to the Swatches palette. You can also select a swatch and choose Delete Swatch from the Swatches palette menu.

COLOR PALETTE

Use the Color palette to mix and edit colors. The icon on the Color palette displays the currently selected color for the fill or stroke, depending on which icon you selected in the Toolbox. Use the triangle on the right side of the palette to select a color model (CMYK and Grayscale for print work; RGB for Web illustrations) and to expand the palette. Unless you choose Show Options from the Color palette's menu, only the CMYK Spectrum for process colors or the Tint Ramp for spot colors will be displayed.

At the right side of the Spectrum Bar and the Tint Ramp are black and white swatches which allow you to select those colors quickly, without having to find them in the Swatches palette.

EXERCISE B

1. In a new document (File/New), press the Shift and Tab keys to hide all the palettes except the Toolbox. Display the Swatches palette (Window/Show Swatches). Click the Default Colors icon in the Toolbox. Use the Rectangle tool to draw a rectangle.

2. Click on the Color button in the Toolbox to display the Color palette. Because the default white fill is active and because the Fill icon is selected, the CMYK sliders for white appear in the Color palette.

3. Click on a swatch in the Swatches palette to fill the rectangle with a new color. Click the Stroke icon in the Toolbox or press x to activate the Stroke icon and assign the object a new stroke color (Figure 4.6).

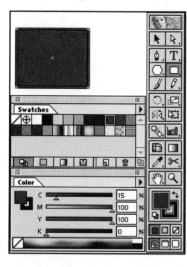

Figure 4.6. When the Fill icon is active, clicking on a process color fills the selected object with that color and displays the color in the Color palette and in the Fill icon in the Toolbox. Because it is a process color, the Color palette also displays the CMYK sliders, allowing you to adjust the color.

Clicking the Color button in the Toolbox displays the Color palette.

Deselect the Non-Global option in a process color's Swatch Options dialog box (version 8 only)to update that color in every object should you edit that color. A non-global process color displays a white triangle (without the dot) in its lower right corner.

FYI

Press the Tab key to hide all the palettes; press the Tab key again to display them. Press the Shift-Tab keys to hide all the displayed palettes except for the Toolbox.

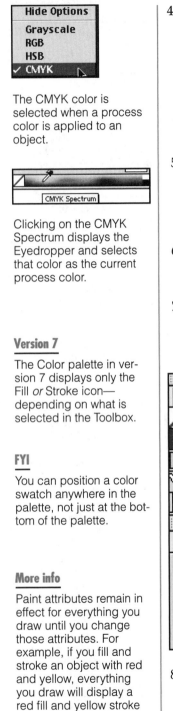

The CMYK color is selected when a process color is applied to an object.

Clicking on the CMYK Spectrum displays the Eyedropper and selects that color as the current process color.

Version 7

The Color palette in version 7 displays only the Fill *or* Stroke icon—depending on what is selected in the Toolbox.

FYI

You can position a color swatch anywhere in the palette, not just at the bottom of the palette.

More info

Paint attributes remain in effect for everything you draw until you change those attributes. For example, if you fill and stroke an object with red and yellow, everything you draw will display a red fill and yellow stroke until you change those paint attributes.

4. When you click on a process color swatch and have an object selected, several things happen: the object fills with the selected color; the color appears in the Fill Color icon in the Color palette and in the Toolbox; the CMYK sliders in the Color palette display the percentages used to create the selected color; and the selected color appears with a white border around it in the Swatches palette, indicating that it is the currently active color. Anything you draw now will be filled with that color.

5. With the rectangle still selected, drag the CMYK sliders to the right and left to change the color. Notice how the changes are reflected in the selected rectangle and in the Fill and Stroke icons (depending on which is active) in the Toolbox and Color palette.

6. Click on a color in the CMYK Spectrum below the CMYK sliders to select a process color with the Eyedropper. The color's CMYK percentages appear in the CMYK sliders.

7. When you have a process color you like, save the color in the Swatches palette. Drag the Fill icon in either the Color palette or in the Toolbox into the bottom row of the Swatches palette (Figure 4.7).

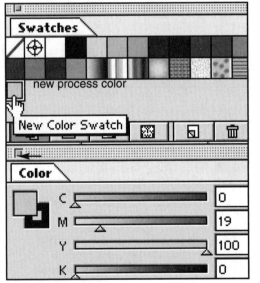

Figure 4.7. The new process color is dragged from either the Toolbox or the Color palette into the Swatches palette, where it will be stored with this document.

8. Double-click on the new swatch in the Swatches palette to display the Swatch Options dialog box. You can change the CMYK percentages here and assign a name to the swatch. Type a name for the color in the Swatch Name field and click on OK.

9. Use the Ellipse tool and press the Shift key as you draw to create a circle. Release the mouse button before releasing the Shift key. Because a color is active, it is applied to the ellipse.

10. Click on the Show Color Swatches button in the Swatches palette to display only the color swatches—not the gradients or patterns. Use the triangle on the right side of the palette to select Name. All the color swatches, even the new one you just created, are now displayed alphabetically by name (Figure 4.8).

11. Each color displays an icon to the right of its name, specifying the color model used to create the color. The new color you just created displays the CMYK icon as opposed to the RGB icon and no icon for spot color, indicating that this is a process color and will print on four plates.

12. Close this file (Command-Ctrl-W). Don't save your changes.

Macintosh Keystrokes
⌘-W File/Close

Windows Keystrokes
Ctrl-W File/Close

This spot color was converted from a process color and displays the Spot Color icon next to the CMYK icon.

Figure 4.8. The new process color is dragged from either the Toolbox or the Color palette into the Swatches palette, where it is named and will be stored with the document.

CONVERTING COLORS

To convert process colors to spot colors or vice versa simply select the color in the Swatches palette, display its Swatch Options dialog box, and select another color mode. Every object filled or stroked with the original color mode is replaced with the color in its new color mode.

Be aware, however, that regardless of any color mode options you select, Illustrator will automatically convert spot colors to process colors when separating the colors at printing. If you don't want this to happen, because it would be cheaper to print one plate instead of four plates, choose Separation Setup from the File menu and deselect the Convert to Process option in the Separation Setup dialog box.

Drag and Drop color

If you don't want to bother selecting an object to color, just drag the color swatch from the Color palette, Swatches palette, or Toolbox onto the object. The object will be filled or stroked with that color, depending on which icon is active in the Toolbox.

⌘-N File/New
F6 Window/Show Color

Ctrl-N File/New
F6 Window/Show Color

Click the New Swatch icon on the Swatches palette to add the current color to the Swatches palette.

FYI

To move the four CMYK sliders in tandem, Command-drag (Macintosh) or Ctrl-drag (Windows) any single slider.

Desaturate Colors

To desaturate a color (reduce its intensity), press the Shift key while dragging any of the CMYK sliders in the Color palette.

The Stroke icon is selected in the Color palette whenever it is selected in the Toolbox— and vice versa.

EXERCISE C

1. In a new document (File/New), display the Swatches palette (Window/Show Swatches). The default Swatches palette contains only process colors.

2. Click on the red swatch in the top row of swatches and click on the New Swatch icon at the bottom of the Swatches palette to create a duplicate red swatch.

3. Double-click on the duplicate red swatch to display the Swatch Options dialog box. Click the Preview button. Type *deep rose* in the Swatch Name field. Use the Color Type pull-down menu to select Spot Color.

4. Drag the Y(ellow) slider to the left until the percentage field reads about 7. The swatch in the dialog box turns a deep rose color, as does the duplicate swatch on the Swatches palette. Click on OK (Figure 4.9).

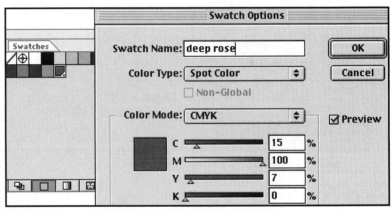

Figure 4.9. Once the spot color is named, it displays a white dot in its lower right corner, indicating that it is a spot color.

5. Notice that the deep rose swatch displays a dot in the lower right corner, indicating that it is a spot color and will print on its own plate on press.

6. Draw an object with any basic shape tool. Display the Color palette (F6). Click the Fill icon on the Toolbox. Drag the Tint Slider on the Color palette to the 50% position or click about halfway across the Tint Ramp to fill the object with a 50% tint (screen) of the deep rose color.

7. Click the Stroke icon in the Color palette. Drag the Tint Slider back to 100% to stroke the object with 100% color (Figure 4.10).

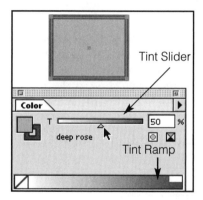

Tint Slider

Tint Ramp

Figure 4.10. A spot color displays a Tint Ramp and Tint Slider. Drag the slider or click inside the ramp to select a tint value of the color.

Macintosh Keystrokes

⌘-W File/Close

Windows Keystrokes

Ctrl-W File/Close

8. Duplicate other colors, double-click on them, name them, specify them as spot colors, and apply them as fills and strokes to objects.

9. Close this file (Command/Ctrl-W). Don't save your changes.

STROKE PALETTE

When you stroke a color, you can set the color of the stroke, its weight (thickness), and the way lines appear when joined. You can also specify a dashed line for a stroke and specify the length of the dash and the length of the gap between dashes. Before you apply a stroke, make sure the object is selected and the Stroke icon is selected in the Toolbox; otherwise you will fill the object, not stroke it.

To work with dashed lines, you must select Show Options from the Stroke palette menu. Without this option, the only thing you can do with a path is change its color and stroke weight.

STROKE WEIGHT

The weight of a stroke is defined in points. When you apply a stroke to an object, it distributes itself across the path with half the weight value on each side of the path. You can select a stroke weight from the pull-down menu on the Stroke palette, type in a value in the Weight field, or use the up and down arrows on the palette to increase or decrease a selected stroked path.

MITER LIMIT

When a path is stroked with the Miter Join (default join), the Miter Limit value applies. It specifies how far out a stroke can extend as it changes its direction along a path before it changes from a mitered (pointed) join to a beveled (squared-off) join. The default value of 4 means that when the length of the join's point becomes four times the stroke weight, Illustrator will automatically change the miter join to a bevel join.

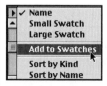

Select a color in the secondary palette and choose Add to Swatches from the palette's menu to add that color swatch to the current document's Swatches palette.

These pairs of lines display the default Butt Cap option (top), Round Cap option (center), and Projecting Cap option (bottom) available from the Stroke palette.

Macintosh Keystrokes

⌘-N File/New
F10 Window/Show Stroke
⌘-W File/Close
F6 Window/Show Color

Windows Keystrokes

Ctrl-N File/New
F10 Window/Show Stroke
Ctrl-W File/Close
F6 Window/Show Color

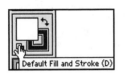

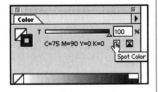

Click and drag the Ellipse
tool to select the Star tool.

The Tint Slider and Tint
Ramp, as well as the Spot
Color icon, appear when
a spot color is active. The
Tint Ramp also displays a
None swatch on the left
and white and 100% color
swatches on the right.

DASHED LINES

The default stroke is a solid line running around or along a path. By typing values in the Dashed Line fields, you can create custom dots and dashes for paths (Figure 4.11). The number entered in the first dash field determines the length of the first dash. You can also create dashes of varying lengths by entering different amounts in the other dash fields.

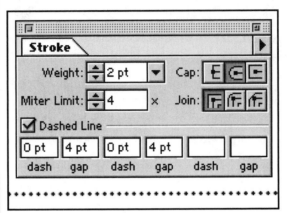

Figure 4.11. To create a dotted line, enter a gap value that is equal to or greater than the Weight value. The dash value is always 0.

EXERCISE D

1. In a new document (File/New), press the Shift and Tab keys to hide all the palettes except for the Toolbox. Click the Default Colors icon in the Toolbox and click the Stroke icon to make it active. Choose Window/Show Stroke to display the Stroke palette (F10). Choose Window/Show Swatches to display the Swatches palette.

2. Use the Star tool (behind the Ellipse tool) and drag to draw a star on the page. Click the Color button on the Toolbox to display the Color palette. It displays the CMYK values for black.

3. Double-click on the dark blue swatch in the first row of swatches to display the Swatch Options dialog box. Use the Color Type menu to select Spot Color. Type a name for the color in the Swatch Name field and click on OK.

4. Drag the Tint Slider to increase or decrease the intensity of the spot color, or click on the Tint Ramp below the slider (the cursor changes to the Eyedropper) to select a percentage of the color.

5. The star appears outlined in blue. Click on the up arrow in the Stroke palette to increase the weight of the stroke. Use the Weight pull-down menu to select 10. This applies a 10-point stroke to the star's path, with 5 points on either side of the path.

6. With the star still selected, click on the Round Join icon in the Stroke palette (the middle icon). The star points appear rounded. Click on the Bevel Join icon to square off the star points (Figure 4.12).

Figure 4.12. The original star (left) displays a round join (center) and a bevel join (right).

7. Click the Miter Join (first Join icon) to restore the default sharp corner points.

8. With the star still selected, click the Dashed Line box in the Stroke palette. The star displays the default 12-point dash. Type 3 in the dash field, press the Tab key, type 6 in the gap field, press the Tab key, type 3 in the dash field, press the Tab key and type 6 in the second gap field. Press Return/Enter. Your star should resemble Figure 4.13.

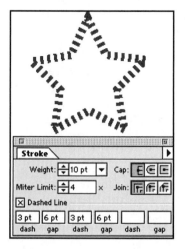

Select a Join from the Stroke palette. The Miter Join is the default join.

Figure 4.13. Change the dash and gap values in the Stroke palette to achieve different effects.

⌘-N File/New
⌘-W File/Close

Windows Keystrokes

Ctrl-N File/New
Ctrl-W File/Close

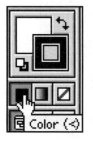

Changing the Startup file

You can change Illustrator's Startup file to include any colors in the default Swatches palette. To create a custom startup file: (1) Back up the current default startup file, *Adobe Illustrator Startup* (Mac) or *Startup.ai* (Windows) in the Plug-ins folder in the Adobe Illustrator 8.0 folder and save it outside that folder. (2) Open the default startup file to use as a template for the custom startup file. Add and/or delete any colors to customize the file and save this new file as *Adobe Illustrator Startup* (Mac) or *Startup.ai* (Windows) in the Plug-ins folder. You must quit Illustrator and restart it to activate the new startup settings.

9. Continue to apply different colors and dashed lines to the star until it twinkles.

10. Close this file (File/Close). Don't save your changes.

SWATCH LIBRARIES

When you first launch Illustrator and display the Swatches palette, that palette is the main or default palette. You can open other swatch palettes in the same document and add their colors to your main palette. Click any color in a secondary Swatches palette to add that color to the Default Swatches palette.

You can also edit the main Swatches palette in an Illustrator document, save the document, and then open its Swatches palette in another Illustrator document.

EXERCISE E

1. In a new document (File/New), use any of the basic shape tools to draw a few shapes on the page. Display the Swatches palette (Window/Show Swatches). Click the Default Colors icon on the Toolbox.

2. Click the Color button on the Toolbox. With one object selected, click on a process color in the Swatches palette to apply it to the selected object. Duplicate that color by dragging its swatch over the New Swatch icon on the Swatches palette. Click on the duplicate to apply it to the selected object. Adjust the CMYK sliders in the Color palette to edit the color. Drag its swatch from the Color palette onto the Swatches palette.

3. Double-click on the new color and type a name for it in the Swatch Options dialog box. Click on OK.

4. Select another object and apply another process color. Edit the color in the Color palette, drag its swatch to the Swatches palette, and double-click on the swatch. Type a name for the swatch and click on OK. You have added two color swatches to the document's default Swatches palette.

5. Save the file as *Color.ai.* in your Projects folder (File/Save As). Close the file (File/Close).

6. Create a new document (File/New) and display the Swatches palette (Window/Show Swatches). The default Swatches palette appears.

7. Choose Window/Swatch Libraries/Other Libraries. Navigate to your Projects folder and highlight the *Color.ai* file you just saved. Click on Select to open, not the file, but the Swatches palette in the current document (Figure 4.14).

Color	
▢ C=80 M=5 Y=0 K=0	⊠
▮ Black, White	
▯ Chrome	
▮ Rainbow	
▢ Yellow & Orange Radial	
▨ Brick	
▢ Confetti	
▨ Leaves – Fall	
▨ Stripes	
▨ sick green	⊠
▢ pumpkin orange	⊠

Figure 4.14. Whenever you open a Swatches library, it displays the Locked icon, indicating that you cannot edit any colors in the library, just apply them to objects.

8. Select Name from the palette's menu and scroll to find your new colors.

9. Drag one of those colors onto the Swatches palette in your document, where it becomes available for filling and stroking objects.

10. To display the default Swatches palette, choose Window/ Swatch Libraries/Default. The default Swatches palette appears next to the Color library. The document's current Swatches palette is still displayed. However, both the Color and Default libraries display the Locked icon at the bottom of the palette, indicating that colors can be removed from the palette, but not added to it.

11. Close this file (File/Close). Don't save your changes.

MANIPULATING COLORS

Nothing is ever final in Illustrator. Colors can be replaced, inverted, changed from spot to process colors (or vice versa) or to grayscale, as well as converted to RGB colors for Web work.

REPLACING COLORS GLOBALLY

In a complicated illustration, it may be necessary to change a single spot color or process color that has been used frequently throughout the document. Instead of selecting each object or path segment to which the same spot color has been applied, simply replace a spot color swatch with a different spot color swatch. To replace a process color in the Swatches palette, however, you must first select the object or objects you want recolored. You can also use the Select

Options
Separate: [Printable Layers] ▼
⊠ Use Default Marks
⊠ Convert to Process
☐ Overprint Black

Deselect Convert to Process if you don't want spot colors converted to process colors when printing.

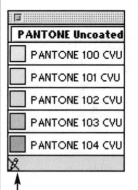

PANTONE Uncoated
▢ PANTONE 100 CVU
▢ PANTONE 101 CVU
▢ PANTONE 102 CVU
▢ PANTONE 103 CVU
▮ PANTONE 104 CVU

Any Swatch library opened in the document displays the Locked icon, indicating that colors can be removed from the palette but not added to it.

Colors to go

To add more than one color to the default Swatches palette, select the first color, then press the Command/Ctrl key and click any other colors you want to select. This lets you select noncontiguous colors. To select contiguous colors, select the first color, press the Shift key, and select the other contiguous colors.

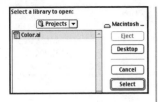

Open a secondary library of color swatches in the active document by selecting the Illustrator file that contains the swatches.

Shift-select

To select multiple objects, select the first object, then press the Shift key and select other objects. To remove a selected object from the multiple selection, click on it while the Shift key is depressed.

The Non-Global option must be selected to replace a process color globally in the document.

Process colors that have their non-global option deselected display their lower right corners in white.

filters under the Edit menu to select all the objects with the same fill and stroke attributes.

CUSTOM LIBRARIES

Illustrator ships with several color libraries needed for print, Web, and video artwork. The Pantone and Trumatch libraries consist of spot colors; the Web library consists of process colors that are browser-friendly. To access these libraries, select the appropriate library from the Swatch Libraries option under the Window menu.

EXERCISE F

1. Create a new file (File/New). Click on the Default Colors icon. Display the Swatches palette. Click on the Fill icon in the Tool-box to apply a fill color to any selected objects.

2. Use the basic shape tools to draw four shapes. Shift-select two shapes and click on a process color in the Swatches palette to assign the same process color to both objects. Deselect the objects.

3. Shift-select the other two objects and assign them the same process color (not the one applied to the first two objects) from the Swatches palette. Deselect the objects (Command/Ctrl-Shift-A).

4. In the Swatches palette, select a different process color, press the Option/Alt key, and drag that color swatch from the Tool-box over the process color swatch used to color the first two objects. Nothing happens because process colors default to a non-global setting.

5. Double-click on the third process color you selected, the one you want to apply globally. In its Swatch Options dialog box, deselect the Non-Global option beneath the Color Type menu. Click on OK.

6. Notice that the swatch now displays a white lower right corner, indicating that it is a process color that can be used to replace a color globally.

7. Now press the Option/Alt key and drag that color over the process color swatch applied to the first two objects. The unselected objects are filled with the new color (Figure 14.15).

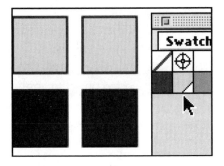

Figure 14.15. The top squares were originally filled with red. Once the Non-Global option was deselected in the yellow swatch's Swatch Options dialog box, Option/Alt-dragging the yellow swatch from the Toolbox over the red swatch filled the objects with yellow.

Add to Swatches

If you delete a color from the Swatches palette, choose Window/ Swatch Libraries/Default to display the Default Swatches palette. Click on the swatch you deleted and choose Add to Swatches from the Default palette menu to add the deleted color to the Swatches palette.

8. Shift-select the two objects filled with the process color. Click on the Color button on the Toolbox to display the Color palette. The selected process color appears in the Fill icon on the Color palette. Move the CMYK sliders to change the color. The selected objects change to reflect the new color. Drag the color swatch from the Fill icon on the Color palette onto the Swatches palette.

9. Shift-select any two objects and select the Stroke icon in the Toolbox. Choose Window/Show Stroke to display the Stroke palette (F10). Apply a 5-point stroke in a spot color to the selected objects. Deselect everything (Edit/Deselect All).

10. Select one of the objects you just stroked. Choose Edit/Select/ Same Stroke Color. Both items with the same stroke color are selected. Deselect everything (Command/Ctrl-Shift-A).

11. Select one of the objects created with the process color. Choose Edit/Select Same Fill Color. Both objects filled with the edited process color are selected.

12. Close this file (File/Close). Don't save your changes.

REVIEW

In this unit you learned that:

1. Objects have paint attributes that include a fill and/or a stroke.

2. The Fill and Stroke icons in the Toolbox and on the Color palette must be selected to apply color to an object's fill or stroke.

3. Clicking the Default Colors icon in the Toolbox restores the fill and stroke colors to the default white fill and 1-point black stroke.

4. Clicking the Swap Colors icon in the Toolbox swaps the fill and stroke colors.

5. Clicking the None button in the Toolbox or on the Color palette strips the selected object of any fill or stroke, depending on which icon is selected in the Toolbox or Color palette.

6. The Fill and Stroke icons can be dragged from the Toolbox, Color, and Gradient palettes onto an unselected object to apply the color to that object.

7. The Color and Gradient palettes are automatically displayed by clicking the Color and Gradient buttons in the Toolbox.

8. A stroke outlines a path with half of the stroke weight (width) on either side of the path.

9. Spot color is a single, premixed color (such as a Pantone or TruMatch color) that prints on a separate plate.

10. Process color is a color created by mixing percentages of cyan, magenta, yellow, and black. Process colors print on four plates, one for each color.

11. Colors are stored in the Swatches palette. Unless a color is stored in the Swatches palette, it will not be saved with the file.

12. Colors can be duplicated, renamed, and converted to process or spot color.

13. The Color palette is used to create and edit colors.

14. The Stroke palette is used to specify stroke width, dashed lines, and the way corners meet.

15. Custom Swatch libraries can be saved and loaded into any Illustrator file.

16. Colors can be replaced globally using the Swatches palette or the Select command.

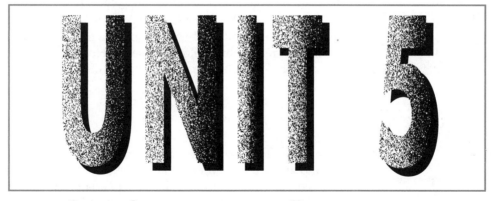

Painting Tools

OVERVIEW

In this unit you will learn how to:
apply color with the Eyedropper and
    Paint Bucket tools
mix colors to create the illusion of transparency
use the freehand painting and drawing tools
use the Pencil, Smooth, and Erase tools
use the Paintbrush tool and set tool options
use and create Calligraphic, Scatter, Art,
    and Pattern brushes
convert brushes to art
create custom brush libraries

TERMS

Art brush
Calligraphic brush
Pattern brush
Scatter brush

HOW IT WORKS

Create the type and duplicate it. Working with the duplicate type object, track about 200% and convert to outlines. Group the paths and fill with a gradient. In Plug-Ins & Scratch Disk Preferences, select the Adobe Photoshop Plug-Ins folder. Rasterize the paths from the Object menu and apply the Mezzotint filter with the Fine Dots option. Drag the original point type behind the artwork to create an offset shadow. Group everything and scale.

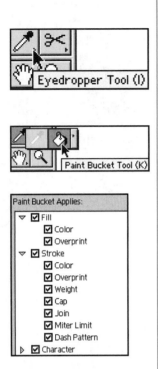

Double-click on the Eye-dropper tool or on the Paint Bucket tool to access their dialog boxes, where you can select which fill and stroke attributes the tool will select and apply.

Tip

Using the Eyedropper tool to update the Fill and Stroke icons is a lot easier than trying to figure out what colors were used, what the line weight is, what the Caps and Joins options are, and what the dash and gap values are for a dashed line.

APPLYING COLOR WITH TOOLS

There are several ways to apply color to objects in Illustrator. Ordinarily you mix a color in the Color palette or select a color from the Swatches palette and apply that color to a selected object. This is fine if you are selecting colors on the fly. However, if you want to apply color from one object in the active Illustrator document, in another Illustrator document, or in an open Photoshop document to another object in the active Illustrator document, it's easier and faster to use tools instead of palettes.

The tools used to select and apply color are the Eyedropper and Paint Bucket tools. You select color attributes with the Eyedropper tool and apply them with the Paint Bucket tool. To switch between the Eyedropper and Paint Bucket tools, press the Option key ((Macintosh) or Alt key (Windows) when either tool is selected.

EYEDROPPER TOOL

The Eyedropper tool is used to sample or select a color that has already been applied to an object, even a text object. When you click with the Eyedropper tool on an object that has been filled or stroked, the Eyedropper samples or "picks up" all the fill and stroke attributes of that object and applies them to the Fill and Stroke icons in the Toolbox and Color palette. If you have any objects selected when you click with the Eyedropper tool, they too will display the fill and stroke attributes the Eyedropper sampled. If no objects are selected, select the Paint Bucket tool to "dump" those color attributes onto unselected objects.

PAINT BUCKET TOOL

The Paint Bucket tool applies the current fill and stroke attributes to any object you click on. You don't have to select an object on which to "dump" color attributes; just clicking on an object with the Paint Bucket tool applies the attributes. For example, if you create one object and duplicate it several times, then remember that all those objects should have a yellow fill with a blue stroke, you mix the colors in the Color palette or use the Eyedropper to select an object that already displays those attributes—just as long as those fill and stroke attributes are displayed in the Fill and Stroke icons in the Toolbox—then select the Paint Bucket tool and click on all the objects you forgot to color yellow and blue.

TOOL OPTIONS

Double-click on the Eyedropper or Paint Bucket tool to access their dialog boxes. There you can select which fill and stroke attributes the tool will select and apply.

EXERCISE A

Macintosh Keystrokes

⌘-N File/New
⌘-Y View/Artwork/Preview
F10 Window/Show Stroke
⌘-Shift-A Edit/Deselect All

Windows Keystrokes

Ctrl-N File/New
Ctrl-Y View/Artwork/
      Preview
F10 Window/Show Stroke
Ctrl-Shift-A Edit/Deselect
      All

1. Create a new file (File/New), and display the Swatches palette (Window/Show Swatches) and the Stroke palette (F10). Click on the Default Colors icon in the Toolbox.

2. Choose View/Artwork (Command/Ctrl-Y). Use the Rectangle tool to draw three rectangles on the page. Because you are in Artwork view, none of the default fills and strokes will appear. Only the outline and center points of the objects are displayed.

3. Use the Swatches palette to assign one rectangle a green fill and a purple stroke with a stroke weight of 8 points.

4. Choose Window/New Window to create another window of the same file. With the new window selected, choose View/Preview (Command/Ctrl-Y). Resize both windows so that they fit on your screen. The filled rectangle appears with its fill and stroke attributes displayed in the new window (Figure 5.1).

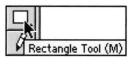

Rectangle Tool (M)

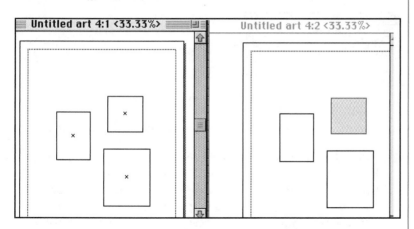

Figure 5.1. The New Window command allows you to view the color and stroke changes made in Artwork view. You can, of course, make changes in both windows, and any changes you make in one window are updated in the other. Both windows belong to the same document.

Now you see it...

Using the New Window command allows you to see the changes made to objects in Artwork view. It's easier to select objects and segments in Artwork view because the stroked paths are easier to select and anchor points are more visible than in Preview view, where the color and Stroke Weight values frequently make selection difficult.

5. Choose Edit/Deselect All (Command/Ctrl-Shift-A), and change the Fill and Stroke colors in the Toolbox to anything you did not use for the rectangle. Change the Stroke Weight value to 1. This will let you better see what happens when you use the Eyedropper tool.

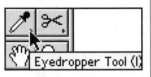

Tip

Select the filled rectangle in the Artwork view window by clicking on its center point. This is easier than clicking all over the filled rectangle to find its center point. You can also select the Area Select option in the General Preferences dialog box, which allows you to select a filled object by clicking anywhere inside the object.

Press the x key on the keyboard to toggle between the Fill and Stroke icons in the Toolbox.

6. Use the Selection tool to select the filled rectangle and notice that now the Fill and Stroke icons in the Toolbox change to reflect the fill and stroke values of the selected object. Also note that the stroke weight value changes from 1 to 8.

7. Click anywhere on the page to deselect the filled rectangle. Use the Selection tool and click on the title bar of the window in Artwork view to activate that window. Shift-select only the two unfilled rectangles.

8. Click on the Eyedropper tool, then click on the center point or on the path of the filled rectangle. Both of the selected rectangles now display the fill and stroke attributes of the first rectangle.

9. Choose Edit/Deselect All (Command/Ctrl-Shift-A) to deselect everything. Click on the window in Preview view to activate it.

10. Click on the Show Pattern Swatches button in the Swatches palette to display just the pattern tiles (Figure 5.2). Make sure the Fill icon is active in the Toolbox. Click on the Brick pattern (or on any pattern) to designate it as the current fill.

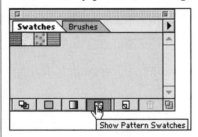

Figure 5.2. Displaying just the pattern tiles makes it easier to see and select an available pattern.

11. Select the Stroke icon in the Toolbox by pressing x on the keyboard. Click on the Show Color Swatches button in the Swatches palette to display just the color swatches (Figure 5.3). Click on any color to designate it as the current stroke color. Because nothing is selected, these new fill and stroke attributes are not reflected in any of the objects in the illustration.

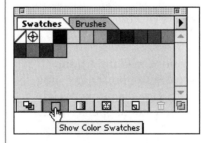

Figure 5.3. Use the buttons at the bottom of the Swatches palette to hide and display swatches.

12. Click on the Paint Bucket tool to select it. The Paint Bucket tool automatically "fills" with the current fill and stroke attributes and becomes a selection tool. Click on one of the rectangles and notice that it fills with the current fill and stroke attributes.

13. Deselect everything (Command/Ctrl-Shift-A) and change the fill and stroke attributes, including the stroke weight value, in the Swatches and Stroke palette. Apply different fill and stroke values to the rectangles. Use the Eyedropper tool to select an object (sample its color attributes), press the Option/Alt key to turn the Eyedropper into the Paint Bucket tool, and click on any other object to apply the sampled attributes.

14. Close this file (File/Close). Don't save your changes.

MIXING COLORS

Although Illustrator does not have the color transparency options that Photoshop has (Figure 5.4), there are ways of faking a transparent look by using the Pathfinder Hard Mix and Soft Mix filters. These filters split the overlapping areas into separate paths and change the fill colors to create the illusion of transparency. In the process the stroke colors are removed. Once you apply the filter, the overlapping objects are grouped.

Figure 5.4. The transparent panel placed over the background and behind the text is possible only with Photoshop's Opacity function, an option not (yet!) available in Illustrator.

HARD MIX FILTER

This Pathfinder filter works like overprinting colors. It takes the highest CMYK values from each object and mixes them where they overlap. You see the "transparency" where the colors were most different.

SOFT MIX FILTER

The Pathfinder Soft filter allows you to change the "transparency" of the overlapping regions of the selected objects. In the Mix Soft dialog box, enter a percent in the poorly named Rate option box. (The option should really be named *Transparency*.) A value of 0%

Macintosh Keystrokes

⌘-Shift-A Edit/Deselect All
⌘-W File/Close

Windows Keystrokes

Ctrl-Shift-A Edit/Deselect All
Ctrl-W File/Close

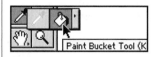

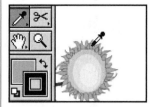

Clicking on any object with the Eyedropper tool applies that object's fill and stroke attributes to the Toolbox icons and to any other selected object in the document. When clicking with the Eyedropper, its tip turns black, indicating that it is sampling the color.

Version 7

In version 7, the Hard and Soft filters are accessed from the Object menu. Choose Object/ Pathfinder/Hard or Soft.

Macintosh Keystrokes

⌘-N File/New
F5 Window/Show Brushes
⌘-D Object/Transform/
   Transform Again

Windows Keystrokes

Ctrl-N File/New
F5 Window/Show Brushes
Ctrl-D Object/Transform/
   Transform Again

FYI

If the fill color in an object is too dark, you won't see the effect of the Hard filter. If one of the colors is dark, make it the front-most object to better see the effect of the filter.

Tip

You can mix more than two overlapping objects and can create lighter effects with the Soft Mix filter by giving the top-most object a white fill and applying a Mixing Rate value between 80% and 100%.

Whoa!

Release the mouse button *before* releasing the Option/Alt keys to create a duplicate object.

means that the frontmost object is not transparent at all and thus is entirely opaque. A value of 100% makes the frontmost object entirely transparent. Values in between mix the colors in the front-most object with those of other objects in the selection.

EXERCISE B

1. In a new document (File/New), use any of the basic shape tools to create two overlapping objects. Display the Swatches palette and Color palette (F6). Display the Pathfinder palette (Window/Show Pathfinder). Use the Color palette menu to select CMYK (Figure 5.5).

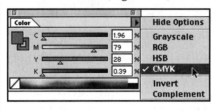

Figure 5.5. Use the Color palette menu to select a color model.

2. Select the first object and apply a fill and stroke color. Select the second object and apply a different fill and stroke color. The fill color should be fairly light, so use the CMYK sliders on the Color palette to make the fill color almost a pastel shade.

3. Use the Selection tool to select both objects and drag them. As you drag, press the Option/Alt key to create a duplicate set. Choose Object/Transform/Transform Again (Command-Ctrl-D) to create a third set.

4. Choose Show Options from the Pathfinder palette menu. This displays the Hard Mix and Soft Mix icons at the bottom of the palette (Figure 5.6).

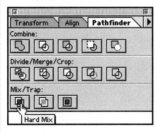

Figure 5.6. The Hard Mix and Soft Mix filters are on the Pathfinder palette.

5. Shift-Select the first set of objects. Click on the Hard Mix icon on the Pathfinder palette. The filter creates separate paths where the objects overlap and mixes the highest CMYK values.

6. Shift-select the second set of objects. Click the Soft Mix icon in the Pathfinder palette. Leave the default 50% Mixing Rate value in the Pathfinder Soft Mix dialog box and click on OK. Your screen should resemble Figure 5.7.

7. Close this file. Don't save your changes.

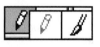

The higher the value in the Mixing Rate field, the more transparent the frontmost object will appear.

Figure 5.7. The original pair of overlapping objects (left) displays the Hard Mix filter (center) and Soft Mix filter (right).

FREEHAND DRAWING AND PAINTING TOOLS

The three freehand drawing tools in Illustrator's Toolbox are the Pen tool, Pencil tool, and Paintbrush tool. The Pen tool is by far the most powerful, versatile, and effective tool for creating illustrations and is covered in another unit. But the Pencil and Paintbrush tools can also be used to create paths that do not require a high level of exactitude.

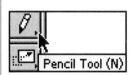

Drag the Pencil tool to display the Paintbrush tool.

PENCIL TOOL

The Pencil tool thinks it's an authentic drawing pencil, but it really is more like a rough crayon. It's hard to control, does not create straight lines, and renders curves as lumpy segments on a lumpy path. It is most useful for sketching a rough drawing that you can later smooth out with the Smooth tool. Once you learn to use the Pen tool, you'll probably never use the Pencil tool.

When you draw with the Pencil tool, Illustrator creates anchor points automatically. The longer and more complex the path, the more anchor points. The fewer anchor points used to create a path, the fewer bumps and lumps in the path, to say nothing about how much more easily a path with fewer anchor points will print! However, you can control the number of anchor points in the Auto Trace Tolerance field in the Type & Auto Tracing Preferences dialog box (Figure 5.8). The Auto Trace Tolerance value defaults to 2 points, which gives you a fairly bumpy path. Its maximum of 10 points will result in a much smoother path.

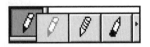

The Smooth tool and Eraser tool live behind the Pencil tool. Use the Tearoff menu to access them more easily.

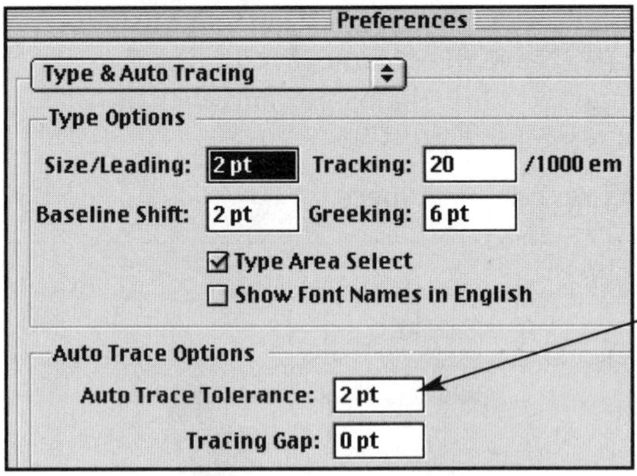

Adding/closing paths

To add to a path drawn with the Pencil tool, select the path, position the tip of the pencil on an end-point, and drag to continue the path.

To close a path drawn with the Pencil tool, Option/Alt to display a loop, and click to close the path.

Version 7

There is no Smooth tool or Erase tool in Version 7.

Figure 5.8. The higher the Auto Trace Tolerance value, the smoother the path drawn with the Pencil and Paintbrush tools.

As you draw a freehand path, a dotted line appears behind the cursor as you are dragging. When you release the mouse button, anchor points will appear on the path with endpoints at each end of the path.

CHANGING A PENCIL TOOL PATH

Once a path has been drawn with the Pencil tool, you can add to that path and you can reshape the path. To add to a path, position the Pencil tool cursor on an endpoint of the path and continue drawing. Be careful! You may find that as you begin to redraw the path you will change a closed path to an open path, change an open path to a closed path, or even lose part of the object's shape.

If you make a mistake while using the Pencil tool, choose Edit/Undo (Command/Ctrl-Z) to undo the last segment drawn.

SMOOTH TOOL

The Smooth tool lets you "iron out" an existing stroke or path section without losing the original shape of the path. The more you run the Smooth tool over a path, the less lumpy it becomes.

ERASE TOOL

Use the Erase tool to remove part of an existing path by dragging the tool along the length of the path segment you want to erase. You'll get better results with this tool if you use a single, smooth, dragging motion.

Unit 5 ★ Painting Tools

EXERCISE C

Macintosh Keystrokes

⌘-N File/New
⌘-W File/Close

Windows Keystrokes

Ctrl-N File/New
Ctrl-W File/Close

1. In a new document, click on the Pencil tool to select it. Choose File/Preferences/Type & Auto Tracing and set the Auto Trace Tolerance value to 8. Select a stroke color and no fill.

2. Click and drag to create the letters in your name. If you release the mouse button, you will create a new path—that's OK. Select the Smooth tool and drag over part of the path to smooth it out.

3. With the Pencil tool selected, click on an endpoint of the selected path and continue drawing to add to the path. If you delete part of the path, choose Edit/Undo and try again.

4. Select the Erase tool and drag the eraser end of the tool over part of the path to delete it (Figure 5.9).

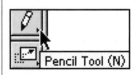

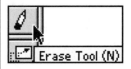

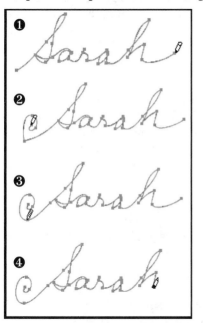

Figure 5.9. Draw with the Pencil tool (1), add to the path (2), smooth out the path with the Smooth tool (3), and erase part of the path with the Erase tool (4).

Press the Caps Lock key to turn the drawing tool cursor into a crosshair. The center of the crosshair is the cursor's "hot spot."

5. Continue to draw, smooth, and erase until you are comfortable with these tools.

6. Close this file (Command/Ctrl-W). Don't save your changes.

PAINTBRUSH TOOL

The Paintbrush tool is very much like the Pencil tool, in that you use it to draw freeform paths on the page. These paths are painted with the currently selected brush in the Brushes palette. Brushes can be as simple as a line or as complex as any artwork you draw.

Version 7

In Version 7 the Paintbrush tool is behind the Pencil tool. Double-click the Paintbrush tool to select the Calligraphic option.

```
┌─ Options ──────────────┐
│  ☐ Fill new brush strokes │
│  ☑ Keep Selected        │
└────────────────────────┘
```

Select options for the brush stroke in the Paintbrush Tool Preferences dialog box.

Version 7

There is no Brushes palette in Version 7. Alas! This also means that there are no Calligraphic, Art, Scatter, or Pattern brushes either.

Closing Brush paths

To close a path drawn with the Paintbrush tool, press the Option/Alt key to display the loop, and click to close the path.

```
┌──┬──┬──┬──┬──┐
│ ✁│ ✐│ 🗔│ 🗑│ ▣│
└──┴──┴──┴──┴──┘
│ Options of Selected Object │
```

Version 7

Double-click the Paintbrush tool to display its Options dialog box, where you can select a brush width and the Calligraphic option.

Brushes operate in two modes, a freehand paint mode and a stroke mode. When you drag the Paintbrush tool with any of the brushes selected, a path is created with the brushstroke following the curvature of the path. When you select an object, highlight the Stroke icon in the Toolbox, and select a brush, the object is stroked with the brush.

BRUSHING PATHS

In the old days (Version 7), creating a path pattern was a complicated process involving a dialog box and several options. In version 8, once you create a brush, you can simply apply it as a stroke to any path. Four kinds of brushes are available: Calligraphic, Scatter, Art, and Pattern brushes.

Actually, you don't even have to paint a path with a brush. Simply select the path and drag any brush from the Brushes palette over the path to apply all its brush attributes to that path. Or, select the path and click on a brush in the Brushes palette to stroke the path with a brush.

BRUSHES PALETTE

All four kinds of brushes are available in the Brushes palette. The preloaded brushes, as well as those brushes you create from artwork or import from Brush libraries, can be all be edited, providing an unlimited number of brushes for drawing and for stroking paths.

Use the Brushes palette menu to display, duplicate, and delete brushes as well as to display the Options dialog box for each brush. Existing brushes can be modified and several brush libraries can be imported into the Illustrator document.

BRUSH TOOL OPTIONS

Double-click the Paintbrush tool to display the Paintbrush Tool Preferences dialog box. The Smoothness value determines the percentage value of the stroke and curve. The higher the value, the smoother the stroke or curve will be. The Fidelity value specifies the number of pixels the stroke is positioned from the center of the path. The higher the Fidelity value, the smoother the stroke or curve.

If you choose the Fill new brush strokes option, paths drawn by the brush are filled. Otherwise, they are unfilled. The Keep Selected option keeps the path you just drew selected so you can move it or edit it.

CALLIGRAPHIC BRUSHES

The Calligraphic brushes create elliptical shapes along the center of a path. As you draw, anchor points appear along the center of the path. These anchor points can be edited with the Direct Selection tool and with the Pencil tool.

SCATTER BRUSHES

These brushes scatter artwork at a specified distance around or along a path, depending on the options selected in the Scatter Brush Options dialog box. Any vector artwork can be turned into a Scatter brush.

ART BRUSHES

Art brushes spread a single object evenly along the length of a selected path. If you are using text as an Art brush (or as a Scatter brush), it must first be converted to outlines before you can define it as a brush. The Art brush can be used not only to stroke a path, but also as a brush. Dragging with the Paintbrush tool, with an Art brush selected, creates a single object along a path every time you click and drag. The object is stretched to fit the shape of the path. Increasing the stroke width widens the artwork, but, depending on the shape of the path, can create a distorted effect.

PATTERN BRUSHES

Patterns are individual tiles that repeat along a path. When you select a Pattern brush, dragging with the Paintbrush tool creates a path along which the pattern tiles are placed. If you stroke an object with a pattern brush, the pattern is applied evenly along the sides of the selected path.

Many patterns include side, inner corner, and outer corner tiles that make the tile fit properly on a path. Because Illustrator ships with many Brush libraries that include properly designed path brushes, you don't have to be an engineer to design patterns that will wrap properly around a path.

ADDING BRUSHES TO THE BRUSHES PALETTE

Once you create artwork that you want to define as a brush, select it and click the New Brush button in the Brushes palette or choose New Brush from the Brushes palette menu. You can also select the artwork and drag it into the Brushes palette. You cannot create a Calligraphic brush this way, only Scatter, Art, and Pattern brushes.

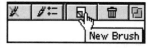

Roundness

The higher the Roundness value in the Calligraphic Brush Options dialog box, the greater the roundness of the line.

FYI

The different brushes in the Brushes palette display an icon next to the brush's name when View by Name is selected from the Brushes palette menu.

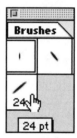

A new brush is named in the Brushes palette.

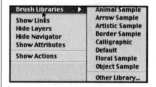

Access Brush libraries from the Window menu.

Sorry!

Brushes cannot be created from artwork containing patterns, gradients, blends, other brushes, gradient mesh objects, or bitmap images.

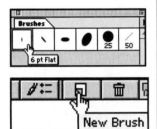

A check mark next to a brush indicates that the brush type is displayed in the palette. Highlight a checked brush type to deselect it.

Version 7

There is no Paintbrush Tool Preferences dialog box for this tool in version 7—only the Paintbrush Options dialog box, which does not contain the same options as version 8.

CREATING CALLIGRAPHIC BRUSHES

A calligraphic brush is a single line drawn along a selected path or directly on the page with the Paintbrush tool. Unless you first select a calligraphic brush in the Brushes palette, any line drawn with the Paintbrush tool defaults to a 6-pt. flat line. If you edit that brush in the Calligraphic Options dialog box, you have the option of applying the edits to any line drawn with the original brush or leaving those lines as they were originally painted. However, if you choose to leave the original lines, the brush you used to create those lines changes to reflect the edits. That's why it's always a good idea to duplicate any brush before editing it.

EXERCISE D

1. In a new document (File/New), double-click on the Paintbrush tool to display the Paintbrush Tool Preferences dialog box. Deselect the Fill new brush strokes option, but select the Keep Selected option. Click on OK.

2. Choose Calligraphic Brushes from the Brushes palette pull-down menu. Click the first brush in the palette, most likely the 6 pt Flat brush, to draw a curved line on the page. The path appears stroked with a 6-pt. flat line, with 3 points on either side of the path.

3. Drag the first brush, the 6 pt Flat brush, down onto the New Brush icon on the Brushes palette to create a duplicate. You could also select the brush and choose Duplicate Brush from the Brushes palette menu.

4. Double-click on the duplicate brush icon in the Brushes palette (now named 6 pt Copy) to display the Calligraphic Brush Options dialog box. Click to select the Preview option.

5. Type 24 in the Name field. Drag the ellipse angle of rotation in the Preview field until 40 appears in the Angle field, or type 40 in the Angle field. Set the Roundness value to 10%.

6. Use the Diameter slider to set the diameter of the line to 24, or type 24 in the Diameter field. Make sure Fixed is the option selected for the Angle, Roundness, and Diameter fields. Click on OK.

7. An alert appears telling you that the stroke is in use. If you select Apply to Strokes, any path stroked with that brush will be changed to reflect the new values. Click the Leave Strokes

button to set the new brush values but not apply them to any object.

8. Select the 6-pt. line with the Selection tool, press the Option/Alt key, and drag down to create a copy of the path. Click on the 24 pt brush icon in the Brushes palette to paint the line with the new brush. Deselect (Command/Ctrl-Shift-A).

9. Use the Direct Selection tool to select the 24-pt. line and drag its anchor points and direction handles to reshape the line. Your screen should resemble Figure 5.10.

10. Close this file (Command/Ctrl-W). Don't save your changes

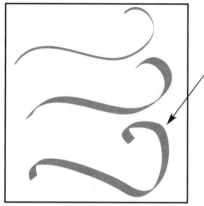

The Smooth tool could be used to smooth out this sharp point.

Figure 5.10. The original line (top) is painted with the new brush (center), and edited with the Direct Selection tool (bottom).

CREATING SCATTER BRUSHES

Scatter brushes are composed of one or more artwork objects that are (usually) grouped and scattered along a selected path or along a path drawn with the Paintbrush tool. You cannot create a Scatter brush with artwork that contains gradients or patterns.

EXERCISE E

1. In a new document (File/New), display the Brushes palette (F5) and the Stroke palette (F10). Use the Spiral tool to draw a small spiral. Assign it a 3-pt. stroke color but no fill.

2. Click on the Selection tool and drag the spiral into the Brushes palette. A dialog box appears asking you to select a brush type. Click the New Scatter Brush option and click on OK. The New Scatter Brush Options dialog box appears.

Macintosh Keystrokes

⌘-Shift-A Edit/Deselect All
F10 Window/Show Stroke
F5 Window/Show Brushes

Windows Keystrokes

Ctrl-Shift-A Edit/Deselect All
F10 Window/Show Stroke
F5 Window/Show Brushes

Selection Tool (V)

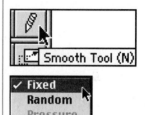

Smooth Tool (N)

Fixed
Random
Pressure

The Angle, Roundness, and Diameter fields allow for Fixed or Random values. The Fixed value keeps the specified value regardless of the way the line curves. Random values specify the range by which the brush characteristic can vary. For example, if the Diameter value is 20 and the Variation value is 5, the diameter can be any value between 15 and 25.

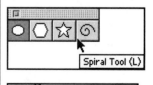

Spiral Tool (L)

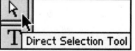

Direct Selection Tool

Macintosh Keystrokes

⌘-D Object/Transform/
Transform Again

Windows Keystrokes

Ctrl-D Object/Transform/
Transform Again

Scatter value

The higher the Scatter value in the Scatter Brush Options dialog box, the farther the objects are from the path. A Scatter value of 0% aligns the objects to either side of the path.

Spacing value

The higher the Spacing value in the Scatter Brush Options dialog box, the more space between objects when the stroke is applied to a path or when you select an object with that brush and the Paintbrush tool active.

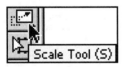

WARNING!

Art brushes and Pattern brushes cannot include type, unless the text has first been converted to outlines (paths).

3. Apply the values in Figure 5.11. Drag the Size slider to 50% or type a value in the Size field to reduce the size of the spiral. Leave the Spacing value at 100%.

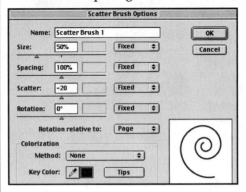

Figure 5.11. The Scatter Brush Options dialog box displays the selected artwork specified as a new brush.Because Fixed is selected, only one slider is available. If Random were selected, two sliders would appear, allowing you to sent the range of options.

4. Type -20 in the Scatter field to reduce the object's distance from the path. Leave the Rotation value at 0%. Use the Rotation relative to pull-down menu to select Path so the spirals will rotate along the path axis, not against the page axis. Click on OK.

5. Make sure Show Scatter Brushes is selected in the Brushes palette menu, where the Spiral Brush appears as the last Scatter Brush.

6. Select the Ellipse tool and click on the page. Type 330 in the Width field. Press the Tab key and type 330 in the Height field. Click on OK to create a circle with a diameter of 330 points.

7. With the circle still selected, click on the Spiral Brush in the Brushes palette to replace the circle's stroke with the spiral. If you don't like how the spirals fit on the circle, select the path and double-click the Scale tool. Increase the Uniform Scale value to 110%. Choose Object/Transform/Transform Again (Command/Ctrl-D) to increase the circle's size in 10% increments until the spirals are properly positioned on the path. Your screen should resemble Figure 5.12.

Figure 5.12. The Spiral brush is applied to a path.

82

Unit 5 ★ Painting Tools

CREATING ART BRUSHES

When creating an Art brush, keep in mind that Illustrator will stretch a *single* object (brush) across a path or reproduce that single object with every stroke of the Paintbrush tool. Like Scatter brushes, Art brushes can be created from grouped objects and can be applied to selected paths or applied as a stroke to a path drawn with the Paintbrush tool.

Macintosh Keystrokes

⌘-N File/New
⌘-Y View/Artwork/Preview
⌘-Shift-A Edit/Deselect All
F5 Window/Show Brushes
F10 Window/Show Stroke

Windows Keystrokes

Ctrl-N File/New
Ctrl-Y View/Artwork/
    Preview
Ctrl-Shift-A Edit/Deselect
    All
F5 Window/Show Brushes
F10 Window/Show Stroke

EXERCISE F

1. In a new document (File/New), display the Brushes palette (F5) and the Stroke palette (F10).

2. Use the Ellipse tool to create a narrow filled and stroked ellipse. Don't make it too big. Use the Selection tool to drag the ellipse into the Brushes palette. In the New Brush dialog box, select the New Art Brush option. Click on OK to display the Art Brush Options dialog box (Figure 5.13).

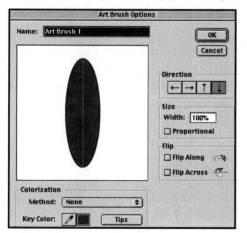

Figure 5.13. Once you select the kind of brush you want to create, its Options dialog box appears and displays the new brush.

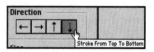

The Direction options in the Art Brush Options dialog box let you select a direction in which you want the art to be drawn as you drag with the Paintbrush tool across the page. In each button, the part of the line with the arrowhead represents the end of the brush stroke; the part without the arrowhead represents the start of the brush stroke.

3. Type *Ellipse Brush* in the Name field. Leave the Direction button set at stroking from top to bottom. Type 50 in the Width field to resize the artwork to 50% of its original size. Click the Proportional button to resize the artwork proportionally; otherwise, it will be longer than it is wide. Click on OK. Make sure that Art Brushes is selected in the Brushes palette menu so that the new brush is visible.

4. Use the Rectangle tool to draw a large rectangle on the page. With the rectangle selected, click on the Ellipse brush in the Brushes palette. The ellipse is stretched to fit around the rectangle (Figure 5.14).

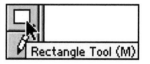

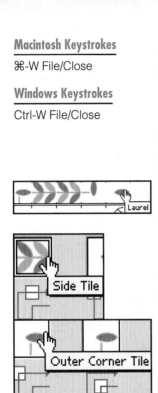

Click on a tile button to display its position on the path.

Tile fitting

The Stretch to fit option is the optimal setting for a path pattern, as it tells Illustrator to stretch the tiles to fit the pattern completely around the path. If you select the Add space to fit option, Illustrator will add empty space between tiles to make them fit on the path. The Approximate path option positions the pattern tiles slightly inside or outside the path instead of centering them on the path.

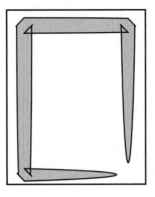

Figure 5.14. The Ellipse Art brush is stretched around the path when applied as a stroke.

5. Keep the rectangle selected and double-click the Ellipse brush in the Brushes palette. Select the Preview option and change the values. Notice how your changes affect the selected rectangle. Click on OK.

6. Close this file (Command/Ctrl-W). Don't save your changes.

CREATING PATTERN BRUSHES

Once you define a pattern, you can convert that pattern to a brush-stroke. The advantage of using a Pattern brush instead of a Scatter brush is that a Pattern brush will follow the curve of a path exactly; a Scatter brush is positioned relative to the x axis of either the page or the path. As with the other brushes, drag with the Paintbrush tool and a selected Pattern brush to create a path stroked with the brush tiles, or select a path and apply the Pattern brush as a stroke.

EDITING PATTERN BRUSHES

Pattern brushes are edited in the Pattern Brush Options dialog box (Figure 5.15). Patterns are tiles that wrap around the inner and outer corners and along the sides of paths, so you can edit any of these tiles to change the way the tile hugs the path.

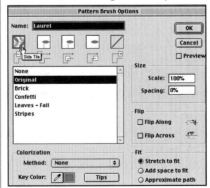

Figure 5.15. The Pattern Brush Options dialog box is where you specify which tiles run along the inner and outer corners and along the sides of a path.

Select the Pattern tile button below the Name field for the tile you want to modify. You can leave the original pattern as it appears in the button, or select another pattern for that tile. For example, you can leave Original selected in the Pattern Brush Options dialog box for the Laurel pattern in Figure 5.15, or you can select another pattern, such as Brick or Stripes, for the side tile in the Laurel pattern. Likewise, selecting the other tiles (such as Outer Corner, Inner Corner, and Start) lets you substitute different patterns for just those tile positions. Selecting None strips that tile position of its pattern.

Use the Scale and Spacing fields in the Size area to reduce or enlarge the pattern and specify the distance between each tile.

EXERCISE G

1. In a new file (File/New), display the Brushes palette (F5). Use the Rectangle tool to draw a large rectangle. Select the Stroke icon in the Toolbox.

2. Choose Show Pattern Brushes from the Brushes palette menu. With the artwork selected, click on any of the Pattern brushes. Deselect the artwork (Command/Ctrl-Shift-A).

3. Click on a different Pattern brush and drag it onto the unselected artwork, where it replaces the previous brush.

4. Click on the Laurel brush in the Brushes palette to select it. Choose Duplicate Brush from the Brushes palette menu. Select the rectangle and click on the Laurel copy brush to stroke the path with that brush.

5. Double-click on the duplicate brush (Laurel copy) to display the Pattern Brush Options dialog box. Click on the Preview button. Type *My Laurel* in the Name field. Because patterns are tiles, you edit the pattern by modifying the tiles that wrap around the inner corners, outer corners, and sides of the path.

6. Click on the Side Tile icon, the first icon under the Name field, and click on another pattern in the scroll box to replace just that tile with another pattern.

7. Click the Start Tile icon and click the Brick pattern to replace that tile with the Brick pattern. Repeat for the Inner Corner tile.

8. Click the Add Space to Fit button to space the pattern tiles instead of stretching them to fit the path. Click the Flip buttons to flip the tiles across the path. Click on OK. Click the Apply to Strokes button at the alert to apply your changes to the rectan-

Macintosh Keystrokes

⌘-N File/New
⌘-Shift-A Edit/Deselect All
F5 Window/Show Brushes

Windows Keystrokes

Ctrl-N File/New
Ctrl-Shift-A Edit/Deselect All
F5 Window/Show Brushes

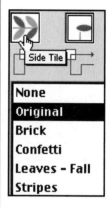

Select a tile and click to select a different pattern for just that tile.

The Flip options in the Art Brush Options dialog box specify how the art is oriented on the path, along the center line of the path, or across one side of the path. This won't make a difference with most geometric patterns, but you can get some interesting effects with more intricate pattern tiles.

Macintosh Keystrokes

⌘-N File/New
⌘-Y View/Artwork/Preview
⌘-Shift-A Edit/Deselect Al
F5 Window/Show Brushes
F10 Window/Show Stroke

Windows Keystrokes

Ctrl-N File/New
Ctrl-Y View/Artwork/
 Preview
Ctrl-Shift-A Edit/Deselect
 All
F5 Window/Show Brushes
F10 Window/Show Stroke

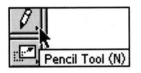

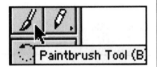

Cut and Clear commands

When you use the
Edit/Cut command, the
selected object (or
objects) is cut from the
document and placed on
the Clipboard, where it is
available for pasting anywhere in that document or
in another Illustrator document. When you choose
Edit/Clear, the selected
object (or objects) is
removed, but does not go
on the Clipboard and can-
not be pasted back into
the document.

gle. Notice that the My Laurel brush in the Brushes palette displays the new tiles you added to that pattern (Figure 5.16).

Figure 5.16. The edited brush in the Brushes palette displays the tiles used to create it.

9. Choose Edit/Select All (Command/Ctrl-Shift-A) and choose Edit/Clear to clear the artwork without placing it on the Clipboard and clogging memory.

10. Use the Pencil tool to draw a leaf—or anything you like. Fill and stroke the artwork. Select all the paths in the artwork with the Selection tool and choose New Brush from the Brushes palette menu.

11. Select the New Pattern Brush option in the New Brush dialog box. Click on OK to display the Pattern Brush Options dialog box. Type a name for the pattern and click on the tiles to select any of the patterns available for the Pattern brush. Click on OK.

12. Select the Paintbrush tool, click on the Pattern brush you just created, and draw with that brush to create a path stroked with the new pattern (Figure 5.17).

13. Close this file (Command/Ctrl-W). Don't save your changes.

Figure 5.17. Dragging with a Pattern brush creates a path stroked with the brush.

COLORIZATION

The Options dialog boxes for the Scatter, Art, and Pattern brushes allow you to change the color of the brush using four different methods. Any changes you make to a brush's color are based on the Key Color and on the current stroke color. If you plan to select a Colorization option, first specify a stroke color in the Toolbox before accessing the brush's Options dialog box. Click the Tips box in the Options dialog box for information about how these four options work.

NONE

The None option displays the brush colors exactly as they appear in the Brushes palette.

TINTS

This option is used with brushes that contain black-and-white art, and where the black turns into another color. Selecting Tints converts the black areas to the stroke color, changes the non-black areas to tints of the stroke color, and leaves the white areas white.

TINTS AND SHADES

Use this option for grayscale brushes, as it maintains the black and white colors but makes everything in between a blend from black to white through the stroke color.

HUE SHIFT

This option uses the key color in the artwork in the Key Color box. Anything in the artwork that is the key color changes to the stroke color. The other colors in the brush artwork are colored with colors related to that stroke color while maintaining black, white, and gray. This is a good option for brushes containing multiple colors. You can change the key color by clicking with the Eyedropper on any color in the Preview box.

CONVERTING BRUSHES TO ART

Many of the brushes in the Brushes palette are simply Illustrator artwork defined as brushes. Illustrator 8 ships with hundreds of brushes, giving you an extensive source of vector artwork. To convert those brushes to editable artwork, drag the brush out of the Brushes palette onto the drawing page. Then select it with any of the selection tools and edit it just as you would your own artwork.

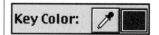

The key color is the primary color in the artwork. A red flower with a yellow center, for example, will display red as the key color in the Key Color box.

Click with the Eyedropper on the Preview in the Scatter Brush Options dialog box to select another Key Color.

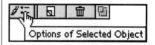

When any object is stroked with a brush, click this icon to display the options for that brush.

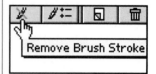

Click this icon to remove a brush stroke from a selected object.

Macintosh Keystrokes

⌘-O File/Open
⌘-Shift-A Edit/Deselect All
F5 Window/Show Brushes
F6 Window/Show Color

Windows Keystrokes

Ctrl-O File/Open
Ctrl-Shift-A Edit/Deselect All
F5 Window/Show Brushes
F6 Window/Show Color

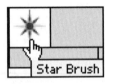

Selection Tool (V)

Star Brush

Important info

The Method Colorization options depend on the color in the Stroke icon in the Toolbox. If you find that nothing is happening when you select different colorization methods, check the stroke color.

EXERCISE H

1. Open the *Brush.eps* file in the Unit 05 folder on the CD-ROM. It displays a rectangle filled and stroked with the default colors. Make sure the Brushes and Color palettes are visible. Use the Brushes palette menu to select Scatter Brushes.

2. Select the rectangle with the Selection tool and click on the Star Brush, the last brush in the Brushes palette. Deselect the rectangle (Command/Ctrl-Shift-A).

3. Select the Stroke icon in the Toolbox and click on the blue process color, Pantone 300 CVU in the Swatches palette, to specify it as the stroke color (Figure 5.18).

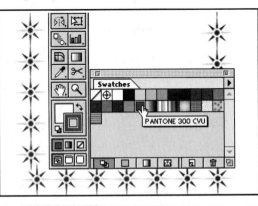

Figure 5.18. Select a spot color for the stroke color.

4. Double-click on the Star Brush in the Brushes palette to display its Options dialog box. Because the blue spot color is the predominant color in the brush, that blue appears in the Key Color box at the bottom of the dialog box. And because None is selected in the Method pull-down menu, the brush appears exactly as it does in the Brushes palette.

5. Select the Preview button. Use the Method menu to select Tints. The stroke changes to tints of the stroke color, the blue color. The non-black areas, including the red circle, become tints of the blue color. The white areas remain white, and the original black areas of the artwork become blue.

6. Use the Method menu to select Tints and Shades. The black and white areas remain, but the gray and red areas become a blend from black to white through the blue stroke color.

7. Choose Hue Shift from the Method menu. Click on the Eyedropper next to the Key Color box and click on the red circle in the Preview area—not in the rectangle. The Key Color changes

to red, which turns any red areas in the brush (in this case the red circle), to the stroke color, blue. The other parts of the brush take on colors related to the blue color family. Click on OK and click Apply to Strokes to return to the document

8. Close this file (Command/Ctrl-W). Don't save your changes.

BRUSH LIBRARIES

Illustrator 8 ships with many different kinds of brush libraries that you can import into your documents. Like imported Swatch libraries, the Brush libraries are locked, allowing you to drag brushes to the primary Brushes palette in the document, but not to delete or modify any brushes in the secondary libraries.

EXERCISE I

1. In a new document, display the Brushes palette (F5). Choose Window/Brush Libraries/Floral Sample. The Floral Sample Brushes palette appears.

2. Click on the Bird of Paradise brush and drag it out onto the page, where it is no longer a brush, but Illustrator art. Select it with the Selection tool and move it around on the page. Use the Rotate tool to rotate it so that it is stem up on the page. Press the Option/Alt key while dragging with the Selection tool to create a copy of the flower (Figure 5.19).

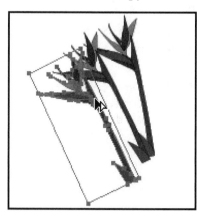

Figure 5.19. Press the Option/Alt key while dragging the artwork to create a copy.

3. Click on the Paintbrush tool and click on the Bird of Paradise brush. Drag the brush on the page from the top to the bottom, so that the flower appears at the top and the stem at the bottom. The longer the drag, the longer the flower.

Macintosh Keystrokes

⌘-N File/New
F5 Window/Show Brushes

Windows Keystrokes

Ctrl-N File/New
F5 Window/Show Brushes

Macintosh Keystrokes

⌘-Shift-A Edit/Deselect All
⌘-C Edit/Copy
⌘-V Edit/Paste

Windows Keystrokes

Ctrl-Shift-A Edit/Deselect
    All
Ctrl-C Edit/Copy
Ctrl-V Edit/Paste

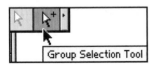

4. Create several flowers. Each flower is on a path, so edit the path by selecting the edge of the path with the Direct Selection tool and moving anchor points and direction handles. Deselect everything (Command/Ctrl-Shift-A). Use the Selection tool to select one of the paths. Click to select one of the anchor points and move the anchor point and its direction handles to reshape the curvature of the path, and therefore the curve of the flower (Figure 5.20).

Figure 5.20. If the path and its anchor points are selected, you will be able only to move the path, not reshape the path. To reshape, select and move only an anchor point or direction handle.

5. Continue to duplicate and reshape the flowers, rotating and resizing them using the Rotate and Scale tools or the Transform Each command (Object/Transform/Transform Each) until you have a bouquet of flowers.

6. Select the Paintbrush tool and click on the Branch brush in the Floral Sample palette. Paint with the Branch brush just as you did with the Bird of Paradise brush.

7. Select one of the branches with the Selection tool and choose Object/Expand. Click OK to expand the object fill, and stroke. You now have artwork, not a brush.

8. Use the Group Selection tool (behind the Direct Selection tool) and triple-click on one leaf to select all the objects in that group. Choose Edit/Copy, then Edit/Paste to paste the leaf on the page. Move it onto the flower stems. Create an arrangement using the flowers and leaves. Your screen should resemble Figure 5.21.

Figure 5.21. The bouquet of Bird of Paradise brush strokes. Because dragging with an Art brush creates one brush, Art brushes can be used to create complex artwork without drawing every element separately.

9. Drag the Bird of Paradise brush out of the Floral Sample palette into the Brushes palette. Repeat for the Branch brush. Close the Floral Sample palette by clicking in its Close box on the title bar.

10. Choose File/Save A Copy. Navigate to your Projects folder. Type *Flowers.eps* in the Save a Copy as field (Macintosh) or Save as type field (Windows), and select Illustrator EPS from the Format pull-down menu. You can now import this EPS file into another program like QuarkXPress or PageMaker.

11. Close this file (Command/Ctrl-W). Don't save your changes.

12. Open the *Flowers.eps file* (File/Open) in your Projects folder. The Brushes palette displays the Bird of Paradise and Branch brushes you saved with the file.

13. Close this file (File/Close). Don't save your changes.

REVIEW

In this unit you learned that:

1. The Eyedropper tool is used to select (sample) colors applied to a text object or art object and make those colors the current fill and stroke colors.

2. The Paint Bucket tool applies the current fill and stroke attributes to any object, even if it is not selected.

3. The Eyedropper and Paint Bucket tools behave according to the options you select in their dialog boxes.

4. It's often easier to select an object's center point in Artwork view.

5. The Hard Mix and Soft Mix filters on the Pathfinder palette are used to create the illusion of color transparency.

6. Clicking with the Eyedropper tool on any object applies the fill and stroke colors to any selected object in the file.

7. The freehand drawing tools in Illustrator's Toolbox are the Pencil tool, Paintbrush tool, and Pen tool.

8. The number of anchor points created with the Pencil tool is determined in the Type & Auto Tracing Preferences dialog box.

9. The higher the Auto Trace Tolerance value, the smoother the path created with the Pencil tool.

Macintosh Keystrokes

⌘-O File/Open
⌘-W File/Close

Windows Keystrokes

Ctrl-O File/Open
Ctrl-W File/Close

FYI

Dragging brushes from an secondary palette into the Brushes palette saves those brushes with the document.

Save a Copy As:		
Flowers.eps		
Format:	Acrobat PDF	
	✓ Illustrator	
	Illustrator EPS	

When you save a copy of the file in EPS format, you can then save the original file in its native Illustrator format.

Windows info

For the operating system-disadvantaged, Windows automatically adds the .eps tag to a file saved in the Illustrator EPS format.

10. A path created with the Pencil tool can be edited with the Direct Selection tool, with the Smooth tool, and with the Eraser tool.

11. Dragging the Smooth tool over a path removes anchor points and "irons out" the path.

12. The Eraser tool removes path segments and is best used in a single, smooth, dragging motion.

13. The Paintbrush tool draws freeform paths painted with a brush selected from the Brushes palette.

14. Calligraphic brushes create elliptical shapes along the center of the path.

15. Scatter brushes scatter artwork at a specified distance around or along a path.

16. Art brushes place a single object evenly along a path.

17. Pattern brushes create a path along which the pattern tiles are placed.

18. Any artwork can be converted to any of the four kinds of brushes.

19. Brushes can be edited with the option of applying the new brush to artwork painted with the original brush.

20. Brush libraries can be imported into a document and those brushes can be added to the document's Brushes palette.

Unit 6
Gradient
Fills

Boy and Fish
by Ralph Warwick

OVERVIEW

In this unit you will learn how to:
create and edit linear and radial fills
create and edit custom gradients
use the Gradient Mesh tool
create and edit a gradient mesh

TERMS

Color Stop
gradient fill
Gradient slider
mesh lines
mesh object
mesh point
mesh segment
Midpoint diamond

HOW IT WORKS

Use the Pen tool and basic shape tools to draw and edit the paths. Create custom gradients and apply at different angles with the Gradient tool.

Macintosh Keystrokes

⌘-N File/New
⌘-Y View/Artwork/Preview

Windows Keystrokes

Ctrl-N File/New
Ctrl-Y View/Artwork/
        Preview

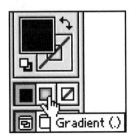

Click the Gradient button in the Toolbox to display the Gradient palette.

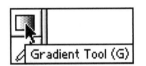

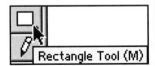

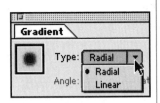

Use the Type menu on the Gradient palette to select a radial or linear gradient.

GRADIENT FILLS

A gradient fill is a graduated blend between colors. Create a gradient in the Gradient palette from one color to another color, or create a gradient containing many colors. Using the Gradient palette, you can specify which colors constitute the gradient, where the colors are equally mixed, and whether the gradient is a linear or radial fill.

You cannot apply gradients to strokes, and you must convert text to paths before filling with a gradient. If you have an object selected while editing a gradient, that object will reflect the changes you make in the Gradient palette. You can also use the Gradient Mesh tool in version 8 to blend multiple colors in different directions to give an object a painted look, the kind you can achieve in a program like Photoshop or Painter.

Like process colors, spot colors, and patterns, several default gradient fills are also loaded into the Swatches palette. Click on the Gradient button in the Toolbox or choose Window/Show Gradient (F9) to display the Gradient palette. Although the Gradient *palette* is used to create custom gradient fills, the Gradient *tool* is used to change the direction of the gradient fill within a selected object.

LINEAR GRADIENTS

Although Illustrator allows only two types of gradients, a linear gradient and a radial gradient, you can change the angle of a linear gradient to create a different effect. The gradient's angle can be specified in the Angle field of the Gradient palette, or it can be applied by dragging the Gradient tool at an angle. Linear gradients change colors from left to right, right to left, top to bottom, and bottom to top, depending on where you start and end with the Gradient tool.

RADIAL GRADIENTS

Radial gradients change colors from the center outward. Any color can be specified as the beginning and ending color or as an intermediate color, giving you unlimited variations. The Angle field is not available for a radial gradient.

EXERCISE A

1. Create a new file (Command/Ctrl-N), choose View/Preview (Command/Ctrl-Y), and display the Swatches palette. Click on the Default Colors icon in the Toolbox.

2. Select the Rectangle tool. Press the Alt/Option key before you click and drag to draw the rectangle from the center outward. Keep the rectangle selected.

Unit 6 ★ Gradient Fills

3. Click on the Fill icon in the Toolbox and click the Gradient button in the Toolbox to display the Gradient palette (Figure 6.1). The selected box fills with the last applied gradient.

Macintosh Keystrokes

⌘-Y View/Artwork/Preview
⌘-W File/Close

Windows Keystrokes

Ctrl-Y View/Artwork/
Preview
Ctrl-W File/Close

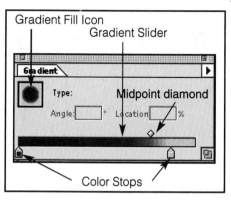

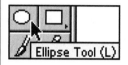

Figure 6.1. The Gradient palette displays a Fill icon, a slider bar, a midpoint marker, and color stops that indicate the start and stop points for the graduated color. The current gradient fill is a radial fill.

4. Select the Ellipse Tool and press the Alt/Option key before you click and drag to draw an oval from the center outward. The oval fills with the current gradient.

5. Click on one of the radial fills in the Swatches palette to fill the selected oval with a radial gradient.

6. With the oval still selected, use the Type pull-down menu on the Gradient palette to select Linear. The gradient retains the same colors but changes to a linear gradient.

7. Close this file (File/Close). Don't save your changes.

GRADIENT TOOL

The Gradient tool is used to change the direction of the gradation in a selected object, to specify the starting and ending points of a gradient fill, and to apply a gradient fill across a group of selected objects.

GRADIENT DRAGGING

How you drag with the Gradient tool affects the gradient's display. The shorter the drag, the more compressed the gradient. The longer the line you drag through the object, the more the gradient expands—sometimes so much that some colors are not even displayed, and a single color in the gradient can fill a whole object.

Dragging outside of the selected object starts the gradient with the first color in the gradient. Although it won't be displayed outside the selection, it is still "used up" in the area where you're dragging. This allows you to create different variations of color using the same gradient (Figure 6.2).

FYI

Once you select any fill, solid color, pattern, or gradient, that fill automatically fills any object you draw until you either change the fill or click the Default Colors icon.

Access the Gradient tool by typing *g*.

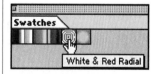

Select a gradient from the Swatches palette. Clicking the Show Gradient Swatches button on the Gradient palette displays only the gradient swatches.

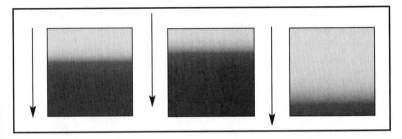

Figure 6.2. Click and drag from the top to the bottom of the rectangle (left). Clicking slightly above the rectangle and dragging reduces the yellow (center). Clicking from the top of the rectangle and extending a few inches beyond the bottom increases the yellow and loses the blue.

Macintosh Keystrokes

⌘-N File/New
⌘-K File/Preferences/
   General

Windows Keystrokes

Ctrl-N File/New
Ctrl-K File/Preferences/
   General

Rectangle Tool (M)

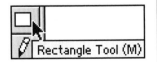

Selection Tool (V)

Use the Swatches palette menu to select a display format for the swatches.

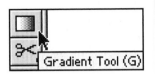

Gradient Tool (G)

EXERCISE B

1. In a new file (File/New), display the Swatches palette and click on the Default Colors icon in the Toolbox. Make sure you are in Preview view (View/Preview).

2. Choose File/Preferences/Units & Undo (Command/Ctrl-K) and use the General pull-down menu to select inches. Click OK.

3. Click once on the Rectangle tool to select it and click in the center of the page. When the Rectangle dialog box appears, type 5 in the Width field and 3 in the Height field. Click on OK. The rectangle will fill with the default white fill.

4. Click on the Gradient button in the Toolbox to display the Gradient palette. The rectangle fills with the last gradient you used.

5. Click on the Show Gradient Swatches button in the Swatches palette to display only the gradient fills (Figure 6.3).

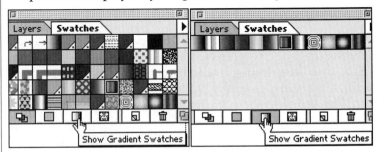

Figure 6.3. When working with gradients and the Swatches palette (left), it's easier to display only the gradient swatches (right).

6. Use the Swatches palette menu to select Name. With the rectangle still selected, scroll through the gradient swatches and click on the fill named *Purple, Red, Yellow*. Make sure the Angle value is set to 0. The rectangle fills with a linear fill starting with purple, moving to red and ending with yellow (Figure 6.4).

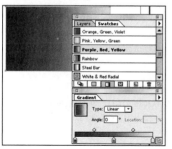

Figure 6.4. Click on the name of a gradient to apply it to a selected object.

7. Click on the Gradient tool to select it. Click on the upper left corner of the selected rectangle and drag to the lower right corner. When the cursor changes to a white arrow, indicating that you have reached the end of the selected object, release the mouse button. The angle of the blend has been repositioned to a 45° angle (Figure 6.5).

Figure 6.5. The original gradient (left), drawing a diagonal line from the top left to bottom right corner (center), and the result of using the Gradient tool (right).

8. Continue to click and drag on the selected rectangle with the Gradient tool until you become comfortable with that tool.

9. Use the Ellipse tool to draw ovals and circles (press the Shift key to constrain the ovals to circles), and fill with different radial fills. Then use the Gradient tool to change the direction of the fills.

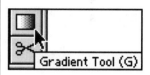

Trouble?

You must use the Gradient tool on a selected object or else nothing will happen when you drag.

10. Draw three circles. Use the Selection tool to Shift-select them.

11. Select the Fill box on the Toolbox and click on the Rainbow gradient to fill all three circles with a six-color gradient. Use the Type menu on the Gradient palette to select Radial.

12. Keep all three circles selected. Select the Gradient tool, press the Shift key, and click and drag from the first circle through the second and third circles. Instead of three separate rainbow

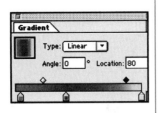

The selected Midpoint diamond displays 80 in the Location field, indicating that the midpoint between the two colors in the gradient occurs 80% across the length of the Gradient Slider.

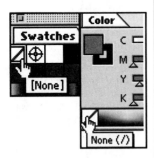

Click the None swatch on the Swatches palette or on the Color palette to deselect the Color Stops on the Gradient palette.

blends, the Gradient tool distributes the blend among the three selected objects and fills from purple, to red, to yellow, depending on the size of the circles. Now reverse the direction, dragging from right to left. The selected circles fill with the same colors but in the reverse order (Figure 6.6).

13. Close this file (File/Close). Don't save your changes.

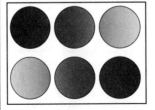

Figure 6.6. Dragging with the Gradient tool from left to right across multiple selected objects distributes the gradient evenly among the objects (top). Reversing the direction applies the same colors but in the opposite direction (bottom).

CUSTOM GRADIENTS

Just as you created, named, and edited custom colors, so you can use the Gradient palette to create, name, and edit a linear or radial gradient fill. You can specify the starting and ending color of the fill as well as add other colors to the fill. When you create a radial fill, the starting point determines the filled object's highlighted (lighter) areas and the ending point defines its shadows (darker areas).

CREATING GRADIENTS

Custom gradients are created in the Gradient palette from colors selected in the Color or Swatches palette. You can also drag a color swatch from the Swatches palette onto the Gradient slider to add that color to the gradient fill. If you *just click* on a swatch in the Swatches palette, that color becomes the fill color, but does not become a color in the gradient. You must *drag* the swatch onto the Gradient slider to add it to the gradient.

Add a color to the custom gradient by

▲ Dragging the Fill icon onto the Gradient slider, where it automatically adds a Color Stop for that color on the Gradient slider.

▲ Select a Color Stop and click on a color in the CMYK spectrum at the bottom of the Color palette.

▲ Select a Color Stop and Option/Alt-click on a color swatch in the Swatches palette.

▲ Select a Color Stop and Shift-click with the Eyedropper tool on any artwork in the document to add that color to the gradient.

To deselect the Color Stops on the Gradient slider, click the None icon on the Color palette or on the Swatches palette. This allows you to specify a fill color without applying it to the gradient.

COLOR STOPS

Colors are applied to the selected Color Stop in the Gradient palette. A selected Color Stop displays a black "roof." If you don't add another Color Stop or select another Color Stop, any changes you make to the color in the Color palette are applied to the selected Color Stop.

MIDPOINT DIAMONDS

The Midpoint diamond visible at the top of the Gradient slider indicates the location in the gradient where the starting and ending colors are of equal amounts.

SAVING GRADIENTS

Once a gradient is created, it must be saved in the Swatches palette if it is to be used again. If you don't save a gradient, unless you apply it to an object, selecting another color from the Swatches palette removes the custom gradient. If you applied that gradient to an object, select the object and drag the Fill icon from the Toolbox to the Swatches palette to save the gradient swatch.

To save a custom gradient, select the object filled with the gradient or deselect the object once its fill color appears in the Fill icon in the Toolbox and do one of three things:

▲ Drag the Fill icon from the Toolbox or Color palette into the Swatches palette.

▲ Choose New Swatch from the Swatches palette menu and name it.

▲ Drag the Gradient Fill icon from the Gradient palette onto the Swatches palette.

DELETING GRADIENT COLORS

To delete a color from a gradient, click on its Color Stop and drag it downward and out of the Gradient slider. There must always be at least two colors in any gradient.

EXERCISE C

1. In a new file (File/New), display the Swatches, Color, and Gradient palettes. Click the Show Gradient Swatches button on the Gradient palette and use the Gradient palette's menu to select Small Swatch. The Gradient palette displays the last gradient you used.

2. Use the Rectangle tool to draw a rectangle. Keep it selected so you will be able to see how the gradient looks as you edit it.

3. Click on the first gradient swatch in the Gradient palette, a linear black-and-white gradient. It displays two Color Stops and

Macintosh Keystrokes

⌘-N File/New
F6 Window/Show Color
F9 Window/Show Gradient

Windows Keystrokes

Ctrl-N File/New
F6 Window/Show Color
F9 Window/Show Gradient

Active Color Stop displays a black "roof."

Midpoint diamond

The diamond above the gradient bar indicates where the starting color and ending color in the gradient are of equal amounts. The more you move this icon to the right, the more of the starting color is assigned to the gradient. Move it to the left to assign more of the ending color to the gradient.

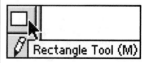

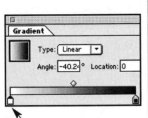

The first Color Stop on the Gradient Slider is selected. This first Color Stop determines the first color in the gradient.

Select a color mode from the Color palette's menu.

FYI

Whenever you create a gradient swatch and save it, it is saved as either a linear or radial swatch, depending on which option you selected from the Type menu in the Gradient palette. You can always save a swatch in one format, change it to the other format in the Gradient palette, and save the second swatch.

a Midpoint diamond. Click on the left Color Stop to activate it. Notice that its "roof" turns black, indicating that it is selected. Once you select a Color Stop, any color selection you make will apply to that Color Stop.

4. The black-and-white linear gradient is a grayscale. To create a color gradient, choose CMYK from the Color palette's menu. Click on a pink color in the CMYK spectrum bar. Because you already selected a Color Stop in the Gradient palette, that pink color is applied to the first color in the gradient (Figure 6.7).

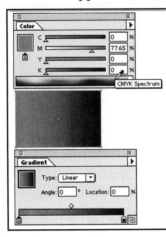

Figure 6.7. Click on a Color Stop in the Gradient palette (below), then select a color from the Color palette to apply that color to the Color Stop (above).

5. Click on the right Color Stop, select CMYK again from the Color palette's menu, and click on a contrasting color in the CMYK spectrum in the Color palette to apply it to the second color in the gradient. Or, Option/Alt-click on a color swatch in the Swatches palette.

6. Use the Midpoint diamond above the Gradient slider in the Gradient palette to specify the point at which the starting and ending colors are equal.

7. The current blend starts with yellow and blends into red. Notice the Color Stops at the beginning and end of the Gradient slider bar. These specify where the first color begins and where the second color ends. The diamond above the bar is the midpoint marker and indicates where the two colors mix in exactly the same amounts. The percentage field on the right displays the color percentage of the color at the start, midpoint, and end of the gradient.

8. When you are satisfied with the gradient, drag the color swatch from the Gradient or Color palette onto the Swatches palette. Double-click on the new gradient swatch and type a name for it in the Swatch Name field. Click on OK. You can

now apply this swatch as a linear or radial gradient to any object in this file.

9. Close this file (File/Close). Don't save your changes.

MULTI-COLORED GRADIENTS

A gradient can have more than two colors, in which case you will have a start color, intermediate colors, and an end color. For every color you add to the gradient, you must add a Color Stop, which must be selected before the color can be applied. And as with two-color gradients, once the multi-color gradient is created, it must be saved in the Swatches palette if you want to use it again.

EXERCISE D

1. In a new document (File/New), display the Swatches, Color, and Gradient palettes. Use the Gradient palette to select Show Options. Use the Color palette menu to select CMYK.

2. Use the Rectangle tool to draw a rectangle on the page and keep it selected so you can see the effect of the gradient you are creating. Fill the rectangle with the default black-and-white gradient in the Swatches palette.

3. Click the Fill icon on the Color palette to activate it. Click on a red color in the CMYK spectrum in the Color palette. The rectangle fills with a solid red.

4. Drag the red Fill icon from the Color palette or from the Tool-box down onto the left side of the Gradient slider on the Gradient palette. Four things happen: (1) The rectangle fills with a white, red, and black gradient; (2) a selected Color Stop appears at the point where the red color starts; (3) a selected Color Stop appears below the Color icon on the Color palette, indicating that the current color is a gradient color; and (4) the Stroke icon disappears from the Color menu, because gradients cannot be applied as strokes (Figure 6.8).

5. Click the right Color Stop on the Gradient slider. Click on another color in the CMYK spectrum on the Color palette to fill the Fill Color icon on the Color palette and to replace the color for the right Color Stop on the Gradient palette.

Macintosh Keystrokes

⌘-N File/New
F6 Window/Show Color
F9 Window/Show Gradient
⌘-W File/Close

Windows Keystrokes

Ctrl-N File/New
F6 Window/Show Color
F9 Window/Show Gradient
Ctrl-W File/Close

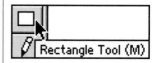
Rectangle Tool (M)

FYI

To quickly apply a color swatch to the Gradient palette, select the Color Stop and Option-click (Macintosh) or Alt-click (Windows) on the color in the Swatches palette.

Problems?

If you find that clicking a color swatch fills the object instead of editing the gradient, that's because you either haven't selected a Color Stop on the Gradient palette or you didn't Option/Alt-click on the color swatch.

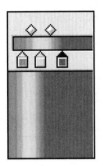

Moving the Color Stops close together creates a sharp transition between the colors.

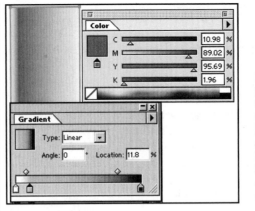

Figure 6.8. The rectangle displays the first color added to the Gradient palette. The Color icon in the Color palette displays a Color Stop below it, and the Fill icon in the Gradient palette displays the new gradient mix.

6. Click below the Gradient slider to add another Color Stop (Figure 6.9). When you do this, the Color Stop adds a color from a mix of the two colors on either side of it and displays that color in the Color icon of the Color palette. With the third Color Stop still selected, drag the CMYK sliders in the Color palette to adjust the color.

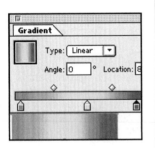

Moving the Color Stops farther apart creates a softer transition between the colors.

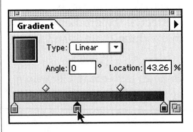

Figure 6.9. Click below the Gradient slider to add another Color Stop.

7. Drag a process color swatch (one without a dot in the corner) from the Swatches palette onto the Gradient slider between the second and third Color Stops to add a fourth color to the gradient (Figure 6.10).

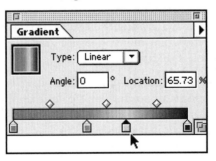

Figure 6.10. Dragging a color swatch from the Color palette to any position on the Gradient slider adds that color to the gradient.

FYI

When adding a color from the artwork to a selected Color Stop on the Gradient palette, you must Shift-click with the Eyedropper tool. Otherwise, the sampled color will fill the object instead of editing the gradient.

8. Drag the Midpoint diamonds to the left and/or right to adjust the point at which the two colors on either side of the diamond are of equal amounts. Dragging the Midpoint diamond closer to a Color Stop creates a sharp transition between the two colors. Likewise, moving Color Stops closer together results in a sharp transition between colors.

9. To delete a Color Stop, drag it off the Gradient Slider.

10. When you have mixed a gradient you like by adding and deleting colors and Color Stops, drag its swatch from the Gradient palette to the Swatches palette, positioning it next to another gradient swatch.

11. Double-click on the new swatch and type a name for it in the Swatch Name field. Click on OK. The new gradient swatch can now be used to fill any object in this document.

12. Close this file (File/Close). Don't save your changes.

Macintosh Keystrokes

⌘-W File/Close

Windows Keystrokes

Ctrl-W File/Close

GRADIENT MESH TOOL

Ordinarily, a gradient spreads horizontally, vertically, or diagonally across an object. The gradient's spread is controlled by the Gradient tool. Drag with the Gradient tool in one direction to blend in that direction or drag in another direction to blend colors in that direction. Period. All this changes with the Gradient Mesh tool. Instead of applying a smooth color transition across one or more objects, as with the Gradient tool, the Gradient Mesh tool transforms the object into a mesh object, one capable of displaying many colors positioned at precise intervals.

These petals filled with the Gradient Mesh tool show subtle transitions between the colors.

GRADIENT MESH OBJECTS

An object is transformed into a gradient *mesh object* when you click on it with the Gradient Mesh tool, or when you select it and choose the Create Gradient Mesh command (for objects filled with a solid color) or the Expand command (for objects filled with a gradient) from the Object menu.

A mesh object, unlike a regular Illustrator object, has multiple lines called *mesh lines* that crisscross the object. Where the mesh lines cross, *mesh points* are created. Mesh points behave like ordinary anchor points except that they are diamond-shaped and can hold color. Their ability to hold color is what makes them so powerful in creating graduated color blends (Figure 6.11).

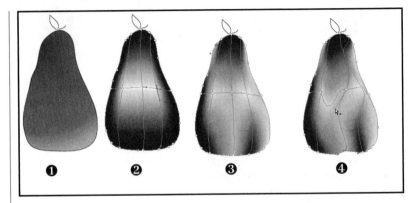

Figure 6.11. The object is filled with a radial gradient (1). Clicking in the center of the object with the Gradient Mesh tool changed it to a mesh object with the first mesh line running vertically down the center. Clicking on ether side of that mesh line with the Gradient Mesh tool created two new vertical mesh segments (2). Selecting the individual mesh points and applying color resulted in different gradients in different directions in the same object (3). Selecting the mesh segments and mesh points with the Direct Selection tool changed the direction of the gradients (4). Because mesh points behave like regular anchor points, the pear's bottom was reshaped with the Direct Selection tool.

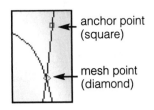

anchor point (square)

mesh point (diamond)

Anchor points are added to a mesh line with the Add Anchor Point tool. Mesh points are added with the Gradient Mesh tool.

MESH LINES, MESH SEGMENTS, AND MESH POINTS

The crisscross lines on a mesh object are called *mesh lines*. Moving these lines changes the color transition between those lines. Where the mesh lines cross, *mesh points* are created. These mesh points can be moved and edited—they have direction handles—to change the intensity of the color shift or to change the extent of the colored area between the points. Mesh points can be added and deleted from a mesh line, changing the color shift as you do so.

Anchor points can also be added to and deleted from a mesh line with the Add Anchor Point and Delete Anchor Point tools, to give you more flexibility in moving the mesh lines. As you move the mesh line, the gradient updates to the new position. It does this in real time, so you don't have to wait for the object to redraw to see how the gradient looks.

The area between any four mesh points is called a *mesh segment*. Selecting any of the mesh points that enclose the mesh segment and applying color to those mesh points shifts the color gradient within the segment (Figure 6.12).

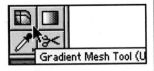

Gradient Mesh Tool (U

Unit 6 ★ Gradient Fills

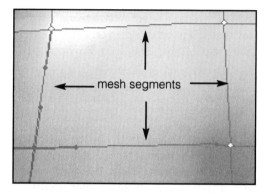

Figure 6.12. The four lines enclosed by mesh points are called mesh segments. Each mesh point was selected and a different color applied to that mesh point.

EXERCISE E

1. Open the *Pears.ai* file in the Unit 06 folder on the CD-ROM. It displays two pears filled with a normal radial gradient. Select one pear with the Selection tool and click on the Default Colors icon in the Toolbox to change the fill and stroke.

2. Select the Gradient Mesh tool and click in the center of the white pear. The fill remains white, but the stroke disappears and a single mesh appears (Figure 6.13).

3. Click with the Gradient Mesh tool to the right and left of the vertical mesh line on the horizontal mesh line o create two vertical mesh lines. If you click with the mesh tool on an empty area of the mesh object, you will create another mesh segment of horizontal *and* vertical lines. Click above and below the horizontal mesh line on the vertical mesh line to create the mesh in Figure 6.13.

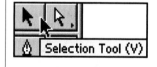

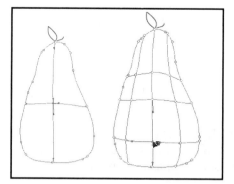

Figure 6.13. Clicking once on the object with the Gradient Mesh tool creates the first crisscross mesh line (left). Clicking elsewhere creates other mesh lines. Selecting the mesh points and applying color creates the controlled gradient fill.

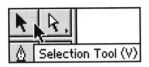

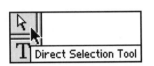

4. Choose Window/New Window and select Artwork view for the new window. Resize the two windows so you can work in Artwork mode and view the color application in Preview view.

5. Deselect everything (Command/Ctrl-Shift-A). Click on the window in Preview view to activate it. Click the Fill icon in the Toolbox. Use the Selection tool to click on any mesh point in the pear to select the entire pear and all its mesh points. Click on a red color in the Swatches palette to fill the pear with red. Deselect the pear. Use the Direct Selection tool to select the pear. This will also select the four mesh points and mesh segments closest to where you click. Click a yellow color in the Swatches palette to apply that color to the area bounded by those four mesh segments (Figure 6.14).

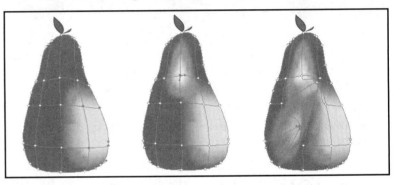

Figure 6.14. Clicking on a mesh object with the Direct Selection tool and clicking a color in the Color or Swatches palette applies the current fill color to the four segments (left). Clicking a mesh point and clicking a color applies it to just that mesh point (center). Clicking and dragging on a mesh point with the Gradient Mesh tool moves the mesh point and its connecting lines, changing the color flow (right).

6. Click another mesh point and click on white in the Swatches palette to apply that color to just that mesh point. Continue to select mesh points and apply colors to them.

7. Select the Gradient Mesh tool, click on a mesh point, and drag to move the mesh points and any mesh lines connected to it (Figure 6.14).

8. Change the fill color in the Toolbox. Select the Paint Bucket tool and click directly on a mesh point or on a mesh segment (one of the four lines bounded by four mesh points) to color it with the current fill color.

9. Select a mesh point with either the Gradient Mesh tool or the Direct Selection tool. Drag a swatch color from the Swatches palette onto that mesh point or click a color in the Color palette

Unit 6 ★ Gradient Fills

to apply that color to the mesh segment bounded by the selected mesh point.

10. Close this file (Command/Ctrl-W). Don't save your changes.

CREATING AND EDITING MESH OBJECTS

Besides clicking on an object with the Gradient Mesh tool to convert it to a mesh object, you can use the Create Gradient Mesh and Expand commands. These commands give you more control over the number and position of the horizontal and vertical mesh lines and allow you to specify the direction of the highlighting in the mesh object.

CREATE GRADIENT MESH COMMAND

Select any object filled with a solid color and choose Object/Create Gradient Mesh. Enter the number of horizontal rows and vertical columns in the appropriate fields and select a direction for the highlight from the Appearance menu (Figure 6.15). The Highlight value specifies a percentage of highlight applied to the mesh object. The 100% value applies a maximum highlight to the object. A lower value reduces the effect of the highlight.

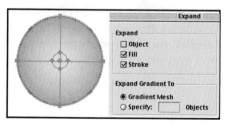

Figure 6.15. The Create Gradient Mesh dialog box.

EXPAND COMMAND

This command is used only with an object containing a gradient fill. Select Fill and/or Stroke in the Expand field and Gradient Mesh in the Expand Gradient field. The selected object displays a single mesh in Artwork view or when selected with the Selection tool (Figure 6.16).

Figure 6.16. The Expand command creates a mesh object from a selected object filled with a gradient.

Appearance:	✓ Flat
Highlight:	To Center
	To Edge

Use the Appearance menu in the Create Gradient Mesh dialog box to specify the direction of the highlight. **Flat** applies the highlight evenly across the surface of the object. **To Center** generates the highlight from the sides to the center of the object. **To Edge** highlights from the center of the object outward to its sides.

Version 7

There is no Gradient Mesh tool in version 7.

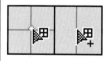

The plain gradient mesh cursor (left) indicates that clicking will select a mesh point. The cursor with the + sign indicates that clicking will create another mesh line.

Macintosh Keystrokes

⌘-N File/New
⌘-Shift-A Edit/Deselect All

Windows Keystrokes

Ctrl-N File/New
Ctrl-Shift-A Edit/Deselect
    All

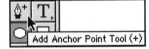
Add Anchor Point Tool (+)

Ellipse Tool (L)

Gradient Mesh Tool (U)

EDITING MESH OBJECTS

A mesh object is edited by adding and deleting mesh points, and by adjusting or editing its mesh points, anchor points, and mesh lines with the Gradient Mesh tool. When you add a mesh point, it fills with the current fill color unless you press the Shift key before clicking a mesh line in an area that does not contain a mesh point. To delete a mesh point and its connected mesh lines, Option/Alt-click directly on the mesh point with the Gradient Mesh tool.

To edit a mesh point, use the Gradient Mesh tool or the Direct Selection tool and click on the mesh point to display its direction handles. Drag these direction handles to edit the mesh point just as you would do with an anchor point. You can also Shift-click and then drag a direction handle to move all the direction handles from the selected mesh point at once.

ADDING MESH LINES

To add a mesh line to a mesh object, select the Gradient Mesh tool and click on an area of the mesh object that does not contain a mesh line. The new mesh line appears with its mesh point at the spot where you clicked.

EXERCISE F

1. In a new document (File/New), choose File/Preferences/ Units & Undo. Make sure the General Units displays Points. Display the Swatches palette (Window/Show Swatches). Select the Ellipse tool and click on the page to display the Ellipse dialog box. Type 300 in the Width field. Press the Tab key and type 300 in the Height field. Click on OK. Fill the circle with a solid color from the Swatches palette.

2. With the circle still selected, choose Object/Create Gradient Mesh. Click the Preview button. Leave the Rows and Columns values at 4, but choose To Edge from the Appearance menu and type 80 in the Highlight field. Click on OK.

3. Select the Gradient Mesh tool and click on any part of the center horizontal mesh line to create another vertical mesh line (Figure 6.17). Click on any vertical mesh line to create another horizontal mesh line. Deselect everything (Command/Ctrl-Shift-A).

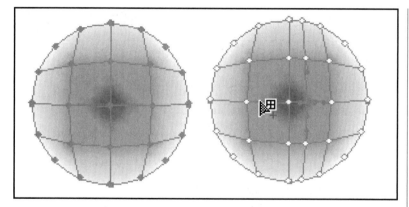

Figure 6.17. The values in the Create Gradient Mesh dialog box change the original ellipse into a gradient mesh object (left). Clicking on an empty section of the mesh creates another mesh line, as indicated by the + sign next to the cursor..

4. Use the Direct Selection tool to click anywhere on the object to select a mesh segment and its surrounding mesh points. Drag a color swatch from the Swatches palette onto a selected mesh point to color the segments connected to that point.

5. Select another mesh point with either the Direct Selection tool or the Gradient Mesh tool. Click on another color in the Swatches palette to color that segment.

6. Use the Gradient Mesh tool to select a mesh segment and drag it to reshape the gradient.

7. Use the Add Anchor Point tool and click on a mesh line to add an anchor point to the mesh line. Use the Direct Selection tool to drag the line and reshape the gradient.

8. Use the Gradient Mesh tool and press the Option/Alt key before clicking on a mesh point to delete that point.

9. Continue to add and delete anchor points and mesh points to reshape the mesh object until you are fairly comfortable with creating mesh gradients.

10. Close this file (Command/Ctrl-W). Don't save your changes.

In this unit you learned

1. That a gradient fill is a graduated blend between colors.

2. That gradients are created and edited in the Gradient palette.

3. That there are linear and radial gradients and that gradients can be duplicated and changed from linear to radial and vice versa.

4. The Gradient tool is used to change the direction of the gradation in a selected object.

5. Colors are added to a gradient by selecting a Color Stop on the Gradient palette before applying a color.

6. Gradients must be saved in the Swatches palette if they are to be applied to another object once the object filled with that gradient is deleted.

7. Gradients can have more than two colors.

8. The Gradient Mesh tool transforms an object capable of displaying many colors positioned at precise intervals.

9. Mesh objects have multiple crisscrossed lines called mesh lines that can be filled with different gradients to create a smooth transition of color.

10. Mesh objects can be edited by dragging mesh lines and mesh points to shift the color transition.

11. Conventional Illustrator objects filled with any color can be converted to gradient mesh objects using the Create Gradient Mesh command.

12. Conventional Illustrator objects filled with a *solid* color can be converted to gradient mesh objects using the Expand command.

UNIT 7
PATTERNS

OVERVIEW

In this unit you will learn how to:
create, save, and edit patterns
move and transform patterns
create geometric patterns
create texture patterns
create brush patterns for paths

TERMS

Bounding Rectangle
path pattern
pattern
pattern tile

HOW IT WORKS

Create the type, create outlines, and make compound paths. Drag the pattern swatch onto the page and edit its color. Drag the new swatch into the Swatches palette and use it to fill the paths. Select the paths and apply a stroke. Use the Drop Shadows filter to apply a drop shadow offset three points from the paths. Use the Group Selection tool to move the individual paths with their drop shadows to "kern" the type outlines so that the paths are not touching.

Macintosh Keystrokes

⌘-N File/New
F10 Window/Show Stroke

Windows Keystrokes

Ctrl-N FIle/New
F10 Window/Show Stroke

Sorry!

You cannot create a pattern from artwork filled or stroked with gradients or other patterns.

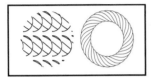

Path Patterns

Although you can stroke a path with a pattern, you will get much better results by creating a Pattern brush and stroking the path with the brush, because stroked patterns run around the x axis of the path (left), whereas Pattern brushes run around the path itself (right).

PATTERN FILLS

Patterns are tiles created from Adobe Illustrator artwork which, when used as fill and stroke attributes, repeat in (fill) or around (stroke) a path. Patterns are constructed from tiles of pattern objects (the artwork), and sometimes are surrounded by a rectangle that allows you to apply a fill and stroke to the pattern's background. You cannot create a pattern with artwork filled with any pattern or with a gradient. Think of patterns as repeating wallpaper or fabric designs and get as creative as you like.

Once you create a pattern and add it to the list of default patterns in the Swatches palette, you can apply that pattern from the Swatches palette just as you would apply any of the default patterns.

MOVING PATTERNS IN OBJECTS

Because a pattern is made up of Illustrator artwork, it can be moved even though it is used to fill an object. To move the pattern tile inside the object, click on the object with the Selection tool and press the tilde (~) key as you drag with the Selection tool. It may seem that the whole object is moving, but it isn't. Only the pattern tiles are being repositioned.

EXERCISE A

1. Create a new file (File/New) and select inches as the unit of measure (File/Preferences/Units & Undo). Display the Swatches palette and Stroke palette (F10).

2. Click on the Show Pattern Swatches button on the Swatches palette to display only the pattern swatches (Figure 7.1).

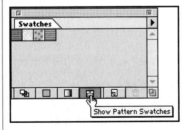

Figure 7.1. Displaying only the pattern swatches keeps the Swatches palette uncluttered.

3. Use the Spiral tool (behind the Ellipse tool) to draw a small spiral. Assign it a fill and stroke color in contrasting colors or tints of the same color.

4. Use the Selection tool to select the spiral. Choose Edit/Define Pattern to display the New Swatch dialog box. Type *Spiral* in the Swatch Name dialog box and click on OK.

5. The new pattern swatch appears in the Swatches palette and remains as artwork on the page (Figure 7.2).

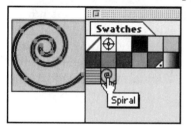

Figure 7.2. The Spiral swatch appears in the Swatches palette and is displayed with the other swatches.

6. Save this file as *Pattern.ai* as an Illustrator file in your Projects folder (File/Save As).

7. Draw a large rectangle or circle on the page. Click the Fill icon in the Toolbox and click the new pattern swatch you just created to fill the object (Figure 7.3).

8. Close this file (File/Close). Don't save your changes.

Figure 7.3. The pattern fills the entire rectangle and can be repositioned inside the rectangle by pressing the tilde (~) key and dragging with the Selection tool.

EDITING PATTERNS

You can edit any pattern you create or any pattern that ships with Illustrator. When you edit a pattern, you can either create a new pattern from the original or overwrite the original pattern with the edited pattern. If you overwrite the original pattern, any objects filled with the original pattern will be updated to reflect the new, edited pattern.

DUPLICATING A PATTERN SWATCH

Once you edit a pattern tile, drag it into the Swatches palette and assign it a new name. This lets you use both the original pattern and the edited pattern as different fill patterns for objects. It's a good idea to duplicate a pattern before editing it, so you can always go back to the original one for use or for editing. To duplicate the pattern, click on the pattern tile in the Swatches palette and click on the New Swatch icon in the Swatches palette. A duplicate swatch appears next to the original. Double-click on the duplicate and type a different name for it in the Swatch Name field.

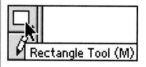

FYI

You can name or rename any swatch by double-clicking on it and typing a name in the Swatch Name field of its Options dialog box.

Version 7

To apply path patterns, choose Filter/Stylize/Path Patterns to display the Path Patterns dialog box.

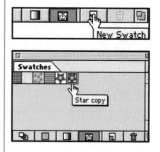

Select the pattern you want to duplicate and click the New Swatch button on the Swatches palette to create a copy of the original pattern.

⌘-O File/Open
⌘-Shift-A Edit/Deselect All

Windows Keystrokes

Ctrl-O File/Open
Ctrl-Shift-A Edit/Deselect
All

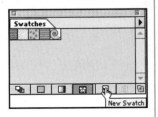

FYI

A pattern can be comprised of more than one object. When those objects are defined as a pattern, they are automatically grouped. To edit the pattern, use the Direct Selection tool to select the different objects in the pattern.

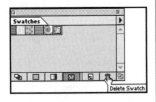

Select a swatch and click the Delete Swatch icon to delete that swatch.

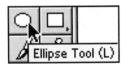

SAVING AN EDITED PATTERN

If you don't want to override the original swatch, select the edited swatch with the Selection tool and define it as a new swatch from the Edit menu. If you want to override the original swatch with the edited swatch, press the Option/Alt key as you drag the edited swatch over the original swatch in the Swatches palette. When you do this, any artwork created with the original swatch is updated to reflect the new pattern swatch.

DELETING A PATTERN SWATCH

Pattern swatches are deleted just like any color or gradient swatch. Click the pattern swatch to select it, and click the Trash icon on the Swatches palette. You can also drag any pattern to the Trash icon on the Swatches palette or choose Delete Swatch from the Swatches palette menu.

EXERCISE B

1. Open the *Pattern.ai* file you created earlier or open the *Pattern.ai* file in the Unit 07 folder on the CD-ROM. Display the Swatches palette (Window/Show Swatches).

2. Click the spiral pattern in the Swatches palette to select it and click the New Swatch icon in the Swatches palette to duplicate the pattern swatch. The duplicate appears next to the original in the Swatches palette and is named *Spiral copy* (Figure 7.4).

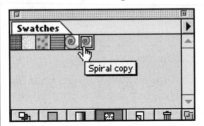

Figure 7.4. Duplicating a pattern swatch using the New Swatch button on the Swatches palette names the pattern with the original name and copy.

3. Double-click on the duplicate and assign it a new name in the Swatch Name field. Click on OK.

4. Drag the original Spiral swatch out of the palette onto the page. It appears selected on the page surrounded by a rectangular Bounding Rectangle. Deselect (Command/Ctrl-Shift-A). Use the Direct Selection tool to select only the spiral, not the rectangle. Change its fill and stroke colors.

5. Use the Ellipse tool to draw a large circle on the page. Click the Fill icon on the Toolbox and click the original Spiral Pattern swatch in the Swatches palette.

6. Use the Selection tool to select the edited pattern swatch on the page and choose Edit/Define Pattern. Type *New Spiral* in the Name field and click on OK.

7. Press the Option/Alt key as you drag the edited (New Spiral) swatch over the original Spiral Swatch in the Swatches palette. When you Option/Alt drag one swatch over another, it replaces the original swatch and updates any artwork filled with the original swatch (Figure 7.5).

8. Close this file (File/Close). Don't save your changes.

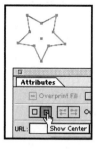

Figure 7.5. When the original Spiral swatch (left) was edited (right), the circle filled with the original pattern updated to fill with the edited pattern, because the edited pattern over-wrote the original one.

USING BOUNDING RECTANGLES

To space pattern tiles, draw a Bounding Rectangle around the pattern. This Bounding Rectangle must be a rectangle or square and must be the backmost object in the artwork. Don't fill or stroke the Bounding Rectangle—those colors will interfere with the artwork and you won't get the space you want between the pattern tiles. To define the pattern, select both the Bounding Rectangle and the artwork.

DISPLAYING THE CENTER POINT

Some objects, such as stars and polygons, do not automatically display their center points as circles and rectangles do. To display center points for these objects, display the Attributes palette and click the Show Center button (Figure 7.6).

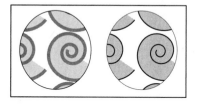

Figure 7.6. Click the Show Center button in the Attributes palette to display center points for objects that do not automatically display a center point. The button to the left of the Show Center button is the Don't Show Center button.

Macintosh Keystrokes

⌘-W File/Close

Windows Keystrokes

Ctrl-W File/Close

Oops!

If you overwrite a pattern swatch you didn't dupli-cate, select any object filled with the original swatch and drag the Fill icon from the Toolbox to the Swatches palette. If you don't have an object filled with the lost pattern, you're out of luck.

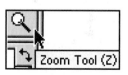

Now you see it...

When you drag a pattern swatch out of the Swatches palette onto the page, it is very small and difficult to see, much less work with. Use the Zoom tool to draw a marquee around the swatch to enlarge it on the page.

Macintosh Keystrokes

⌘-N File/New
F10 Window/Show Stroke
⌘-U View/Smart Guides

Windows Keystrokes

Ctrl-N File/New
F10 Window/Show Stroke
Ctrl-U View/Smart Guides

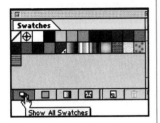

Click the Show All Swatches button to display colors, gradients, and patterns.

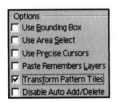

Select the Transform Pattern Tiles option in the General Preferences dialog box to transform a pattern fill when dragging with one of the transformation tools.

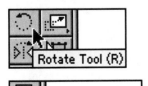

TRANSFORMING PATTERNS

When transforming objects by dragging the Scale, Shear, Rotate, and Reflect tools, you have the option of transforming only the object or the object and its pattern fill. For example, you could create a rectangle that is six inches high and fill it with a pattern based on half-inch objects. If you decide to reduce or enlarge the rectangle *by dragging* with the Scale tool, you can also choose to reduce or enlarge the pattern fill as well. This decision is made in the General Preferences dialog box. Select the Transform Pattern Tiles option to transform pattern tiles when dragging with the transformation tools.

If you transform (scale, rotate, reflect, or shear) objects using the tool's dialog box, you can opt to transform the pattern in the dialog box, regardless of any options you select in the General Preferences dialog box.

CREATING GEOMETRIC PATTERNS

Once a pattern tile is created, it can be duplicated to create another pattern. This will fill more of the area and allow for more interesting graphic effects. In order to create precise patterns, however, use the center point of every object in the pattern to properly align the objects.

EXERCISE C

1. Create a new file (File/New). Make sure inches is the unit of measure (File/Preferences/Units & Undo), and Snap to Point is selected in the View menu.

2. Display the Swatches palette (Window/Show Swatches) and Stroke palette (F10). Click the Show All Swatches button on the Swatches palette to display all the colors, gradients, and patterns in the palette.

3. Select the Fill icon in the Toolbox and select red for the fill color. Select black for the stroke color.

4. Choose View/Smart Guides (Command/Ctrl-U). Use the Rectangle tool and click on the page. Type .5 in the Width field; press the Tab key and type .5 in the Height field to create a square. Use the Zoom tool to enlarge the view.

5. With the square selected, double-click on the Rotate tool and type 45 in the Rotate dialog box. Click on OK.

6. Use the Selection tool and press the Option/Alt key before clicking on the center point of the square. Drag a duplicate square below the original at a 45° angle. Release the mouse button *before* releasing the modifier key. Use the Smart Guide to control the movement so that the sides of the two squares just touch (Figure 7.7).

Macintosh Keystrokes

⌘-D Object/Transform/
  Transform Again
⌘-Shift-[Object/Arrange/
  Send to Back

Windows Keystrokes

Ctrl-D Object/Transform/
  Transform Again
Ctrl-Shift-[Object/
  Arrange/Send to Back

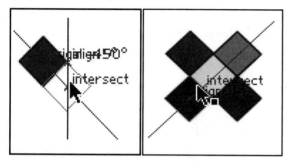

Figure 7.7. Use Smart Guides to position the rotated copy below the original square.

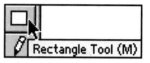

7. Choose Object/Transform/Transform Again (Command/Ctrl-D) to create a third square, also at a 45° angle. Fill the two duplicate squares with different primary colors (Figure 7.7).

8. Select the Rectangle tool and press the Option/Alt key before clicking on the center point of the center diamond to draw from the center of the square outward. (Figure 7.8). *Center point* is displayed when you click on the center point. Assign the Bounding Rectangle no fill and no stroke.

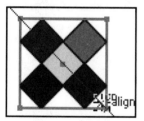

Tip

A fill pattern should be about ½ to 1 inch square. Side tiles for patterns should be no larger than ½ inch to 1 inch high by 1 inch to 2 inches wide. Corner tiles must be the same height as the side tiles and should be square. If you don't want to do all this math, use or edit one of the dozens of Pattern brushes that ship with Illustrator and come with corner and side tiles already created.

Figure 7.8. Drag with the Rectangle tool and the Option/Alt key pressed to draw a rectangle outward from the center of the center diamond.

9. With the square (the Bounding Rectangle) still selected, choose Object/Arrange/Send to Back (Command/Ctrl-Shift-[).

10. With the squares and Bounding Rectangle still selected, choose Edit/Define Pattern. Type *Squares* in the Name field of the Swatch Options dialog box and click on OK.

Macintosh Keystrokes

⌘-W File/Close

Windows Keystrokes

Ctrl-W File/Close

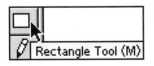

Many path patterns include outer and inner corner patterns.

11. Use the Rectangle tool to draw a large rectangle on the page. Select the Fill icon in the toolbox and click on the Squares swatch in the Swatches palette. Your screen should resemble the left fill in Figure 7.9.

12. Select the Squares swatch in the Swatches palette and choose Duplicate Swatch from the Swatches palette menu or click on the New Swatch icon in the palette. Drag the duplicate swatch onto the page and use the Direct Selection tool to select the Bounding Rectangle. Assign it no fill and a black stroke.

13. Select the Bounding Rectangle and the tiles and choose Edit/Define pattern. Type *Outline Squares* in the Swatch name field and click on OK.

14. Draw a large rectangle and fill with the Outline Squares pattern. Your screen should resemble the right fill in Figure 7.9.

15. Close this file (File/Close). Don't save your changes.

Figure 7.9. The geometric pattern on the left was created without a stroke on the Bounding Rectangle, as was the pattern on the right. (The stroke on the right was applied later.)

BRUSH PATTERNS FOR PATHS

The major difference between a path stroked with a pattern and a path to which a brush pattern is applied is in the direction of the stroke/path. Patterns tile from left to right from the ruler origin. Brush patterns tile perpendicular to the path, and therefore display the entire pattern (Figure 7.10). Brush patterns also allow placement of corner tiles.

Figure 7.10. The circle on the left was stroked with the Laurel *pattern swatch*, which lies perpendicular to the path. The circle on the right was stroked with the Laurel *Pattern brush*, which follows the path exactly.

CREATING TEXTURE PATTERNS

Texture patterns are irregular fill patterns that tile seamlessly. To create an irregularly textured path pattern, select and define as a pattern only the textured artwork within the Bounding Rectangle, not the Bounding Rectangle itself as you do for a textured fill pattern.

If you use the Pencil or Paintbrush tools to create the texture, be careful not to draw the lines too closely together. If you get within two points of another line, you will edit that line instead of creating a new line.

EXERCISE D

1. In a new document (File/New), click on the Default Colors icon. Select the Rectangle tool and click on the page. Make sure Snap to Point is selected under the View menu.

2. Type 72 pt in the Width field, press the Tab key, and type 72 pt in the Height field. Click on OK to create a square.

3. Use the Pencil tool and draw a squiggly line that intersects only the left side of the Bounding Rectangle (Figure 7.11).

4. Select both the line and the rectangle with the Selection tool and place the pointer on the lower left corner of the rectangle. Start dragging the rectangle to the right, then press the Option-Shift keys (Macintosh) or the Alt-Shift keys (Windows) and drag the rectangle to the right to create a copy and constrain the move to the horizontal axis. When the upper left corner point of the copy snaps to the upper right corner of the original Bounding Rectangle, release the mouse button, *then* release the Option/Alt keys (Figure 7.11). This creates a duplicate of the squiggly line on the opposite side of the original rectangle.

Macintosh Keystrokes

⌘-N File/New
⌘-Shift-[Object/Arrange/
    Send to Back

Windows Keystrokes

Ctrl-N File/New
Ctrl-Shift-[Object/
    Arrange/Send to Back

Rectangle Tool (M)

Pencil Tool (N)

Selection Tool (V)

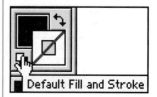
Default Fill and Stroke

Macintosh Keystrokes

⌘-Shift-[Object/Arrange/
   Send to Back
⌘-W File/Close

Windows Keystrokes

Ctrl-Shift-[Object/
   Arrange/Send to Back
Ctrl-W File/Close

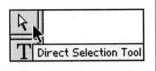

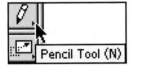

Select a library to open:

The Other Libraries folder in the Adobe Illustrator folder contains more fill patterns, gradients, and path patterns that can be dragged from the secondary palettes into the Swatches palette.

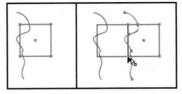

Figure 7.11. Drag the original Bounding Rectangle and line to the right. The double cursor appears when the lower points snap together.

5. Deselect everything (Command/Ctrl-Shift-A). Select the right rectangle—not the line—with the Direct Selection tool and delete it.

6. Use the Pencil tool and draw another squiggly line that intersects the top side of the remaining rectangle.

7. Select the Bounding Rectangle and the line you just drew at the top of the rectangle. Click on the lower left point of the rectangle, start dragging, and press the Option/Alt key. Drag down until the corner points snap (Figure 7.12).

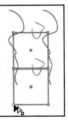

Figure 7.12. Drag the original Bounding Rectangle and line that intersects the top of the Bounding Rectangle down to create a duplicate of the box and line.

8. Deselect everything by clicking on an empty area of the page.

9. Select the lower rectangle and delete it.

10. Use the Pencil tool to draw a few squiggly lines in the center of the rectangle. Don't intersect any of the rectangle's edges or you will throw off the tiling. Apply stroke colors to any of the lines (Figure 7.13).

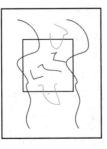

Figure 7.13. The squiggly lines form the texture once the Bounding Rectangle is stripped of fill and stroke attributes.

11. Select just the Bounding Rectangle and assign it no stroke and no fill.

12. With the rectangle still selected, Choose Object/Arrange/ Send to Back (Command/Ctrl-Shift-[).

13. Use the Selection tool to select the rectangle and all the squiggly lines. Choose Edit/Define Pattern. Type *Texture* in the Swatch Name field and click on OK. The swatch appears in the Swatches palette.

14. Draw a large rectangle on the page. Click on the Fill icon in the Toolbox and select the Texture pattern in the Swatches palette to fill the rectangle with the new texture. Your screen should resemble Figure 7.14. Close this file. Don't save your changes.

Macintosh Keystrokes

⌘-Shift-[Object/Arrange/ Send to Back

Windows Keystrokes

Ctrl-Shift-[Object/ Arrange/Send to Back

Arrange menu

Use the commands under the Arrange menu to stack objects in front and behind each other on a single layer.

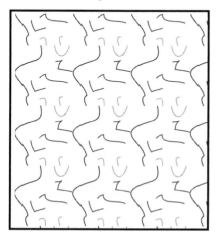

Figure 7.14. The texture tiles create a seamless pattern fill in the rectangle.

REVIEW

In this unit you learned that:

1. Patterns are tiles created from Illustrator artwork.

2. It is better to stroke a path with a path pattern brush than with a regular pattern.

3. Patterns can be moved inside an object without affecting the object itself.

4. A pattern can be edited and saved in the Swatches palette as a new pattern or used to override an existing pattern.

5. Patterns can be duplicated. The duplicate pattern can be edited to create a new pattern tile.

6. Patterns can be named and renamed in the Swatches palette Swatch Options dialog box.

7. When a pattern is deleted, the artwork painted with that pattern is not affected, and retains the deleted pattern's fill and/or stroke.

8. If a pattern is deleted, selecting an object filled or stroked with that pattern allows you to drag the icon from the Color palette or from the Toolbox into the Swatches palette.

9. Bounding Rectangles can be used to space pattern tiles.

10. To display the center point of objects that do not normally display a center point, such as stars and polygons, select the Show Center option on the Attributes palette.

11. Objects filled with patterns can be transformed without transforming the pattern fill unless the Transform Pattern Tiles option is selected in the General Preferences dialog box.

12. Geometric patterns can be created with the help of Smart Guides.

13. The major difference between a path stroked with a pattern and a path to which a brush pattern is applied is in the direction of the stroke/path. Brush patterns allow use of corner tiles.

14. To create an irregularly textured path pattern, select and define as a pattern only the textured artwork within the Bounding Rectangle, not the Bounding Rectangle itself.

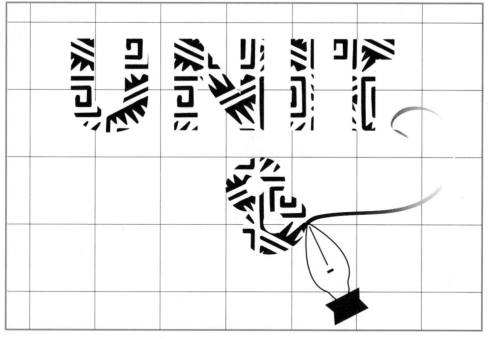

The Pen Tool

OVERVIEW

In this unit you will learn how to:
draw straight and curved lines with the Pen tool
draw open and closed paths
edit paths by adding, deleting, and converting
   anchor points
duplicate, split, and join paths
change the direction of a curve

TERMS

continuous curve
direction point
noncontinuous curve
ruler guide

HOW IT WORKS

Use the Pen tool to draw a pen. Create the type and convert to outlines. Fill with a pattern from Illustrator's additional patterns (Window/Swatch Libraries/Other Library) in the Illustrator folder on the hard drive. Use the Paintbrush tool with the Calligraphic option to draw the ribbon. Create the grid background by drawing a single line, duplicating it, and then applying the Repeat Transform command.

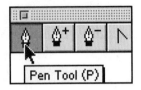

Click on the Pen tool to display other Pen tools, and drag the Tearoff Tab to keep the Pen tools handy.

When you first click to select the Pen tool and move onto the drawing page, a small x appears next to the cursor. This tells you that your first click will set the first anchor point in the path.

FYI

Illustrator automatically fills an open path with the default fill and stroke colors unless you select None for the Fill and Stroke before drawing.

THE PEN TOOL

The Pen tool is the most powerful drawing tool in Adobe Illustrator. With it, you can draw straight lines in any direction and curved lines with any slope. You can resize, reposition, and reshape any straight or curved segment drawn with the Pen tool by adjusting either its anchor points, the direction handles attached to those anchor points, or the segments between the anchor points.

There's good news and great news about the Pen tool. The good news is that it takes a little practice to learn how to use it skillfully; the great news is that once you learn—it's like climbing Mt. Everest—you never forget, and you don't have to think about what you're doing. You click a little, drag a little, and bingo! It's art!

SELECTING PEN TOOLS

The Pen tool is a multiple tool giving access to the Add Anchor Point, Delete Anchor Point, and Convert Anchor Point tools. Press the *p* key to access the Pen tool and Shift-*p* to cycle through the four Pen tools.

DRAWING STRAIGHT LINES

The Pen tool is easiest to use when drawing straight lines. The important thing to remember about drawing lines, however, is that you do not drag to create the line. You click to set the anchor points and Illustrator connects them for you. If you ever played "Connect the Dots," this is your tool!

When you draw an open path (line), the last anchor point remains selected (filled) and all the other anchor points are hollow, or deselected. To keep that last anchor point active while changing its position, press the spacebar and drag the anchor point to another position.

CONSTRAINING STRAIGHT LINES

Press the Shift key while clicking with the Pen tool to constrain the line to the nearest 45° angle. If the Pen tool is positioned in what appears to be a straight line from the original point and you press the Shift key before clicking the second point, you will create a straight line as opposed to a slanted line.

COMPLETING A PATH

Once you start drawing with the Pen tool, you must either close the path or, in the case of an open path, click the Pen tool, or Command/Ctrl-click anywhere away from the path. To close a path, move the cursor next to the first anchor point you set; when a small loop appears, click to close the path.

Macintosh Keystrokes

⌘-N File/New
⌘-Y View/Artwork/Preview

Windows Keystrokes

Ctrl-N File/New
Ctrl-Y View/Artwork/
   Preview

1. Create a new file (File/New), choose View/Artwork (Command/Ctrl-Y), and display the Swatches palette. Set both the fill and stroke to None in the Toolbox.

2. Click once on the Pen tool to select it. Move onto the drawing page and notice the x next to the cursor. This tells you that your first click will create the first anchor point in the path.

3. Click once in the middle of the page and release the mouse button. Do not drag. Move up or down a few inches and click again. Notice the line (segment) that appears between the first and second anchor points.

4. Move the cursor close to the second anchor point and notice that a caret appears to the right of the cursor. This tells you that the next segment will be connected to the selected anchor point (Figure 8.1).

Pen Tool (P)

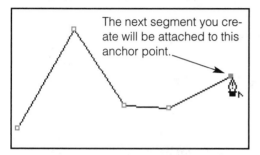

The next segment you create will be attached to this anchor point.

Figure 8.1. A caret appears next to the cursor when it is near a selected anchor point, indicating that the next time you click, the new segment will be anchored to the selected anchor point.

FYI

There are five ways to deactivate the Pen tool: close the path with the Loop cursor; select a different tool; click once on the Pen tool in the Toolbox; press the Command/Ctrl key and click on an empty area of the page; or choose Edit/Deselect All.

5. Click again to set another anchor point and to create another segment.

6. Move the cursor down at an angle and press the Shift key before clicking again to constrain the line to a 45° angle. You are now ready to deactivate (but not deselect) the Pen tool.

7. Click once on the Pen tool in the Tool palette to deactivate the Pen tool and create an open path. All of the anchor points on the path are hollow except for the last one, which remains selected. The Pen tool is still selected, and it will begin a new path the next time you click.

8. With the path still active and the Pen tool selected, move the cursor onto the last, selected anchor point. Because you are going to *add a segment to a completed, open path*, the cursor displays a slant line to its right (Figure 8.2). This symbol tells you

Macintosh Keystrokes

⌘-Shift-A Edit/Deselect All
⌘-W File/Close
⌘-Y View/Artwork/
 Preview

Windows Keystrokes

Ctrl-Shift-A Edit/Deselect
 All
Ctrl-W File/Close
Ctrl-Y View/Artwork/
 Preview

FYI

Remember: Closing a path is one way to deactivate the Pen tool, even though the path remains selected.

This three-sided open path automatically displays the current fill and stroke values.

that when you click on the selected anchor point, you will continue to draw the original path.

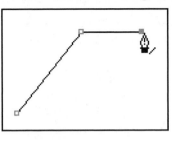

Figure 8.2. Clicking with the Pen tool on the selected anchor point of a completed path displays a slant line to the right of the cursor, indicating that the next segment will be connected to the selected anchor point.

9. Continue to click and add a few more straight line segments to this path. When you have finished, click once on the Pen tool.

10. Move the cursor around the drawing page, away from the selected endpoint of the path you just drew, and notice that the x is displayed next to the cursor. This tells you that you are ready to draw another path.

11. Choose Edit/Deselect All (Command/Ctrl-Shift-A) to deselect the path.

12. Close this file (File/Close). Don't save your changes.

DRAWING AN OPEN PATH

A path with two endpoints (anchor points on each end of the path) is called an *open path*. This is the kind of path you created in Exercise A. You can also use the Pen tool to create a closed path, a path in which you cannot see where the first segment begins and the last one ends.

FILLS AND STROKES FOR OPEN PATHS

When working in Preview view, any paths drawn with the Pen tool will display the current fill and stroke values specified in the Fill and Stroke icons in the Toolbox and Stroke palette. This makes the object appear to be a closed path, but it is not! If the lines of the open path are not straight, the fill will appear jagged between the two endpoints.

EXERCISE B

1. In a new file (File/New), display the Swatches palette. Click the Default Colors icon. Choose View/Preview (Command/ Ctrl-Y).

2. Click on the Pen tool to select it and move onto the drawing page. You will draw a triangle. Click once to set the first

anchor point. Release the mouse button. Move up and to the right and click to set the second anchor point and create the first segment. Release the mouse button. Move down and to the right and click to set the third anchor point and create the second segment. Release the mouse button.

3. Move to the left, onto the first anchor point. As you come onto it, the cursor displays a loop, which tells you that the next time you click, you will be clicking on the first anchor point and you will close the path (Figure 8.3). Click on that first anchor point to close the path.

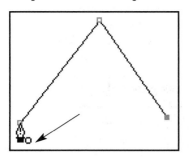

Figure 8.3. When you move the cursor onto the first anchor point, a loop is displayed next to the cursor, indicating that the next time you click, you will close the path.

Closed means shut!

You cannot add segments to a closed path in the same way as you continued to draw and add segments to an open path. The only way to reshape a closed path is to add anchor points along the segments. You can also cut the path with the Scissors tool and reshape from the resulting endpoints.

4. Not only have you closed the path, but you have returned the Pen tool to its "start position." Notice that as soon as you click, the cursor displays the **x**, indicating that if you click again, you will start a new path (Figure 8.4). The completed, closed path, however, displays the selected last anchor point until you click to start another path.

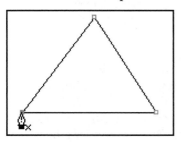

Figure 8.4. The cursor displays an **x** when it is ready to begin a new path.

5. Continue to draw closed paths until you are comfortable with drawing the straight lines and finding the first anchor point needed to close the path.

6. Close this file (File/Close). Don't save your changes.

The cursor changes to an arrowhead when drawing curve segments.

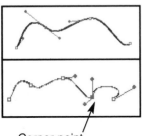

Corner point

The top path is comprised of all smooth points. The bottom path has a corner point before the endpoint.

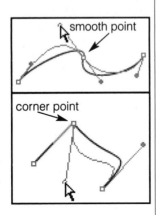

Moving the direction handle on a smooth point (top) moves the curves on either side of the point. Dragging the direction handle on the corner point (bottom), moves just the curve on the same side of that point.

CURVED SEGMENTS

You don't drag when drawing straight lines because dragging with the Pen tool produces curved segments. Curve segments are connected by anchor points which display one or two direction handles with direction points. Click on the direction points to move the handles to change the shape of a curve.

CONTINUOUS AND NONCONTINUOUS CURVES

Curves connected by smooth points are called *continuous curves*. Rolling waves, for example, would be created with continuous curves. If you change the direction of a curve by adding a corner point, you create a *noncontinuous curve*. When you move the direction handle of a smooth point, the curves on both sides of the anchor point adjust simultaneously. However, when you move the direction handle attached to a corner point, only the curve on the same side of that point is repositioned (Figure 8.5).

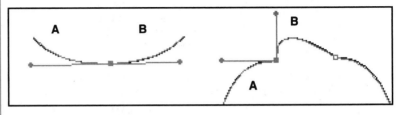

Figure 8.5. The path on the left displays a selected curve point. If either direction handle is moved, both segments A and B will be repositioned. The path on the right displays a selected corner point. If the left direction handle is moved, only segment A will be repositioned. If the right direction handle is moved, only segment B will be repositioned.

CURVE CHARACTERISTICS

Every curve has slope and height or depth. The slope of a curve is determined by the slope of each direction handle. The height of the curve is determined by the length of the direction handle. So, dragging a direction handle changes the slope of the curve; shortening or lengthening the direction handle shortens or lengthens the height or depth of the curve (Figure 8.6).

When you move the direction handle attached to a smooth point, the curves on both sides of the point adjust simultaneously. However, when you drag a direction handle attached to a corner point, only the curve on the same side of the corner point's direction handle is moved.

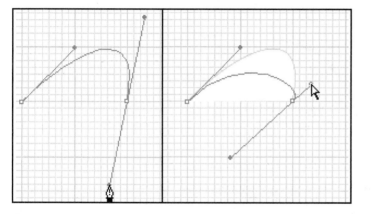

Figure 8.6. The slope of the original curve (left) is changed by moving the direction handle. Because that direction handle was shortened, the depth of the curve was reduced (right). Use the grid (View/Show Grid) to align the points more accurately.

DRAWING CURVES

There are two ways to draw curves in Illustrator: the right way and the easy way. The right way is to click with the Pen tool and drag in the direction of the curve before releasing the mouse; then release the mouse and click to complete the curve (Figure 8.7).

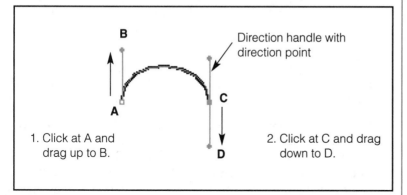

Figure 8.7. Direction handles appear when you drag to create a curve segment. Because this curve is an open path, A and C are endpoints.

The other way is to click and release the mouse button, then click at the high point of the curve and drag to the right, then click at the endpoint to complete the curve (Figure 8.8).

Now you see it...

If you click away from the segment when the Direct Selection tool is active, the segment becomes deselected and the anchor points with their direction handles are no longer visible. If that happens, just click on the segment again with the Direct Selection tool to make the anchor points and direction handles visible.

Hiding edges

To hide the anchor points and direction handles, choose View/Hide Edges (Command/Ctrl-H). You will still be able to edit the path, but the points and selection edges won't be visible.

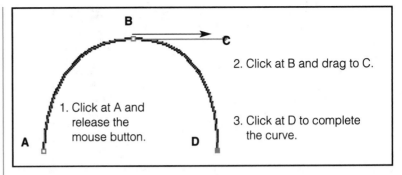

2. Click at B and drag to C.

1. Click at A and release the mouse button.

3. Click at D to complete the curve.

Figure 8.8. Dragging at B outward instead of dragging from A upward also sets the slope (arc) of the curve. The last endpoint remains selected.

The first way produces a more elegant curve (from a technical viewpoint), because it utilizes only two anchor points. The second way requires three anchor points, but many users find this a much easier and quicker way to create curves.

EXERCISE C

1. Create a new file (File/New). Choose View/Artwork (Command/Ctrl-Y. Click the Default Colors icon in the Toolbox.

2. Choose View/Show Rulers (Command/Ctrl-R). Rulers will appear on the top and left sides of the screen. Click in the horizontal ruler and drag a ruler guide down to the middle of the page. Drag another ruler guide down about two inches above the first guide.

3. Click on the Pen tool to select it. Click on the bottom guide (A) and drag straight up to the top guide. Release the mouse button. The anchor point will appear selected (filled), and the direction handle will extend from the anchor point (A) to the top guide (Figure 8.9). Notice the direction handle that appears when you release the mouse button. You'll use this handle later to adjust the slope of the curve.

Pen Tool (P)

The cursor becomes hollow when it touches the ruler guide.

Guides & Grid

Your ruler guides will appear as either lines or dots depending on the options you select in the Guides & Grid Preferences dialog box.

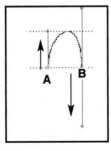

Figure 8.9. Click and drag *up* at A—always in the direction of the curve or the "hump"—and release the mouse button when the direction handle is about one third the size of the curve. Click and drag *down* at B to complete the curve.

4. Click on the bottom guide about two inches away from the selected anchor point and drag down to complete the curve. Always drag away from the "hump" to complete the curve.

5. When you release the mouse button, the selected anchor point displays two direction handles, one going up and one going down. You'll use these also to adjust the curve (Figure 8.10).

6. Option/Alt-click in that last selected anchor point to set a smooth point and drag up. Click on the lower guide and drag down to complete the curve.

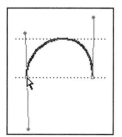

Figure 8.10. Click on the anchor point to display a second direction handle from the anchor point.

7. Repeat steps 3–5 until you are comfortable making "picket fence" curves. Don't worry if they're crooked; you'll fix them later.

8. Choose Edit/Deselect All (Command-Shift-A). Save this file as *Practice Curves.ai* (File/Save As). You will need it for the next exercise.

EDITING PATHS

Any path, whether it's a line or curve segment, can be edited. You may want to shorten or lengthen it, extend or compress a curve, or even remove part of it. All editing (except for duplicating) is best done with the Direct Selection tool, as it leaves the anchor points hollow and allows you to select only the ones you want to work with.

A path can be edited by moving an anchor point or by adjusting the direction handles by dragging on the direction points. When you adjust a corner point, you have only the anchor point to work with, because corner points don't have direction handles.

DUPLICATING PATHS

Paths are duplicated just as any Illustrator object is duplicated. Select the path with the Selection tool, which selects every anchor point on the path, and press the Option/Alt key while dragging to create the duplicate path. If you select the path with the Direct Selection tool, you will duplicate only the selected segment and, in the case of a curved segment, distort the curve as you Option/Alt-drag.

Macintosh Keystrokes

⌘-Shift-A Edit/Deselect All

Windows Keystrokes

Ctrl-Shift-A Edit/Deselect All

When you click on the smooth endpoint, the cursor displays a caret, indicating that you can Option/Alt-click on this anchor point to create a corner point. The Status Bar in the lower left corner of the screen also displays Pen: Make Corner.

Pen : Make Corner

FYI

Option/Alt-clicking with the Pen tool creates a corner point. Ordinarily, corner points don't display direction handles, but when they are set in conjunction with a smooth point, they will display the smooth point's first direction handle. It is the corner point's direction handle which appears when you Option/Alt-click and drag up.

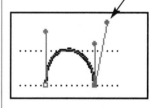

SPLITTING AND JOINING PATHS

Use the Scissors tool to split a path in the middle of a segment. This creates two new endpoints, one on top of the other, and leaves one endpoint selected. Then deselect everything and use the Direct Selection tool to adjust the new anchor points and/or new path segment or to select the new path segment and delete it.

Just as you can cut anchor points, you can also join them by selecting two endpoints and using the Object/Path/Join command to close an open path. This lets you fill and stroke the object with more accuracy.

EXERCISE D

1. If necessary, open the *Practice Curves.ai* file (Command-O) and display the Swatches palette. Make sure that the Fill and Stroke options are set to None and that nothing is selected. Choose View/Artwork (Command/Ctrl-Y).

2. Click on the Direct Selection tool to select it and click once on the first curve. It displays a direction handle on either side of the two anchor points. The endpoints are hollow because only the curve segment is selected, not the anchor points (Figure 8.11).

Figure 8.11. When you click on a curve path with the Direct Selection tool, direction handles appear on each side of the curve.

3. With the Direct Selection tool, click on the direction point of any direction handle. You move the handle by clicking and dragging this point. Notice that you can move the slope of the curve to the right and left as well as up and down (Figure 8.12). Notice also that only the curve segment moves; the anchor point remains stationary.

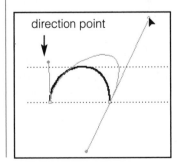

direction point

Figure 8.12. Click on the direction point and drag the direction handle to change the slope and height of the curve segment.

Unit 8 ★ The Pen Tool

4. Choose Edit/Undo (Command/Ctrl-Z) to return the curve to its original shape.

5. Click on the direction point extending from the other anchor point on the curve segment. Move it up and down and back and forth. Notice how the curve segment moves in the direction of the moving handle.

6. Choose Edit/Undo (Command/Ctrl-Z) to restore the curve to its original shape.

7. With the Direct Selection tool, click on the left anchor point to display another direction handle from that anchor point (Figure 8.13). Click on its direction point and drag to the right and left. You cannot use this handle to move the curve up and down.

Macintosh Keystrokes

⌘-Z Edit/Undo
⌘-W File/Close

Windows Keystrokes

Ctrl-Z Edit/Undo
Ctrl-W File/Close

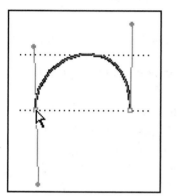

Figure 8.13. Click on the anchor point to display a second direction handle from the anchor point.

8. Click on the right anchor point to display its second direction handle. Use all four handles to adjust the shape of the curve.

9. Select the other curves and use their direction handles to adjust their arc and shape.

10. Close this file (File/Close). Don't save your changes.

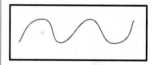

Continuous curves are connected by smooth points.

CHANGING THE DIRECTION OF A CURVE

Thus far, the curves you have been drawing are continuous curves—curves connected by smooth points. You drew the first segment, then placed the pointer where you wanted the next segment to end, and dragged in the opposite direction of the curve's "hump." To create a noncontinuous curve—curves connected by corner points—such as a series of curves in a picket fence, position the pointer on the last anchor point, press the Option/Alt key, and drag in the opposite direction to complete the curve.

⌘-N File/New
⌘-Y View/Artwork/Preview
⌘-R View/Show Rulers
⌘-Z Edit/Undo

Windows Keystrokes

Ctrl-N File/New
Ctrl-Y View/Artwork/
    Preview
Ctrl-R View/Show Rulers
Ctrl-Z Edit/Undo

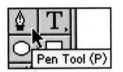

Pen Tool (P)

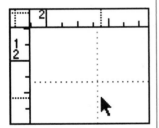

Click inside the horizontal
ruler and drag a ruler
guide down. Click inside
the vertical ruler and drag
a ruler guide out.

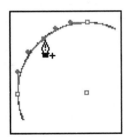

Clicking with the Add
Anchor Point tool adds a
selected anchor point to
the path.

EXERCISE E

1. Create a new file (Command/Ctrl-N). Choose View/Artwork (Command/Ctrl-Y). Click the Default Colors icon on the Toolbox or select another stroke color.

2. Choose View/Show Rulers (Command/Ctrl-R). Drag two horizontal rulers down onto the drawing page, about one inch apart. You will use these ruler guides as start and stop positions when creating curves.

3. Select the Pen tool. Move onto the drawing page and notice that a small x appears next to the pen cursor. This tells you that your first click will create the first anchor point in the path.

4. Click on the lower ruler and drag up to begin the curve. Release the mouse button. You always drag in the direction of the curve when you set the first anchor point in the curve. Although nothing appears to happen, the next time you click, you will be able to complete the curve.

5. Click on the lower ruler and drag down to complete the curve. Always draw away from the "hump" when completing a curve.

6. Click and drag in the last anchor point you just created and drag up to start the next curve. Notice that when you click and drag in the same point, instead of moving to another position as you did when drawing continuous curves, the segment moves down and the curve becomes distorted (Figure 8.14).

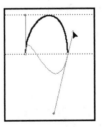

Figure 8.14. Clicking and dragging in the last placed anchor point causes the segment to flip. Option/Alt-click in the anchor point before dragging to set a corner anchor point and establish the direction (up) of the next curve.

7. Choose Edit/Undo (Command/Ctrl-Z) to return to the original curve.

8. Press the Option/Alt key, *then* click and drag up to set a corner anchor point and direction handle for the next curve. Move to the right and click and drag down to complete the curve.

9. Continue to create more sets of noncontinuous curves. When you're finished, click on the Pen tool to deactivate it. Your screen should resemble Figure 8.15.

10. Close this file (File/Close). Don't save your changes.

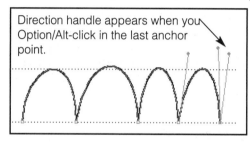

Direction handle appears when you Option/Alt-click in the last anchor point.

Figure 8.15. A series of noncontinuous curves connected by corner points and created by Option/Alt-clicking in the last anchor point of the previously completed curve.

EXERCISE F

1. Choose File/Open (Command/Ctrl-O) and open the *Mixed Template.ai* file in the Unit 08 folder on the CD-ROM. Display the Swatches palette and select None for the fill and a red color for the stroke. Choose View/Artwork (Command/Ctrl-Y).

2. Use the Pen tool to draw each of the straight and curved segments. Don't forget to click on the Pen tool to select it when you have finished drawing each object.

3. Use the Direct Selection tool to select a path. When you have finished drawing the path, use the direction handles to adjust the curves.

4. Save the file (File/Save As) as *Mixed Templates.ai* in your Projects folder. The .ai suffix tells you that the file contains the actual Illustrator artwork, not just the template. You will use this file later.

ADDING ANCHOR POINTS

No Illustrator path is ever set in stone. You can always add and delete anchor points for reshaping a path. Illustrator provides you with an Add Anchor Point tool accessed from behind the Pen tool.

Click with the Add Anchor Point tool anywhere on a path—it doesn't have to be selected—to add an anchor point. Adding anchor points is frequently an easy way to adjust a segment, because it gives you extra direction handles (smooth point) or just another corner point to manipulate.

If you have a path selected and move over that path with the Pen tool, the Pen tool automatically changes to the Add Anchor Point tool, letting you click on the path to add an anchor point.

Macintosh Keystrokes

⌘-O File/Open
⌘-Y View/Artwork/Preview
⌘-R View/Show Rulers
⌘-Z Edit/Undo
⌘-Shift-A Edit/Deselect All

Windows Keystrokes

Ctrl-O File/Open
Ctrl-Y View/Artwork/
    Preview
Ctrl-R View/Show Rulers
Ctrl-Z Edit/Undo
Ctrl-Shift-A Edit/Deselect
    All

Pen Tool (P)

Direct Selection Tool

Add Anchor Point

FYI

You can switch between the Add and Delete Anchor Point tools by pressing the Option/Alt key.

Macintosh Keystrokes

⌘-N File/New
⌘-Y View/Artwork/Preview

Windows Keystrokes

Ctrl-N File/New
Ctrl-Y View/Artwork/
Preview

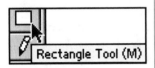

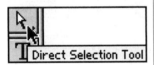

ADD ANCHOR POINTS COMMAND

When adding an anchor point between a pair of anchor points, use the Add Anchor Points command (Object/Path/Add Anchor Points). This command positions the new anchor point exactly between the existing points and will give you better results if you apply any of the Distort filters. The object must be selected before the Add Anchor Points command can be applied.

DELETING ANCHOR POINTS

The Delete Anchor Point tool removes anchor points from a path. Deleting an anchor point simplifies the path and reshapes the object. To delete an anchor point, position the Delete Anchor Point tool over the anchor point and click.

EXERCISE G

1. Create a new file (File/New). Display the Swatches palette and select a light fill color. Leave the stroke at None. Choose View/Preview (Command/Ctrl-Y).

2. Reset the Toolbox by pressing the Command-Shift (Macintosh) or Ctrl-Shift (Windows) keys and double-clicking on any tool.

3. Select the Rectangle tool. Drag to draw a rectangle. Click and drag on the Pen tool to select the Add Anchor Point tool.

4. With the rectangle still selected, click with the Add Anchor Point tool on the top segment of the rectangle. A selected anchor point appears, and the other four anchor points on the rectangle become deselected (hollow) (Figure 8.16).

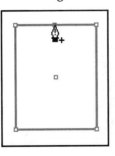

Figure 8.16. When you click with the Add Anchor Point tool, a selected anchor point appears on the path and the path becomes deselected.

5. Click on the Direct Selection tool and click on the newly created selected point. Drag that point up to change the appearance of the rectangle to a roofed building (Figure 8.17).

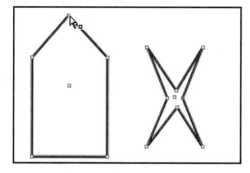

Figure 8.17. Use the Direct Selection tool to drag the newly created anchor point up to reshape the rectangle. Adding another three anchor points, for a total of eight anchor points, lets you reshape the rectangle into a star.

Add Anchor Point

6. Click with the Add Anchor Point tool on the other three segments. Use the Direct Selection tool to drag all four points inward to create a shape similar to the one shown in Figure 8.17. The object now has a total of eight anchor points.

7. Use the Direct Selection tool to select the star. Press the Command and Shift keys (Macintosh) or Ctrl and Shift keys (Windows) simultaneously and double-click on any tool to reset the Toolbox. Drag out the Pen tool and select the Delete Anchor Point tool.

Direct Selection Tool

8. Click on any of the anchor points with the Delete Anchor Point tool. Notice how the shape of the star changes as you delete anchor points.

9. Close this file (File/Close). Don't save your changes.

Delete Anchor Point

CONVERTING ANCHOR POINTS

The third tool that appears when you drag the Scissors tool out is the Convert Direction Point tool. Use this tool to convert a corner point (selected with the Direct Selection tool) to a smooth point by clicking on the corner point and dragging. Clicking on a smooth point with this tool converts the smooth point with its two direction handles to a corner point with no direction handles.

FYI

If you use the Add Anchor Point command (Object/Path/Add Anchor Point), the anchor points will be added at the exact center of every segment on the rectangle.

REVIEW

In this unit you learned that:

1. Clicking with the Pen tool creates straight lines.

2. Pressing the Shift key when clicking the second point on a straight line segment constrains the line to either a straight line or a line at 45°.

3. An open path must be closed before a new path can be drawn.

FYI

Dragging the direction handle of a smooth point with the Convert Direction Point tool does two things: It converts the smooth point to a corner point and adjusts the angle of the segment connected to that newly converted anchor point.

4. The Pen tool must be deactivated after drawing an open path before a new path can be drawn.

5. The Pen tool is deactivated by closing the path, by clicking on the first point created in the path, by selecting a different tool, by clicking once on the Pen tool in the Toolbox, by pressing the Command/Ctrl key and clicking on an empty area of the page, or by choosing Edit/Deselect All.

6. An open path (line) can be filled and stroked.

7. The only way to reshape a closed path is to add anchor points to the path and use the Direct Selection tool to reshape the path.

8. Clicking and dragging with the Pen tools creates curved line segments.

9. Curves have slope and height which can be edited by dragging the anchor point connecting the curve segments, or by dragging the direction handles attached to the curve segments.

10. To hide anchor points and direction handles without deselecting the object, use the View/Hide Edges command.

11. Ruler guides appear as either lines or dots, depending on the options selected in the Guides & Grid Preferences dialog box.

12. Selected paths and path segments can be edited, deleted, and duplicated.

13. Paths can be split with the Scissors tool and joined with the Join command.

14. Change the direction of a curve to create noncontinuous curves by Option/Alt-clicking on the last anchor point and dragging in the opposite direction to complete the curve.

15. Anchor points can be added to a path with the Add Anchor Point tool or with the Add Anchor Point command and deleted from a path with the Delete Anchor Point tool. They can also be converted to and from smooth and curve points with the Convert Anchor Point tool.

UNIT 9
Layers

Scorpion, by Michael Zielinski

OVERVIEW

In this unit you will learn how:
to organize artwork on separate layers
stacking order affects display
to cut, copy, and paste parts of an image to and from
    different layers
to paste into a Photoshop file
to create, duplicate, merge, and delete layers
groups appear on layers
to use templates
to import and export layers between
    Illustrator and Photoshop

TERMS

Anti-alias
backmost object
Clipboard
Copy
Cut
Flatten Artwork
frontmost object
group
layer
Lock/Unlock
Merge Layers
Paste
Paste in Back
Paste in Front
Paste Remembers Layers
raster image
Revert
template

HOW IT WORKS

Use layers, the Reflect tool, and the Transform Again command to create the artwork. Fill with custom gradients.

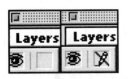

The Eye icon refers to what is *visible* on the layer, and the Pencil icon to what can be *edited* on that layer. A visible Eye icon means that the layer can be viewed (left). A Pencil icon with a bar across it, the Locked Layer icon (right), means that you cannot edit that layer.

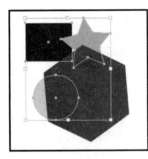

The rectangle, star, and circle were created on different layers and grouped. They now appear on the frontmost layer behind the polygon.

The Hollow Eye icon indicates that artwork will be displayed in outlines on that layer.

STACKING ORDER

Each object created in a document is stacked in front of the one previously created. For example, if you draw a circle, then a rectangle, and then a star, the circle is the backmost object in the stacking order and the star is the first object, even if no objects are overlapping or touching. This arrangement of objects in their painting order is called the *stacking order* or *painting order*.

Objects can be arranged in a file in two ways: they can be stacked on a single layer (like the circle, rectangle, and star in the example above), or they can be placed individually or stacked on different layers in the same document.

LAYERS

A layer is a specific level on which artwork is placed and edited. A layer can be hidden so that the artwork on that level cannot be viewed or edited. A layer can be locked so that the artwork on that layer can be viewed but not edited. Artwork on any layer can be printed or not printed with the rest of the document.

When you first launch Adobe Illustrator, the drawing page appears and Layer 1 is automatically created and selected (highlighted). To access any layer, use the Layers palette from the Window menu (Window/Show Layers or F7).

LAYERS AND GROUPS

Grouped objects always appear on the same layer. If you select an object on Layer 1 and another object on Layer 2 and group them, both objects appear grouped on the frontmost layer of the group behind the frontmost object on that layer.

THE LAYERS PALETTE

Use the Layers palette (Window/Show Layers) to create, hide, lock, and delete layers. Each layer has its own options, which allows you to specify the printing and display options for that layer.

LAYERS PALETTE ICONS

When you display the Layers palette for a new document, the **Eye icon** appears, telling you that the artwork on that layer is visible (or will be when you draw it). If you select Preview from the Layer Options dialog box, artwork will appear as outlines even in Preview view and a **Hollow Eye icon** is displayed. A **Pen icon** appears on the selected layer indicating that anything you draw will be created on that layer. A crossed pen, the **Locked Layer** icon, indicates that the layer is locked and cannot be edited.

When you select artwork on a layer, a colored dot called a Selection Square, appears to the right of the layer's name, indicating that there is selected artwork on that layer.

Clicking in the second column to the left of a layer's name locks that layer and makes it unavailable for editing. When you lock a layer, a Crossed Pencil icon appears. Click the Crossed Pencil icon to unlock the layer. When no Crossed Pencil icon appears, that layer is available for drawing and editing (Figure 9.1).

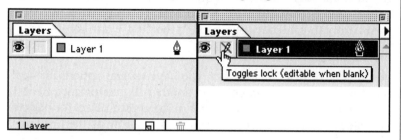

Figure 9.1. The Layers palette as it appears in a new document displays only Layer 1, which is both visible and available for editing (left). Clicking the column to the right of the Eye icon displays the Locked Layer icons (crossed pencil on left; crossed pen on right), indicating that you cannot edit any artwork on that layer.

The Pen icon on the right side of Layer 3 indicates that anything you draw will appear on Layer 3. The colored dot (Selection Square) next to Layer 2 indicates that an object is selected on that layer.

SELECTING LAYERS

Any artwork you create will appear on the currently selected layer. Select a layer by clicking on it to highlight it. To select multiple layers, Option/Alt-click on a layer name in the Layers palette or Option/Alt-drag through the layer names, which selects all the objects on the selected layers.

To select contiguous layers, Shift-click on the layer name. To select or deselect noncontiguous layers, Command/Ctrl-click on the layer name.

Keep in mind that anything you draw appears on the currently selected layer, and anything you select takes you to the layer on which that object appears—unless the layer is locked, in which case you can't select anything on the layer.

FYI

Locking an object makes it unavailable for editing. You cannot select it to display its anchor points.

PASTING OBJECTS

When you copy and paste objects on a layer, the pasted object appears as the frontmost object on that layer. If you paste the same object or another object on that layer, it becomes the frontmost object in the stacking order. The Paste commands, however, affect how objects are pasted depending on what you have selected in the document.

COPY AND CUT COMMANDS

When you copy an object (or objects) with the Edit/Copy command, that object is placed on the Clipboard, an area of memory reserved for holding copied items. Once an object is copied to the Clipboard, it remains there until you copy another object, which will overwrite the previously copied object. The copied object remains in the document until you delete it or cut it.

If you cut an object with the Edit/Cut command, that object is not only copied to the Clipboard, but it is also *removed* from the document. You can get it back again using the Edit/Undo command.

PASTE COMMAND

When you copy or cut an object, you have several options for pasting it back in that document or in another Illustrator document. If you choose the Edit/Paste command, the copied object (or objects) is pasted in the center of the document window as the frontmost object.

PASTE IN BACK COMMAND

The Paste in Back command pastes the contents of the Clipboard behind a selected object. If no object is selected, the object is pasted behind the backmost object on the layer, making the pasted object the backmost object.

PASTE IN FRONT COMMAND

The Paste in Front command pastes the contents of the Clipboard in front of a selected object. If no object is selected, the object is pasted in front of the frontmost object on the layer, making the pasted object the frontmost object.

PASTE REMEMBERS LAYERS COMMAND

Ordinarily, when you cut or copy an object and then paste it, it is pasted onto the *selected* layer. To ensure that the copied or cut object is pasted on the layer *where it originated*, select the Paste Remembers Layers option in the General Preferences dialog box or from the Layers palette menu.

PASTE INTO PHOTOSHOP

You can copy objects in Illustrator and paste them into Photoshop documents. When you select the Paste command in Photoshop, the Paste dialog box gives you the option of pasting the vector artwork as pixels, in which case Photoshop rasterizes the Illustrator art into pixels. Or, you can paste the vector artwork as paths. Selecting this option lets you manipulate the object in Photoshop as you could any path created directly in Photoshop.

Select the Paste Remembers Layers option in the General Preferences dialog box to paste cut or copied objects on the same layer from where they originated.

When you select the Paste as Pixels option in Photoshop, Illustrator art is pasted as raster art, not as paths.

Macintosh Keystrokes

F7 Window/Show Layers
⌘-Shift-A Edit/Deselect All
⌘-2 Object/Lock
⌘-Option-2 Object/
   Unlock All
⌘-W File/Close

Windows Keystrokes

F7 Window/Show Layers
Ctrl-Shift-A Edit/Deselect
   All
Ctrl-2 Object/Lock
Ctrl-Alt-2 Object/ Unlock
   All
Ctrl-W File/Close

1. Create a new document (File/New) and choose Window/ Show Layers (F7) to display the Layers palette. It appears displaying Layer 1 as visible and editable. Display the Swatches palette. Click on the Fill icon in the Toolbox and select a color from the Swatches palette.

2. Use the Rectangle tool to draw a rectangle. Then use the Ellipse tool to draw an oval. Keep the oval selected.

3. Notice that a blue Selection Square appears next to the Pen on the right side of the Layers palette (Figure 9.2). This tells you that a selected object exists on this layer. The visible Eye icon indicates that the artwork on this layer is visible. The blank field next to the Eye icon indicates that the layer is unlocked and available for editing. Deselect the oval (Command-Shift-A) and the square disappears because nothing is selected on the layer.

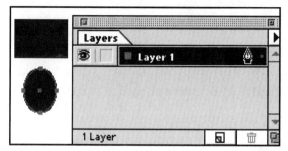

Figure 9.2. The Selection Square to the right of the Eye icon indicates that the selected object is editable.

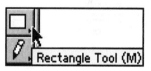

4. Use the Selection tool to select the rectangle. Choose Object/ Lock. Notice that the blue Selection Square next to the Pen disappears, indicating that there is a locked (uneditable) object on that layer.

5. Choose Object/Unlock All to display the blue Selection Square next to the Pen icon on Layer 1.

6. Continue to select and deselect, lock and unlock single and multiple objects on Layer 1, while watching the icons on the Layers palette, until you are familiar with what the Selection Square means.

7. Close this file (File/Close). Don't save your changes.

Macintosh Keystrokes

⌘-N File/New
⌘-X Edit/Cut
⌘-V Edit/Paste
⌘-B Edit/Paste in Back
⌘-F Edit/Paste in Front

Windows Keystrokes

Ctrl-File/New
Ctrl-X Edit/Cut
Ctrl-V Edit/Paste
Ctrl-B Edit/Paste n Back
Ctrl-F Edit/Paste in Front

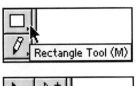

EXERCISE B

1. In a new document (Command/Ctrl-N), use the Rectangle tool to draw a rectangle, the Pen tool to draw a slightly smaller triangle, and the Ellipse tool to draw a circle slightly smaller than the triangle.

2. Use the Swatches palette to fill and stroke them with contrasting colors and patterns (Figure 9.3).

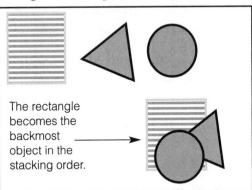

The rectangle becomes the backmost object in the stacking order.

Figure 9.3. Even though the rectangle was the first object drawn, once the triangle and oval are placed in front of it, the rectangle becomes the backmost object in the stacking order.

3. Use the Selection tool to drag the triangle on top of the rectangle so that half of the triangle extends beyond the right edge of the rectangle. Drag the oval over the triangle so that it extends beyond the edge of the triangle (Figure 9.3).

4. Use the Selection tool to select the triangle. Choose Edit/Cut (Command/Ctrl-X) to remove the triangle and place it on the Clipboard.

5. Select the rectangle and choose Edit/Paste in Back (Command/Ctrl-B) to place the cut triangle behind the selected rectangle. If you had chosen Edit/Paste, the triangle would have been pasted in the center of the drawing page as the frontmost object. By pasting the triangle behind the rectangle, the triangle becomes the backmost object in the stacking order.

6. With the triangle still selected, choose Edit/Paste in Front (Command/Ctrl-F). Nothing appears to happen, but the triangle has been pasted in front of itself. Use the Selection tool to drag the selected pasted copy away from the other objects. The original triangle remains behind the rectangle.

7. Select the circle and choose Edit/Paste (Command/Ctrl-V) to paste the triangle from the Clipboard in front of the selected circle, making the triangle the frontmost object on Layer 1.

Because the pasted triangle is still selected, the Selection Square appears next to the Pen on Layer 1.

8. Save this file as *Layers.ai* as an Illustrator file in your Projects folder (File/Save As). You will need it for the next exercise.

CREATING NEW LAYERS

Every new Illustrator document is created with one layer, Layer 1. There are three ways to add new layers to a document: (1) Use the pull-out menu on the Layers palette and drag to select New Layer. Once you select New Layer, that layer is created, is named Layer 2, and the New Layer dialog box is displayed. (2) Click the New Layer icon on the Layers palette. (3) Duplicate a selected layer.

DUPLICATING LAYERS

When you select the Duplicate Layer command from the Layers palette menu, that duplicate layer is placed above the original layer and duplicates not only all the artwork on the original layer, but also all the options selected for that layer. You can also drag a layer over the New Layer icon on the Layers palette to create a duplicate of that layer. Duplicate layers display *copy* after the layer's name.

MERGING AND FLATTENING LAYERS

To merge multiple layers into one layer, Shift-select the layers you want to merge, and choose Merge Layers from the Layers palette menu. This command puts all the artwork from the selected layers onto the topmost selected layer. The artwork retains its original stacking order on the merged layer.

Merging layers does not affect any artwork on the merged layers, but flattening layers does. When you choose Flatten Artwork from the Layers palette menu, all visible layers are merged into the bottommost layer and all hidden layers and their artwork are deleted. It's a good idea to flatten a file only when you have finished working on it, or else use the Edit/Undo Flatten Artwork command right away.

DELETING LAYERS

To delete a layer, select it and choose Delete Layer from the Layers palette menu. If you have artwork on that layer, an alert will appear, giving you the option of cancelling the Delete command. You can also drag a layer to the Trash icon on the Layers palette to delete it or select a layer and click on the Delete Selected Layers (Trash) icon at the bottom of the Layers palette.

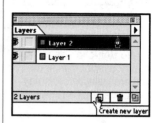

Click the New Layer button to add a new layer to the Layers palette.

The duplicate layer is named a copy of the original layer.

Selecting an item on a layer and choosing the Delete command from the Layers palette gives you an alert dialog box where you can choose to cancel the deletion.

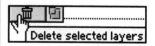

To delete any layer, select it and click the Trash icon in the Layers palette.

Create new layer

Option/Alt-click on the New Layer button in the Layers palette to display the Layer Options dialog box for the new layer.

Layers shortcuts (Macintosh)

Command-click the New Layer button to create a new layer below the selected layer.
Command-Option-click the New Layer button to create a new layer at the top of the Layers palette.

Layers shortcuts (Windows)

Ctrl-click the New Layer button to create a new layer below the selected layer.
Ctrl-Alt-click the New Layer button to create a new layer at the top of the Layers palette.

FYI

Double-click on any layer to display its Layer Options dialog box.

NEW LAYER OPTIONS

Once you select New Layer from the Layers palette, the Layer Options dialog box is displayed (Figure 9.4). It is here that you name the layer and specify display and printing options for only that layer or level of artwork. It defaults to another color for the outlines of selected objects. You can change this selection color from the Color menu in the Layer Options dialog box.

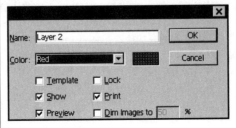

Figure 9.4. Select New Layer from the Layers palette menu to display the new layer's Options dialog box.

The layer also defaults to being visible and in Preview view, and to being a printing layer. If you place a template on that layer, you should check the Dim Images option so you can trace the template. You can also lock the layer, making any artwork on that layer uneditable as well as not allowing any artwork to be created on that layer.

Whenever you create a new layer by clicking on OK in the New Layer dialog box, that new layer becomes the active layer in the document. Until you specify otherwise, any objects you create will be placed on that layer.

RASTER IMAGES ON LAYERS

A raster image such as one created in Photoshop can be placed on any layer where it will appear and print in all its glorious color—unless you choose otherwise in the Layer Options dialog box.

Select the Dim Images option in the Layer Options dialog box to dim the image, making it easier to trace it or to edit artwork created over the image.

NEW LAYER BUTTON

Click the New Layer button at the bottom of the Layers palette to add a new layer to the document. Using this button does not display the Layer Options dialog box (unless you Option/Alt-click on the button), but does number the layer sequentially and specify another color for the edges of selected objects.

DUPLICATE LAYER COMMAND

When you choose Duplicate Layer from the Layers palette menu, the selected layer is given the same name as the original layer with the "copy" extension. All artwork from the original layer is copied to the duplicate layer.

MOVING OBJECTS FROM LAYER TO LAYER

Although it's good practice to define the layers in a piece of artwork before you begin drawing, many times we get so carried away by the fact that the drawing is actually looking like something someone would pay for that we end up with many objects on one layer. This makes it difficult to edit individual objects, as it's hard to select single objects surrounded by many other objects. Even though the Layers palette is not displayed, objects are being drawn on the currently selected layer (usually Layer 1), so it is frequently necessary to move objects to new layers in the artwork.

To move objects from one layer to another, cut them, select the new layer, and paste the objects on that new layer. Another way to move objects from layer to layer is to use the Layers palette. Select the object to be moved and drag the colored Selection Square next to the Pen icon on the right side of the Layers palette up or down to the new layer. As you do this, the colored Selection Square turns into a hollow square. When you have reached the new layer, release the mouse button. The selected artwork has been moved from its original layer to the new layer (Figure 9.5).

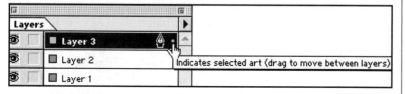

Figure 9.5. Click on the colored Selection Square that indicates an object is selected, and drag the square to another layer to move the selected object to that layer.

DUPLICATING ARTWORK BETWEEN LAYERS

To duplicate selected artwork as you move it to a new layer, press the Option/Alt key before you begin dragging the layer's Selection Square. As you drag, a plus sign appears next to the cursor hand. When you get to the new layer, release the mouse button before releasing the Option/Alt key.

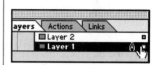

Select this option from the Layers palette menu to display the layers in smaller rows, thus letting you display more layers without resizing the Layers palette too much.

When dragging an object from one layer to another, a white square appears under the Hand cursor, indicating that an object is being moved.

The + sign indicates that you are duplicating—not moving— selected art from one layer to another.

Macintosh Keystrokes

⌘-O File/Open
F7 Window/Show Layers
⌘-X Edit/Cut
⌘-V Edit/Paste

Windows Keystrokes

Ctrl-O File/Open
F7 Window/Show Layers
Ctrl-X Edit/Cut
Ctrl-V Edit/Paste

Select New Layer from the Layers palette menu.

FYI

Selecting an object automatically takes you to that layer and selects the layer.

EXERCISE C

1. If necessary, open the *Layers.ai* file you created in the last lesson (File/Open) or create a new file with three different objects on one layer. Choose Window/Show Layers (F7) to display the Layers palette. Layer 1 is highlighted, indicating that it is the active layer; any objects you draw will be placed on that layer.

2. Use the Selection tool to select the rectangle. Layer 1 remains highlighted, indicating that the object is on that layer. Deselect the rectangle by clicking on an empty area of the page.

3. Click on the triangle in the right corner of the Layers palette to display the pull-down menu. Deselect Paste Remembers Layers if it is selected.

4. Use the Layers palette menu again to select New Layer. The New Layer dialog box appears, displaying Layer 2 as the highlighted name of the new layer.

5. Type *Triangle* in the Name field. Change the selection color if you like, and make sure that Show, Print, and Preview are checked. Click on OK. The Triangle layer appears as the topmost layer in the Layers palette. However, it does not display any square on the right side of the palette next to the Pen icon, because there are no objects on the Triangle layer.

6. Use the Selection tool to select the rectangle. Layer 1 on the Layers palette becomes highlighted, because an object on that layer has been selected. And because the triangle is available for editing, a colored Selection Square appears next to the Pen icon on the right side of the Layers palette.

7. Choose Edit/Cut (Command/Ctrl-X). Click once on the triangle layer to select that layer and choose Edit/Paste (Command/Ctrl-V). The triangle is pasted on the Triangle layer and, because it is selected and available for editing, a Selection Square appears next to the Pen icon on the right side of the palette (Figure 9.6).

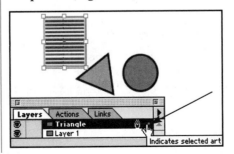

Figure 9.6. Copying the triangle and pasting it on the Triangle layer displays a colored Selection Square next to the Pen icon, indicating that an object is selected on the Triangle layer.

148

8. Because you selected Show in the New Layer dialog box, all objects on the Triangle layer are displayed. The triangle is displayed with all of its fill and stroke attributes because Preview (viewing mode) was selected, and all the objects on this layer will print when you print the file because Print was selected in the New Layer dialog box.

9. Use the pull-out menu on the Layers palette to create a new layer. Type *Circle* in the name field of the New Layer dialog box. Make sure that only Show is selected. Click to deselect Print and Preview. Click on OK. The Circle layer, now the first layer in the Layers palette, is highlighted, indicating that it is the active layer and that anything you draw will appear on that layer.

10. Click on the circle, which deselects the Circle layer and highlights Layer 1 because the selected object (the circle) is on Layer 1.

11. Click with the Selection tool on the colored Selection Square next to the Pen icon on the right side of the palette and drag it up to the Circle layer. A hand appears as you drag, and once the object is placed on the new layer, a colored Selection Square appears where the finger is pointing (Figure 9.7), indicating that the selected object has overcome all transportation hazards and been safely moved through all the layers onto the designated layer.

FYI

A layer's name appears in italics when the Print option is deselected in its Options dialog box.

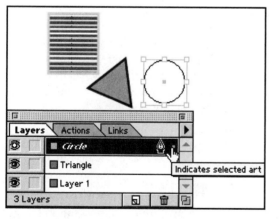

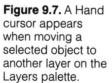

Figure 9.7. A Hand cursor appears when moving a selected object to another layer on the Layers palette.

12. Because Preview was deselected in the New Layer dialog box, the circle appears on the Circle layer in Artwork view, even though the objects on the other two layers are displayed in Preview view.

Macintosh Keystrokes

⌘-P File/Print
⌘-X Edit/Cut
⌘-Edit/Paste

Windows Keystrokes

Ctrl-P File/Print
Ctrl-X Edit/Cut
Ctrl-V Edit/Paste

The Locked Layer icon appears when any layer is locked in its Options dialog box.

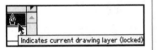

Tip

When the Direct Selection tool is selected, press the Option/Alt key (quickly!) to access the Group Selection tool.

13. Choose File/Print (Command/Ctrl-P) to display the Print dialog box. Click on OK. Because the Print check box was not selected in the Circle layer's dialog box, only the rectangle and triangle print.

14. Click the New Layer button in the Layers palette to create Layer 4. Double-click on Layer 4 and type *Rectangle* in the Name field. Click to select Show, Preview, Print, and Lock. Click on OK. The Layers palette now displays four layers, the Rectangle layer as the topmost layer, the Circle and Triangle layers, and Layer 1. Notice that the Locked Layer icons appear next to the Eye icon and next to the layer's name. Because the Rectangle layer is a locked layer, no items can be added to that layer and nothing already on that placed on that layer can be edited (Figure 9.8).

Figure 9.8. The Locked Layer icons appear to the left and right of the Rectangle layer.

15. Click with the Selection tool on the rectangle and notice that Layer 1 is highlighted, because that is where the rectangle is. Choose Edit/Cut (Command/Ctrl-X). Click once on the Rectangle layer to access it, and choose Edit/Paste (Command-V). An Alert dialog box appears telling you that this is a hidden or locked layer. Click on OK to simultaneously unlock the layer and paste the rectangle on the Rectangle layer.

16. Save this file as *Layers1.ai* as an Illustrator file. You will use it in the next exercise.

LAYERS PALETTE OPTIONS

You can view and hide layers, lock and unlock layers, and change any layer's display mode from the Layers palette menu. Remember: when the Eye icon is displayed, a layer's contents are visible; when a Crossed Pencil icon or Crossed Pen icon is displayed, a layer is locked.

EXERCISE D

1. If necessary, open the *Layers.ai* file you worked on in the last exercise or open (File/Open) the *Layers1.ai* file on the Unit 09 folder on the CD-ROM.

2. Display the Layers palette (F7). As the file is now, the Rectangle, Triangle, and Layer 1 layers can all be viewed and edited. Those layers are also displayed in Preview view. The Circle layer can be viewed in Artwork view and can be edited.

3. Click once on the Eye icon for the Rectangle layer. Two things happen: (1) the Eye icon disappears, indicating that the Show check box in the Rectangle layer's dialog box has been deselected; and (2) the Pen icon displays a slash, indicating that the objects on the Rectangle layer cannot be edited.

4. Double-click on the Rectangle layer's name to display its Options dialog box, and notice that the Show check box is empty. Click to select it and click on OK. The Eye icon now reappears next to the Rectangle layer's name, because the layer is now visible, and the slash line is removed from the Pen icon on the right side of the Layers palette, because items on that layer can now be edited.

5. Click on the triangle to highlight the Triangle layer. The Selection Square next to the Pen icon is displayed, indicating that there is a selected object on that layer.

6. Click once in the blank area next to the Eye icon for the Triangle layer. Three things happen: (1) The colored square disappears, indicating that although the objects on that layer are visible, they are locked and not available for editing. (2) The Locked Layer icon appears next to the Eye icon, indicating that the layer is locked and cannot be edited. (3) A slashed line appears across the Pen icon to the right of the layer's name as another indication that the objects on that layer cannot be edited (Figure 9.9). This is not something you can easily miss!

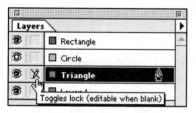

Figure 9.9. The Locked Layer icon and Crossed Pen icon indicate that the Triangle layer is locked and cannot be edited.

Macintosh Keystrokes

⌘-O File/Open
F7 Window/Show Layers
⌘-B Edit/Paste in Back
⌘-F Edit/Paste in Front
⌘-V Edit/Paste

Windows Keystrokes

Ctrl-O File/Open
F7 Window/Show Layers
Ctrl-B Edit/Paste in Back
Ctrl-F Edit/Paste in Front
Ctrl-V Edit/Paste

When the Eye icon is deselected, the Show option is automatically deselected in that layer's Options dialog box.

FYI

Hidden layers cannot be edited.

7. Double-click on the Triangle layer's name to display its Options dialog box. Notice that the Lock check box is selected, indicating that all the objects on that layer are locked and cannot be edited.

8. Try clicking on the triangle itself, and notice that you cannot select it because it is locked.

9. Click the Locked Layer icon next to the Eye icon on the Triangle layer to unlock the layer.

10. Close this file (File/Close). Don't save your changes.

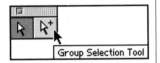

LAYERS AND GROUPS

Thus far you have worked with single objects on single layers. The rules change when you are grouping individual objects on different layers. When objects on one layer are arranged in a stacking order, grouping two or more objects results in the non-grouped objects being moved behind the group.

Because all grouped objects must exist on a single layer, if you group objects drawn on different layers, that group of objects is placed on the frontmost (top) layer of the group directly behind the frontmost object on that layer. In other words, the group takes a back seat on the layer.

CREATING GROUPS

FYI

You can group as many objects and groups together as you like into one group.

A *group* is two or more selected objects to which the Group command has been applied. When objects are grouped, they can be moved and transformed as one object. For example, if you select and group three objects, applying the Scale command to the group will scale all three objects in the group, unless you use the Transform Each command which transforms even grouped objects separately.

GROUP SELECTION TOOL

WARNING!

To move one object in a group or one group in a multiple-grouped object, click once with the Group Selection tool *and release the mouse button.* Use the Selection or Direct Select tool to edit the selected object. Otherwise, the next click will select the the whole group.

Because you can group one group or many groups with another group to create a multiple grouped object, it's easier to select objects and groups with the Group Selection tool. Access the Group Selection tool by dragging out the Direct Selection tool or by pressing *a* to toggle between the Direct Selection and Group Selection tools.

To use the Group Selection tool, click once on the group to select a single object in the group. Then click again on that same object to select the entire group of which that single object is a part. If you click again on that object, you will select the next larger group of which the first group is a part.

Macintosh Keystrokes

⌘-O File/Open
F7 Window/Show Layers
⌘-G Object/Group

Windows Keystrokes

Ctrl-O File/Open
F7 Window/Show Layers
Ctrl-G Object/Group

1. Open the *Layers1.ai* file in the Unit 09 folder on the CD-ROM (File/Open). Display the Layers palette (F7).

2. Double-click on the name of the Circle layer in the Layers palette to display the Layer Options dialog box. Click in the Preview check box to display any artwork on that layer in Preview view. Click on OK.

3. Use the Selection tool to Shift-select both the circle and the triangle (Figure 9.10).

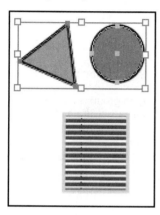

Figure 9.10. Use the Selection tool and press the Shift key to select only the circle and triangle.

4. Notice the colored Selection Squares that appear on the right side of the Layers palette next to the Circle and Triangle layers. These colored squares indicate that objects on those layers are selected (Figure 9.11).

Figure 9.11. The colored Selection Squares indicate that objects are selected on those layers.

Macintosh Keystrokes

⌘-Shift-A Edit/Deselect All
⌘-G Object/Group
⌘-Shift-G Object/Ungroup
⌘-W File/Close

Windows Keystrokes

Ctrl-Shift A Edit/Deselect
     All
Ctrl-G Object/Group
Ctrl-Shift-G Object/
     Ungroup
Ctrl-W File/Close

Group Selection Tool

Revert risks

Once you click the Revert button, any unsaved changes made to the file will be lost. If you're not sure you want to do this, click the Cancel button. If you haven't made any changes to the file since you last saved it, the Revert command is not available.

5. With both the circle and the triangle selected, choose Object/ Group. Both objects are grouped and placed on the Circle layer, because it is the frontmost of the two layers.

6. Click once on the Eye icon for the Rectangle, Triangle, and Layer 1 layers. Notice that now only the selected circle- and- triangle group is visible, because the other three layers are now hidden (Figure 9.12).

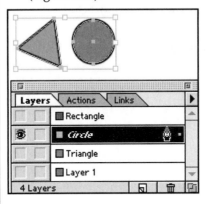

Figure 9.12. Hiding the other three layers results in display-ing only the group on the one visible layer, the Circle layer.

7. Choose Edit/Deselect All and choose the Group Selection tool. Click once on the circle to select just the circle, and click again to select the second item in the group, the triangle. Drag the group around the page.

8. Choose File/Revert and click on the Revert button to revert to the last saved version of this file. Use the Pen tool to draw dif-ferent shapes on different layers. Shift-select and group the shapes (Command/Ctrl-G). Then group the groups. Use the Group Selection tool to first select any object in any group, then click again to select the group of which that object is a part. Click again to select the next group in the larger group. Ungroup that group (Command/Ctrl-Shift-G).

9. Close this file (File/Close). Don't save your changes.

REORDERING LAYERS

By dragging a layer up or down on the Layers palette, you reposi-tion the artwork on that layer in the document. For example, if you have a rectangle on the bottommost layer and drag that layer above any other layer in the Layers palette, that rectangle is no longer the bottommost object in the document.

EXERCISE F

1. In a new document, display the Layers palette (F7). Use any of the drawing tools to draw a rectangle on Layer 1.

2. Click the New Layer icon at the bottom of the Layers palette to create a new layer which is also selected. Draw an ellipse on Layer 2 which overlaps the rectangle on Layer 1. Notice that the ellipse on Layer 2 is the frontmost of the two objects.

3. Click on Layer 2 and drag it down below Layer 1. Because you moved the artwork with the layer, the rectangle on Layer 1 becomes the frontmost object (Figure 9.13).

4. Close this file (Command/Ctrl-W). Don't save your changes.

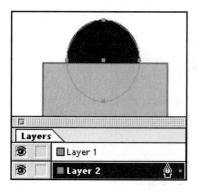

Figure 9.13. When Layer 2 was moved below Layer 1, the ellipse on Layer 2 became the backmost object in the document.

WORKING WITH TEMPLATES

A *template* is any kind of artwork—vector or raster—that is used as the basis for new artwork. For example, you might use a Photoshop image of a tree as a template in Illustrator to use the tree as a guide for tracing a vector tree. Illustrator, lets you set options for a template so that it doesn't interfere with your drawing.

When placing an image with the Place command, if you click the Template option in the Place dialog box, that placed image appears on a separate, bottommost layer in the document. It is dimmed, locked, and will not print.

Macintosh Keystrokes

⌘-N File/New
F7 Window/Show Layers
⌘-W File/Close

Windows Keystrokes

Ctrl-N File/New
F7 Window/Show Layers
Ctrl-W File/Close

Create new layer

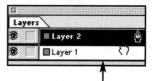

When dragging a layer to a new position, a black line appears, indicating that the layer has been repositioned.

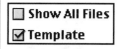

Clicking Template in the Place dialog box dims the image and places it on a separate layer.

Pen Tool (P)

Layers

👁 ☐ ▢ Layer 1

🐟 ✗ ☐ *Template PHONE* ✍

When art is placed as a template or when a layer is specified as a template layer, the Template icon appears on the far left side of the Layers palette.

FYI

To show or hide all the template layers in the Layers palette, press Command/Ctrl-Shift-W.

More info

To hide all the inactive layers, first select the layer or layers you want to view. Then Option/Alt-click on its Eye icon. This will hide any nonselected layers. You can also select the layers you want to view and choose Hide Others from the Layers palette menu—if no other layers are hidden.

EXERCISE G

1. In a new document (File/New), choose File/Place. Display the Layers palette (F7). Navigate to the Unit 09 folder on the CD-ROM and highlight the *Parrot.tif* file. Click on Place (Macintosh) or Open (Windows). The image appears in full color on Layer 1.

2. Double-click on Layer 1 or choose Options for Layer 1 from the Layers palette menu to display the Layer Options dialog box. Click the Template check box (version 8) or the Dim checkbox (version 7) and click OK.

3. Selecting the Template option dims the Show, Preview, Lock, and Print options and automatically dims the image so you can work around it (Figure 9.14).

Layer Options

Name: Layer 1   OK

Color: Light Blue ⬍ ▢   Cancel

☑ Template ☑ Lock
☑ Show   ☐ Print
☑ Preview   ☑ Dim Images to: 50 %

Layers
🐟 ✗ ▢ *Layer 1*   ✍

1 Layer

Figure 9.14. Clicking Template in the Layer Options dialog box (version 8) or Dim Images (version 7) dims the image and locks the layer (Crossed Pencil and Template icons on the Layers palette in version 8), making it unavailable for editing.

4. Click the New Layer icon in the Layers palette to create a new, editable layer. Select a fill of None and a black stroke and use the Pen tool to trace the parrot, using the template as a guide (Figure 9.15).

5. When you have finished, select the template layer and choose Delete Layer from the Layers palette menu.

6. Close this file (File/Close). Don't save your changes.

Figure 9.15. Use the template as a guide to create artwork on another layer.

IMPORTING AND EXPORTING LAYERS BETWEEN ILLUSTRATOR AND PHOTOSHOP

You can import a Photoshop file into Illustrator, which will bring in every Photoshop layer. If the Photoshop file has multiple layers, those layers are flattened and the file is placed as a single-layer file in Illustrator.

However, when exporting Illustrator files to Photoshop 5, because the file is exported as a Photoshop 5 file, you can specify that Illustrator keep all the layers intact when exporting the Illustrator file. When you open the Photoshop 5 file (that began life as an Illustrator file), all the Illustrator layers are intact and can be edited individually in Photoshop. If you have Photoshop 4 or Photoshop 5 installed on your hard drive, complete the next exercise.

EXERCISE H

1. In a new file (File/New), choose File/Place. Navigate to the Unit 09 folder on the CD-ROM and highlight the *Parrot1.tif* file. Click on Place (Macintosh) or Open (Windows). The file appears displaying the image and text on one layer, although the original Photoshop image contained two layers, one for the bird and the other for the text.

2. Double-click on Layer 1, the one with the image, and type *Bird* in the Name field. Click on OK. Deselect the image.

Export This Document As:

Polly.psd

Format: [Photoshop 5 ◆]

You must export the file in Photoshop 5 format to preserve the layers.

Version 7

Version 7 does not support multiple layers in Photoshop files.

Layers for Web work

Exporting layers to Photoshop where you are creating Web files lets you manipulate each element separately in Photoshop.

3. Option/Alt-click the New Layer button in the Layers palette and type *Cracker* in the Name field. Click OK.

4. Select the Type tool and type *Polly want a cracker?* on the Cracker layer. Format it any way you want. Click on an empty area of the page to deselect the type.

5. Option/Alt-click the New Layer button again and type *Name* in the Name field. Click on OK. Select the Type tool and type *My name isn't Polly.* on the Name layer. Deselect the type. Your screen should resemble Figure 9.16.

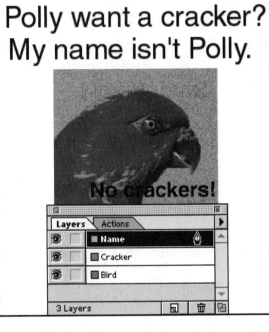

Options

☑ **Include Placed Files**

If you select this option in the Illustrator Format dialog box, Illustrator will embed the image with the file.

Figure 9.16. This Illustrator document contains three layers, one for the image and two for the type.

6. Choose File/Export. Navigate to your Projects folder. Type *Polly.psd* in the Export This Document As field. Select Photoshop 5 from the Format pull-down menu (Macintosh) or from the Save as type menu (Windows), and click on Save.

7. When the Photoshop Options dialog box appears (Figure 9.17), click the Screen button in the Resolution field; this automatically sets the resolution at 72 pixels per inch. If you are going to print the file, select the resolution appropriate for your printer.

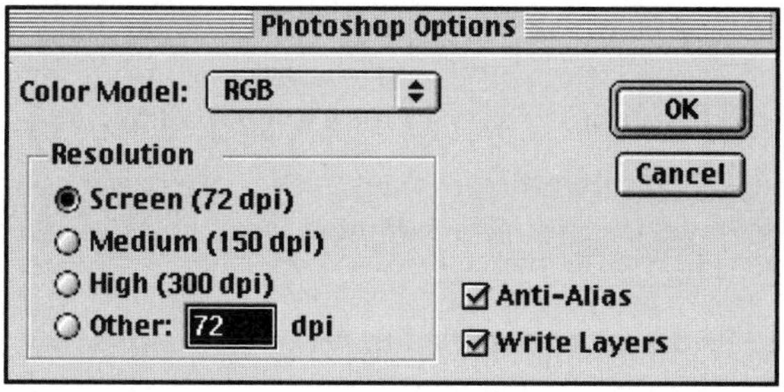

Figure 9.17. The Photoshop file with three separate text layers.

Resolution choices

To print to an ink jet printer, select Medium. To print to a high-resolution imagesetter, choose High.

8. Make sure the Anti-Alias option is selected. To export the individual Illustrator layers to the Photoshop file, select the Write Layers option. Click on OK.

9. Choose File/Save As and save the file as *Polly.ai* in Illustrator 8 format in your Projects folder. Select the Include Placed Images option in the Illustrator Format dialog box.

10. Launch Photoshop, version 4 or 5. Choose File/Open and open the *Polly.psd* file. It appears with the image on one layer and the type on three separate layers.

11. Quit out of Photoshop (File/Quit). Close all files. Don't save your changes.

REVIEW

Sorry!

If you open the *Polly.psd* file in Photoshop 5, the text layers are not editable. The type is rendered when Illustrator exports the file as a Photoshop document.

In this unit you learned that:

1. Objects are arranged in a stacking order with the most recently created objects on top.

2. The Layers palette is used to organize and arrange artwork.

3. Artwork on layers can be hidden or displayed, locked or unlocked.

4. Objects pasted on a layer appear as the frontmost object on the layer.

5. The Paste Remembers Layers command pastes a copied selection, not on the selected layer, but on the layer from which the selection was copied.

6. Objects can be copied and pasted into Photoshop.

7. Layers can be duplicated; this duplicates all the artwork on the layer.

8. The Merge command from the Layers palette menu merges multiple layers into one layer, putting all the artwork from the selected layers on the topmost layer in the Layers palette.

9. The Flatten Artwork command from the Layers palette menu merges all visible layers into the bottommost layer and deletes all hidden layers—and their artwork.

10. The Layers Options dialog box is used to set printing, preview, and display options for a selected layer.

11. Selected objects can be moved from layer to layer by dragging the Selection Square from one layer to another. Pressing the Option/Alt key while dragging the Selection Square, moves *and* duplicates the selected artwork.

12. A Crossed Pencil icon next to a layer indicates that the layer is locked and cannot be edited.

13. Unless the Eye icon is visible next to a layer's name, the artwork on that layer cannot be viewed.

14. The Group Selection tool is used to select individual objects in grouped objects and to select groups themselves.

15. Artwork can be rearranged in a document by dragging layers from one position to another on the Layers palette.

16. If the Template option is selected when placing an image in an Illustrator file, the image appears on a separate, bottommost layer. The layer is dimmed, locked, and will not print.

17. A Photoshop file imported *into* Illustrator flattens all layers before it is imported. When an Illustrator file is exported as a Photoshop 5 file, you have the option of flattening the layers or keeping individual multiple layers.

Gardenia, Joseph Dai

UNIT 10
Tracing, Measuring, and Moving Objects

OVERVIEW

In this unit you will learn how to:
use the Auto Trace tool to trace a template
display ruler guides
create guide objects
measure and move objects a specified distance
use the Info palette
hide and lock objects
work with a grid

TERMS

Auto Trace Tolerance
guide object
Include Placed Files
ruler origin
Tracing Gap

HOW IT WORKS

Place the scanned TIFF image in Illustrator, and use the Auto Trace and Pen tools to create an outline of the flower. Then use the Gradient Mesh tool to fill the mesh points with different colors. Save the file as an Illustrator EPS file so it can be imported into other applications.

THE AUTO TRACE TOOL

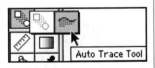

The Auto Trace tool is accessed from the Toolbox by clicking and dragging out on the Blend tool. It is used to trace images, thus creating new PostScript art from bitmapped images. The Auto Trace tool automatically traces any image you bring into Illustrator, with various degrees of success, depending on how simple or complex the image is. To trace complex images, place the image on a separate layer, select Template from the layer's Options dialog box, and use the Pen or Pencil tools to trace the image.

There's bad news and good news about the Auto Trace tool. The good news is that if the image you want to trace is big enough and simple enough—that is, if it contains hard edges that define the tracing area—the Auto Trace tool works very well. The bad news is that if there are any open areas in the image—that is, if the image is somewhat complex, or if it is too small—the Auto Trace tool is useless. You're better off tracing the image with the Pen tool or using a dedicated tracing program like Adobe Streamline.

SETTING TOLERANCE AND GAP PREFERENCES

The accuracy of the Auto Trace tool is affected by the values set in the Type & Auto Tracing Preferences dialog box (Figure 10.1). Both the Auto Trace Tolerance and Tracing Gap values determine what the Auto Trace tool does with the pixels it encounters on its trip around the image.

FYI

There really is no such thing as a "white pixel," but it's helpful to think of the white areas between black pixels as white pixels.

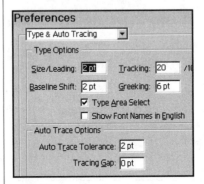

Figure 10.1. A low Auto Trace Tolerance value traces the object more accurately. The higher the Tracing Gap setting, the more anchor points are created.

The Auto Trace Tolerance value controls the number of anchor points created in the tracing process. It can be set from 0 to 10 points. A value of 0 tells Illustrator to skip zero pixels on the template. A value of 10 tells Illustrator to skip large jagged areas of the template by placing fewer anchor points. This creates a smoother line, but makes the trace less precise.

Unit 10 ★ Tracing, Measuring, and Moving Objects

The Tracing Gap value determines the minimum pixel width a gap "white pixels" must be in order to be traced. The higher the Tracing Gap value, the more anchor points are created.

The Tracing Gap value can be set from 0 to 2. A value of 1 tells Illustrator to trace the image by moving from one black pixel to the next, ignoring gaps created by one or less than one white pixel. A value of 2 specifies that the Auto Trace tool will ignore gaps existing between the black pixels of two or less than two white pixels.

TEMPLATE LAYERS

When you place an image in Illustrator that you want to trace, that image should be placed on a Template layer. There it is dimmed so it doesn't confuse the image lines with the tracing lines. If you select the Template option in the Place dialog box, Illustrator automatically dims the image and places it on a Template layer.

You can place just about any kind of image in Illustrator with the Place command, then assign it its own layer. Choose Template from the Layer Options dialog box, which dims the image and lets you trace it with any of the drawing tools. Even if you select the Include Placed Files option when you go to save the document, that image on the Template layer will not print. The only reason to include it with the Illustrator file would be to change it from a nonprinting template image to a normal placed file, or to retrace it on the Template layer.

LINKING FILES

When placing an image from another application such as Photoshop, you have the option of embedding that placed image in the Illustrator document or linking it to the document. If you don't select the Include Placed Files option at the time you save the document, Illustrator imports a low-resolution version of the image into the document and establishes a link to the high-resolution image. When the Illustrator document is printed, Illustrator follows that link to the high-resolution image and prints it instead of the jaggy, low-resolution image. This creates smaller files, but requires that Illustrator be able to access the linked high-resolution image. If you move the image, you will have to reestablish the link when you open or print the file. The good news, however, is that if you modify the placed image in its originating application like Photoshop, Illustrator will automatically update that image in the Illustrator document. To ensure that the placed image is always available to Illustrator, select the Included Placed Files option—if you and your media can live with the large file size.

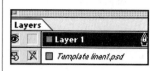

When the *linen.psd* file was placed, Template was selected in the Place dialog box. This told Illustrator to place the image on a separate, Template layer and to dim the image.

Select the Include Placed Files option if the Illustrator document contains placed files and you want those files embedded in the document. Other applications need access to these files, or at least the ability to follow the link, in order to print them.

The Links palette tells you if Illustrator can or cannot locate a linked image.

Macintosh Keystrokes

⌘-N File/New
F7 Window/Show Layers

Windows Keystrokes

Ctrl-N File/New
F7 Window/Show Layers

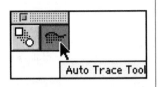

Auto Trace Tool

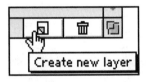

Create new layer

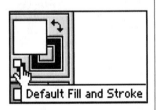

Default Fill and Stroke

Tip

Try deleting the first path you traced and click somewhere else on the object with the Auto Trace tool to get a better trace.

EXERCISE A

1. Create a new file (File/New). Display the Layers palette (F7). Choose File/Place and navigate to the Unit 10 folder on the CD-ROM. Highlight the *Cupid.tif* file. Click the Link button to place only a low-resolution version of the image in the Illustrator document. Click the Template check box to place the image on a Template layer and click on Place.

2. The image appears on a new Template layer with the name of the image, all in italics, indicating that this is a locked layer (Figure 10.2).

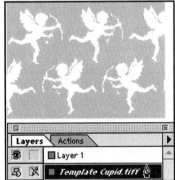

Figure 10.2. Locking the template prevents you from moving it as you trace around it.

3. Click and drag on the Blend tool to select the Auto Trace tool.

4. Choose File/Preferences/Type & Auto Tracing and type 6 in the Auto Trace Tolerance field. Press the Tab key and type 0 in the Tracing Gap field. Click on OK.

5. Click the New Layer button on the Layers palette to create Layer 2. Click on the Default Colors icon in the Toolbox.

6. Click once with the crosshair cursor on the top of any cherub and release the mouse button. The Cupid is outlined by a path (Figure 10.3).

Figure 10.3. Clicking on the edge of an object with the Auto Trace tool automatically traces an outline of the object.

7. Click on the Eye icon next to the Template layer to hide the layer and reveal only the path (Figure 10.4). This gives you a good idea of the accuracy of the trace and lets you see where you have to make corrections.

Macintosh Keystrokes

⌘-P File/Print
⌘-W File/Close

Windows Keystrokes

Ctrl-P File/Print
Ctrl-W File/Close

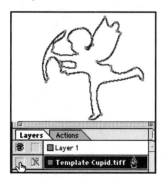

Figure 10.4. Hide the Template layer to display just the outlined path.

8. Click the Fill icon in the Toolbox and click on a color in the Color palette to fill the path you just traced. You may not have traced the area between the wings or the arrows in Cupid's hand, and filling the object is a good way to see what's missing.

9. Drag with the Auto Trace tool along the edge between the wings to create a path between them.

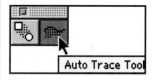

10. Use the Direct Selection tool to adjust the points and direction handles on the path, turning the Template layer on and off so you can compare your drawing to the original.

11. Choose File/Print (Command/Ctrl-P) and print the file. Only the path prints, because nothing on a Template layer will print. Then go back to the file and use the Direct Selection tool to make any corrections in the object's shape,

12. Close this file (File/Close). Don't save your changes.

TRACING PART OF A SHAPE

Sometimes you may want to trace only part of a path or trace the template one path at a time. This allows you to control the fill and stroke options for different parts of an image. To trace part of a template, click and drag the auto trace crosshair cursor from the point where you want the path to start to the position where the path should end. Then release the mouse button. You must start and stop dragging within two pixels of the shape's edge.

Double your view

Choose Window/New Window to display a duplicate of the current drawing page. This lets you work in Artwork view while viewing the illustration in Preview view. Any changes made in one window are automatically applied to the second window.

Macintosh Keystrokes

⌘-N File/New
⌘-Y View/Artwork/
   Preview
⌘-K File/Preferences
   General
⌘-W File/Close

Windows Keystrokes

Ctrl-N File/New
Ctrl-Y View/Artwork/
   Preview
Ctrl-K File/Preferences
   General
Ctrl-W File/Close

1. Create a new file (File/New). Choose Edit/Preferences/General (Command/Ctrl-K) and set the Auto Trace Tolerance to 4 and the Auto Trace Gap to 2. Click on OK. Display the Layers palette (F7).

2. Choose File/Place and navigate to the Unit 10 folder on the CD-ROM. Highlight the *Art.tif* file, select the Link option, and click on Place. The image appears on Layer 1 in the Layers palette.

3. Double-click Layer 1 and select the Dim and Lock options. Deselect the Print option. Click on OK.

4. Click the Default Colors icon in the Toolbox or select another stroke color from the Color palette.

5. Select the Auto Trace tool and click and drag inside one of the designs. Be sure the Auto Trace tool is dragging, then release the mouse button (Figure 10.5). The top part of the design is traced.

Figure 10.5. Dragging with the Auto Trace tool draws a path around part of the image.

6. You can continue to select different pieces of the design and use the Join command to connect the endpoints of each path segment. It would be easier, however, just to click and select the whole design. Or, you could also select the Pen tool, click in one of the endpoints and draw the rest of the design (Figure 10.6).

7. Close this file (File/Close). Don't save your changes.

Figure 10.6. Sometimes is easier to use the Pen tool to clean up a traced image.

MEASURING DISTANCES

There are several ways to measure distances between anchor points when creating precision drawings. The rulers display the unit of measure selected in the Units & Undo Preferences dialog box, and you can use the ruler guides to position objects at exact points on the ruler. The ruler guides can be turned into objects just as objects can be turned into ruler guides. When the Measure tool is used to measure the distance between anchor points or the dimension of an angle, those values are displayed in the Info palette.

DISPLAYING RULERS

When you first launch Illustrator, the rulers are not visible on the drawing page in the new document. To display the rulers, choose View/Show Rulers (Command/Ctrl-R). This command toggles between showing and hiding the rulers.

When you choose View/Show Rulers, a horizontal ruler displaying the unit of measure specified in the Units & Undo Preferences dialog box appears along the top of the page. A vertical ruler appears on the left side of the page. The ruler origin, intersecting dotted lines, is displayed in the corner where the two rulers meet (Figure 10.7).

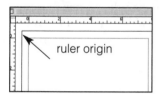

Figure 10.7. When rulers are displayed, they appear along the top and left edges of the drawing page.

RULER ORIGIN

The ruler origin (zero point) on the ruler is useful in establishing precise measurements. For example, to position an object a certain distance from another object, you could use the Move command after drawing the object, or you could use a ruler guide and move the ruler origin so that the ruler guide would be at the 0 position for the x axis (horizontal) and 0 position for the y axis (vertical). This allows you to place a ruler guide at the precise point on the ruler.

RULER GUIDES

Ruler guides are nonprinting guidelines that are "stored" in the rulers. Click on the horizontal ruler and drag a ruler guide down; click on the vertical ruler and draw a ruler guide out.

MOVING AND DELETING RULER GUIDES

Ruler guides must be unlocked from the View menu before they can be moved with any selection tool. To delete a guide, click on it,

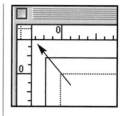

The ruler origin or zero point (dotted lines) is at the intersection of the horizontal and vertical rulers.

Show Guides
✓ **Lock Guides**
Make Guides
Release Guides

The Guides options are available under the View menu. When Lock Guides is selected (the default state), ruler guides are locked and cannot be moved or deleted; they can only be displayed or hidden.

FYI

Objects will snap to a guide if they are moved to within two pixels of the guide. You can customize guides in the Guides & Grid Preferences dialog box.

Macintosh Keystrokes

⌘-N File/New
⌘-R View/Show Rulers
⌘-Y View/Preview/Artwork
⌘-Option-; View/Lock/
    Unlock Guides
⌘-Option-5 View/Release
    Guides

Windows Keystrokes

Ctrl-N File/New
Ctrl-R View/Show Rulers
Ctrl-Y View/Preview/
    Artwork
Ctrl-Alt-; View/Lock/
    Unlock Guides
Ctrl-Alt-5 View/Release
    Guides

When the selection tool's cursor changes to an arrowhead, the guide can be deleted. To delete all the guides at once, choose View/Clear Guides.

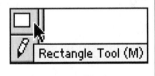

Select the Snap to Point option in the View menu so that when you drag an object with the Selection tool by an anchor point, it will snap to a guide or to an anchor point on another object—if the selected object is moved within two pixels of the guide or anchor point.

and when the cursor turns to an arrowhead, press the Delete key (Macintosh) or the Backspace/Delete key (Windows). To delete all the guides at once, choose View/Clear Guides or drag the unlocked guides back into the rulers.

The Lock Guides option under the View menu determines whether a guide is locked in place or unlocked. Unless Lock Guides is unchecked (the default position), ruler guides cannot be moved. To unlock a guide so that you can reposition it or drag it off the page, choose View/Lock Guides [Command-Option-; (Macintosh) or Ctrl-Alt-; (Windows)] to toggle the Lock Guides command on and off.

EXERCISE C

1. In a new file (File/New), choose View/Show Rulers (Command/Ctrl-R). Display the Swatches palette and choose View/Preview (Command/Ctrl-Y).

2. Use the Rectangle tool to draw a rectangle and fill it with any color.

3. Click on the ruler origin and drag the intersecting lines down and out of the rulers onto the drawing page so that they fit over the left and top segments of the rectangle. Notice that the zero points on the ruler are at the top and left sides of the rectangle (Figure 10.8).

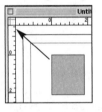

Figure 10.8. Click on the ruler origin and drag the intersection to the upper left corner of the rectangle to set the zero points on the horizontal and vertical rulers at the upper left point of the rectangle.

4. Click inside the vertical ruler and drag a ruler guide out to the one-inch mark on the horizontal ruler.

5. Pull down the View menu and make sure the Snap to Point option is selected.

6. Draw another rectangle and fill it. While it is still selected, click on one of its anchor points and drag it to the ruler guide. The rectangle snaps to the guide (the cursor turns white) and is positioned exactly one inch from the zero point on the horizontal ruler. Remember that the center point is not an anchor point.

7. Choose View/Lock Guides. This toggles the Lock command (default) to the unlock position by removing the check mark before Lock Guides. You can now move and remove the ruler guide.

8. Move the ruler guide to the two-inch position on the horizontal ruler, and then select the second rectangle and move it against the guide at its new position.

9. Close this file (File/Close). Don't save your changes.

CREATING GUIDE OBJECTS

A guide object is a ruler guide that started life as a path in any shape. When an object is changed into a guide, it loses its paint attributes and its path outline becomes a dashed line. To restore guide objects to their original object state, select the guide object and choose View/Release Guides. Guide objects are especially useful when you want to align several objects.

Macintosh Keystrokes

⌘-N File/New
⌘-D Object/Transform/
    Transform Again
⌘-5 View/Make Guides

Windows Keystrokes

Ctrl-N File/New
Ctrl-D Object/Transform/
    Transform Again
Ctrl-5 View/Make Guides

EXERCISE D

1. In a new file (File/New), use the Ellipse tool and press the Shift key while dragging to draw a circle.

2. Pull down the View menu and make sure that the Snap to Point option is checked. This allows you to drag an object by an anchor point and have it snap to a guide—whether it's a ruler guide or a guide object.

3. Use the Selection tool to drag the circle and press the Option/ Alt key to drag a copy of the circle directly down. Before releasing any keys, press the Shift key. Pressing the Option/Alt key creates the duplicate; pressing the Shift key constrains its movement to the vertical axis. When the second circle is directly below the first, release the mouse button, *then* release the Option/Alt and Shift keys.

4. Shift-select both circles and choose Object/Arrange/Transform Again (Command/Ctrl-D). This command repeats the last drawing action; in this case, it duplicates the second circle and moves it directly below the second circle.

5. With the third circle still selected, choose Object/Arrange/ Transform Again to create a fourth circle. Use the Selection tool to drag a marquee around all four circles to select them. Choose Object/Guides/Make (Command/Ctrl-5). The outline of the circles changes from any stroke to a dashed line (Figure 10.9).

FYI

An object must be selected before it can be made into a guide.

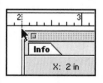

FYI

To drag a guide to a specific point on the ruler, eye the hashmark on the ruler as you drag. Use the Info palette to verify the guide's position.

Figure 10.9. The four circles appear as dashed lines when you use the Make Guides command.

Macintosh Keystrokes

⌘-Option-; View/Lock/
    Unlock Guides
⌘-Option-5 View/Release
    Guides
⌘-W File/Close

Windows Keystrokes

Ctrl-Alt-; View/Lock/
    Unlock Guides
Ctrl-Alt-5 View/Release
    Guides
Ctrl-W File/Close

Pen Tool (P)

Selection Tool (V)

Important info

Once you create guides
from an object, those
guides are locked unless
you select View/Release
Guides.

6. Use the Pen tool to draw a straight line about two inches long. Select the line with the Selection tool and drag it by its left anchor point to the edge of the first circle. The cursor turns white when the line snaps to the guide.

7. Select the line with the Selection tool and drag it, pressing the Alt/Option key to create a duplicate line. Drag the duplicate by its left anchor point to the center line of the second circle.

8. Continue to duplicate and place lines, creating a design similar to that in Figure 10.10.

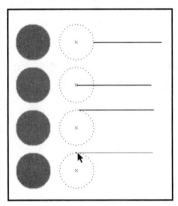

Figure 10.10. Drag a line by its anchor point to snap it to the guide.

9. Pull down the View menu. If Lock Guides is checked, highlight it to select it and to unlock the four circle guides. Then use the Selection tool to Shift-select the four circles, clicking on their outside paths so as not to select the lines. Choose View/Release Guides. The selected circles return to being art objects and are no longer guides (Figure 10.11).

10. Close this file (File/Close). Don't save your changes.

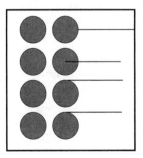

Figure 10.11. Once the guide objects are released, they return to being art objects with fills and strokes.

MEASURING AND MOVING OBJECTS

Use the Measure Tool to calculate the distance or angle between any two anchor points in an illustration. This value appears on the Info palette and is used as the default value in the Move dialog box. Always move an object immediately after measuring it, because any operation performed between measuring and moving changes the values in the Info palette and in the Move dialog box.

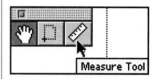
Measure Tool

MEASURE TOOL

This tool calculates the distance from one anchor point to another anchor point and displays this value in the unit of measure specified in the Units & Undo Preferences dialog box. As soon as you click on an anchor point with the Measure tool, the Info palette appears.

INFO PALETTE

The Info palette displays the horizontal and vertical distances from one point to another, the absolute distance from the object's starting point, and the angle from the starting point (Figure 10.12).

FYI

The Measure tool is useful for measuring the length of open paths. Just click on one endpoint, then on the other, and read the length in the W field of the Info palette.

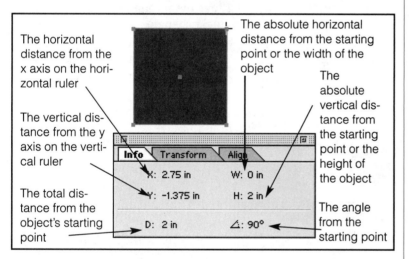

The horizontal distance from the x axis on the horizontal ruler

The vertical distance from the y axis on the vertical ruler

The total distance from the object's starting point

The absolute horizontal distance from the starting point or the width of the object

The absolute vertical distance from the starting point or the height of the object

The angle from the starting point

Info · Transform · Align

X: 2.75 in W: 0 in
Y: -1.375 in H: 2 in
D: 2 in ∠: 90°

Figure 10.12. The Info palette displays the following information about the selected square after clicking first the lower right corner, then the upper right corner with the Measure tool: Its upper right corner is 2.75 inches from the zero point on the horizontal ruler (X) and -1.375 inches down on the vertical ruler (Y).The upper right corner is 2 inches from the lower right corner (H) with a total distance of 2 inches from the two corners (D) and forms a 90-degree angle.

Macintosh Keystrokes

⌘-Option-" View/Snap to
Point
F8 View/Show Info
⌘-Y View/Artwork/Preview
⌘-S File/Save
⌘-W File/Close

Windows Keystrokes

Ctrl-Alt-" View/Snap to
Point
F8 View/Show Info
Ctrl-Y View/Artwork/
Preview
Ctrl-S File/Save
Ctrl-W File/Close

FYI

You can group as many
objects and groups
together as you like into
one group.

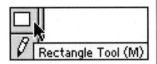

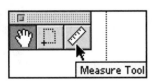

EXERCISE E

1. In a new file (File/New), choose View/Snap to Point. This will force the Measure tool to snap to anchor points and guide objects. Choose inches as the unit of measure (File/Preferences/Units & Undo).

2. Click the Default Colors icon in the Toolbox.

3. Choose Window/Show Info (F8) to display the Info palette. When you display the Info palette in a document where nothing is selected, the X and Y values display the horizontal (X) and vertical (Y) position of the cursor.

4. Press F8 or click in the Close box of the Info palette to close it.

5. Click on the Rectangle tool and click on the drawing page to display the Rectangle dialog box. Type 3 in the Width field and 4 in the Height field. Click on OK.

6. Use the Selection Tool and Option/Alt-drag the rectangle to create another rectangle. Move the second rectangle a few inches away from the original rectangle.

7. Click on the Measure tool (behind the Hand tool), and click on the lower left corner of the first rectangle. Then click on the lower right corner of the second rectangle. The Info palette appears automatically and displays the horizontal distance between the rectangles in the W field and the total distance measured in the D field (Figure 10.13).

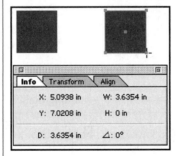

Figure 10.13. The Info palette displays the horizontal (W) and absolute distance (D) between two points of the two rectangles.

8. The X and Y values indicate the right rectangle's horizontal (X) and vertical (Y) position from the x and y axes, or the zero point on the rulers. Because no angle exists between the two selected points, the angle field displays 0.

9. Close this file (File/Close). Don't save your changes.

Unit 10 ★ Tracing, Measuring, and Moving Objects

MOVING OBJECTS

As helpful as the Info palette is, it's often much easier to use the Move command to specify the distance an object should be moved on the drawing page. You can also use the arrow keys to move an object the distance specified in the General Preferences dialog box. This is an excellent way of making lines straight, because you can't constrain a line segment to a 45-degree angle once it is drawn.

Macintosh Keystrokes

⌘-N File/New
⌘-K File/Preferences/
    General
⌘-Z Edit/Undo
⌘-R View/Show Rulers

Windows Keystrokes

Ctrl-N File/New
Ctrl-K File/Preferences/
    General
Ctrl-Z Edit/Undo
Ctrl-R View/Show Rulers

EXERCISE F

1. In a new document (File/New), choose File/Preferences/Units & Undo, and select inches from the Ruler Units pull-down menu.

2. Draw two objects with any of the drawing tools.

3. Click on one of the objects and choose Object/Transform/Move or double-click on the Selection tool to display the Move dialog box (Figure 10.14).

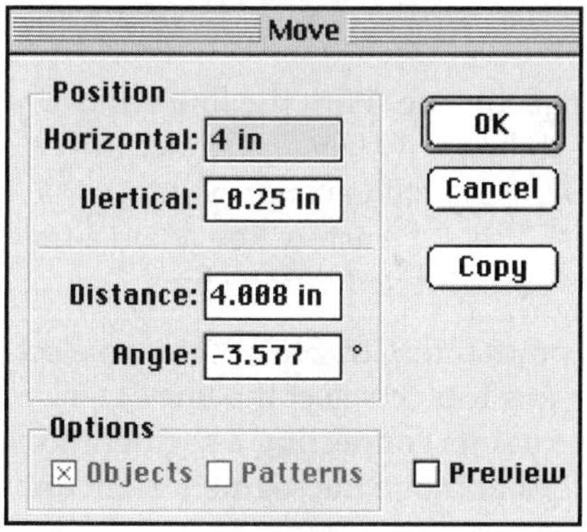

Figure 10.14. The positive number in the Horizontal field indicates that the object will be moved to the right; the negative number in the Vertical field indicates that the object will be moved *down*. The Distance and Angle fields are filled automatically once you input values in the upper panel of the dialog box.

FYI

Negative numbers in the Move dialog box move the selected object down or to the left.

4. Type 3 in the Horizontal and -1 in the Vertical field to move the selected object 3 inches to the right and 1 inch down. Click to select the Preview button. Click on OK. Notice that the object has moved 3 inches to the right and 1 inch down.

5. Choose Edit/Undo Move (Command/Ctrl-Z), and with the object selected, double-click on the Selection tool to display the Move dialog box again. Type in a negative value in the Horizontal field and a positive value in the Vertical field. Click on Copy. Notice that a copy of the selected object moves to the left and up on the drawing page.

6. Display the rulers (Command/Ctrl-R). Choose File/Preferences/General and type .5 in the Cursor Key field under Keyboard Increments. This specifies the distance the cursor will

The value in the Cursor Key field determines how far an object moves when using the arrow keys.

Macintosh Keystrokes

⌘-K File/Preferences/
    General
⌘-Shift-A Edit/Deselect All
⌘-W File/Close

Windows Keystrokes

Ctrl-K File/Preferences/
    General
Ctrl-Shift-A Edit/Deselect
    All
Ctrl-W File/Close

move when you press the arrow keys. The lower the value, the more control you have over the distance the selected object moves when it is being positioned.

7. With the object still selected, press any of the arrow keys on the keyboard, and notice that the object moves half an inch in that direction.

8. Choose File/Preferences/General again and type 0.01 in the Cursor Key field. Use the Pen tool to draw a line with several segments. Don't press the Shift key before clicking; you don't want a perfectly straight line. Once you finish drawing the path, only the last endpoint is selected (Figure 10.15).

Cursor Key: 0.01 in

The smaller the Cursor Key value, the smaller the object or anchor point's movement when moved with the keyboard arrows.

Figure 10.15. As you click with the Pen tool to draw straight lines, only the last anchor point is selected.

9. Zoom in on the last segment of the line. With the line's endpoint still selected, press the right arrow key and notice how only the segment attached to the selected anchor point moves—almost imperceptibly. Press the arrow key again a few more times or until you have straightened out the line.

10. Choose Edit/Deselect All (Command/Ctrl-Shift-A) to deselect the line. Use the Direct Selection Tool to select the line again and Shift-click on two anchor points connecting a segment to select them. Use the arrow keys to move the segment right and left, up and down to change its position.

11. Close this file (File/Close). Don't save your changes.

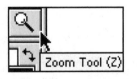
Pen Tool (P)

Zoom Tool (Z)

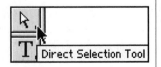
Direct Selection Tool

HIDING AND LOCKING OBJECTS

When you're working with a complex illustration, it's frequently easier to see what you're doing when only the part of the illustration you're working with is visible. You can choose to hide objects while working with other illustration elements and then display them. You can also lock objects, which prevents you from accidentally selecting and editing them.

The Lock/Unlock commands apply only to selected objects. When you lock a layer on the Layers palette, every object on that layer is locked and cannot be edited.

EXERCISE G

Macintosh Keystrokes

⌘-N File/New
⌘-Y View/Artwork/Preview
⌘-3 Object/Hide
  Selection
⌘-Option-3 Object/Show
  All
⌘-2 Object/Lock
⌘-Option-2 Object/
  Unlock All
⌘-H View/Hide Edges

Windows Keystrokes

Ctrl-N File/New
Ctrl-Y View/Artwork/
  Preview
Ctrl-3 Object/Hide
  Selection
Ctrl-Alt-3 Object/Show All
Ctrl-2 Object/Lock
Ctrl-Alt-2 Object/Unlock
  All
Ctrl-H View/Hide Edges

1. Create a new file (File/New). Choose View/Preview (Command/Ctrl-Y). Display the Swatches palette.

2. Reset the Toolbox by pressing the Command/Ctrl and Shift keys while double-clicking on any tool.

3. Select the Rectangle tool and draw two rectangles. Fill each with a different color.

4. Use the Selection Tool to select one rectangle. Choose Object/ Hide Selection (Command/Ctrl-3) to make the selected rectangle disappear.

5. Choose Object/Show All [Command-Option-3 (Macintosh) or Ctrl-Alt-3 (Windows)] to make the hidden rectangle visible on the screen.

6. Select the other rectangle. Choose Object/Lock (Command/ Ctrl-2). Now try selecting it—you can't. Although the locked object is visible, it is not available for editing (Figure 10.16).

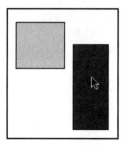

Figure 10.16. Once you lock an object, you cannot select it with any of the selection tools.

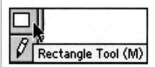

7. Choose Object/Unlock All [Command-Option-2 (Macintosh) or Ctrl-Alt-2 (Windows)] to unlock the object and make it available for editing.

8. Create more objects and practice hiding and showing them and locking and unlocking them.

9. Close this file (Command/Ctrl-W). Don't save your changes.

HIDING SELECTION EDGES

When you select an object, its edges and anchor points appear. If you want to keep the object selected, perhaps to work with it, but do not want to be distracted by the selection edges, choose View/Hide Edges (Command/Ctrl-H). To display the edges again, choose View/Show Edges. When the selection edges of an object are hidden, the object is still visible and selected.

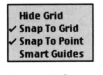

Snap to Grid

You must select Snap to Grid from the View menu to have objects snap to the gridlines.

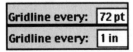

You can override the unit of measure by typing the appropriate abbreviation in the Gridline every field (top). Illustrator will automatically convert it to the established unit of measure (bottom).

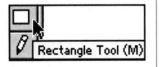

WORKING WITH A GRID

When you select the Show Grid command from the View menu, a grid appears behind all the artwork. Like guides and guide objects, a grid is a series of nonprinting lines to which you can snap objects for alignment purposes. Unlike guides, however, gridlines cannot be moved or deleted. Customize grids in the Guides & Grid Preferences dialog box.

The advantage of using a grid behind the artwork is that you can lay out objects symmetrically by having them snap to the grid at a specified location by positioning the gridlines and subdivision lines at the appropriate intervals.

EXERCISE H

1. In a new document (File/New), choose File/Preferences/General (Command/Ctrl-K) and deselect the Use Bounding Box option.

2. Choose File/Preferences/Units & Undo and select inches as the unit of measure. Choose View/Show Grid (Command/Ctrl-"). Choose File/Preferences/Guides & Grid to display the Guides & Grid Preferences dialog box (Figure 10.17).

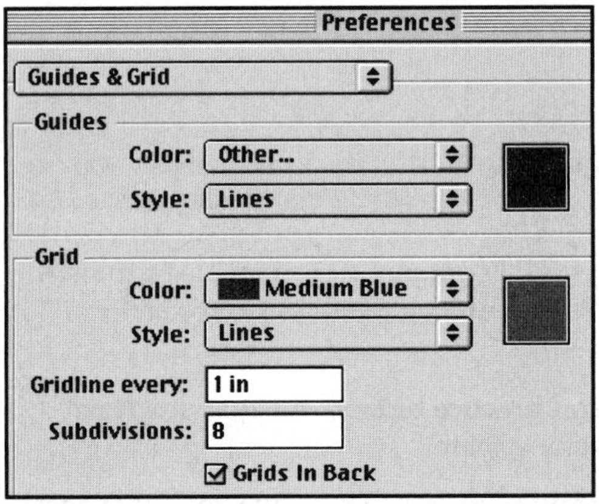

Figure 10.17. The Guides & Grid Preferences dialog box lets you set color and style options for ruler guides and for the gridlines.

3. Select Color and Style options in the Grid field, and set the primary gridlines to appear every 1 inch with eight subdivisions. Make sure Grids in Back is selected so that the grid will appear behind any artwork. Click on OK. The grid appears on the page. Choose View/Snap to Grid.

4. Use the Rectangle tool to draw a square that fits between the first two gridlines on the left side of the page. Assign it a fill

and stroke color. The strokes will create the lines between the calendar boxes you will be creating.

5. Display the Info palette (F8). The W field should read 1 in and the H field 1 in (Figure 10.18). If the values in the Info palette are not correct, move or resize the rectangle until the correct readings appear.

Macintosh Keystrokes

F9 Window/Show Info
⌘-D Object/Transform/
   Transform Again
⌘-Shift-; View/Snap to
   Grid

Windows Keystrokes

F9 Window/Show Info
Ctrl-D Object/Transform/
   Transform Again
Ctrl-Shift-; View/Snap to
   Grid

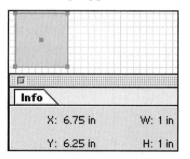

Figure 10.18. Because the grid is set for one-inch increments and Snap to Grid is selected, dragging through one set of gridlines creates an object one inch wide. The X and Y values specify the object's position on the horizontal (x) and vertical (y) axes.

6. Drag the selected square while pressing the Option/Alt key to create a duplicate square to the right of the original square in the next one-inch grid space. Choose Object/Transform/Transform Again five times to create seven squares on the horizontal axis.

7. Drag a selection marquee around the seven squares and drag down into the next set of grids, pressing the Option/Alt key to create a duplicate set of squares. Choose Object/Transform/Transform Again three times to create a total of five lines of squares (Figure 10.19).

Figure 10.19. The Repeat Transform command positions all the squares exactly one inch apart on the grid.

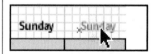

Option/Alt-drag point type and when it snaps to the grid, use the Repeat Transform command.

8. Use the Type tool to create the days of the week and position them on the left side of the squares above the top row, snapping the point type to the grid. You will have to turn off the Snap to Grid option to center some of the days over the square.

9. Use the Guides & Grid Preferences dialog box to change the Subdivisions value to 14. This creates 14 spaces across and 14 spaces down inside the one-inch grid and gives you more room to move the objects and still snap to the grid.

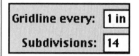

Tip

Drawing objects using the Snap to Grid feature and the Repeat Transform command can be a quick way to create symmetrical illustrations.

10. Repeat for the numbers, snapping the point type to the lower right area of the grid in each square. Delete any unnecessary squares. Your screen should resemble Figure 10.20.

11. Close this file. Don't save your changes.

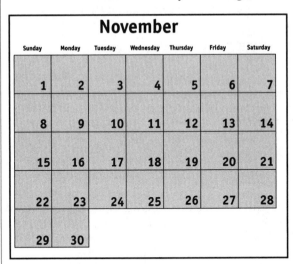

November						
Sunday	Monday	Tuesday	Wednesday	Thursday	Friday	Saturday
1	2	3	4	5	6	7
8	9	10	11	12	13	14
15	16	17	18	19	20	21
22	23	24	25	26	27	28
29	30					

Figure 10.20. Using the grid, the boxes and numbers are perfectly aligned.

REVIEW

In this unit you learned that:

1. Setting Tolerance and Gap preferences affects the precision of the Auto Trace tool.

2. Images imported as templates appear on a locked, dimmed, Template layer.

3. Dragging with the Measure tool displays the drag distance in the Info palette.

4. Ruler guides can be used to precisely position objects.

5. Any object can be converted to a guide object; it then functions just like any horizontal or vertical ruler guide.

6. Objects can be moved horizontally, vertically, or at a specified distance in the Move dialog box.

7. Objects can be displayed or hidden, locked or unlocked; hidden and unlocked objects cannot be selected.

8. Selection edges can be hidden while still keeping the object(s) selected.

9. Grids are helpful in creating symmetrically arranged objects.

UNIT 11
TRANSFORMATION TOOLS

OVERVIEW

In this unit you will learn how to:
use the transformation tools to scale, rotate,
    skew, reflect, and shear objects
repeat transformations
distort objects

TERMS

point of origin
reflect
rotate
scale
shear
skew

HOW IT WORKS

Create a single leaf. Scale it using the Copy option, and then use the Repeat Transform command to create more scaled leaves. Select all the leaves; rotate and reflect
them using the Copy option. Fill leaves with different colors and gradients. Continue to duplicate and transform the objects until you have enough for a background. The unit type was converted to outlines with a .75 stroke and no fill
applied.

179

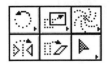

The transformation tools are the Rotate, Scale, and Twirl tools (top) and Reflect, Shear, and Reshape tools (bottom).

No center point?

To display a selected object's center point, click the Show Center button in the Attributes palette.

The Origin Pointer. When the object is transformed, it will be transformed from this point, which remains stationary during the transformation.

FYI

Option/Alt-clicking with the Scale, Rotate, Reflect, and Shear tools displays their respective dialog boxes and sets the point of origin for that function at the point where you clicked.

TRANSFORMING OBJECTS

Transforming an object means changing its size, shape and/or orientation without changing its color characteristics. When you select a transformation tool (Rotate, Twirl, Scale, Reflect, Shear, and Free Transform tools), you can drag on the page to eyeball the transformation, transform the object using the bounding box, or double-click on the transformation tool and enter values in that tool's dialog box.

Using the dialog box gives you the option of creating a copy of the transformed object, leaving the original object untouched. Otherwise, pressing the Option/Alt key when dragging with a tool creates a duplicate (transformed) object.

DEFINING THE POINT OF ORIGIN

Whenever you transform an object, you do so in relation to a fixed point on or around the object. This fixed point is called the *point of origin*; the object's center point is the default point of origin. Click on another anchor point to specify that point as the point of origin.

ORIGIN POINTER

If you click on a page or on an object with a transformation tool, you set an Origin Pointer. When you drag to transform the object, the transformation starts at that Pointer and the object remains stationary there (Figure 11.1).

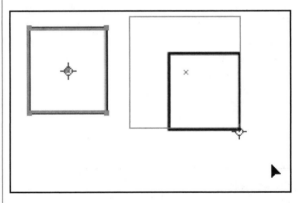

Figure 11.1. When the rectangle was selected and the Scale tool selected, the Origin Pointer appears in the center of the object (left). Clicking with the Scale tool on the lower right corner set the Origin Pointer there (right). Dragging with the Scale tool outward enlarged the rectangle from that point of origin.

Unit 11 ★ Transformation Tools

FREE TRANSFORM TOOL

To scale or rotate an object visually, select the object or objects and select the Free Transform tool. Because the Free Transform tool works only on the Bounding Box handles, Illustrator displays those handles once you select the Free Transform tool even if you haven't selected that option in the General Preferences dialog box.

Drag a Bounding Box handle to reduce or enlarge the object or drag *outside* a Bounding Box handle to rotate the selected object from that point. If you Shift-drag a handle, the object is proportionately scaled.

RESHAPE TOOL

The Reshape tool stretches, bends, and pinches paths to reshape them. Unlike the other transformation tools, the Reshape tool does not transform around any point of origin. Instead, it stretches the selected path that remains anchored by the two points on either side of the path segment.

When you click with the Reshape tool on a section of the path that does not have an anchor point, an anchor point is added. Drag the new anchor point to reshape the path.

SCALING OBJECTS

You can reduce or enlarge an object by scaling it either horizontally, vertically, or both horizontally and vertically. Unless you specify a point of origin, all scaling takes place from the center point of the selected object. If you click on any anchor point of the object to set an Origin Pointer, scaling takes place from that point inward or outward, depending on the direction you drag.

SCALE TOOL

To scale visually with the Scale tool, select the object, click on the Scale tool, and click on the object to set the point of origin. Release the mouse button. Move the cursor away from the object, then click and drag inward to reduce the size of the object or drag outward to enlarge the object.

To scale with the Bounding Box, drag a Bounding Box handle in or out to resize the object. Pressing the Option/Alt key scales the object from the center instead of from the opposite handle. Pressing the Shift key while dragging on any Bounding Box handle resizes the object proportionately.

To specify exact scaling dimensions, use the Scale dialog box. To scale visually, click and drag an object with the Scale tool or with the Free Transform tool.

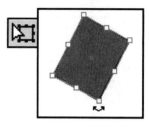

Drag with the Free Transform tool to scale or rotate an object. Press the Command-Option-Shift keys (Macintosh) or Ctrl-Alt-Shift keys (Windows) while dragging a handle to change the perspective of the object.

Version 7

There is no Free Transform tool inversion 7.

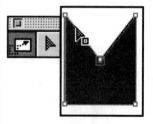

Drag with the Reshape tool to reshape paths via anchor points and direction handles.

FYI

Option/Alt-click on the object with the Scale tool to set the point of origin and display the Scale dialog box.

Macintosh Keystrokes

⌘-N File/New
⌘-Z Edit/Undo

Windows Keystrokes

Ctrl-N File/New
Ctrl-Z Edit/Undo

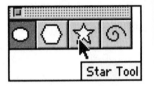

Star Tool

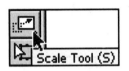

Scale Tool (S)

FYI

When scaling with the Bounding Box, you cannot set a point of origin. All scaling takes place from the handle you're dragging. Press the Option/Alt key to scale from the center of the Bounding Box.

EXERCISE A

1. Choose File/New (Command/Ctrl-N) and display the Swatches palette. Use the Fill and Stroke icons in the Toolbox to select fill and stroke colors. Use the Units & Undo Preferences dialog box to select inches as the unit of measure.

2. Select the Star tool and click on the page to display the Create Star dialog box. Create a five-pointed star using the values in Figure 11.2 and click on OK. A star appears selected on the drawing page.

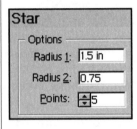

Figure 11.2. These values will create a five-pointed star.

3. With the star still selected, select the Scale tool. Then click on one of the star points and drag away from the object to enlarge it; drag toward the object to reduce it. Notice that in dragging this way, the star is becoming distorted. Choose Edit/Undo (Command/Ctrl-Z) to restore the star to its original shape.

4. Select the star. Select the Scale tool and notice that the point of origin appears at the star's center. Once you start dragging outside of the star, the cursor changes to an arrowhead. Choose Edit/Undo to restore the original star.

5. Click on one of the star points and drag away from the center. The original star is displayed as the object is enlarged (Figure 11.3). Release the mouse button.

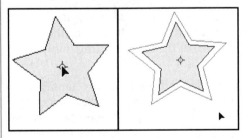

Figure 11.3. One click with the Scale tool sets the point of origin for the scale (left). The object will be enlarged or reduced from this point. When you drag with the scaling cursor, the original object (inside star) remains displayed as it is reduced or enlarged.

Unit 11 ★ Transformation Tools

6. Choose Edit/Undo Scale (Command/Ctrl-Z) to restore the original image.

7. Select the star again. Click with the Scale tool on any star point and drag away from the star. Notice that dragging away from the object enlarges it; dragging toward the object reduces it. Likewise, depending on the direction in which you drag, the star can become distorted.

8. Choose Undo Scale (Command/Ctrl-Z) until you return to the original star. Double-click on the Scale tool to display the Scale dialog box. Click on the Preview button to see what the scaled object will look like. Click the Uniform button to select it and type 50 in the percent field to reduce the object to half its current size. Select Scale Stroke Width to scale the stroke along with the object. This avoids heavy strokes around smaller objects. Then click the Copy button to create a copy of the selected object without changing the original object (Figure 11.4).

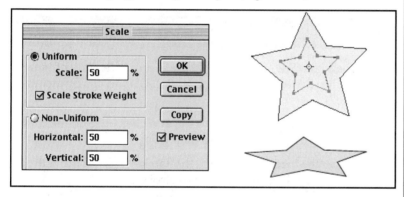

Figure 11.4. Double-clicking on the Scale tool displays the Scale dialog box (left). Click on Copy to exit the dialog box and display a copy of the selected object, now scaled to the specified size (top). Selecting non-uniform values creates a star that is wider than it is long (bottom).

9. Use the Selection tool to move the small star onto a blank area of the drawing page. Double-click on the Scale tool again to display the Scale dialog box.

10. Click on the Non-Uniform button and type 150 in the Horizontal field to enlarge the object 50% beyond its current size in a horizontal (wide) direction. Type 50 in the Vertical field to reduce the object to 50% of its current size in a vertical (high) direction. Click on OK. Your screen should resemble the bottom star in Figure 11.4.

11. Close this file (File/Close). Don't save your changes.

Macintosh Keystrokes

⌘-Z Edit/Undo
⌘-W File/Close

Windows Keystrokes

Ctrl-Z Edit/Undo
Ctrl-W File/Close

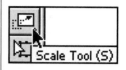

FYI

If you click in the Scale Stroke weight box, the stroke of any stroked path will be scaled along with the scaled object.

Version 7

In version 7 the Scale Line Weight option appears in the Scale dialog box.

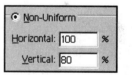

Scaling values

If you scale using the Non-Uniform option, type 100 in the Horizontal or Vertical fields to constrain the scale to the direction that isn't 100%. For example, scaling a shadow vertically 120%, while leaving the Horizontal value at 100%, lengthens the object without adding to its width.

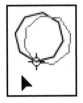

Click on an anchor point with the Rotate tool to set the point of origin.

ROTATING OBJECTS

As with the Scale function, there are several ways to rotate an object in Illustrator:

▲ Rotate by dragging a selected object around the object's midpoint, around a point of origin, or around another anchor point with the Rotate tool.

▲ Specify an angle of rotation in the Rotate dialog box.

▲ Rotate an object with the Free Transform tool.

TRANSFORM AGAIN

Once you transform an object, you can repeat the transformation using the Transform/Transform Again command. If you copied the object when you first transformed it, a transformed copy of the *transformed object*, not the original object, is made. You must choose this command immediately after you transform the object.

EXERCISE B

1. In a new file (File/New), make sure inches is the unit of measure (File/Preferences/Units & Undo). Display the Swatches palette.

2. Click on the Ellipse tool to select it, and click once on the drawing page to display the Ellipse dialog box.

3. Type 1 in the Width field; press the Tab key and type 2 in the Height field. Click on OK. Fill and stroke the oval.

4. Click once on the Rotate tool and click on the lower point of the oval. This sets the point around which the oval will rotate (point of origin).

5. Move the arrowhead cursor away from the oval and click. Once you have begun to drag, press the Alt/Option key. Drag to rotate the oval about 30° to the left. Release the mouse button (Figure 11.5).

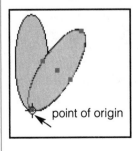

point of origin

Figure 11.5. To rotate an object from a specific point, first click that point with the Rotate tool, then move away from the object and drag. Pressing the Option key while dragging creates a rotated copy of the original object.

6. Choose Object/Transform/Transform Again (Command/Ctrl-D) to repeat the copy/rotate action. Continue to press Command-D until the rotated ovals create a flower (Figure 11.6).

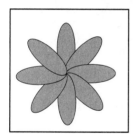

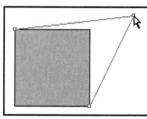

Figure 11.6. The first oval was Option/Alt-rotated. Then the Repeat Transform command created the rest of the flower's petals.

7. Choose Edit/Select All (Command/Ctrl-A) and press the Delete key.

8. Use the Rectangle tool to draw a square (Shift-drag). Deselect it (Command/Ctrl-Shift-A).

9. Use the Direct Selection tool to select the square and click on one of the corner anchor points to select it. Drag that anchor point out so that the square becomes reshaped into a kite (Figure 11.7). Use the Pencil tool to draw a tail on the kite.

Figure 11.7. Select the square with the Direct Selection tool. Then select one anchor point and drag it to reshape the square into a kite.

10. Choose Edit/Select All (Command/Ctrl-A) and group all the objects (Command/Ctrl-G). Leave the group selected.

11. Click on the Rotate tool to select it. Click anywhere on the page and drag to rotate the kite from its center point. Release the mouse button.

12. Now click with the Rotate tool on one of the selected anchor points of the kite. This sets the point of origin around which the kite (object) will rotate.

13. Move the arrowhead away from the point you just clicked and drag in a circular motion to rotate the kite.

14. Press the Shift key while rotating to constrain the rotation to 45 degrees.

15. Close this file (File/Close). Don't save your changes.

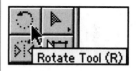

Rotate Tool (R)

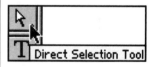

Direct Selection Tool

Pencil Tool (N)

FYI

Before selecting with the Direct Selection tool, always deselect first. You cannot select individual paths while an object is still selected with the Selection tool.

Macintosh Keystrokes

⌘-N File/New
⌘-Z Edit/Undo
⌘-W File/Close

Windows Keystrokes

Ctrl-N File/New
Ctrl-Z Edit/Undo
Ctrl-Z File/Close

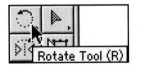

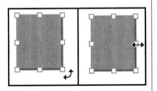

The round arrows that appear when you select the Free Transform tool (left) are used for rotating an object. The horizontal arrows (right) are used for scaling.

EXERCISE C

1. In a new file (File/New), use any of the drawing tools to create an object. Keep the object selected.

2. Double-click on the Rotate tool to display the Rotate dialog box.

3. Type 35 in the Angle field. Click on the Copy button to rotate a copy of the original object 35 degrees from its center point to the left.

4. With the copy still selected, double-click on the Rotate tool again. Type –75 in the Angle field and click on OK to rotate the selection 75 degrees to the right.

5. Choose Edit/Undo (Command/Ctrl-Z). Select the object with the Selection tool. Select the Free Transform tool. Click and drag outside one of the Bounding Box handles to display the rounded arrows. Drag to rotate the object.

6. Close this file (File/Close). Don't save your changes.

TRANSFORM COMMANDS

All the transform commands are available from the Object menu when an object is selected. Choosing a transform command displays the same dialog box you see when you click on the page with a transformation tool.

TRANSFORM EACH

When you have multiple objects selected, an invisible bounding box appears around those multiple-selected objects (unless you turn on the Bounding Box option). If you use the Scale tool or the Rotate tool to transform (scale, rotate) them, that invisible bounding box is also transformed, scaling or rotating all the selected objects as if they were one object. The Transform Each command allows you to scale and/or rotate and/or move each selected object without transforming the Bounding Box because the transformation occurs relative to the objects' center points.

If you select the Random option in the Transform Each dialog box, Illustrator will randomly transform the objects within the range of the values you selected in the Scale, Rotate, and Move fields. For example, if you set the Horizontal scale value to 200% (doubling the size of the selected objects), Illustrator will scale the objects using different values between 100% and 200%.

EXERCISE D

1. In a new file (File/New), create three objects on the page and use the Selection tool to draw a selection marquee around them.

2. Choose Object/Transform/Transform Each. In the Transform Each dialog box, click to select the Preview box at the bottom of the dialog box. This allows you to see how the values you input will affect the selected objects.

3. Type 50 in the Horizontal and Vertical Scale fields. Type values in the Horizontal and Vertical Move fields. Notice how those values affect the selected objects. Make changes and click on OK (Figure 11.8).

4. Close this file. Don't save your changes.

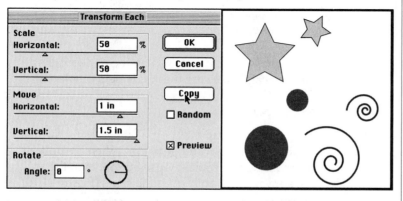

Figure 11.8. The three objects are each scaled and moved.

REFLECT TOOL

Use the Reflect tool or the Reflect command to create a mirror image of an object. Illustrator reflects across the axis that runs through the selected anchor point. Press the Option/Alt key or click on the Copy button in the Reflect dialog box to create the mirror image.

Because the Reflect command flips only what is selected, you can select part of a path with the Direct Selection tool and flip only that section. Or you could Shift-select several objects in a drawing and flip (reflect) only them. To create a mirror image of the whole object, select the object with the Selection tool to ensure that all the paths are selected.

Macintosh Keystrokes

⌘-N File/New
⌘-J Object/Path/Join
⌘-W File/Close

Windows Keystrokes

Ctrl-N File/New
Ctrl-J Object/Path/Join
Ctrl-W File/Close

Preview update

To update the preview in a dialog box, press the Tab key after making a selection. Otherwise, you have to deselect, then select the Preview check box again.

Reflecting with the Free Transform tool

To reflect a selected object with the Free Transform tool, click on the Bounding Box handle at the opposite corner of where you want to reflect (left) and drag until the object is reflected (right). You will see the object cross over as you drag. If you don't drag an opposite handle, you will scale, not reflect the object.

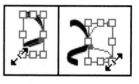

Macintosh Keystrokes

⌘-O File/Open
⌘-Y View/Preview/Artwork
⌘-Shift-A Edit/Deselect All
⌘-J Object/Path/Join

Windows Keystrokes

Ctrl-O File/Open
Ctrl-Y View/Preview/
   Artwork
Ctrl-Shift-A Edit/Deselect
   All
Ctrl-J Object/Path/Join

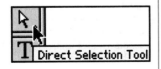

Selection Tool (V)

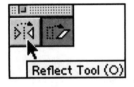

Reflect Tool (O)

Direct Selection Tool

EXERCISE E

1. Open (Command-O) the *Vase.ai* file in the Unit 11 folder on the CD-ROM. Choose View/Artwork (Command/Ctrl-Y). The screen displays one side of a vase.

2. Select the object with the Selection tool. Select the Reflect tool (behind the Shear tool) and click on the endpoint at the end of the horizontal line at the bottom of the drawing (Figure 11.9).

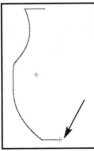

Figure 11.9. Selecting the Reflect tool displays the center point for the selected object. Click on the anchor point from which you want the object reflected (flipped).

3. Double-click on the Reflect tool to display the Reflect dialog box. Click on Vertical. Make sure the Angle field displays 90 degrees. Click on Copy to create a reflected copy of the object from the selected point.

4. Use the Selection tool to drag the copy while pressing the Shift key to constrain the drag to a straight path. When the bottom horizontal lines meet, release the mouse button, then the Shift key. The vase appears with both sides the same (Figure 11.10).

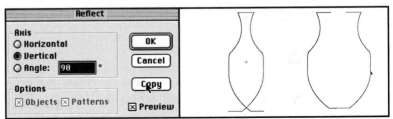

Figure 11.10. Reflecting the object from the bottom point creates a copy that must be dragged into position to complete the artwork. These are still two open paths that must be joined.

5. Deselect the path (Command/Ctrl-Shift-A). Use the Direct Selection tool to draw a selection marquee around the two endpoints at the top of the vase. Choose Object/Path/Join (Command/Ctrl-J) to create a segment that joins the two paths.

6. Drag another selection marquee around the two endpoints at the bottom of the vase where you dragged the reflected copy. Choose Object/Path/Join (Command/Ctrl-J) to create a closed path. Use the Selection tool to move the vase, now a single closed path, around the page.

7. Close this file (Command/Ctrl-W). Don't save your changes.

SHEAR TOOL

What the rest of the world calls "skew," Adobe Illustrator calls "shear." The Shear tool is used to slant an object along a specified axis. It is most useful for creating shadows when the Option/Alt-key is pressed while dragging with the Shear tool.

The Shear Tool is tricky to use, especially when you are skewing a path with many segments. It's sometimes easier to access the Shear dialog box, plug in a small angle like 10 degrees, and then repeat the transformation until the object is slanted properly.

Another way to control the skewing is to shear along an angle that is a multiple of 45 degrees in relation to the current x axis by pressing the Shift key while dragging with the Shear Tool. Choose View/Smart Guides to display the 45° guideline along which you can drag. Pressing the Shift and Option/Alt keys while dragging with the Shear Tool will create a copy of the original object (Option/Alt) and constrain the shearing (Shift).

DISTORTING OBJECTS

To vary the size and shape (perspective) of an object (or objects), first select it with the Selection tool. Select the Free Transform tool, and begin dragging on a corner handle (not a side handle). Once you start dragging, press the Command key (Macintosh) or Ctrl key (Windows) and continue dragging to distort the shape of the object.

EXERCISE F

1. Create a new document (File/New) and use the Pen tool to draw something that resembles a palm tree. Make sure you have a closed path and fill it with a tropical green color.

2. Select the tree with the Direct Selection tool. Select the Reshape tool and click on the edge of a path to place a new anchor point. Drag the anchor point to reshape the path.

Macintosh Keystrokes

⌘-J Object/Path/Join
⌘-W File/Close

Windows Keystrokes

Ctrl-J Object/Path/Join
Ctrl-W File/Close

Because the two endpoints overlap, you will not be able to see them, but dragging a selection marquee will select both points.

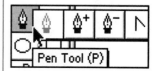

Click on the Pen tool to display other pen tools.

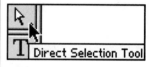

Macintosh Keystrokes

F7 Window/Show Layers
F10 View/Show/Hide
    Stroke

Windows Keystrokes

F7 Window/Show Layers
F10 View/Show/Hide
    Stroke

3. Select the tree and click on the Shear tool. Click on the base of the tree to set the point of origin (Figure 11.11).

Figure 11.11. Click with the Shear tool on the base of the tree to set the point from which the object will be skewed.

4. With the Shear tool still selected, move the cursor away from the base of the tree and drag, pressing the Option/Alt key to create a (slanted) duplicate of the object. When you have the slant you want, release the mouse button, *then* the Option/Alt key (Figure 11.12).

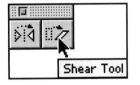

Shear Tool

Figure 11.12. Dragging from a selected point with the Shear tool while pressing the Option/Alt key creates a slanted copy of the original object.

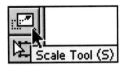

Create new layer

5. The Sheared duplicate appears selected. Fill it with black.

6. Display the Layers palette (F7). Click on the New Layer icon on the Layers palette to create Layer 2. Click the Selection Square on Layer 1 and drag it up to Layer 2, placing the sheared tree on a separate layer.

7. Double-click on Layer 2 and type *Shadow* in the Name field. Click on OK.

Tip

The further away from the point of origin that you start dragging with the Shear tool, the more control you have over it.

8. Because the shadow must appear behind the tree, click on the *Shadow* layer and drag it down below Layer 1 to change the stacking order (Figure 11.13).

9. On the *Shadow* layer, select the black tree and double-click the Scale tool. Select Uniform and type 80 in the Scale field. Click on OK.

Scale Tool (S)

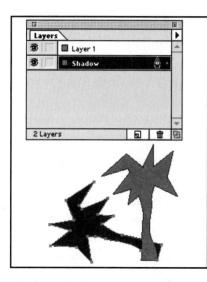

Figure 11.13. Drag the Shadow layer down below Layer 1 to position the sheared shadow behind the green tree.

Tip
You will have more control over the shear process if you start dragging farther from the point of origin.

10. Use the Selection tool to drag the black shadow so that the base of the shadow matches the base of the tree. You may want to experiment with scaling and rotating values to get a realistic shadow. Fill the black tree with a black-and-white gradient. Your screen should resemble Figure 11.14. Enjoy the beach!

11. Close this file (Command/Ctrl-W). Don't save your changes.

Figure 11.14. Scale the sheared shadow and fill it with a gradient.

REVIEW

In this unit you learned that:

1. Transforming objects means to scale, shear, rotate, twirl, reflect, or reshape objects.

2. All transformation occurs from a specified point of origin.

3. The point of origin is set by clicking anywhere on the page.

4. Pressing the Option/Alt key while dragging with the Scale tool scales the object from the center instead of from the opposite handle.

5. The Free Transform tool scales and/or rotates an object from its Bounding Box handles.

6. Selected objects can be transformed by dragging on a point of origin or by using the tool's dialog box.

7. Selected objects can be transformed using the commands under the Object menu.

8. The Transform Each command transforms individual objects within the same Bounding Box without transforming the Bounding Box contents as a single unit.

9. The Reflect tool can create a mirror image of a selection.

10. Pressing the Command/Ctrl key while dragging with the Free Transform tool distorts the object while transforming it.

11. The Shear tool slants or skews objects at a specified angle.

UNIT 12
Transformation Filters

OVERVIEW

In this unit you will learn how to:
use filters to enhance artwork created with basic
  shapes
use the Transform palette
align objects using the Align palette
arrange objects in the stacking order

TERMS
align
arrange
distribute
transform

HOW IT WORKS

Use the Star tool to draw stars of varying sizes and with different numbers of
points. Apply the Zig Zag and Punk & Bloat filters using various Amount and
Ridges values. Use the Smooth and Corner Points option for different effects.

TRANSFORMATION FILTERS

Although the transformation tools are powerful, in that you can enter values in a dialog box or visually transform a path or entire object, sometimes it's easier and quicker to use one of Illustrator's Distort filters to transform an object.

All of the Distort filters have dialog boxes with a Preview option, letting you make adjustments in real time. However, they do not contain a Copy button, so it's a good idea to duplicate an object before applying any of the filters.

TWIRLING POINTS

Illustrator provides two ways of twirling path points, the Twirl tool and the Twirl filter. Both twirl points around an object's center, but the Twirl tool, with its drag capabilities, lets you see the effect of the twirl as you drag, as well as enter values in the Twirl dialog box. The Twirl filter has only the Twirl dialog box, which does not contain a Preview option.

TWIRL TOOL

Access the Twirl tool by dragging on the Rotate tool. Select an object and click on any anchor point. As you drag in a clockwise motion around the center of the object, the edges curve around the center of the object. The more you turn (drag), the more twirls are created (Figure 12.1).

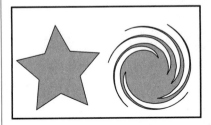

Figure 12.1. Clicking on a point of the star with the Twirl tool and dragging around the center of the star a few times creates the twirls.

TWIRL FILTER

To use the Twirl filter, select the object and choose Filter/Distort/Twirl. Type a value in the Angle field—at least 50 to see anything—and click on OK. The greater the value in the Angle field, the more pronounced the twirl (Figure 12.2).

Figure 12.2. The Twirl filter with an Angle value of 50 gently twirls the edges of the star.

Preview update

Press the Tab key in any dialog box with a selected Preview button to update the preview.

Distort	▶	Punk & Bloat...
Pen and Ink	▶	Roughen...
Stylize	▶	Scribble and Twea
		Twirl...
Artistic	▶	Zig Zag...

The Distort filters transform paths, points, and selected objects. They work only on vector images, not on raster images, such as Photoshop images placed in the document.

The Twirl tool appears next to the Rotate tool in the Toolbox and on a Tearoff menu.

DISTORT FILTERS

The Distort filters provide an easy way to create interesting effects with all kinds of objects. If you don't like the distortion, there's always the Undo command.

PUNK & BLOAT

The Punk & Bloat filter contains two distortion options for curving objects inward and outward from their anchor points. The Punk filter curves the object inward and the Bloat filter curves the object outward (Figure 12.3).

Dragging the slider to the left punks the selection; dragging to the right bloats it.

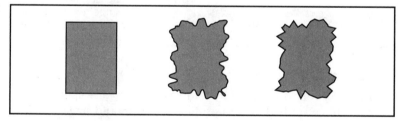

Figure 12.3. The original object (left) is distorted by the Punk option (center) and Bloat option (right) in the Punk & Bloat filter dialog box.

ROUGHEN FILTER

The Roughen filter creates a jagged edge to a path by moving the anchor points in random directions. The Smooth option creates softer edges than the Corner option, which creates sharper edges. You can also set the size of the distortion and the details per inch in the Roughen dialog box (Figure 12.4).

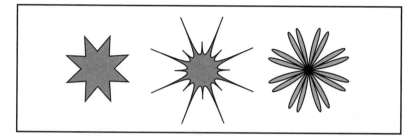

In the Roughen dialog box, the Size slider controls the size of the distortion. The Detail slider controls the number of paths per inch needed to roughen the path.

Figure 12.4. The original object (left) is distorted by the Roughen filter using the Smooth option (center) and Corner option (right) in the Roughen dialog box.

SCRIBBLE AND TWEAK

The Scribble and Tweak filter does not add anchor points to an object, but moves the existing anchor points and their direction handles in random directions and at a random distance from the original position. The only difference between the two filters is that the Scribble option moves anchor points and direction handles a specified percentage of the longest segment, whereas the Tweak option measures those movements in points. Fortunately, the Preview option saves you the trouble of figuring this out (Figure 12.5).

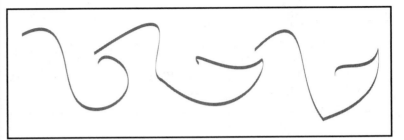

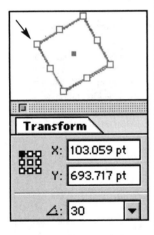

Click a square to set the point from which the transformation occurs.

Figure 12.5. The original object (left) is distorted by the Scribble and Tweak filter using the same values for the Scribble option (center) as for the Tweak option (right).

ZIG ZAG

The Zig Zag filter distorts an open or closed path by adding anchor points and then moving some of those points upward or downward from the line or to the right or left of the line. The effect depends on whether you choose the Smooth Point or Corner Point option (Figure 12.6).

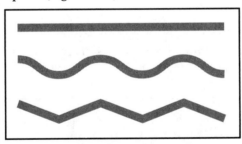

Figure 12.6. The original line (top) is distorted by the Zig Zag filter using the Smooth Point option (center) and the Corner Point option (bottom).

Clicking the upper left Reference handle rotates the square 30° from the upper left Bounding Box handle.

TRANSFORM PALETTE

Because it is very difficult to transform objects to any specification after you have applied the Distort filters, you should size the object as closely as possible to its intended size before applying the filter. An easy way to do this without using any of the transformation tools is to use the Transform palette.

The Transform palette lets you enter values for the position and size of a selected object as well as specify rotation and shearing (skew) values. If you select a rotate or skew value from the menu, the value is applied immediately. If you type a value in any of the fields, you must press Enter/Return to execute the command.

Unit 12 ★ Transformation Filters

The Transform palette displays values based on the bounding boxes of the selected objects. It uses the center point of an object to calculate position, size, and orientation (Figure 12.7).

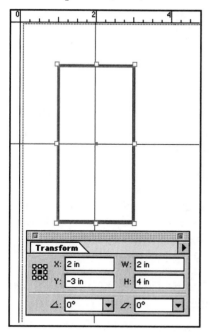

Macintosh Keystrokes

⌘-N File/New
⌘-R View/Show Rulers
F11 Window/Show
        Attributes

Windows Keystrokes

Ctrl-N File/New
Ctrl-R View/Show Rulers
F11 Window/Show
        Attributes

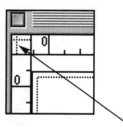

The Star tool is selected on the Tearoff palette.

Figure 12.7. The Transform palette indicates that the center of the selected rectangle is two inches across and three inches down from the zero point. It is two inches wide and four inches high and has not been rotated or skewed.

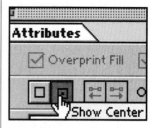

The two crossed dotted lines are dragged down onto the page to set the zero point.

EXERCISE A

1. In a new document (File/New), display the Swatches palette and the Attributes palette (F11). Use the Units & Undo Preferences dialog box to select inches as the unit of measure.

2. Select the Star tool with the Selection tool. Press the Up Arrow key as you drag to create a star with at least 8 points. Fill and stroke the star. Click on the Show Center button in the Attributes palette to display the star's center point.

3. Use the Selection tool to position the star in the upper left corner of the drawing area. Choose View/Show Rulers (Command/Ctrl-R) and drag the zero point to the inner corner of the page, the imageable area of the document.

4. Display the Transform palette (Window/Show Transform). With the star selected, type in the position and size values displayed in Figure 12.8.

Macintosh Keystrokes

⌘-D Object/Transform/
Transform Again

Windows Keystrokes

Ctrl-D Object/Transform/
Transform Again

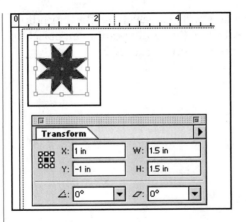

Figure 12.8. The star is positioned one inch from the left side of the page and one inch down from the top of the page.

You may want to scale down the first distorted star so it doesn't extend beyond the artboard, as well as add a title for the document.

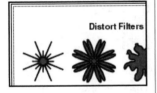

Tip

Double-click on the Selection tool to display the Move dialog box.

5. Select the star with the Selection tool. Drag the star to the right, pressing the Shift and Option/Alt keys as you drag to constrain the movement to a 45° angle and to create a copy of the star. Release the mouse, *then* the modifier keys. You could also select the Move dialog box (Object/Transform/Move) and type 2 in the Horizontal field to move the star horizontally, 0 in the Vertical field to constrain the horizontal movement, and 2 in the Distance field to move it 2 inches from the original. Click on Copy to create the duplicate star.

6. As soon as you create the duplicate star, press Command/Ctrl-D twice to create a total of four stars across the top of the page.

7. Drag a selection marquee around the four stars with the Selection tool and Option/Alt-drag down to create a duplicate row of stars. Press Command/Ctrl-D to create a third row. Your screen should resemble Figure 12.9. Deselect (Command/Ctrl-Shift-A).

Figure 12.9. Use the Repeat Transform command to create three rows of stars.

Unit 12 ★ Transformation Filters

8. Select the first star. Choose Filters/Distort/Punk & Bloat. Click the Preview button. Drag the slider to the right to display -100 or type -100 in the % field. A negative number punks the object; a positive number bloats it. Click on OK.

9. Use the Text tool to type -100%. Click the Selection tool and drag the point type under the first star.

10. Use the Selection tool to select the second star in the top row. Press Command-Option-E (Macintosh) or Ctrl-Alt-E (Windows) to display the last filter dialog box. Click the Preview button. Drag the slider to the right to the 80% mark or type 80 in the % field. Click on OK.

11. Use the Selection tool to Option/Alt-Shift-drag the point type under the second star. Select the Type tool, triple-click on the text to select the paragraph, and type *Bloat 80%*.

12. Select the third star in the first row and choose Filter/Distort/Roughen. Click the Preview button. Click the Smooth option in the Points field to add curve points, and drag the Size slider to specify how far the anchor points can be moved. Drag the Detail slider to specify how many points will be added to each inch of the path segments. Click on OK.

13. Select the Selection tool. Option/Alt-Shift-drag the type under the third star. Triple-click with the Type tool and type *Roughen/ Smooth*.

14. Select the fourth star, press Command-Option-E (Macintosh) or Ctrl-Alt-E (Windows) to display the Roughen dialog box again. Click the Preview button. Click the Corner option in the Points field to add corner points to the object. Adjust the sliders and click on OK. Option/Alt-drag the point type and use the Type tool to change it to *Roughen/Corner*. Your screen should resemble Figure 12.10.

Macintosh Keystrokes

⌘-E Filter/Apply last filter
⌘-Option-E Filter/Display last filter

Windows Keystrokes

Ctrl-E Filter/Apply last filter
Ctrl-Alt-E Filter/Display last filter

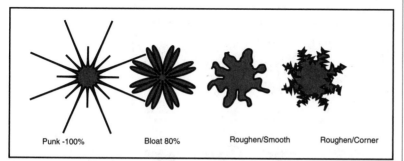

Punk -100%   Bloat 80%   Roughen/Smooth   Roughen/Corner

Figure 12.10. The first line of stars has been filtered with the Punk, Bloat, and Roughen Distort filters.

Macintosh Keystrokes

⌘-E Filter/Apply last filter
⌘-Option-E Filter/Display
last filter

Windows Keystrokes

Ctrl-E Filter/Apply last filter
Ctrl-Alt-E Filter/Display last
filter

Select Scribble or Tweak
from the pull-down menu
in the filter's dialog box.

15. Repeat the type function for the rest of the stars. This gives you a sampler page of the different Distort filters.

16. Select the first star in the second row. Choose Filter/Distort/ Scribble and Tweak. Choose Scribble from the pull-down menu to move the points randomly. Drag the Horizontal and Vertical sliders to move the points as a percentage of the longest segment of the object. Because each segment in the star is the same length, you will just get a muddle. If you select the Anchor Points option, the anchor points will be "scribbled." If you deselect this option, they will remain anchored while the filter is applied to the rest of the object. The In and Out control points refer to which points on the path will be randomly moved: the In points lead into other anchor points on the path; the Out points lead out of anchor points on the path. Click on OK.

17. Select the second star in the second row; press Command-Option-E (Macintosh) or Ctrl-Alt-E (Windows) to return to the Scribble and Tweak dialog box. Choose Tweak from the pull-down menu. Use the Horizontal and Vertical sliders to specify the amount the anchor points and the inner and outer control points will be moved. Click on OK.

18. Select the next star and choose Filter/Distort/Zig Zag. Click the Preview button. Select the Smooth option in the Points field. Drag the Amount slider to 10, the distance you want the points moved on the path. Drag the Ridges slider to 4 or type 4 in the Ridges field. This is the number of ridges per unit of measure. Because inches is the unit of measure, this value will create four ridges on every inch of the path. Click OK.

19. Select the fourth star in the second row and press Command-Option-E (Macintosh) or Ctrl-Alt-E (Windows) to return to the Zig Zag dialog box. Click the Preview button. Select the Corner option. Type 3 in the Amount field and 5 in the Ridges field. Click on OK. Your screen should resemble Figure 12.11.

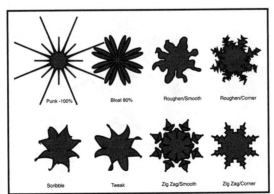

Figure 12.11. The second line of stars has been filtered with the Scribble, Tweak, and Zig Zag Distort filters.

20. Select each star in the fourth row and apply a different variation of the Distort filters to each one. Include the text label beneath each filtered star.

21. When you have finished, save the file (File/Save As) as *Distort.ai* in your Projects folder. You will need it for the printing exercise in a later unit.

Macintosh Keystrokes

⌘-Shift-S File/Save As

Windows Keystrokes

Ctrl-Shift-S File/Save As

ALIGNING AND DISTRIBUTING OBJECTS

All objects live on an x (horizontal) and y (vertical) axis, and often it is necessary to align multiple objects along a specific point on either or both axes or to distribute multiple objects along the same axis. To do this more easily than using the Info palette, select the objects to be aligned and use the Align palette.

ALIGN COMMANDS

The Align palette is used to align or distribute selected objects. The top row contains the align icons. The first three icons in the top row align objects horizontally along the left edges (leftmost anchor point), through their centers, or along their right edges using the rightmost anchor points (Figure 12.12).

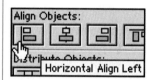

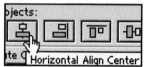

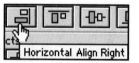

The first three icons in the top row of the Align palette align selected objects horizontally across the x axis.

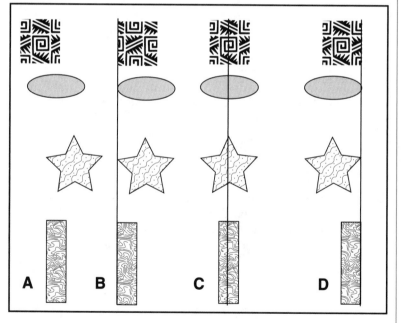

Figure 12.12. The original four objects (A) are aligned from their leftmost anchor points (B), from their centers (C), and from their rightmost anchor points (D).

The second three icons in the top row align objects vertically along their topmost anchor points, center points, and bottom anchor points (Figure 12.13).

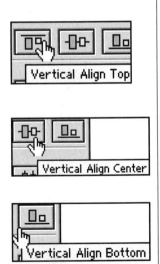

The last three icons in the top row of the Align palette align objects vertically on the y axis.

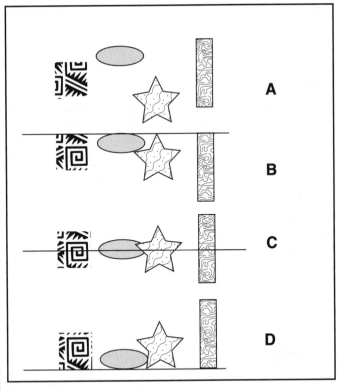

Figure 12.13. The original four objects (A) are aligned from their topmost anchor points (B), vertically through their centers (C), and from their bottommost anchor points (D).

DISTRIBUTE COMMANDS

The second row of the Align palette displays icons used to distribute objects evenly along the horizontal or vertical axis. The Distribute commands even out the space between the edges or between the center points of the objects' bounding boxes (Figure 12.14).

FYI

The Distribute commands only work when three or more objects are selected. Because these commands compare the space between objects, you have to have at least two spaces to compare.

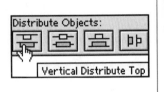

Figure 12.14. The original objects (left) were distributed vertically along the top edges, creating an equal amount of space between the top edges of each object (right).

Unit 12 ★ Transformation Filters

ARRANGING OBJECTS

When you create objects sequentially, the last object created is in the topmost position in the stacking order. If it is moved over an object created earlier, it will obscure that object. To arrange objects so that they display properly, use the Arrange commands under the Object menu (Figure 12.15).

Arrange	▶	Bring To Front	⇧⌘]
		Bring Forward	⌘]
Group	⌘G	Send Backward	⌘[
Ungroup	⇧⌘G	Send To Back	⇧⌘[

Figure 12.15. The Arrange commands under the Object menu are used to position objects relative to their display order.

EXERCISE B

1. Open the *Align.ai* file in the Unit 12 folder on the CD-ROM. Display the Align palette (Window/Show Align) and the Attributes palette (F11).

2. Select the first three vertical objects on the left side of the page, the circle, rectangle, and star. Click the Show Center button in the Attributes palette to display the star's center point.

3. Click the Horizontal Align Left button in the Align palette, the first button in the top row. The objects are aligned by their left-most anchor points. Click the Horizontal Center Align button, the second button in the top row. Click the Horizontal Align Right button in the Align palette.

4. Select the second column of objects. Click the Show Center button on the Align palette and click the Vertical Align Top button to align the objects vertically along the top anchor points.

5. Repeat for the third column of objects, clicking the Vertical Align Center button to align the objects on their center points. Select the fourth column of objects and click the Vertical Align Bottom button to align the objects along their bottommost points.

6. Use the Selection tool to drag a selection marquee around all the colored objects at the bottom of the page. Click the Horizontal Align Center button, then the Vertical Align Center button to align all the objects from their center points.

Macintosh Keystrokes

⌘-O File/Open
F11 Window/Show Attributes

Windows Keystrokes

Ctrl-O File/Open
F11 Window/Show Attributes

Bring to Front

The selected object is positioned in front of every other object on the layer.

Bring Forward

The selected object is positioned in front of the object directly in front of it.

Send to Back

The selected object is positioned behind every other object on the layer.

Send Backward

The selected object is positioned behind the object directly behind it on that layer.

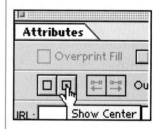

⌘-O File/Open
⌘-[Object/Arrange/Send
    Backward
⌘-Shift-[Object/Arrange/
    Send to Back
⌘-] Object/Arrange/Bring
    Forward

Ctrl-O File/Open
Ctrl-[Object/Arrange/
    Send Backward
Ctrl-Shift-[Object/
    Arrange/Send to Back
Ctrl-} Object/Arrange/
    Bring Forward

7. Select the red circle, the topmost object, and choose Object/ Arrange/Send Backward to move it behind the gradient object.

8. Select the gradient object, now the frontmost object, and choose Object/Arrange/Send to Back to make it the bottom-most object in the stacking order.

9. With the gradient object still selected, choose Object/Arrange/ Bring Forward to move it in front of the yellow square.

10. Continue to select and arrange objects until you are comfort-able with the commands.

11. Close this file. Don't save your changes.

REVIEW

In this unit you learned that:

1. The Twirl tool manually distorts a selected object, whereas the Twirl filter uses specific values to effect the transformation.

2. The Punk & Bloat filter curves the edges of an object inward or outward.

3. The Scribble and Tweak filter moves existing anchor points randomly to distort the object.

4. The Zig Zag filter adds anchor points to create jagged or wavy lines from open or closed paths.

5. The Transform palette is used to enter values for the position and size or angle of rotation or shear angle of a selected object.

6. Objects can be precisely aligned and distributed horizontally and vertically using the Align palette.

7. Objects' stacking order can be changed using the Arrange com-mands to bring objects to the front or back of the stacking order or forward or backward relative to other objects in the stacking order.

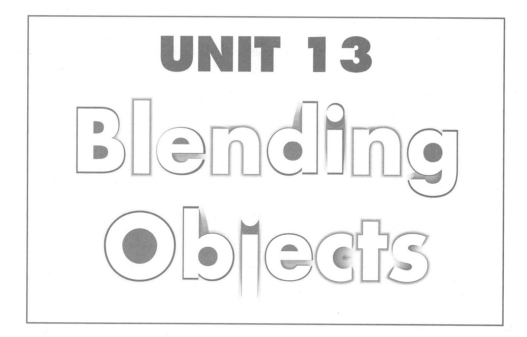

OVERVIEW

In this unit you will learn how to:
use the Blend tool and Make Blends command
  to blend multiple objects
create and edit blends
blend open paths
blend similar closed paths
blend dissimilar paths
apply blends to paths

TERMS

blend
blend object
blend path

HOW IT WORKS

Create the type and convert to outlines. Choose Object/Path/Offset Path. Type a value in the Offset dialog box. Fill the offset paths with a light color and send them to the back. Copy the original text. Blend the offset path to the original text path in the same number of steps as the offset value (about 5). Paste the copied text in front and fill with a light color.

In Version 7 you must Shift-select anchor points on the objects you are blending, then click on each selected point with the Blend tool. This displays the Blend dialog box, where you can either accept Illustrator's recommended blend steps or type in your own values. Blends are not live, and the only way to edit them is to select an intermediate object with the Direct Selection tool and edit it. There is no blend path to edit.

The original blend on the left changes as the blend objects are moved and resized (right).

Sorry!

You cannot blend between two gradient mesh objects.

BLENDING OBJECTS

Blending objects creates a series of intermediate colors that can be expanded to objects between two or more objects. Blending shapes (sometimes called *morphing*) is a useful technique for creating high-lighting and shading effects that make illustrations more realistic.

Any object that is selected and to which the Make Blends command is applied is a blend object. Any object you click on with the Blend tool to make part of a blend is also a blend object.

BLEND PATH

When you first create a blend, a straight path is created between the objects. This path can be edited by dragging anchor points on the path. You can also use the Pen tools to add and delete anchor points from the blend path. Dragging those anchor points reshapes both the blend path and the blend objects (Figure 13.1).

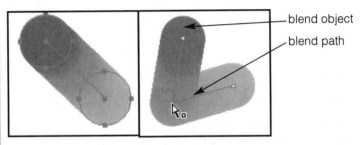
blend object
blend path

Figure 13.1. The blend between two circles displays the blend path (left). Adding an anchor point to that path and dragging it reshapes both the blend path and the blended objects (right).

LIVE BLENDS

In Illustrator 8 blends are live—as in *alive*. This means that the blend objects change as you edit them, reshaping the entire object. To edit the blend, select points and segments in the original blend objects, or select the blend path itself with the Direct Selection tool. Then drag to reshape the blend objects or the blend path, which reshapes the entire blend.

EDITING BLENDS

Adding and deleting anchor points to and from blend objects and the blend path also allows you to edit the blend object. When you add an anchor point to a blend object or to the blend path, you can use the Convert Direction Point tool to convert the point to a curve point and drag its direction handles to edit the blend.

RULES FOR BLENDING

There are a few rules to observe when blending:

▲ You can Blend more than two objects—actually, an unlimited number of objects—at one time.

▲ If you blend one object containing spot color with another object containing process color, Illustrator will automatically paint the transition objects with blended process colors.

▲ You can blend between gradients and solid colors, but not between gradient mesh objects.

▲ If you blend between two patterned objects, the intermediate objects will display the pattern fill of the frontmost object.

▲ Illustrator automatically calculates the steps for a blend unless you specify otherwise in the Specified Steps option of the Blends Options dialog box.

▲ When preparing illustrations containing blends to be color-separated, use tints to reduce the number of separations. When blending a custom color with white, do not use process white. Instead, use a zero percent tint of the same custom color.

▲ To end the blend path, deselect the blended objects or select another tool.

CREATING BLENDS

There are two ways to create a blend between objects: the Blend tool and the Make Blends command. When using the Blend tool, the current value in the Specified Steps field of the Blend Options dialog box determines how many steps (intermediate objects) Illustrator uses to create the blend.

BLEND TOOL

To blend objects with the Blend tool, click the objects to be blended (blend objects) in the order in which you want them blended. Doing so will create a straight line (blend path) from one object to the next through the center point of each object. You don't have to select objects to blend them. Just click anywhere on the blend object. If the objects are unselected or if only one anchor point is selected, Illustrator automatically selects the two points from which to start and end the blend.

Clicking anchor points with the Blend tool determines where the blend starts and ends. By clicking on different anchor points, you can create the effect of rotating the blend from the selected anchor points (Figure 13.2).

Macintosh Keystrokes

⌘-Z Edit/Undo

Windows Keystrokes

Ctrl-Z Edit/Undo

Version 7

You can blend only two objects in version 7.

Clicking on an object with the Blend tool displays an X next to the Blend cursor, indicating that the object will be part of the blend.

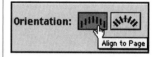

The Orientation field in the Blend Options dialog box displays icons for selecting how a blend is positioned relative to the page or to the blend path.

It's over!

When you have finished clicking on blend objects, click the Blend tool again to deactivate it. Otherwise, the next object you click on with the Blend tool will connected to the current blend path.

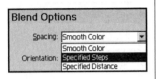

The Blend Options dialog box is where you specify how Illustrator creates the blends.

A Blend created with the Smooth Color option generates as many intermediate objects as necessary to create a smooth transition between colors.

A Blend created by entering 2 in the Specified Steps command of the Blend Options dialog box.

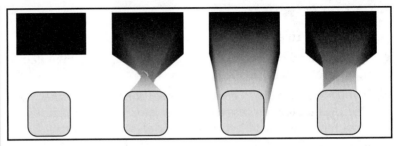

Figure 13.2. The original objects (left) are blended from the top left to the lower right anchor points, from the centers of the objects, and from the top right to the lower left anchor points.

BLEND OPTIONS DIALOG BOX

The Blend Options dialog box displays three options for spacing the intermediate objects. The Orientation icons apply to how the blend aligns when it is applied to a separate path.

SMOOTH COLOR

The Smooth Color option tells Illustrator to calculate the number of intermediate steps needed for the blend's smooth transition of color. If the objects are filled and/or stroked with different colors, or if they are filled with patterns or gradients, Illustrator automatically calculates the number of steps needed to create a smooth color transition. It bases this value on the difference in CMYK percentages between the objects and assumes that the file will be printed to a high-resolution output device.

SPECIFIED STEPS

Type a value in the field next to this option to tell Illustrator how many intermediate objects to create between the start and end of the blend.

SPECIFIED DISTANCE

This value tells Illustrator the distance to space the steps in the blend. This value overrides any value entered in the Specified Steps field.

BLENDING OPEN PATHS

When blending open paths, click with the Blend tool on any part of the path or on an anchor point on the path to create the blend. Shift-select anchor points on each path, and click on each anchor point with the Blend tool to create a different blend angle. You can always move the blend path or blend objects to reshape the final blend (Figure 13.3).

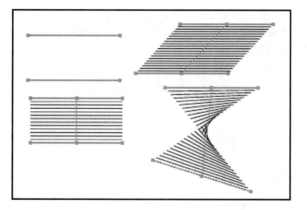

Macintosh Keystrokes

⌘-N File/New
F10 View/Show Stroke

Windows Keystrokes

Ctrl-N File/New
F10 View/Show Stroke

Figure 13.3. The two lines are blended, and the blend path is moved to slant the object. The bottom blend object is moved with the Direct Selection tool to create the twist.

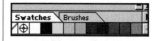

Process colors

The colors in the top row of the Swatches palette are process colors. They do not display the dot in the corner as do the spot color swatches.

EXERCISE A

1. In a new document (File/New), display the Swatches palette and the Stroke palette (F10). Make sure the unit of measure is inches (File/Preferences/Units & Undo). Click the Default Colors icon in the Toolbox.

2. Use the Pen tool to draw a straight horizontal line about three inches long. Press the Shift key before clicking to set the second point. Assign it a 3-point stroke in any process color and no fill.

3. Select the whole line with the Selection tool, because only the last point is selected when you click to set the second point, and anything you do will affect only that point. Double-click the Selection tool to display the Move dialog box. Type 0 in the Horizontal field because you want the copied line to move only vertically. Type -3 (inches) in the Vertical field, because a negative number in the Vertical field moves an object down.

4. Click on Copy to move a copy of the selected line 3 inches *down* on the page (Figure 13.4).

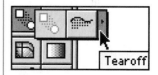

Drag the Blend tool to display its Tearoff Tab and drag the smaller tool strip onto the page, making the Blend tool available anywhere on the drawing area.

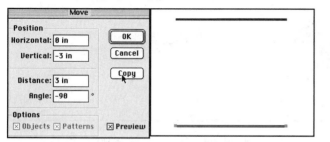

Figure 13.4. Typing a negative number in the Vertical field of the Move dialog box moves the copied line down on the page.

5. With the new bottom line still selected, click on another process color in the Swatches palette. Each line should now be a different process color.

6. Double-click on the Blend tool to display the Blend Options dialog box. Select Specified Steps from the Spacing menu, type 25 in the text field, and click on OK.

7. Click with the Blend tool on the left edge of each line to create 25 intermediate objects between the two lines (Figure 13.5).

blend path

Figure 13.5. The Blend tool creates 25 intermediate objects along a blend path with gradations of color between the original two objects.

8. Choose View/Hide Edges (Command/Ctrl-H) to view the blend without the selection edges. Choose View/Show Edges to display the selection points again. Deselect the blend (Command/Ctrl-Shift-A).

9. Use the Direct Selection tool to select the bottom object in the blend. Drag it to reshape the blend. Drag the top or bottom object to reshape the blend.

10. Select the Add Anchor Point tool and click in the center of blend path to add a point. Drag just that anchor point around to reshape the blend.

11. Double-click on the Blend tool and type 75 in the Specified Steps field. Click on OK. The blend automatically updates, rebuilding the blend with 75 steps instead of the original 25 steps. Your screen should resemble Figure 13.6.

12. Close this file (Command/Ctrl-W). Don't save your changes.

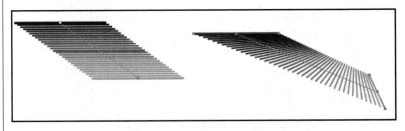

Figure 13.6. Dragging the blend path, adding anchor points to the blend path, adding and deleting steps in the blend, and dragging a blend object from any anchor point are all ways to reshape blends.

BLENDING SIMILAR CLOSED PATHS

Blending similar closed paths creates interesting three-dimensional effects. As with blending open paths, editing the blend objects or the blend path changes the direction of the blend.

EXERCISE B

1. On a clean drawing page (File/New), display the Swatches palette (F5) and Stroke palette (F10). Make sure the unit of measure is inches (File/Preferences/Units & Undo).

2. Use the Star tool to create a five-pointed star. Fill and stroke the star with a .25 stroke width.

3. With the star still selected, double-click on the Selection tool to display the Move dialog box. Type 1 (inch) in the Horizontal field and 1 (inch) in the Vertical field. Click on Copy. Another star appears, 1 inch to the right and 1 inch above the original star. Choose Edit/Transform Again (Command/Ctrl-D) to create a third star.

4. Fill the two new stars with a different color, but leave the .25 stroke value.

5. Select the Blend Tool and click anywhere on the first star, then on the second star, and then on the third star. Illustrator builds the blend as a straight line through the center of each object. This is easier to see in Artwork view. Your screen should resemble Figure 13.7.

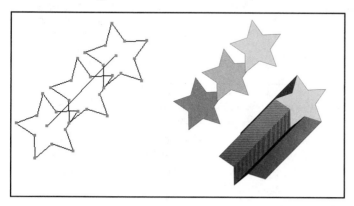

Figure 13.7. A blend between three objects creates a 3D effect. The blend path appears in Artwork view (left) and creates the blend between the three star objects (right).

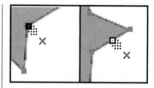

When the Blend cursor displays a black square, you have clicked on an anchor point (left). When it displays a white square, you have clicked on a path (right).

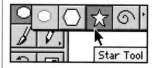

The Star tool is part of the Tearoff menu connected to the Ellipse tool.

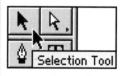

Macintosh Keystrokes

⌘-O File/Open
⌘-Shift-A Edit/Deselect All

Windows Keystrokes

Ctrl-O File/Open
Ctrl-Shift-A Edit/Deselect
    All

BLENDING DISSIMILAR PATHS

When you blend dissimilar objects, Illustrator transforms the first selected object into the second, then the second object into the third, and so on. The subtlety or obviousness of this transformation depends on the number of steps specified for the blend. The greater the number of steps, the more subtle the transformation. Remember, however, that because the blend command creates a series of intermediate objects, these steps take time, memory, and processing power to create.

EXERCISE C

1. Open the *ABC.ai* file in the Unit 13 folder on the CD-ROM. It displays three letters which have been converted from text characters to paths.

2. Double-click the Blend tool and choose Specified Steps from the Spacing menu. Type 6 in the text field and click on OK.

3. Click with the Blend tool on each of the three objects to blend them (Figure 13.8). Deselect (Command/Ctrl-Shift-A).

Figure 13.8. The original items are blended along the blend path. Selecting the blend path and adding anchor points lets you reshape the blend.

4. Choose Window/New Window. In the new window, choose View/Artwork (Command/Ctrl-Y) to switch to Artwork view. Choose View/Fit in Window (Command/Ctrl-0). Use the Direct Selection tool to select the blend path running through the center of the objects. Click on the top endpoint and drag the path to reshape the blend.

5. Select the Add Anchor Point tool and click on the blend path to add another anchor point. Use the Direct Selection tool to drag that anchor point out and reshape the blend. Continue to add anchor points and reshape the blend path.

6. Close this file (Command/Ctrl-W). Don't save your changes.

212

BLEND COMMAND

The Make Blends command blends all the selected objects relative to their center points. You can also select individual points on an object and blend from those points.

DELETING BLENDS

To delete a blend, select the blended objects and choose the Release command from the Blends menu. You can also use the Edit/Undo command to release a blend.

EXPANDING BLENDS

Unless you use the Expand command, you will not be able to edit the intermediate objects in a blend, as you could do in earlier versions of Illustrator. However, once you create a blend and expand it, the intermediate objects are available for editing and/or deletion.

EXERCISE D

1. Open the *Leaf.ai* file in the Unit 13 folder on the CD-ROM. It displays a leaf composed of three stroked objects. Display the Color palette (F6).

2. Select the Fill icon in the Toolbox. Use the Selection tool to select the outer object and click on a green in the Color palette. Select the center object and click on a lighter green. Select the inner object and click on yellow in the Color palette.

3. Use the Selection tool to draw a selection marquee around all three objects. Click the Stroke icon in the Toolbox and click the None icon to remove the stroke from all three objects.

4. Choose Object/Blends/Blend Options. Select Smooth Color from the Spacing menu. Click on OK.

5. Choose Object/Blends/Make. The three objects are blended (Figure 13.9).

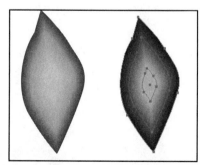

Figure 13.9. The blended leaf (left) still contains the original three blend objects (right). The Make Blends command does not create a blend path.

Macintosh Keystrokes

⌘-O File/Open
F6 Window/Show Color

Windows Keystrokes

Ctrl-O File/Open
F6 Window/Show Color

Selection Tool (V)

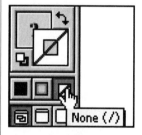

None (/)

The Fill icon for the selected leaf objects displays a question mark, because each leaf is filled with a different color.

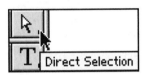

Direct Selection

Selection Tool (V)

Rectangle Tool

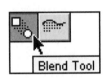

Ellipse Tool

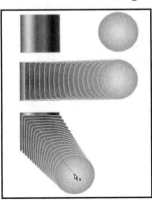

Blend Tool

6. Use the Direct Selection tool to select one of the three blend objects. This might be easier to do in Artwork view (Command/Ctrl-Y) and in a new window (Window/New Window). Select a point or segment and drag to reshape the object. The blend automatically reblends to fit the new shape.

7. Select each of the blend objects and change the fill color.

8. Use the Selection tool to draw a selection marquee around all three objects. Choose Object/Blends/Expand. Use the Selection tool to select individual objects in the blend and drag them out of the blend. Use the Direct Selection tool to select other intermediate objects and reshape them without affecting the shape of the entire blend.

9. Choose Edit/Select All (Command/Ctrl-A) and choose Edit/Clear to delete everything.

10. Use the Rectangle tool to draw a rectangle and the Ellipse tool to draw a circle about two inches to the right of the rectangle. Fill the rectangle with a linear gradient and the circle with a radial gradient.

11. Double-click on the Blend tool, select Specified Steps from the Spacing field, and type 15 in the text field. Click on OK.

12. Click with the Blend tool on the rectangle, then on the circle to create the blend (Figure 13.10).

Figure 13.10. The rectangle and circle are blended. The blend path is moved to change the perspective of the newly blended object.

13. Use the Direct Selection tool to select just the blend path. Click on the right endpoint to select it and drag it to the right. The blend object takes on a new perspective depending on how far to the right (or left) you drag the blend path (Figure 13.10).

14. Use the Selection tool to draw a selection marquee around all three objects. Choose Object/Blends/Release. The blend is released and the objects display the last assigned fill color.

15. Close this file (Command/Ctrl-W). Don't save your changes.

BLENDS AND PATHS

Any blend you create can be applied to any path, which makes it easy to wrap a blend around an object or to create special effects. The blend follows the outline of the path in the orientation specified in the Blend Options dialog box.

By default, blends are created perpendicular to the x axis of the page, not to the blend path. You can change this by clicking the Align to Path button in the Blend Options dialog box.

REVERSE SPINE

When you apply a blend to a path, the blend starts with the first blend object and ends with the last object in the blend. If you select Reverse Spine from the Blends menu, the blend wraps around the path starting with the last blend object.

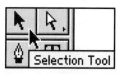

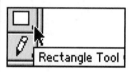

Set the grid spacing in the Guides & Grid Preferences dialog box.

EXERCISE E

1. Create a new document (Command/Ctrl-N). Choose View/Show Grid. Display the Swatches palette.

2. Use the Rectangle tool to draw a rectangle inside one of the grid marks. Fill and stroke it with two different colors.

3. Double-click on the rectangle and double-click the Scale tool. Type 70 in the Uniform field and click on Copy. The smaller square appears inside the larger one. Use the Selection tool to drag the smaller square five grid squares away from the original square. Fill and stroke the smaller square with different colors (Figure 13.11).

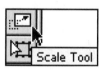

Figure 13.11. The smaller square is moved on the grid away from the original.

Tip

If you're creating a blend to achieve a gradation of color and are not interested in the morphing effect of a blend, or if your blend is wider than seven inches, use a gradient fill instead of the blend tool. This will reduce the possibility of banding (visible steps between blends).

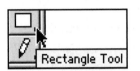

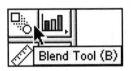

Shortcut

To quickly reshape a blend path around another path, Shift-select the blend path and the other object. Choose Object/Blends/Reverse Spine.

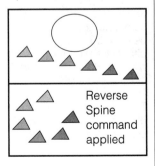

Reverse Spine command applied

4. Use the Selection tool to draw a selection marquee around both squares, press the Option/Alt key, and drag a copy of the two squares down to the bottom of the page. Release the mouse button, *then* the modifier key.

5. Double-click the Blend tool and select Specified Steps from the Spacing menu. Type 6 in the text field. Click the Align to Page button in the Orientation field. Click on OK.

6. Drag another selection marquee around the original squares to select them. Choose Object/Blends/Make to create six intermediate objects between the original squares.

7. Use the Rectangle tool to draw a square across four of the grid squares. Select both the rectangle and the blended squares with the Selection tool. Choose Object/Blends/Replace Spine. The large square's fill and stroke disappear and the blend runs around the path, the outline of the square. Notice that the blend objects are perpendicular to the x axis of the page (Figure 13.12).

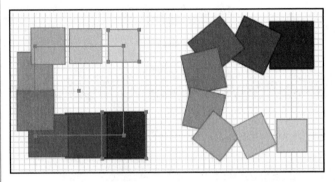

Figure 13.12. The Align to Page option in the Blend Options dialog box causes the blend objects to align to the x axis of the page (left). The Align to Path option aligns the blend objects to the path itself.

8. Double-click on the Blend tool and click the Align to Path button in the Orientation field. Leave the Spacing value at 6. Click on OK. Select the two squares at the bottom of the page and choose Object/Blends/Make.

9. Draw another square on four grid areas. Shift-select the blend and the large square—the path—and choose Object/Blends/Replace Spine. The blend replaces the outline of the square with the blend objects perpendicular to the path (Figure 13.12).

10. Keep the path selected and choose Object/Blends/Reverse Spine. The blend wraps around the path beginning with the last blend object and ending with the first.

11. Close this file (Command/Ctrl-W). Don't save your changes.

EXERCISE F

Macintosh Keystrokes

⌘-N File/New
⌘-W File/Close
F6 Window/Show Color

Windows Keystrokes

Ctrl-N File/New
Ctrl-W File/Close
F6 Window/Show Color

1. In a new document (File/New), use the Pencil or Pen tool to draw a wavy S line. The more curve to the ends of the line, the deeper the ribbon created by the blend. Display the Color palette (F6).

2. Select the line with the Selection tool and assign it a process color from the Color palette. With the line still selected, press the Option/Alt key and drag to the right and down to create a duplicate line slightly below the original (Figure 13.13).

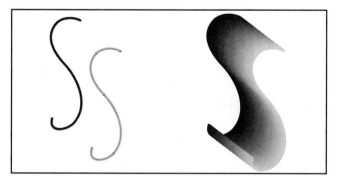

Figure 13.13. The two objects (left) are blended to create a ribbon (right).

3. Assign the duplicate line a different color. Double-click the Blend tool and select Smooth Color from the Spacing menu.

4. Select both lines and choose Object/Blends/Make to create the ribbon.

5. Use the Direct Selection tool to select one of the two blend objects and adjust the color in the Color palette by moving one of the CMYK sliders. Your screen should resemble Figure 13.13.

6. Close this file (Command/Ctrl-W). Don't save your changes.

FYI

You cannot stroke a blend object once the blend is applied, so stroke the blend objects before creating the blend.

In this unit you learned that:

1. When two or more objects are blended, a blend path is created connecting the objects.

2. The blend path can be edited to change the direction of the blend.

3. Blending objects containing both spot and process colors results in the transition objects being painted with blended process colors.

4. Blends are created with the Blend tool and the Make Blends command.

5. When you have finished selecting all the objects to be blended, you must deactivate the Blend tool by clicking on the Blend tool or any other tool in the Toolbox.

6. Clicking different anchor points with the Blend tool on a blend object affects the rotation of the blend.

7. Intermediate objects can be spaced to achieve smooth color, in a specified number of steps and at a specified distance from each other in the Blend Options dialog box.

8. You can blend open and closed paths in the same blend.

9. The Blends command blends all the selected objects relative to their center points unless you have selected anchor points.

10. To blend objects using the Make Blends command, select the objects and apply the Make Blends command from the Object menu.

11. Blends can be deleted with the Blends/Release command from the Object menu.

12. To edit the intermediate objects in a blend, select the objects and apply the Expand command from the Object menu.

13. Blends applied to paths follow the orientation specified in the Blend Options dialog box.

OVERVIEW

In this unit you will learn how to:
set horizontal and vertical type
select and edit type
use the Character palette to apply text attributes
create and edit type containers
copy and apply type attributes
link/unlink text containers
create type in and on paths
import text

TERMS

area (rectangle) type
leading
Overflow Indicator
path type
point type
text object
type container
vertical type

HOW IT WORKS

These text characters are Adobe Type 1 fonts from the *Wild Things* collection. Converting the type to outlines gives you Illustrator art which can be manipulated and edited just like any other art object.

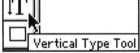

The Type tool (left) is the default tool. Drag on the black triangle on the icon to access the Area Type tool, the Path Type tool, the Vertical Type tool, the Vertical Area Type tool, and the Vertical Path Type tool. Press the *t* key to toggle among the different Type tools. Click on the arrow to tear the type tools off the Toolbox and create a separate floating Type palette.

Baseline

The baseline is the imaginary, nonprinting line on which type sits.

FYI

Triple-click on any text block to select the entire text block.

TYPE IN ILLUSTRATOR

Four kinds of type can be created with the six Type tools in Adobe Illustrator 8.0:

1. *Point type* is created with the Type tool anywhere on the page. Click with the Type tool and type. The text appears with its baseline visible. Point type does not exist in relation to any path.

2. *Area (rectangle) type* is created with either the Type tool or the Vertical Type tool. Use either tool to draw an unfilled and unstroked rectangle into which the text fits. The rectangle acts as a bounding area for the text. If you create a path of any shape, use the Area Type tool to type *inside* that enclosed path, which, like the rectangle, acts as a bounding area for the type.

3. *Path type* is type placed *along* an open or closed path with either the Type tool or the Path Type tool.

4. *Vertical type* positions type vertically on a path or within an object. Use the Vertical Type and Vertical Path type tools to create type that runs vertically from right to left.

The Type tool is the default tool. Drag on the black triangle in the Type Tool icon to access the other type tools or press t to toggle between the tools. You can also tear away the entire Type Tools palette by clicking on the tab after the last tool.

POINT TYPE

Point type is created with the Type tool and can be positioned anywhere on the page. It does not exist on, around, or inside a path. Rather, it exists at the point where it was created and displays a baseline which is used to move the type to any area of the page. Like all type created in Illustrator, point type can be edited with any of the type tools.

VERTICAL TYPE

The Vertical Type tool creates point type by positioning text characters underneath each other. If you drag with the Vertical Type tool to create a text rectangle, the type will flow from top to bottom and from right to left inside the rectangle.

SELECTING TYPE

Type must always be selected before it can be edited. Edit Illustrator type just as you would in a word processor, in the following ways:

▲ Double-click with any type tool and use the I-beam cursor to select a word, or triple-click to select a paragraph.

▲ Use the I-beam cursor to select characters, press the Shift key, and click to select additional adjacent characters.

▲ Press Command-Shift-Up Arrow or Down Arrow (Macintosh) or Ctrl-Shift-Up Arrow or Down Arrow (Windows) to select the previous paragraph or the next paragraph respectively.

▲ Click anywhere in the type with any type tool and choose Edit/Select All. This selects all the type on the type path or in the type container.

▲ Select text with any type tool or with the Selection tool and press the Delete key to delete the text. Selecting text with the Selection tool selects the whole path or type container, and pressing the Delete key will delete all the type, not just individual characters.

Once text is selected, you can change its typeface and size as well as add other paint characteristics. And because type in Illustrator is a text object, it can be manipulated with the transformation tools. For example, if you're trying to size text so it fits over a rectangle, it's frequently easier to drag the alignment point on point type with the Scale tool and eyeball the type size instead of selecting different type sizes from the Type/Size menu or Character palette.

CHARACTER PALETTE

Although many of the type options are available from the Type menu, you may find it easier to apply text editing from the Character palette. If you select Show Options from the Character palette menu, all the type options are available (Figure 14.1).

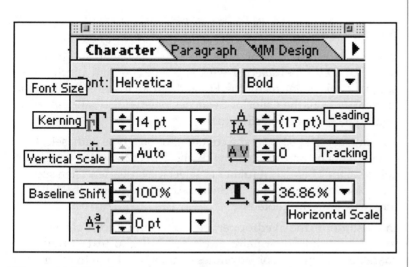

Figure 14.1. The Character palette displays options for editing and restyling text.

FYI

The text object or individual characters must be selected before any type editing can be applied.

FYI

When creating point type, the text will move along a straight line right off the page. To control its placement, press the Return or Enter keys. This causes the text to drop to the next line.

Type tool cursor displays a horizontal bar and is surrounded by a dotted box when it is not on or near any path.

Resizing type visually

(1) Click on the baseline point of origin with the Scale tool; (2) release the mouse button; (3) move the cursor below the baseline; and (4) drag to visually resize the type.

When you click on the Selection tool after creating point type, all the type becomes selected and can be edited.

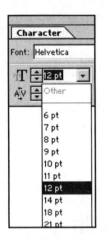

The Size pull-down menu on the Character palette.

Version 7

In Version 7 you can copy type paint attributes to other type blocks and art objects, but you cannot copy text attributes, such as typeface, type size, and paragraph attributes.

RESIZING TYPE SIZE MANUALLY

Use the keyboard commands to manually resize type. Select the type, and press Command-Shift->/< (Macintosh) or Ctrl-Shift->/< (Windows) to increase or decrease type in the increment set in the Size/Leading field of the Type & Auto Tracing Preferences dialog box. The default increment is 2 points, which means that when you select type and press the Command/Ctrl-Shift-> keys, the type size will increase by two points.

ADJUSTING LEADING

Leading is the amount of vertical space between baselines of type and is usually measured in points. The type you're reading now is is 10-point type set on 12 points of leading, and is referred to as type set 10/12 or 10 on 12.

To specify leading in the Character palette, do one of the following:

▲ Select the type by triple-clicking on the paragraph and enter a value in the Leading field. Press Return/Enter to execute the change. Or,

▲ Select the type by triple-clicking on the paragraph and select a value from the Leading pull-down menu. Or,

▲ Select the text block with the Selection tool and change the Leading value in the Character palette.

To manually adjust the Leading value from the keyboard, select the paragraph and press Option/Alt and the Up or Down Arrow keys to increase or decrease the leading of the selected text.

PAINTING TYPE

You can apply color to the type, to a type container, and to a type path. To paint type, select it with any type tool and specify a fill and/or stroke color using the Fill and Stroke icons in the Toolbox and colors from the Color or Swatches palette. You can also select point type with the Selection tool.

To paint just the text in a type container or on a type path, select the type container or type path with the Direct Selection or Group Selection tool, being careful not to select the baselines. Then specify the color from the Color or Swatches palette, using the Fill and Stroke icons in the Toolbox.

In Illustrator 8, the Eyedropper and Paint Bucket tools can be used to copy not only type paint attributes, but also text attributes—character and paragraph attributes—and apply them to other type and non-type objects.

EXERCISE A

Macintosh Keystrokes

⌘-N File/New
⌘-T Type/Character

Windows Keystrokes

Ctrl-N File/New
Ctrl-T Type/Character

1. In a new document (File/New), click once on the Type tool to select it. Move onto the drawing page and notice that the cursor is an I-beam which displays a dotted box around it, indicating that it will create point type—type that does not exist in relation to any path.

2. Click at any point on the page and the I-beam changes to a flashing cursor. Type your name using upper- and lower-case letters.

3. When you finish typing, click once on the Selection tool. This deselects the Type tool and selects the text, which is now a text object. Notice that the baseline is displayed and an alignment point appears to the left of the first character (Figure 14.2).

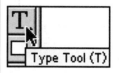

Figure 14.2. Once type is created with the Type tool, press the Selection tool to display the type's baseline and alignment point.

4. With the Selection tool active, click on the alignment point at the left end of the baseline and move the text around the page.

5. Pull down the Type menu, drag to select Font, and highlight another typeface. Because the *text object* is selected, as opposed to selected characters and words, the entire text object reflects the new typeface.

6. Pull down the Type menu, drag to highlight Size, and select a larger size. Again, the entire text object reflects the size change.

7. Display the Swatches palette. Use the Selection tool to select the type you just created, or use the Type tool to type your name again, clicking the Selection tool when you have finished typing.

8. Click on the Type tool and place the I-beam after the last letter in your name. Click once. The baseline and alignment point disappear and a flashing cursor appears. Press the Delete key and delete your name. Click on the Type tool again and type a few words.

9. Double-click on one word in the text object. Click on the Fill icon in the Toolbox and click on a color in the Swatches palette.

10. Drag to select the first letter in the text object. Choose Type/Character (Command/Ctrl-T) to display the Character palette. Type 72 in the Size field and press Return/Enter. You must

Oops!

If you should inadvertently deselect the text object, use the Selection tool to click on its baseline or on the alignment point. You can see the alignment point in Artwork view when the text is not selected.

Type can be resized by dragging the Bounding Box handles.

Macintosh Keystrokes

⌘-Y View/Artwork/Preview
⌘-W File/Close

Windows Keystrokes

Ctrl-Y View/Artwork/
  Preview
Ctrl-W File/Close

The Area Type cursor displays a round dotted line when it is not on a path.

FYI
—
When you draw the rectangle with the Type tool, you can enter the type with the Type tool. To use the Area Type tool, first create the rectangle with the Type tool, then click on the top of the rectangle with the Area Type tool to enter the type.

press Return or Enter to accept any changes typed in any of the palette fields. Or, drag down the Size menu and select 72. You don't have to press Return or Enter when selecting menu items.

11. Change the fill color and apply a stroke to the capital letters from the Swatches palette.

12. Choose View/Artwork (Command/Ctrl-Y). Click with the Selection tool on the alignment point to select the text object.

13. Double-click on the Reflect tool to display the Reflect dialog box. Click on Horizontal and click on Copy. The reflected text object appears selected.

14. Use the Selection tool to grab its alignment point and move it down below the original text.

15. Apply a fill of black and use the Tint slider to make it 50% black. Click on the Stroke box and select None. Your screen should resemble Figure 14.3.

16. Close this file (Command/Ctrl-W). Don't save your changes.

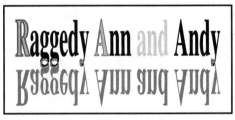

Figure 14.3. A text object in which individual characters and words were edited before the entire text object was reflected.

RECTANGLE TYPE

Use either the Type tool or the Area Type tool to create type inside a rectangle. The text automatically wraps to fit the boundary of the rectangular path, and if the text overflows, you can either duplicate and link the rectangles or create another rectangle into which the text will flow. A rectangle created with a type tool is called a *type container*, because it can be resized and reshaped just like any other Illustrator path.

RESIZING TYPE CONTAINERS

There are two ways to resize a type container: with the Direct Selection tool and with the Bounding Box handles. Select the type *container* with the Direct Selection tool, being careful not to select any of the type baselines. This is easier to do in Artwork view. Click on a path or on an anchor point and drag to reshape the path. You can also add and delete anchor points to reshape the path. When you release the mouse button, the cursor reverts to the I-beam.

To resize using the Bounding Box, make sure the option is selected in the General Preferences dialog box. Select the text container with the Selection tool and drag a handle on the Bounding Box to reshape the container. Press the Shift key before dragging to keep the sides straight.

EXERCISE B

1. In a new document (Command/Ctrl-N), select the Type tool. Click and drag with the Type tool to create a small rectangle. When you release the mouse button, the flashing cursor appears in the upper left corner.

2. Choose a font (Type/Font) and small type size (Type/Size) and type a few words inside the rectangle. Or, choose Font/Character (Command/Ctrl-T) and use the palette pull-down menus to select a typeface and type size. Use the Leading menu on the Character palette to increase the leading.

3. Notice how the text automatically wraps within the confines of the rectangular path. Click on the Type tool or Selection tool again to indicate an end to typing and to select both the text and the rectangle (Figure 14.4).

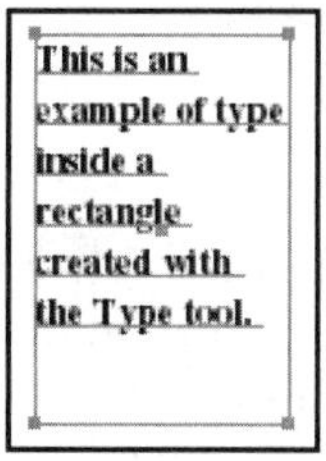

This is an example of type inside a rectangle created with the Type tool.

Figure 14.4. Clicking the Type tool or Selection tool when the Type tool is active selects both the text and the rectangle (type container).

4. Choose Edit/Deselect All (Command/Ctrl-Shift-A) to deselect everything. Click on the Direct Selection tool. Select Artwork view (Command/Ctrl-Y).

5. Because you are in Artwork view, the outline of the rectangle is visible even though it has not been stroked. Select the Direct Selection tool and drag a selection marquee around the two bottom corners to select them. Then click on the bottom segment of the rectangle, press the Shift key, and drag it up or down to resize the rectangle (Figure 14.5). Release the mouse button.

6. Click on the bottom bar of the rectangle again, press the Shift key, and drag up with the Direct Selection tool, making the rectangle too small to contain the text.

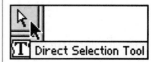

Macintosh Keystrokes

⌘-J Object/Path/Join
⌘-W File/Close

Windows Keystrokes

Ctrl-J Object/Path/Join
Ctrl-W File/Close

This is an example of type created inside a rectangle. Notice how the type stays inside the bounds of the rectangle.

Figure 14.5. First drag a selection marquee around the two bottom corners to select just those two anchor points. Pressing the Shift key before releasing the mouse button constrains the segment to a straight line while being resized.

7. With only the rectangle selected—not the text—apply a stroke and fill from the Swatches palette. Choose View/Preview (Command/Ctrl-Y) to view the effects of the fill and stroke. Notice the box with a plus sign that appears above the lower right point of the rectangle, indicating text overflow. Click on an empty area of the page to deselect everything (Figure 14.6).

8. Close this file (Command/Ctrl-W). Don't save your changes.

When clicking on selected text with the Eyedropper tool, the cursor displays a **†**, indicating that type attributes are being sampled.

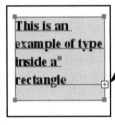

This is an example of type inside a rectangle

Figure 14.6. The Overflow Indicator appears when more text than can fit in the type container is imported into or typed in that type container.

COPYING TYPE ATTRIBUTES

If you have formatted text and want to copy those attributes (character and paragraph attributes) to new or existing text, you can do so with the Eyedropper and Paint Bucket tools. In this process, the text from which you are copying attributes is the source text. The text to which you are copying the attributes is the destination text.

COPYING ATTRIBUTES WITH THE EYEDROPPER TOOL

Copying and applying text attributes is Copy and Paste on steroids. To copy type attributes (size, leading, typeface, fill, and stroke) from one text block to another *selected* text block, do the following:

1. Format the source text the way you want it and deselect it.

2. Select the destination text with the Selection tool.

3. Select the Eyedropper tool and click on the source text. Notice that the Eyedropper displays a **†**, indicating that you are sampling type attributes, and the selected destination text displays the color and text attributes of the source (sampled) text. The Fill and Stroke icons in the Toolbox also display the sampled fill and stroke colors.

The Character palette:

| Character |
| Font: Helvetica ▾ Regular |
| T ⇕12 pt ▾   ÌA ⇕(14.5 pt) |
| A⃗V̬ ⇕(0) ▾   AV̬ ⇕ Other |
| Auto |
| 6 pt |
| 7 pt |
| **8 pt** |
| 9 pt |
| 10 pt |
| 11 pt |

The Leading menu on the Character palette.

To copy (paste) those sampled type attributes to other *nonselected* text objects, either point type or type in a type container, or to copy those attributes to any other artwork (destination text and art), select the Paint Bucket tool and click the text or art to which you want the sampled attributes applied.

COPYING ATTRIBUTES WITH THE PAINT BUCKET TOOL

To copy attributes from the source text to the destination text, do the following:

1. Select the source text with the Selection tool to display its base-lines.

2. Select the Paint Bucket tool. Click with the Paint Bucket tool on the baseline of the source text to display the t above the Paint Bucket cursor.

3. Click the type or type container of the destination text.

To apply (paste) the text attributes to selected destination text, drag with the Paint Bucket cursor over the characters you want selected. The attributes are copied from the source text to the selected desti-nation text.

You don't have to select the destination text with the Selection tool because the Paint Bucket tool acts like a selection tool when you click on text. As long as it displays the t, you know you've sampled the text.

EXERCISE C

1. In a new document (File/New), select the Type tool and type *Source Text*. Click on the Selection tool to select the text and dis-play its baseline. Display the Character palette (Command/Ctrl-T) and format the selected text any way you like.

2. Use the Type tool to create another text block (point type). Type *Destination Text*, click the Selection tool, and format that text differently from the first text block. Deselect everything (Command/Ctrl-Shift-A).

3. Drag the Eyedropper tool out and click on the Tearoff Tab to create a floating palette of just the Eyedropper and Paint Bucket tools.

4. Select the Eyedropper tool and click the *Source Text* text block. The t appears over the Eyedropper, indicating that the type attributes have been sampled (copied).

5. Select the Paint Bucket tool and click on the baseline of the *Destination Text* text block to apply (paste) the attributes from the sampled source text to the destination text.

Macintosh Keystrokes

⌘-N File/New
⌘-T Type/Character
⌘-Shift-A Edit/Deselect All
⌘-W File/Close

Windows Keystrokes

Ctrl-N File/New
Ctrl-T Type/Character
Ctrl-Shift-A Edit/Deselect All
Ctrl-W File/Close

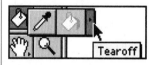

Shortcut

You don't have to select text before clicking with the Paint Bucket tool; it's just easier to find the baseline when the text is selected.

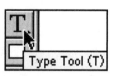

Type Tool (T)

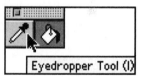

Eyedropper Tool (I)

Tip

Press the Option/Alt key to switch from the Eye-dropper to the Paint Bucket tool.

Macintosh Keystrokes

⌘-Shift-A Edit/Deselect All
⌘-W File/Close

Windows Keystrokes

Ctrl-Shift-A Edit/Deselect All
Ctrl-W File/Close

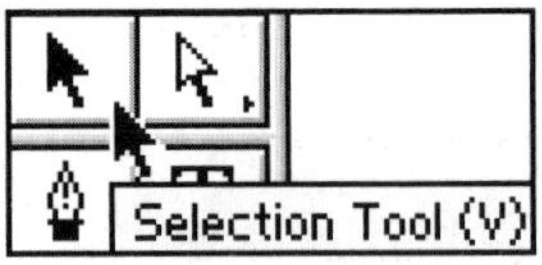

Tip

To select all of the text automatically when the Area Type tool is selected, click on the Selection tool. Any changes you now make will be applied to all the text inside the path.

Linked text containers can be any shape or size.

6. Deselect everything (Command/Ctrl-Shift-A). Use the Selection tool to select the *Source Text* text block and format it differently. Repeat for the *Destination Text* text block.
7. Select the *Source Text* text block. Select the Paint Bucket tool and click the type path of the *Destination Text* text block. The Paint Bucket cursor displays a ↑, indicating that it is applying attributes from the selected text.
8. Close this file. Don't save your changes.

LINKING TEXT

When the Overflow Indicator appears on an open or closed path that has been filled with text, you must either enlarge the text path to contain the text or create additional linked text containers to hold the overflow text. Remember, overflow text does not print.

ENLARGING TEXT CONTAINERS

When enlarging text containers to hold overflow text, always select the rectangle text box with the Direct Selection tool. This tool selects only the box and not the text. If you select the text rectangle with the Selection tool, the text will also be selected and enlarged when the rectangle text box is enlarged. It's easier to enlarge text containers in Artwork view because you can see the unstroked segments of the rectangle text box.

LINKING TEXT CONTAINERS

To link the overflow text box to additional text boxes, draw rectangles with the Rectangle tool and select all the rectangles (including the original text rectangle) with the Selection tool. Then choose Type/Blocks/Link and the text will flow from the original text box to the other rectangles, filling them in the order in which you drew them. When you apply the Link command, any fill and stroke colors applied to the new rectangles are removed.

UNLINKING TEXT CONTAINERS

Once an object is filled with type, it becomes a type object. And once it is linked to another object, it becomes a linked type object, grouped with the original type object. To break the link between all the linked boxes for one type object, Shift-select or marquee-select all the boxes in the grouped type object with any selection tool and choose Type/Blocks/Unlink. The objects will unlink, and although the type will remain in the separate, unlinked objects, those objects are no longer linked together.

DUPLICATING TEXT CONTAINERS

If you don't want to draw additional text boxes, but want to link the text to additional boxes like the original, Option/Alt-drag a selected rectangle (or other shape box) to create a duplicate box into which the text flows. There are two ways to do this:

1. In Artwork view, click on a segment with the Direct Selection tool to select only the text container, not the text. Then use the Attributes palette to display its center point. Click on the center point and drag while pressing the Option/Alt key to create a duplicate, linked text object. Release the mouse button, *then* the modifier key (Option/Alt key). Don't click and release the mouse button on the center point or you will select the text as well as the object. Just click and drag right away.

2. Use the Group Selection tool to click on a segment of the text container, not the text baselines, and drag, pressing the Option/Alt key to create a duplicate.

EXERCISE D

1. Open the *Text.ai* file in the Unit 14 folder on the CD-ROM. Choose View/Artwork (Command/Ctrl-Y) to display the text rectangle.

2. Display the Attributes palette and click the Show Center button to display the text rectangle's center point.

3. Use the Direct Selection tool and click on the center point of the text rectangle to select *only the rectangle* with the Overflow Indicator, not its text.

4. Double-click on the Scale tool, type 200 in the Uniform field, and click on OK. The text rectangle enlarges to display all the text and the Overflow Indicator disappears.

5. Choose Edit/Undo (Command/Ctrl-Z) to return to the original text rectangle displaying the Overflow Indicator. Make sure you are in Artwork view, because you need to see the segments of the unstroked rectangle. Select the Direct Selection tool and click on the right segment of the text rectangle. Press the Shift key to constrain the axis of the segment, and drag to enlarge the rectangle until all the text fits. Release the mouse button, *then* the Shift key (Figure 14.7).

Macintosh Keystrokes

⌘-O File/Open
⌘-Y View/Artwork/Preview
⌘-Z Edit/Undo

Windows Keystrokes

Ctrl-O File/Open
Ctrl-Y View/Artwork/
    Preview
Ctrl-Z Edit/Undo

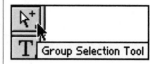

Click the Show Center button on the Attributes palette to display the center point of a text object.

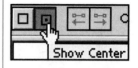

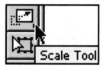

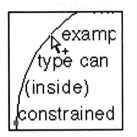

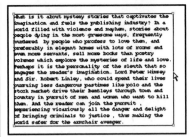

The Group Selection tool selects only the path when you click directly on the path. If you click any-where else, you will select both the path and the type.

Tip

Once you Option/Alt-drag to create a linked text object, press Command/Ctrl-D (Object/Transform/Repeat Transform) to cre-ate another linked object until all the text is dis-played.

6. Choose File/Revert. Click on the Revert button to revert to the original *Text.ai* file without saving any changes.

7. Still in Artwork view, use the Direct Selection tool and click on the right side of the text object to select only the rectangle, not the text. Use the Attributes palette to display the center point Click on the center point, start dragging, and press the Option/Alt key to create another linked text object.

8. In Preview view, click on any of the two text objects to select both the rectangles and the text. Notice that the duplicate, linked rectangle displays a + sign (the Overflow Indicator), indicating that the text still does not fit in the linked text boxes (Figure 14.8).

What is it about mystery stories that captivates the imagination and fuels the publishing industry? In a world filled with violence and mayhem, stories about people dying in the most gruesome ways, frequently murdered by people who profess to love them, and preferably in elegant homes with lots of rooms and even more servants, sell more books than poetry volumes which explore the mysteries of life and love. Perhaps it is the personality of the sleuth that so engages the reader's imagination. Lord Peter Wimsey and Sir. Robert Linley, who could

Figure 14.8. The linked rectangles still display the Overflow Indicator.

9. Use the Pen tool to draw an object (a closed path) that looks like a lethal weapon, or use any of the drawing tools to draw another closed path. Select the two text rectangles and the new path, and choose Type/Blocks/Link. The text flows from the second rectangle to the new text path (Figure 14.9). If the Over-flow Indicator appears (in Preview view only) on the new text object, create another closed path, select the four objects, and choose the Link command again (Type/Blocks/Link).

230

Unit 14 ★ Type

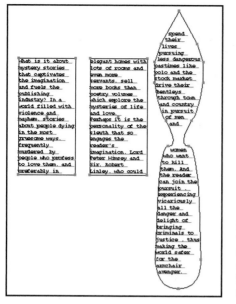

⌘-Y View/Artwork/Preview
⌘-A Edit/Select All
⌘-T Type/Character
⌘-W File/Close

Windows Keystrokes

Ctrl-Y View/Artwork/
    Preview
Ctrl-A Edit/Select All
Ctrl-T Type/Character
Ctrl-W File/Close

Figure 14.9. When the three text objects are selected and the Link command is applied, the overflow text flows into the third text object.

10. Return to Preview view and use the Direct Selection tool to select each object. Apply a different fill and stroke to each of the objects.

11. Select the Type tool, click in any text object, and choose Edit/ Select All to select all the linked type. Use the Character palette to apply a different typeface and type size. Your screen should resemble Figure 14.10.

12. Close this file (Command/Ctrl-W). Don't save your changes.

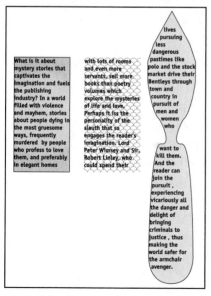

FYI

You can resize a text object by dragging the Bounding Box handles without resizing the type inside the text object.

Figure 14.10. The three text objects are each assigned a different fill and stroke, and the type is selected with the Type tool and edited.

Macintosh Keystrokes

⌘-N File/New
⌘-M Type/Paragraph
⌘-Y View/Artwork/Preview

Windows Keystrokes

Ctrl-N File/New
Ctrl-M Type/Paragraph
Ctrl-Y View/Artwork/
    Preview

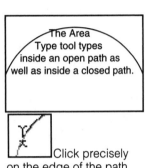

Click precisely on the edge of the path with the Area Type tool.

Area Type Tool

Ellipse Tool

Justify Full Lines

AREA TYPE TOOL

Use the Area Type tool to enter type inside any closed path or along the inner perimeter of an open path. If you use this tool on an open path, Illustrator creates an imaginary line between the endpoints of the path to define the path for type to follow.

To edit the path, use the Direct Selection tool. To edit the text, use any of the Type tools to select text, or the Selection tool to select the entire text block (Figure 14.11).

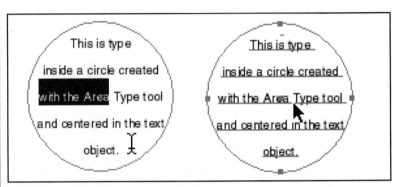

Figure 14.11. The area type on the left is selected with any type tool. Unless you choose Edit/Select All or triple-click on the text, you can only select the text you highlight by dragging. The area type on the right is selected with the Selection tool and any editing will affect all the text in the text object.

EXERCISE E

1. On a clean drawing page (File/New), use the Ellipse tool to draw a circle by pressing the Shift key while dragging.

2. Choose View/Artwork (Command/Ctrl-Y). Use the Swatches palette to assign the circle a fill and 6-pt. stroke.

3. Click on the Area Type tool to select it. Click directly on the circular path to begin entering type inside the path. As soon as you click on the path, the fill and stroke disappear.

4. After typing a few words, click the Justified Alignment icon on the Paragraph palette (Command/Ctrl-M) to fit the text within the confines of the circle (Figure 14.12).

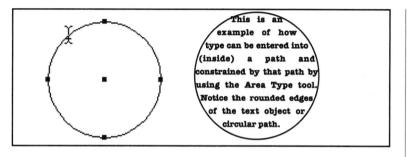

Figure 14.12. Use the Area Type cursor to enter text inside a closed path. The text was justified in the path and the path was stroked for emphasis.

5. With the Area Type tool still selected, choose Edit/Select All to select all of the text. Format the text from the Character palette (Command/Ctrl-T).

6. Close this file (Command/Ctrl-W). Don't save your changes.

EDITING TEXT PATHS

In the last exercise, once the circle was drawn and the type entered inside the path, only the type was edited using the Type tool, Area Type tool, or the Selection tool. To edit the path, use either the Direct Selection tool or the Group Selection tool to select the path.

When working with type in or along paths, it's a good idea to use Artwork view, at least until you have the path selected. This allows you to see the path's outline even though it has not been stroked. Once the path is selected, you can always switch to Preview view.

COPYFITTING

Illustrator's Fit Headline command (Type/Fit Headline) is useful for tracking a single line of type to the edge of the text object. To do this, select the line of type to be tracked outward, and choose the Fit Headline command from the Type menu (Figure 14.13). It is used to fit type across the width of a text path in a text object. The command is available only when type is entered into a text rectangle or into a text area. You cannot use this command for text on an open path.

Always format the headline before applying the Fit Headline command, because this command applies a specific tracking value to the type, and changes you make to the type will affect the width of the headline.

Set in stone: This is bad news.

Once you click on a path with any of the path type tools, the path "memorizes" that path tool and won't let you use a different path type tool on the same path—even if you delete the text. For example, if you click on a path with the Area Type tool, then change your mind and switch to the Path Type tool, you won't get the Path Type tool to "hook" onto the path. Draw another path and then use the Path Type tool. Even better, duplicate a complex path before using the path type tools, just in case you change your mind.

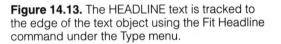

HEADLINE
What is it about mystery stories that captivates the imagination and fuels the publishing industry? In a world filled with violence and mayhem, stories about people dying in the most gruesome ways, frequently murdered by people who profess to love them, and preferably in elegant homes with lots of rooms and even more servants, sell more books than poetry volumes which explore the mysteries of life and love. Perhaps it is the personality of the sleuth that so engages the reader's imagination. Lord Peter Wimsey and

Figure 14.13. The HEADLINE text is tracked to the edge of the text object using the Fit Headline command under the Type menu.

IMPORTING TEXT

Text can be typed directly into any object or along any path using the Area Type tool or any of the text path tools. To import text into an object, click on the edge of the object with the appropriate type tool and begin typing. Or, click on the edge of the object with the Area Type tool and choose File/Place, highlight the name of the file you want to place, and click on Place (Macintosh) or Open (Windows). The text flows into the selected text object.

If you don't select an object into which the type can be imported, when you use the Place command with the Type tool selected, the placed type will appear on the page inside a text rectangle. If you use the Open command, Illustrator also automatically creates a rectangle into which the type is imported.

Ellipse Tool

Area Type Tool

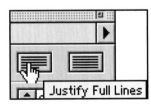

Justify Full Lines

EXERCISE F

1. In a new document (File/New), display the Swatches, Stroke, Character, and Paragraph palettes.

2. Use the Ellipse tool and press the Shift key to draw a circle. With the circle selected, click on its edge with the Area Type tool. Choose File/Place and highlight the *Circle.txt* file in the Unit 14 folder on the CD-ROM. Click on Place (Macintosh) or Open (Windows) to place the text inside the circle.

3. Choose Edit/Select All to select all the text in the circle. Format it in any typeface.

4. Click on the Justify Full Lines icon in the Paragraph palette to justify the text between the sides of the circle.

5. Deselect everything (Command/Ctrl-Shift-A).

6. Choose View/Artwork (Command/Ctrl-Y). Click on the Group Selection tool and click on the path to select it. Then choose View/Preview (Command/Ctrl-Y).

7. Apply a radial fill to the background of the circle. Apply a stroke to the outside of the path.

8. Choose Edit/Deselect All (Command/Ctrl-Shift-A) to deselect everything. Use the Group Selection tool and click inside the circle to select the text object and all of the text.

9. Use the Character palette to apply a new typeface and type size to the selected type.

10. Use the Leading field on the Character palette to select a leading value greater than the type size. This will help to vertically justify the text in the circle.

11. Click the Align Center icon on the Paragraph palette to center the text inside the circle. If necessary, select only the circle with the Group Selection tool, double-click on the Scale tool, and reduce or enlarge the circle to fit the text. Your screen should resemble Figure14.14.

12. Close this file (Command/Ctrl-W). Don't save your changes.

Macintosh Keystrokes

⌘-Shift-A Edit/Deselect All
⌘-Y View/Preview/Artwork
⌘-W File/Close

Windows Keystrokes

Ctrl-Shift-A Edit/Deselect All
Ctrl-Y View/Preview/Artwork
Ctrl-W File/Close

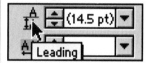

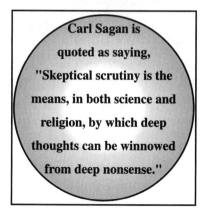

Figure 14.14. The text path was selected with the Group Selection tool and a radial fill applied to it.

REVIEW

In this unit you learned that:

1. There are four kinds of type in Illustrator: point type, area type, path type, and vertical type.

2. Type must always be selected before it can be edited. Double-click with any type tool to select a word; triple-click to select a paragraph.

3. Type attributes can be selected from the Type menu or from the Character palette.

4. Type can be resized manually using the Scale tool or the keyboard shortcuts.

5. Painting attributes (fill and stroke) can be applied to type.

6. The Direct Selection tool is used to select the type in a type container without selecting the container.

7. The Eyedropper and Paint Bucket tools can be used to copy (sample) and paste type paint attributes and apply them to other type and non-type objects.

8. Dragging with the Type tool creates a type container.

9. Type containers can be resized with the Direct Selection tool and with the Bounding Box handles.

10. Type containers can be linked to create more room for over-flow text. Linked type containers can be unlinked.

11. The Area Type tool is used to enter type inside any closed path or along the inner perimeter of an open path.

12. To edit a type path or type container, select it with the Direct Selection tool.

13. The Fit Headline command stretches a single line of text between the edges of the type container.

OVERVIEW

In this unit you will learn how to:
create type on an open and closed path
resize and reshape text paths
position type on a path
wrap text around an object
convert text to paths
transform type and type containers
use type as a mask

TERMS

baseline
baseline shift
compound paths
mask (masking object)
masked object
text outlines
text path

HOW IT WORKS

Create one circle for the Unit 15 type and another for the Type Effects text, using the Path Type tool to set and edit the type. Select the top circle, copy, and paste in front. With that third circle selected, apply a path pattern. Use kerning, tracking, and baseline shift to position the text above and below the type paths.

PATH TYPE TOOLS

Use the Path Type tools to place type horizontally or vertically along an open or closed path. Once you click with this tool on a path, that path becomes a text path, allowing you to manipulate the text and its path separately.

Text can be placed on only one side of the same path, but it can be moved using the I-beam cursor. Don't press the Return/Enter key after entering text on a path, because you can place only one line of text on any path.

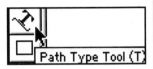

PATH TYPE TOOL

To use the Path Type tool, first create the path. If you paint and/or stroke the path before entering the text, those paint attributes will be reset to None once you enter the text. You can always use the Direct Selection or Group Selection tool to select and edit the path later. The path-type cursor displays a slant line when it is not on a path.

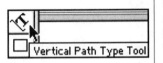

VERTICAL PATH TYPE TOOL

The Vertical Path Type tool creates vertical type around an open or closed path. As you type, the text runs up from the cursor and is positioned vertically on the path (Figure 15.1).

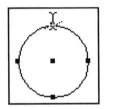

When using the Path Type tool, make sure the dotted line on the cursor crosses the path before you click.

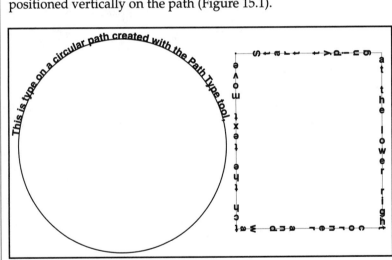

Figure 15.1. Type created around a circle with the Path Type tool and type created around a rectangle with the Vertical Path Type tool.

Using a graphic typeface such as Botanical MT and the Vertical Path Type tool creates a flowered border around the path.

EXERCISE A

Macintosh Keystrokes

⌘-Y View/Preview/Artwork
⌘-T Type/Character
⌘-Shift-A Edit/Deselect All

Windows Keystrokes

Ctrl-Y View/Preview/
    Artwork
Ctrl-T Type/Character
Ctrl-Shift-A Edit/Deselect
    All

1. On a clean drawing page (File/New), choose View/Artwork (Command/ Ctrl-Y). Display the Swatches palette and the Character palette (Command/Ctrl-T). It should be docked with the Paragraph palette.

2. Use the Pencil tool to draw a curvy path about six inches long.

3. Deselect everything (Command-Shift-A).

4. Click on the triangle in the Type tool icon and drag to select the Path Type tool.

5. Click the Align Left icon on the Paragraph palette and click at the beginning of the path. The cursor changes from an I-beam with a slant line to a flashing cursor. Type a few words on the path.

6. Click on the Selection tool to indicate that the typing has stopped and to select all of the text.

7. Use the Character palette to select a typeface and type size.

8. Deselect everything (Command/Ctrl-Shift-A). Click on the Path Type tool and double-click to select one word on the path. Use the Character palette to change its typeface and type size.

9. Deselect everything. Choose View/Artwork (Command/Ctrl-Y). Choose Window/Show Attributes and click on the Show Center button to display the center point for the text path. Select the Group Selection tool and click on the center point of the path to select only the path. Return to Preview view and apply a stroke color from the Swatches palette. Your screen should resemble Figure 15.2.

10. Save this file (File/Save As) as *Path1.ai* as an Illustrator file in your Projects folder.

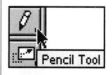

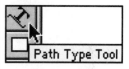

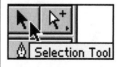

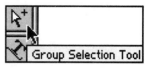

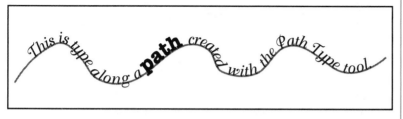

Figure 15.2. A curved path with text that has been styled. The path was selected with one click of the Group Selection tool at its center point in Artwork view and stroked with a 2-point colored stroke.

Macintosh Keystrokes

⌘-O File/Open
⌘-Y View/Preview/Artwork
⌘-Shift-A Edit/Deselect All

Windows Keystrokes

Ctrl-O File/Open
Ctrl-Y View/Preview/
    Artwork
Ctrl-Shift-A Edit/Deselect
    All

FYI

When you click on the Selection tool after creating point type, all the type becomes selected and can be edited.

The Overflow Indicator (+) indicates that there is more text on the path than the path can display.

RESIZING/RESHAPING AN OPEN PATH TEXT OBJECT

Once you have added text to an open path, you can resize it and reshape the path. Reshape the path and thereby change the position of the text on that path by first using the Direct Selection or Group Selection tool to select the path and then selecting and moving anchor points and direction handles.

Resizing the text object is a little more complicated. If the path is too long and is not stroked, it really doesn't matter how long it is, because it won't display or print. But if the path is to be stroked, then length is an issue.

To shorten the text path, you must add an anchor point and then delete it and all the subsequent anchor points. To lengthen the path, simply drag one of the endpoints out until the text fits the path.

EXERCISE B

1. Open the *Path Type Practice.ai* file in the Unit 15 folder on the CD-ROM (Command-O).

2. Choose View/Artwork (Command/Ctrl-Y). Notice that the path is too short to fit the text, *Lend a helping hand*. Choose View/New View 1. to magnify the right endpoint.

3. Use the Direct Selection tool to select the path. Then click on the right endpoint. Drag the endpoint to the right until the Overflow Indicator disappears and all the text is displayed (Figure 15.3). Deselect everything (Command-Shift-A).

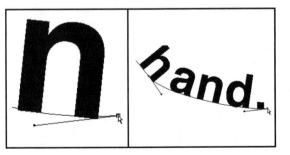

Figure 15.3. Use the Direct Selection tool to stretch a path object (left) until it can display all of the text (right).

4. Once all the text is displayed, use the Direct Selection tool again to select the path. Click on the right endpoint again and drag it out a few inches so that it is longer than necessary (Figure 15.4).

Figure 15.4. Use the Direct Selection tool to stretch the path beyond the last text character, the period.

5. To cut the excess path, select the endpoint with the Direct Selection tool and drag it close to the period after the *d.* You can shorten a text path as far back as the first anchor point.

6. If the path is still too long, use the Add Anchor Point tool and click once on the path *after the period* in the text. An anchor point appears (Figure 15.5).

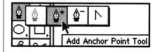

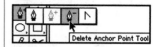

Figure 15.5. Use the Add Anchor Point tool to add an anchor point to the path you want to shorten. You can then use the Delete Anchor Point tool to delete the new anchor point and all subsequent anchor points to shorten the path.

7. Use the Delete Anchor Point tool and click on the extra anchor points to delete them. Leave the endpoint, because every open path must have an endpoint.

8. Use the Direct Selection tool to select anchor points and direction handles and move them to reshape the path. Remember, using the Direct Selection tool selects the path, not the text.

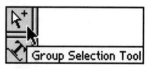

9. You can now use the Type tool to select the text and apply font, size, and paint attributes to the text. You can also use the Selection tool to select the entire text object so that font, style, and size changes will apply to all the text in the text object.

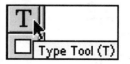

10. Use the Direct Selection tool or the Group Selection tool to select the path (use Artwork view) and apply fill and/or stroke attributes to the path. Your screen might resemble Figure 15.6.

11. Close this file. Don't save your changes.

Figure 15.6. The text path is resized and reshaped, and the text is edited.

What you see is not what you get!

When you select a text object like an open path with type running along it with the Selection tool, the path appears to be selected, but it is not. Only the text is selected.

Tip

You can also resize type and/or use the Letter spacing and Word spacing fields in the Paragraph palette to copyfit type on a path.

Select Empty Text Paths from the Cleanup dialog box (Object/Path/ Cleanup) to remove any unused text paths and/or type containers.

The dotted bar on the Path Type cursor must cross the path before clicking to create path type.

POSITIONING TYPE ON A PATH

In the last exercise you worked with type positioned on top of the path. You can also move the type along the path and flip the type so that it runs along the bottom of the path. Flipping is a useful maneuver when you want to create text above and below a circle.

MOVING TYPE

Move type on a path by first selecting the path. If you select with the Selection tool, the I-beam cursor appears. Drag the I-beam cursor to the right or left (Figure 15.7). If you select the path with the Direct Selection tool, you must click with a horizontal type tool to display the I-beam. When moving type along a path, be careful not to move the cursor down or you will flip the type.

Figure 15.7. Drag with the I-beam cursor to move type on a path or to flip it from one side of the path to the other.

DELETING EMPTY TYPE PATHS

To avoid printing problems, delete any unused type containers or type paths from a finished document. To do this, use the Cleanup dialog box under the Object/Path menu. If there are no empty paths to delete, a message will appear telling you so.

FLIPPING TYPE

Flip type on a path by dragging the I-beam cursor down or up to position the type upside down or right side up on the path (Figure 15.7). You can also double-click on the I-beam cursor to flip type in either direction. If you drag or flip type and are dissatisfied with the way it looks, use the Edit/Undo command (Command/Ctrl-Z) to undo the last command.

EXERCISE C

1. Open the *Path1.ai* file in the Unit 15 folder on the CD-ROM (Command/Ctrl-O) or create text on an open path.

2. Use the Selection tool and click on the path to select it. Click on the I-beam. Drag it to the right across the path and release the mouse button.

3. Double-click with the Selection tool on the I-beam. The type flips to the bottom of the path.

4. Click on the I-beam and drag it to the right (or left) until the text is fully displayed. As you drag, notice the Overflow Indicator, which appears only when you are moving the I-beam.

5. Close this file (Command/Ctrl-W). Don't save your changes.

CREATING TYPE AROUND CIRCULAR PATHS

To create type above or below a circle, you need only one circle. However, to create type above *and* below the circle, you must use two circles as paths and then position one circle on top of the other to create the illusion of type above and below one circle.

An easier way to do this is to click on the part of the I-beam inside the circle, drag it down, and press the Option/Alt key to create a duplicate of the type. Then edit the duplicated type.

EXERCISE D

1. In a new file (Command/Ctrl-N), choose View/Artwork (Command/Ctrl-Y). Display the Color palette (F6), Swatches palette, the Character palette (Command/Ctrl-T), and the Paragraph palette (Command/Ctrl-M) if it isn't docked to the Character palette.

2. Use the Ellipse tool to draw an oval or circle about two inches wide. While it is selected, Option/Alt-Shift-drag down with the Selection tool to create a duplicate circle directly below the original.

3. Select the Path Type tool and click on the top circle. Click the Align Center icon on the Paragraph palette to center the type along the path. Type a few words. If the Alert message is displayed, try again, making sure that the dotted line on the Path Type tool crosses the oval's path.

4. With the Path Type tool still active and the insertion bar flashing in the text (click with the Path Type tool to make it flash), choose Edit/Select All (Command/Ctrl-A) to select all the text. Format it from the Font menus or from the Character palette.

5. Choose Window/Swatch Libraries/Other Library. Navigate to the Adobe Illustrator folder on the hard drive, open the Other Libraries folder, open the Pattern Samples folder, and double-click on the *Pattern1.ai* folder to load the new pattern file into the document. It will appear there as a secondary palette.

Macintosh Keystrokes

⌘-W File/Close
⌘-N File/New
⌘-Y View/Preview/Artwork
⌘-T Type/Character
⌘-M Type/Paragraph
F6 Window/Show Color

Windows Keystrokes

Ctrl-W File/Close
Ctrl-N File/New
Ctrl-Y View/Preview/
   Artwork
Ctrl-T Type/Character
Ctrl-M Type/Paragraph
F6 Window/Show Color

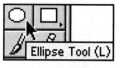

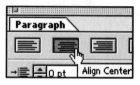

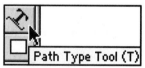

Easy does it!

An easier way to create type above and below a circle is to create the type above the circle and click the Selection tool to display the I-beam. Click on the bottom bar of the I-beam and drag it down, pressing the Option/Alt key to create the duplicate circle. Then select the text on the lower circle and format it.

Baseline Shift

Selecting a positive number from the Baseline Shift pull-down menu or typing a positive number in the text field moves the selected text above the path; a negative number moves it below the path.

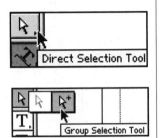

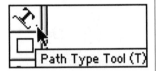

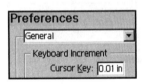

FYI

Pressing Command-Option-Shift (Macintosh) or Ctrl-Alt-Shift (Windows) and pressing the Up or Down Arrow keys shifts the baseline of the selected text in 10-point increments. Pressing Option/Alt-Shift and the Up or Down Arrow moves the baseline the number of points set in the Baseline Shift field of the Keyboard Increments dialog box.

6. Scroll to locate the *Leaves-fall* pattern and use the Selection tool to drag it onto the page (Figure 15.8).

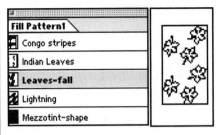

Figure 15.8. Open a pattern file and drag a pattern onto the page to edit it.

7. Select the Fill icon in the Toolbox. Select each leaf in the pattern with the Direct Selection tool and click on an autumn color in the Color palette to fill the leaf. When all the leaves are a different color, use the Selection tool to drag a selection marquee around all the leaves and the rectangle behind them. Drag the tile into the Swatches palette, where it becomes a new pattern.

8. Make sure the Fill icon is active in the Toolbox. Use the Direct Selection or Group Selection tool to select the path—not the text—and click on the new pattern swatch you just created to fill the circle.

9. Click the Stroke icon in the Toolbox and apply a stroke color to the path.

10. To move the text above the path, select the text with any type tool by triple-clicking on the text. Choose Show Options from the Character palette menu and use the Baseline shift command to position the text (Figure 15.9).

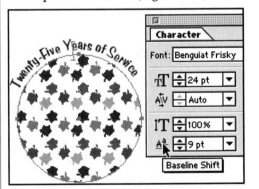

Figure 15.9. Select the text and use the Baseline Shift command to move the text above the path.

11. Select the Path Type tool and click on the bottom of the second circle. Type a few more words. Double-click on the I-beam cursor to flip the text right side up. Triple-click on the text and format it, then apply a negative Baseline Shift value to move it below the path. Don't fill or stroke the path.

Unit 15 ★ Type Effects

12. Make sure Snap to Point is selected under the View menu. Switch to Artwork view (Command/Ctrl-Y). Use the Direct Selection or Group Selection tool to select the lower circle from its center point. Press the Shift key and drag it upward until it fits on top of the original circle. You'll know this happened when the cursor snaps to the center point.

13. Use the Direct Selection tool to select any circle (they're on top of one another), and apply a stroke color. Your screen should resemble Figure 15.10.

14. Close this file (Command/Ctrl-W). Don't save your changes.

Figure 15.10. Select the text and use the Baseline Shift command to move the text above the path. Drag the pattern out of the Swatches palette, select one of the leaves with the Group Selection tool, and position it around the circle. Duplicate the leaf and position it on the other side of the circle between the type.

TEXT WRAP

The text wrap or text runaround function in Illustrator works in a manner similar to the way it works in a page layout program. The Wrap command under the Type menu wraps text in a rectangle or in another text container around any open or closed path. When wrapping text, the object must be in front of the text container in the stacking order on the drawing page. If you find the Wrap command not available (dimmed), select the object and choose Arrange/Bring to Front. Once it wraps the text in the text object around the wrap object, Illustrator groups both objects.

Text wrapped around an object can be unwrapped by selecting the group (text object and wrap object) and choosing Wrap/Release from the Type menu.

EXERCISE E

1. On a new drawing page, choose View/Artwork (Command/Ctrl-Y). Display the Swatches palette and the Paragraph palette (Command/Ctrl-M).

2. Select the Rectangle tool and drag to draw a rectangle.

3. Select the Area Type tool and click on the top of the rectangle. You must click on the path with this tool. Choose File/Place

Macintosh Keystrokes

⌘-Y View/Artwork/Preview
⌘-N File/New

Windows Keystrokes

Ctrl-Y View/Artwork/
    Preview
Ctrl-N File/New

Tip

Type can be offset from the graphic object by selecting the text and inputting values in the Left and Right Indentation fields on the Paragraph palette.

Another way to achieve type offset is to wrap the type around a path to which you have applied a fill and stroke of none. The graphic object is then positioned on top of the "dummy" path.

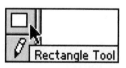

Sorry!

The type container cannot be grouped with another object if it is to wrap around an object.

Macintosh Keystrokes

⌘-Shift-A Edit/Deselect All
⌘-W File/Close

Windows Keystrokes

Ctrl-Shift-A Edit/Deselect
  All
Ctrl-W File/Close

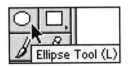

Problems?

If you find the Wrap/Make command dimmed, it's probably because you don't have two objects selected.

Sorry!

You must convert all the type in a text block to outlines, not just individual characters. To create outlines from an individual text character, create that character as a separate text block.

and navigate to the Unit 15 folder on the CD-ROM. Highlight the *Text.txt* file and click on Place. Don't worry if the Overflow Indicator appears.

4. Use the Ellipse tool and press the Shift key to draw a circle that covers part of the rectangle. The text will eventually wrap around the arc of the circle—later!

5. *Select both objects* and choose Type/Wrap/Make. The text wraps around the arc of the circle and both objects are grouped (Figure 15.11).

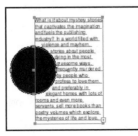

Figure 15.11. The Wrap command wraps the text around the intruding object (arc of the circle) and groups both items.

6. With the group still selected, click on the Up Arrow of the Left Indent icon on the Paragraph palette to move the type away from the arc (Figure 15.12). Choose Edit/Deselect All to see the effect of the wrap.

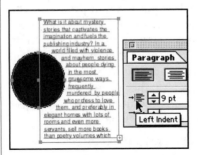

Figure 15.12. Increasing the Left Indent value moves the text away from the wrap object.

7. Choose Type/Wrap/Release. Use the Selection tool to move the circle away from the text object.

8. Close this file. Don't save your changes.

CONVERTING TEXT TO PATHS

One of the most versatile functions in Illustrator is the Create Outlines command, which transforms type into editable artwork. This is a useful technique for creating text-based logos, because you can edit the path to make the former text character conform to the design. Once type is in outline form, it no longer retains its text qualities, and it is edited with the selection tools, rather than with the type tools.

FONT ISSUES

For this command to work, the Type 1 or TrueType font outlines for that typeface must be installed in your system, because it is from those fonts that Illustrator takes the paths it creates. If the printer (outline) font is not available when you choose the Create Outlines command, you will get an alert. Click OK and choose another font.

OUTLINE COMPOUND PATHS

If the type you convert to outlines has an interior path, called a *counter*, such as in the letters *P*, *e*, *g*, and *q*, Illustrator creates a compound path from the two resulting paths, thus making the counter transparent against the page. A compound path unites two or more path objects into one object, and where the paths overlap (as with the counters), a hole is created that is transparent against the page.

EXERCISE F

1. On a clean drawing page (File/New), choose View/Preview (Command/ Ctrl-Y). Restore the original values to the Character palette; otherwise the Baseline Shift values from the last exercise will apply.

2. Select the Type tool and click anywhere on the page. Type *PLOP*. Click on the Selection tool to select the text.

3. Format it in a large-point typeface. Be sure to choose a typeface with the outline (printer) font installed in your system.

4. With the type still selected by the Selection tool (the baseline and alignment point are visible), choose Type/Create Outlines (Command/Ctrl-Shift-O). The type appears as four selected paths. Click on an empty area of the page to deselect everything.

5. Use the Selection tool to select the second *P*. Apply a fill and stroke to just that object (it isn't a text character anymore!).

6. Click on the Rotate tool and click on the upper left corner of the *P*. Move the cursor away from the object and drag to rotate it to the right. Press the Shift key to constrain the rotation to 90°.

7. Use the Selection tool to move the rotated object a little below the other objects. Drag a selection marquee around all four objects and apply a gradient fill. Stroke the objects. Use the Selection tool to select each text object and, where necessary, position the object closer to the one next to it. Your screen should resemble Figure 15.13.

Macintosh Keystrokes

⌘-Y View/Artwork/Preview
⌘-Shift-O Type/Create
    Outlines

Windows Keystrokes

Ctrl-Y View/Artwork/
    Preview
Ctrl-Shift-O Type/Create
    Outlines

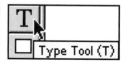

FYI

The only way to reset the Character and Paragraph palettes to their default values is to select Auto or 100% from the individual menus.

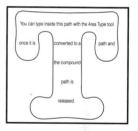

If you select a type outline and choose Object/Compound Paths/Release, you can use those type outlines as type containers.

Macintosh Keystrokes

⌘-Shift-O Type/Create
    Outlines
⌘-Option-8 Object/
    Compound Paths/
    Release

Windows Keystrokes

Ctrl-Shift-O Type/Create
    Outlines
Ctrl-Alt-8 Object/
    Compound Paths/
    Release

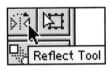

Dragging with the Scale
tool on the alignment
point of a selected text
character reduces or
enlarges the text.

When the text character O
was converted to an out-
line path, the counter and
outside rim were joined
into compound paths,
making the center
(counter) transparent
against the page.

Figure 15.13. Once text has been converted to path outlines, it can be manipulated just like any other path object.

8. Use the Selection tool and drag the O out of the group of
   objects. Notice that it contains an interior and exterior path.
   Choose Object/Compound Paths/Release. Drag the large circle away and notice the smaller, nontransparent circle next to
   it. It is these two circles that were formed into the compound
   path with the transparent center.

9. Type the letter K and click the Selection tool. Use the Scale tool
   to drag on the alignment point to enlarge the type. With the
   type still selected—it's still type—choose Type/Create Outlines
   (Command/Ctrl-Shift-O). Double-click on the Reflect tool and
   select Vertical. Type 90 in the Angle field and click on Copy.

10. Use the Selection tool and press the Shift key to drag the
    reflected K (now a path) to the right of the original (Figure
    15.14). Select both paths and choose Edit/Define Pattern. Draw
    a rectangle and click the new pattern in the Swatches palette.
    Your screen should resemble Figure 15.14.

11. Close this file (Command/Ctrl-W). Don't save your changes.

Figure 15.14. The original text
character is converted to outlines, reflected, and defined as
a fill pattern.

TRANSFORMING TYPE

Selecting a type path or type container with the Selection tool
allows you to use any of the transformation tools on that path or
container. You can transform the path or container and the type
together, or transform just the type or container.

To transform only the type path or type container without transforming the type, use the Group Selection tool to select just the path
(type container). If the baselines appear, the type will also be transformed with the path or container.

TRANSFORMING LINKED TYPE CONTAINERS

You can also transform individual type containers in a series of linked type containers by using the Direct Selection tool to select the linked type containers you want to transform.

EXERCISE G

1. In a new document (File/New), use the Type tool to draw a small rectangle. Drag the arrow on the Direct Selection tool and click on the Tearoff Tab to create a separate palette of selection tools. Select the Area Type tool, click on the rectangle, and type more words than will fit in the rectangle.

2. Draw another rectangle, select both rectangles, and choose Type/Blocks/Link. Use the Direct Selection tool to select the second text block and enlarge it so that it contains all the rest of the text.

3. Use the Direct Selection tool to select each rectangle and apply a stroke so you can better see what's happening.

4. Select any rectangle with the Selection tool, which selects both type containers and their type. You know the type is selected because the baselines appear. Choose Object/Transform/Rotate. Type a value in the Rotate dialog box and click on OK to rotate both containers and their text (Figure 15.15).

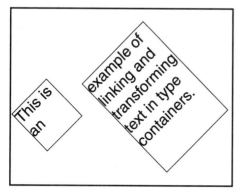

Figure 15.15. Two linked text boxes containing no overflow type.

5. Choose Edit/Undo (Command/Ctrl-Z). Click on an empty area of the page to deselect everything.

6. Use the Direct Selection tool to select the first type container. Make sure the baselines are selected. Choose Object/Transform/Rotate. Type a value in the Rotate dialog box and click OK to rotate the single type container and its type contents.

Direct Selection Tool

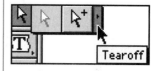
Tearoff

Area Type Tool

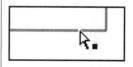

The Direct Selection tool displays a black square when it is over a path. Click to select the path, not its contents.

Selection Tool

Macintosh Keystrokes

⌘-Z Edit/Undo
⌘-N File/New
⌘-T Type/Character
⌘-Shift-O Type/Create
  Outlines
⌘-8 Object/Compound
  Paths/Make

Windows Keystrokes

Ctrl-Z Edit/Undo
Ctrl-N File/New
Ctrl-T Type/Character
Ctrl-Shift-O Type/Create
  Outlines
Ctrl-8 Object/Compound
  Paths/Make

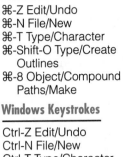

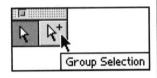

Select this option in the General Preferences dialog box to select a path by clicking inside it with the Direct Selection tool.

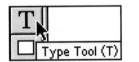

What is that masked object?

A **mask** or **masking object** is a "stencil" placed in front of another object, called the **masked object**. The mask reveals only those parts of the masked object that fit inside the masking object's parameters.

7. Choose Edit/Undo again. Deselect everything. Use the Group Selection tool to select the other type container. Notice that the baselines don't appear, indicating that you are selecting only the path, not the type. Choose Object/Transform/Rotate. Type a value in the Rotate field and click on OK. The path is rotated but not the type. Your screen should resemble Figure 15.16.

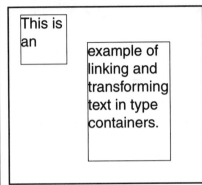

Figure 15.16. Selecting a path with the Group Selection tool selects only the path, not the type.

TYPE AS A MASK

Once you convert type to outlines, you create objects that can be filled with patterns and can be used as mask objects. Masked type is used frequently with Photoshop where type is filled with a graphic. The same technique is available in Illustrator, with the significant difference that the type object in Illustrator started life as a PostScript type character, not a bitmapped text object.

EXERCISE H

1. In a new file (File/New), choose File/Place. Navigate to the Unit 15 folder on the CD-ROM and highlight the *Sunrise.jpg* file. Click on Place (Macintosh) or Open (Windows).

2. Select the Type tool and type SUNRISE. Use the Font menu or Character palette (Command/Ctrl-T) to format the type in a bold typeface at 100 points. Click the Selection tool to select the type's baseline.

3. Choose Type/Create Outlines (Command/Ctrl-Shift-O) to convert the text to paths.

4. Choose Object/Compound Paths/Make (Command/Ctrl-8) to create one path from the former text characters.

5. Use the Selection tool to drag the compound path on top of the graphic, making sure the text object (the mask) is in front of the graphic.

6. Use the Selection tool to drag a selection marquee around both the graphic and the type mask (Figure 15.17).

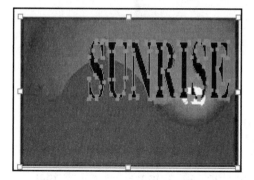

Figure 15.17. Drag the type mask on top of the graphic. Selecting the Bounding Box option lets you use the handles to manually resize the type mask so it fits on the graphic.

7. With both the graphic and the type mask selected, choose Object/Masks/Make (Command-Ctrl-7). The graphic is masked by the type outlines.

8. Deselect everything (Command/Ctrl-Shift-A). Choose Edit/Select/Masks. The mask displays its selection borders. Click on the Stroke icon in the Toolbox and select a stroke color from the Swatches or Color palette to outline the mask. Your screen should resemble Figure 15.18.

Figure 15.18. The type outlines mask the graphic, displaying only what fits inside the mask.

9. Use the Selection tool to select just the graphic. It's easier to do this in Artwork view. Drag the graphic around and notice that when the graphic does not appear under the mask, the mask is empty and displays only its stroke (Figure 15.19).

10. Close this file (File/Close). Don't save your changes.

This is the masked object:

In the *Sunrise* file, the graphic is the masked object and the text is the masking object.

Figure 15.19. Drag the graphic around behind the mask to create different effects. Only the stroked mask is visible where the graphic has been moved below the tops of the masking object.

REVIEW

In this unit you learned that:

1. The Path Type tool is used to create type around a closed path or on an open path.

2. Text paths can be resized and reshaped using the Direct Selection tool.

3. Type can be aligned on any path or positioned by moving the I-beam cursor with the Selection tool. Double-clicking on the I-beam cursor flips the type.

4. To create type around the top and bottom sides of a circular path, two paths must be created.

5. Text in a type container can wrap around another object if the object is in front of the type container in the stacking order. Wrapped text can be unwrapped.

6. The Create Outlines command converts selected text to editable paths.

7. When type is converted to outlines (paths), Illustrator creates a compound path from the two resulting paths in letters such as *R*, *e*, and *g*.

8. Type in a type container, as well as point type, can be transformed using any of the transformation tools.

9. Type in a type container can be transformed without transforming the type container. Or, the type container can be transformed without transforming the type.

10. To transform only the type path or type container without transforming the type, select the container or path with the Group Selection tool.

11. Once type has been converted to outlines (paths), it can be used as a mask.

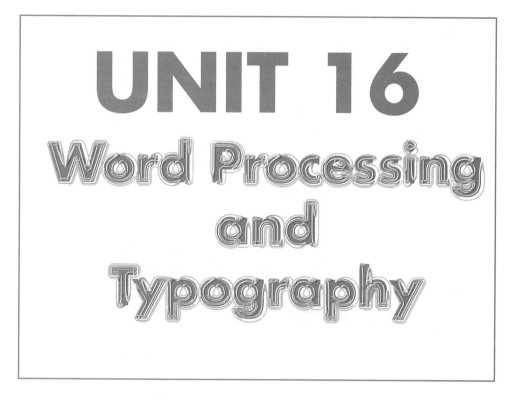

UNIT 16
Word Processing and Typography

OVERVIEW

In this unit you will learn how to:
use the typographic functions of the Character
    palette
format paragraphs from the Paragraph palette
find and change fonts
check spelling
use typographic punctuation
display hidden characters

TERMS

discretionary hyphen
font family
kerning
letter spacing
ligatures
tracking
word spacing

HOW IT WORKS

The type was converted to outlines and compound paths. The Paper Clip brush was duplicated and saved as a new Art brush. It was then reduced 50% in its Options dialog box and applied as a stroke to the type outlines.

The Multinational Options fields can be left at their default values unless you're working in a language other than English.

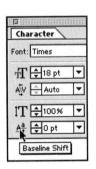

FYI
—
A font family is the complete set of characters in one style for a specific typeface. Palatino, for example, is a font family. Palatino Bold is a style of Palatino.

To quickly select a font name from the Font menu on the Character palette, click Font and type the first letter of the font family to display the font family's name.

CHARACTER PALETTE

Many of the text attributes accessed from the Font menu are also (and more easily) available from the Character palette. Like all palettes in Illustrator, when you type a value in any field, you must press the Return/Enter key to execute the value. You don't have to press the Return/Enter key when making menu selections.

OPTIONS

Click the triangle on the right side of the palette to hide or display the Show Options menu item. Unless you select Show Options, only the font, weight, size, leading, and tracking values appear. Selecting Show Options also displays fields for adjusting horizontal and vertical scale and the baseline shift (Figure 16.1).

Figure 16.1. The Character palette displays the default and optional text fields.

MM (MULTIPLE MASTER) DESIGN PALETTE

Docked to the Character palette is the MM Design palette. If you have Multiple Master fonts installed (customizable Type 1 fonts only), you can use this palette to create new fonts based on extremes (light/bold, wide/narrow, etc.) of the Multiple Master Font.

FONT NAME AND FONT SIZE

Any font installed in your system will appear in the Font menu along the Menu Bar at the top of the drawing page and from the Font pull-down menu on the Character palette. The left Font field displays the name of the font family, like Helvetica or Times. The field next to it displays the style of that font family—regular, bold, italic, etc. Use the pull-down menu on the right to select a different font family and font style.

The Font Size pull-down menu or arrows are used to choose a type size for the selected type. If the size you want is not displayed, type the value in the Type Size field and press Return/Enter. Size is always measured in points, but you don't have to type the abbreviation (pt) in the Size box; Illustrator does it for you.

LEADING

Leading (pronounced *leding*, as in *bedding*) is the amount of vertical space between the lines of type. Like type size, leading is always measured in points. A common leading value is 120 percent of the largest type size in the paragraph. If you select Auto from the Leading pull-down menu, Illustrator will calculate the leading value this way. For example, if the type size is 10 points, the automatic leading value would be 12 points (.10 X 120 = 12).

Leading doesn't work in Illustrator the way it does in programs like QuarkXPress and Microsoft Word, where, to select a paragraph, you click anywhere in the paragraph and the leading value you apply affects every line in the paragraph. In Illustrator, you can apply a different leading value to each line in a paragraph, and you must drag to select at least one character in the line; clicking anywhere in the paragraph doesn't select the paragraph (Figure 16.2).

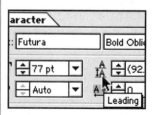

Use the Leading menu or arrows to increase or decrease space between lines of type. Or, select the text and press the Option/Alt key and the Up and Down Arrows to increase or decrease leading.

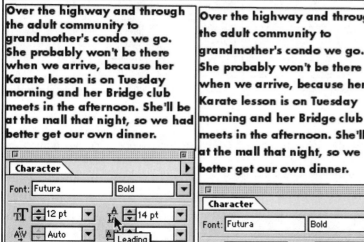

Figure 16.2. The paragraph on the left has 14 points of leading applied to every line in the paragraph. In the paragraph on the right, one line has 18 points of leading applied, moving only that line 18 points below the previous line in the same paragraph.

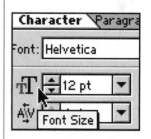

Use the Font Size pull-down menu to select a type size, or type the new size in the Font Size field and press Return/Enter.

Macintosh Keystrokes

⌘-N File/New
⌘-T Type/Character

Windows Keystrokes

Ctrl-N File/New
Ctrl-T Type/Character

Tip

To adjust tracking and kerning from the keyboard, press the Option/Alt key and the left and right arrows respectively to remove and add space.

KERNING

Kerning is adding or decreasing space between two adjacent characters. It is especially important to kern when setting type in a large point size, such as headlines, because excessive character spacing can make it difficult to read the type. As a rule of thumb, body type under 14 points doesn't need kerning because the kerning pairs built into most typefaces automatically adjust the space between those two characters.

TRACKING

Tracking is adding or deleting space between a range of characters. Select three or more characters and use the kerning arrows, or type a positive number in the Tracking field to add space between the selected characters and a negative number to reduce space between the selected characters (Figure 16.3).

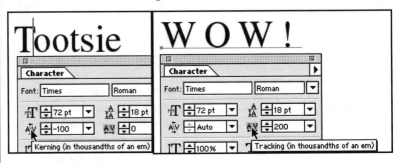

Figure 16.3. The first two characters in the word on the left are kerned -100, thus reducing the space between them by 100 units. The whole word at the right is tracked 200 units (a positive number), thus adding 200 units of space between all the selected characters. You must press Return/Enter if you type a value in any of the fields, but not if you make a selection from any of the menus.

Who cares?

Kerning and tracking values are measured in 1/1000 of an em space. An em space is an invisible character the width of the type's height. An em space for 10-pt. type is 10 points wide. Don't you feel better knowing that?

EXERCISE A

1. Create a new document (File/New). Select inches as the unit of measure (File/Preferences/Units & Undo). Display the Swatches palette and the Character palette (Command/Ctrl-T). Choose Show Options from the Character palette's pull-down menu on the right side of the palette.

2. Click once with the Rectangle tool on the drawing page to display the Rectangle dialog box. Type 2 in the Width field; press the Tab key and type 3 in the Height field. Click on OK.

3. Click on the Area Type tool to select it and click on the top bar of the rectangle to display the flashing cursor. Type *If you see someone without a smile, give him one of yours.* Click on the Selection tool to select the entire text block. Format the type in 14-pt. Times. Select Auto from the Leading pull-down menu.

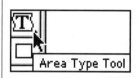

4. Use the Zoom tool to draw a marquee around the word *you*. Select any type tool and click between the *o* and the *u* in the word *you* in the first line.

5. Type -80 in the Kerning field to remove 80 units of space from between the two letters on either side of the flashing cursor. Notice how the two characters move closer together.

6. Drag to select *him one of.* Type 130 in the Tracking field to add space uniformly between all the characters and words in the selected text. Your screen should resemble Figure 16.4.

7. Close this file (Command/Ctrl-W). Don't save your changes.

> If you see someone without a smile, give him one of yours.

Figure 16.4. Kerning two characters with a negative number removes space and moves them closer together. Tracking three or more selected characters with a positive number adds space between them.

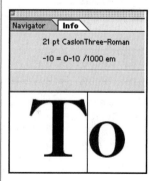

BASELINE SHIFT

When you first create type and click on the Selection tool, the baseline appears under the type. Using the Baseline Shift command, you can raise or lower the type above or below this imaginary baseline to create superscripts or subscripts, or move type around a path for infinite graphic effects.

When inputting values in the Baseline Shift field or when selecting a value from its menu, a positive number raises the selected type above the baseline; a negative number moves the type below the baseline. To restore the type to its default baseline, type 0 in the Baseline Shift field.

HORIZONTAL SCALE

When you apply kerning, tracking, or baseline shift values to type, you only affect the space between characters and words and the space between type and the baseline. Changing the horizontal scale of type, however, changes the actual letterforms themselves by changing the specified proportion between the height and width of characters relative to the baseline.

Viewing kerning values

To view kerning values, click the insertion point between two characters and choose Window/ Show Info. The Info palette displays the total spacing value for the two characters. In the example above, the space between the *T* and the *o* is decreased by 10 units.

Macintosh Keystrokes

⌘-N File/New
⌘-T Type/Character
⌘-D Object/Transform/
    Transform Again
⌘-W File/Close

Windows Keystrokes

Ctrl-N File/New
Ctrl-T Type/Character
Ctrl-D Object/Transform/
    Transform Again
Ctrl-W File/Close

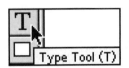

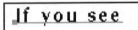

The baseline and alignment point appear when type is selected with the Selection tool.

Resizing type with the Scale tool also affects the type's horizontal and vertical scale.

When you first type a character, its horizontal scale value is 100%, that is, it is horizontally and vertically proportioned the way the fontographer designed it. Typing a number greater than 100% in the Horizontal scale field on the Character palette expands the selected text; typing a value less than 100% compresses the text. To restore selected type to its original shape, type 0 [zero] in the Horizontal scale field.

EXERCISE B

1. On a new page, use the Type tool to type a short word, then click on the Selection tool to select the type and display its baseline.

2. Click on the baseline or on the alignment point and drag the type down, pressing the Option/Alt key before releasing the mouse button to create a duplicate of the type.

3. Choose Object/Transform/Repeat Transform (Command/ Ctrl-D) to create a second copy of the original type. You now have three lines of type on the screen.

4. Display the Character palette (Command/Ctrl-T). Click on the palette's triangle and select Show Options. It displays the last values input into the palette. Restore the values to 0 or to 100% where applicable.

5. Use the Type tool to select one character in the second line of type. Type 200 in the Horizontal scale field of the Character palette or choose 200 from the Horizontal Scale menu. Press Return or Enter to expand the type to twice its normal width.

6. Use the Type tool to select any one character in the third line of type. Type 50 in the Horizontal scale field. Press Return/Enter to compress the character to half its original width. Your screen should resemble Figure 16.5.

7. Close this file (Command/Ctrl-W). Don't save your changes.

Harry Houdini

Harry Houdini

Harry Houdini

Figure 16.5. The *H* in the second line of type is expanded, and the *y* in the third line of type is contracted using the Horizontal Scale command.

PARAGRAPH PALETTE

Paragraphs are formatted only from the Paragraph palette (Figure 16.6). The top panel displays alignment icons; the second panel displays the indent arrows and fields; the third panel displays Word Spacing and Letter Spacing fields; and the fourth panel is where you select other options for paragraphs and text. Only type created with the Area Type tool can be indented.

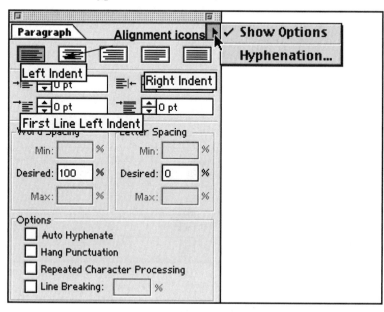

Figure 16.6. The Paragraph palette displays alignment icons, indent fields, Word and Letter Spacing fields, and other text options.

PARAGRAPH ALIGNMENT

The alignment icons in the first panel of the Paragraph palette are used to set paragraphs created with any of the type tools to left, center, right, justify, or right justify alignment. You don't have to select the entire paragraph to set alignment; just click anywhere in the paragraph to select the entire paragraph.

PARAGRAPH INDENTS

Paragraphs (area type only) can be indented from the left edge of the text block, and/or from the right edge of the text block. You can also indent only the first line of the first paragraph, which is what you should do instead of pressing the spacebar to indent a paragraph.

Unlike other palettes, the Character and Paragraph palettes are accessed from the Type menu, not from the Window menu.

Tip

As soon as you finish typing the text, click once on the type tool you used to create the text and the entire text object becomes selected.

FYI

Avoid using the Justify Last Line option, because this tracks the last line of text to make it fit between the left and right margins. It is often an ugly format—just   like   this.

SPACE BEFORE A PARAGRAPH

To create space between paragraphs, never press the Return/Enter key. This generates invisible paragraph returns that contain formatting information over which you have lost control. Instead, apply a Space Before value to a paragraph to separate it from the previous paragraph. The higher the value, the more space appears (Figure 16.7).

To add space before every paragraph in a text block or in a series of linked text blocks, select all the text with either the Selection tool or by using the Select All command when any type tool is active. Selecting all the text ensures that there is the same amount of space between all paragraphs.

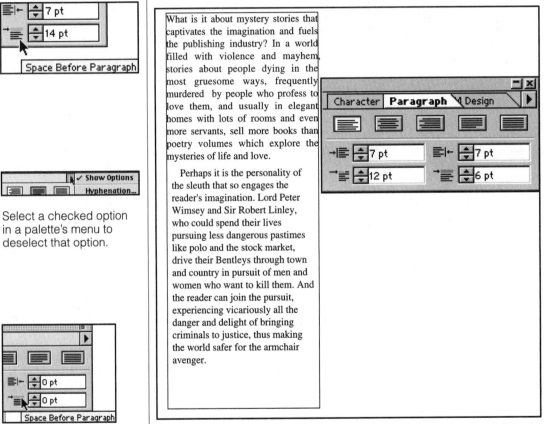

Select a checked option in a palette's menu to deselect that option.

Figure 16.7. The second paragraph is left aligned and displays left and right indents of 7 points from the edge of the text block. The first line of the paragraph is indented 12 points from the left edge of the text block, and 6 points of space have been added between the top of the second paragraph and the bottom of the first paragraph. To add space before a paragraph, just click anywhere inside the paragraph and type a value in the Space Before field in the Paragraph palette.

Macintosh Keystrokes

⌘-N File/New
⌘-T Type/Character
⌘-M Type/Paragraph
⌘-Y View/Preview/Artwork

Windows Keystrokes

Ctrl-N File/New
Ctrl-T Type/Character
Ctrl-M Type/Paragraph
Ctrl-Y View/Preview/
    Artwork

1. In a new document (File/New), select inches as the Ruler units (File/Preferences/Units & Undo).

2. Display the Character palette (Command/Ctrl-T) and the Paragraph palette (Command/Ctrl-M). Deselect Show Options from the palette menus.

3. Click on the Type tool and click and drag on the page to create a rectangle about 3 inches wide and 4 inches long.

4. Select the Area Type tool and click on the top of the rectangle. When the fill and stroke colors disappear, choose File/Place. Navigate to the Unit 16 folder on the CD-ROM and highlight the *Congreve1.txt* file. Click on Place (Macintosh) or Open (Windows). The text flows into the rectangle. There are two paragraphs; the second paragraph is the credit line.

5. Both the Character and Paragraph palettes display the most recently input values. Restore the palettes to their default values by typing 0 or 100 and selecting Auto where appropriate.

6. Select the text block with the Selection tool and assign it any typeface in 14-pt. type with 18 points of leading from the Character palette.

7. In Artwork view (View/Artwork), select only the rectangle with the Direct Selection tool. Click on one of the segments and drag to resize it, pressing the Shift key to constrain the lines. Make it large enough to hold the text and remove the Overflow Indicator.

8. Click anywhere in the first paragraph and click the Justify Full Lines icon on the Paragraph palette.

9. Triple-click in the first paragraph to select it and apply the indent values displayed in Figure 16.8.

Type Tool (T)

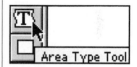

Area Type Tool

Selection Tool

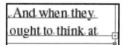

The Overflow Indicator tells you that there is more text in the text block than can be displayed.

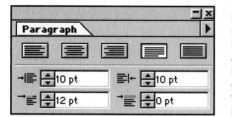

Figure 16.8. The selected paragraph is assigned 10 points of space from the right and left edges of the text block. The first line of the paragraph is indented 12 points from the edge of the text block.

Justify Full Lines

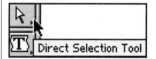

Direct Selection Tool

Align Right

10. Triple-click to select the second paragraph, the credit line. Click the Align Right icon in the Paragraph palette. Assign it the indent and spacing values displayed in Figure 16.9.

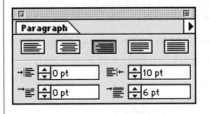

Figure 16.9. The selected paragraph is right aligned, indented 10 points from the right edge of the text block, and assigned 6 points of space before it to separate it from the first paragraph.

11. With the credit line still selected, change its typeface to italics and reduce its size to 12 points.

12. In Artwork view (Command/Ctrl-Y), click on the rectangle with the Direct Selection tool to select just the rectangle, not the type. Assign it a stroke color. Your screen should resemble Figure 16.10.

13. Close this file (Command/Ctrl-W). Don't save your changes.

> Aye, aye dear Marwood, if we will be happy, we must find the means in ourselves, and among ourselves. Men are ever in extremes, either doting or averse. While they are lovers, if they have fire and sense, their jealousies are insupportable. And when they cease to love (we ought to think at least) they loathe; they look upon us with horror and distaste; they meet us like the ghosts of what we were, and as such, fly from us.
>
> *William Congreve*

Figure 16.10. Both paragraphs display character and formatting styles.

Select Hyphenation from the Paragraph palette's menu to display the Hyphenation Options dialog box.

PARAGRAPH OPTIONS

The lower panel of the Paragraph palette contains four additional formatting objects. Selecting these options affects the way your text flows within the text object.

AUTO HYPHENATE

The Auto Hyphenate option automatically hyphenates text based on the selections made in the Hyphenation dialog box. Here you specify the number of characters before and after a hyphen and the maximum number of hyphens in a row Illustrator can allow.

HANG PUNCTUATION

Ordinarily, the first and last punctuation marks in a paragraph, such as quotation marks and periods, appear at the edge of the text block. Using the Hang Punctuation option in the Paragraph palette will cause them to hang outside the edge of any text block filled with area type. The edge of the text block is defined by the left margin of the text, not by any stroke applied to the block itself.

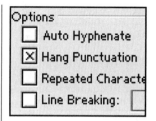

HYPHENATING TEXT

Unless you select the Auto Hyphenate check box in the Paragraph palette, Illustrator will not hyphenate the text, and text will drop to the next line in the text block. If you select the Auto Hyphenate option (click in its check box), Illustrator will hyphenate any text that normally would extend beyond the right edge of the text block.

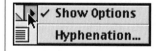

HYPHENATION OPTIONS

If you don't specify hyphenation controls, Illustrator will break words whenever it can and wherever it can. This is frequently unacceptable (editors don't like to see more than two hyphens in a row, and they want at least two, if not three, characters before and after a hyphen), so use the Hyphenation Options dialog box, available from the Paragraph palette's menu (Figure 16.11).

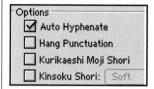

Select the Auto Hyphenate option in the bottom panel of the Paragraph palette.

Figure 16.11. The Hyphenation Options dialog box.

Hyphenation options default to two letters at the beginning of a word before a hyphen will be inserted, and to two letters at the end of a word after the hyphen. For example, with these values, Illustrator would hyphenate *re-solute* because there are at least two characters before and after the hyphen. It would not, however, hyphenate *apex*, because only one character, the *a*, would appear before the hyphen.

DISCRETIONARY HYPHENS

A discretionary hyphen is a hyphen inserted manually using a keyboard command. If the word has to be hyphenated because it will not fit on a line, Illustrator will break the word at the point of the discretionary hyphen, overriding any Auto Hyphenation setting. If the text flow changes and the whole word will fit on the line, the discretionary hyphen disappears and the whole word is displayed on the line.

FYI

You can manually hyphenate a word by entering a discretionary hyphen. Press Command-Shift-hyphen (Macintosh) or Ctrl-Shift-hyphen (Windows) and Illustrator will override the hyphenation settings and break the word at that point. If the word isn't hyphenated, the discretionary hyphen won't force it to break. Likewise, if the word isn't broken but becomes broken if the text reflows, Illustrator will break it using the discretionary hyphen. This is a good way to hyphenate terms such as *ninety-eight* instead of *nine-ty-eight*.

Macintosh Keystrokes

⌘-N File/New
⌘-T Type/Character
⌘-M Type/Paragraph
⌘-W File/Close

Windows Keystrokes

Ctrl-N File/New
Ctrl-T Type/Character
Ctrl-M Type/Paragraph
Ctrl-W File/Close

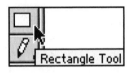

Rectangle Tool

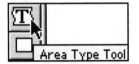

Area Type Tool

Selection Tool

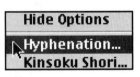

Select Hyphenation from the Paragraph palette menu to display the Hyphenation Options dialog box.

EXERCISE D

1. In a new document (File/New), select inches as the unit of measure (File/Preferences/Units & Undo). Display the Paragraph palette (Command/Ctrl-M). Choose Show Options from the Paragraph palette's menu.

2. Click with the Rectangle tool on the drawing page to display the Rectangle dialog box. Type 1.5 in the Width field; press the Tab key and type 4 in the Height field. Click on OK.

3. Select the Area Type tool and click on the upper line of the rectangle. The flashing insertion point appears and the fill and stroke disappear.

4. Choose File/Place. Navigate to the Unit 16 folder on the CD-ROM. Highlight the *Text2.txt* file and click on Place (Macintosh) or Open (Windows). The text appears in the rectangle. Click on the Selection tool to select the entire text object.

5. Notice that the passage is not hyphenated. Click on the Auto Hyphenate check box in the bottom panel of the Paragraph palette. Several words are now hyphenated and the right rag is decreased (Figure 16.12).

> Some people consider themselves much too highbrow to read mystery stories. Maybe that's because they're not bright enough to figure anything out.
> ☐ Auto Hyphenate
>
> Some people consider themselves much too highbrow to read mystery stories. Maybe that's because they're not bright enough to figure anything out.
> ☒ Auto Hyphenate

Figure 16.12. The paragraph at the left is not hyphenated by default and displays more white space (too much rag) than the hyphenated paragraph on the right.

6. Choose Hyphenation from the Paragraph palette's menu to display the Hyphenation Options dialog box. Type 5 in both Hyphenate fields and click on OK. The hyphenation disappears because you specified that a word must have 5 characters before and 5 characters after the hyphen.

7. Close this file (Command/Ctrl-W). Don't save your changes.

WORD SPACING AND LETTER SPACING

The spacing options in the Paragraph palette allow you to add and delete the horizontal space between words and the space between characters. These spacing options are most helpful when working with justified type where Illustrator has to make decisions about spacing in order to spread the text evenly across a text object. Text must be selected to activate these options.

Word Spacing and Letter Spacing values are measured as percentages of the width of the current type size. Each option allows for minimum, desired, and maximum spacing.

DEFAULT SPACING VALUES

The default Desired spacing values (Figure 16.13) indicate the spacing specified by the fontographer for that typeface. Any value over 100% increases spacing; values below 100% decrease spacing.

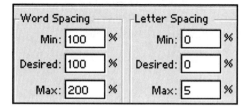

Figure 16.13. Increasing the Desired value increases word or letter spacing.

SETTING TABS

The Tab Ruler palette allows you to set left, right, center, and decimal tabs. A visual guide appears in the selected text, so you can tell where the text is flowing even if the text path is rotated or wrapped around another object. Tab positions are measured using the selected Ruler Units measurement in the Units & Undo Preferences dialog box.

DISPLAYING HIDDEN CHARACTERS

When working with text, especially when setting tabs, it's often easier to see where the rows and columns will fall by viewing the invisible tab characters that appear each time you press the Tab key. Choose Type/Show Hidden Characters to view nonprinting marks that are embedded in the document. Just as in word processors and page layout programs, these invisible characters in Illustrator indicate keyboard actions such as spaces, returns, tabs, discretionary hyphens, and other characters.

Should you find text disappearing when you press the Tab key, because the text block is too small, deselect everything and select the text block with the Direct Selection tool. Then use that tool to Shift-select the two bottom anchor points and drag the bottom line

Space cadet

The Desired value determines how tight or loose the paragraph should be. Increasing or decreasing a 100% Desired value adds or removes space between letters and/or words. A Desired letter spacing value of 20% inserts 20% of the width of a space created by pressing the spacebar between each pair of letters in the paragraph. A negative value reduces the space between characters and moves them closer together.

FYI

When the Word Spacing value is set to 100%, no space is added between text characters. Likewise, when 0% is specified for Letter Spacing, no space is added between the text characters.

FYI

If text is not justified, only the Desired fields are active. Text must be selected to activate the Word and Letter Spacing fields.

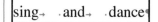

This tab symbol appears as an arrow and the space as a dot when you choose Type/Show Hidden Characters.

Version 7

There is no Show Hidden Characters command in version 7.

Macintosh Keystrokes

⌘-N File/New
F8 Window/Show Info
⌘-T Type/Character
⌘-Shift-T Type/Tab Ruler

Windows Keystrokes

Ctrl-N File/New
F8 Window/Show Info
Ctrl-T Type/Character
Ctrl-Shift-T Type/Tab Ruler

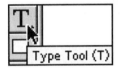

Type Tool (T)

Selection Tool

Zoom Tool (Z)

Drag a segment to enlarge a text rectangle. Press the Shift key to keep the segment straight as you drag it. Release the mouse button, then the Shift key.

down to enlarge the rectangle. Press the Shift key before releasing the mouse button to keep the sides straight.

EXERCISE E

1. On a clean drawing page, select the Type tool and choose File/Place. Navigate to the Unit 16 folder on the CD-ROM and highlight the *Tabs.txt* file. Click on Place. The text appears in a text rectangle. Click on the type with the Selection tool to display its baselines.

2. Choose Window/Show Info (F8) to display the Info palette. Click the Default Colors icon in the Toolbox. Make sure inches is the unit of measure (File/Preferences/Units & Undo).

3. Display the Character palette (Command/Ctrl-T) and change the selected type to 18-point Helvetica. Assign a Leading value of 36 points in the Leading field. Press Return or Enter if you typed the values instead of using the arrows or menus.

4. Choose Type/Show Hidden Characters to display the spaces and tab marks.

5. Use the Zoom tool to magnify the text area so you can see the spaces between the words. Select the Type tool and press the Tab key where indicated by the tab symbols in Figure 16.14. Depending on the size of the text block, text will move down and possibly out of sight. If the Overflow Indicator appears (plus sign in a box), use the Direct Selection tool to select the bottom anchor points and drag them down to enlarge the text block.

Item	Date Issued	Price¶
Computer	March, 1997	$2,000.00¶
Software	May, 1998	$895.90¶
Video Card	May, 1998	$2,400.00¶
Monitor	August, 1997	$1,325.79 ¶

Figure 16.14. Press the Tab key between the item and the date and again between the date and the price. Displaying the hidden characters lets you see exactly where you pressed the Tab key.

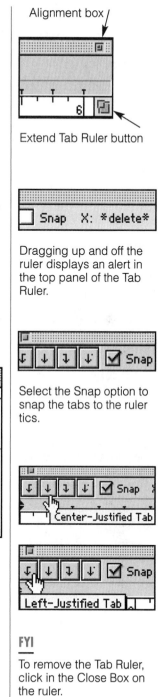

6. Use the Type tool and drag to select the entire text block or choose Edit/Select All (Command/Ctrl-A).

7. Choose Type/Tab Ruler to display the Tabs palette. If necessary, click on the Alignment box in the upper right corner to align the Tab Ruler with the left margin.

8. If necessary, click on the Extend Tab Ruler button in the lower right corner of the palette to extend the ruler.

9. Click in the Snap check box above the ruler to snap the tabs to the ruler units as you drag them.

10. Because you have already placed the tab markers, all you have to do now is position them. Select the first line of text, the heading line, with the Type tool. You can click anywhere in the line to select the whole line. Click on the Center-Justified tab, and click on the 3-inch mark and on the 6-inch mark on the Tab Ruler. If you need to enlarge the text rectangle, deselect evrything, and select the text rectangle with the Direct Selection tool, and Shift-drag to enlarge the text rectangle horizontally. If you have the Bounding Box option selected in the General Preferences dialog box, click on the upper right handle and drag to enlarge the box. Your screen should resemble Figure 16.15.

Alignment box

Extend Tab Ruler button

Dragging up and off the ruler displays an alert in the top panel of the Tab Ruler.

Select the Snap option to snap the tabs to the ruler tics.

Center-Justified Tab

Left-Justified Tab

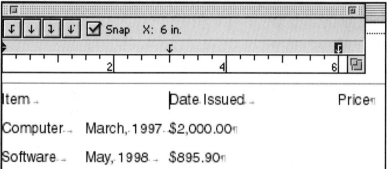

Figure 16.15. When you select the Snap option, the tab snaps to the ruler units on the Tab Ruler. When you click on the Tab Ruler, the tab position appears next to the x value. Here, the Tab Ruler was clicked at the six-inch mark.

11. Select the last four lines with the Type tool. Click on the Left-Justified Tab icon (the first Tab icon) and click at the 2.5-inch mark and on the 5.75-inch mark on the Tab Ruler. When you click on the Tab Ruler, the current tab position appears in the Tab Rule.

FYI

To remove the Tab Ruler, click in the Close Box on the ruler.

12. To change the Left-Justified tab to a Decimal-Justified tab, *keep the 5.75-inch tab selected* and click on the Decimal-Justified icon on the Tab Ruler. The prices will all align under the decimal points. Drag the 5.75 tab a little to the right. Your screen should resemble Figure 16.16.

13. Close this file (Command/Ctrl-W). Don't save your changes.

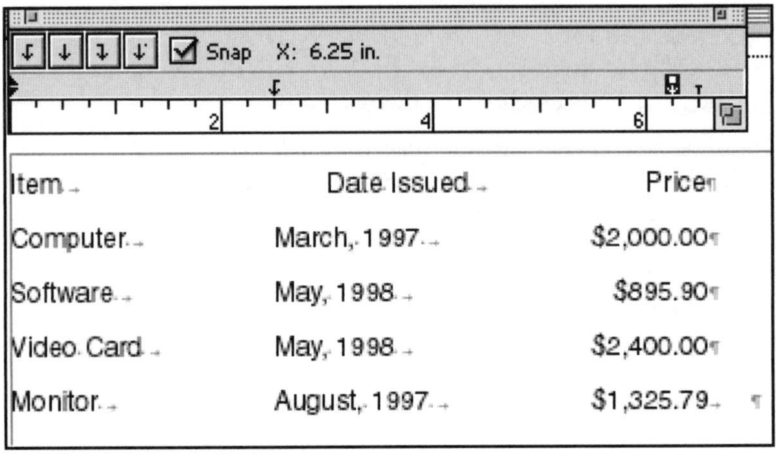

Item	Date Issued	Price
Computer	March, 1997	$2,000.00
Software	May, 1998	$895.90
Video Card	May, 1998	$2,400.00
Monitor	August, 1997	$1,325.79

Figure 16.16. The heading line is formatted with Center-Justified tabs, and the last four lines are aligned with Left-Justified tabs and a Decimal-Justified tab.

DELETING TAB STOPS

To delete a tab from the ruler, click on it and drag it up and off the ruler. As you do, *delete* appears in the upper part of the Tab palette.

WORKING WITH TEXT

There are several other text features in Illustrator that can make working with text-intensive documents much easier, as well as ensuring proper formatting. These include the Find/Change, Find Font, Check Spelling, Change Case, Smart Punctuation, and Rows and Columns functions. You may not need all of them all the time, but you may need most of them at some point if you are working seriously in Illustrator.

FYI

To remove a tab marker, click on it and drag it up and off the top of the ruler or to the left and off the ruler.

Problems?

If you have trouble getting the correct tab to appear on the Tab Ruler even though you're clicking the appropriate Tab icon, select the tab you want to change, *then* click on the Tab icon you want. Any selected Tab stop on the Tab Ruler changes to the Tab icon you click.

FIND/CHANGE

The Find/Change command locates a word and/or phrase and replaces it with another word or phrase. You can limit the search to a whole word and make it case-sensitive. A Wrap Around option allows you to search from the insertion point to the end of the linked text objects, then continue searching from the most recently created object .

FIND FONT

The Find Font command not only finds and replaces typefaces in linked text objects, but also gives you a list of every font used in the document. When a font is replaced, the new typeface retains the original type's formatting.

CHECK SPELLING

Use Illustrator's (quite good) built-in dictionary to check the spelling of all text in linked text objects. You can also create an editable custom dictionary that Illustrator checks along with its own dictionary (Figure 16.17).

Figure 16.17. Create a custom dictionary by clicking Add to List in the Check Spelling dialog box.

CHANGE CASE

To use the Change Case command, type must be selected with any of the type tools. Text can be changed to all upper case, all lower case, or mixed case where the initial character in every word is converted to upper case.

SMART PUNCTUATION

Options selected in the Smart Punctuation dialog box transform straight quotes to curly quotes, certain *ff, fi,* and *fl* letter pairs to ligatures when using fonts that support ligatures, and three periods to a true ellipse (Figure 16.18), among other options. If you have the necessary Adobe Expert Font installed, you can change separate characters representing fractions, which require three characters to their single-character equivalents, such as ½ and ¾. You must select the text with any of the type tools or the conversions will apply to the entire document.

The Change Case command is available only when text is selected with any of the type tools.

Very important info!

If you are printing an illustration to anything other than the printer attached to your computer or network, save the list so you will be sure that your printer has the fonts you used. Click the Save List button in the Find Font dialog box or choose File/Document Info, select Fonts from the Info menu, and click on Save. This saves the font list as a text file you can print out from any word processor.

Type a word in the text field at the bottom of the Learned Words dialog box and click on Add to add that word to the custom dictionary. You can add words to the custom dictionary that are not in the document.

If no results are reported, it's because you didn't select the text block with a type tool.

The word at the top displays straight quotes and no ligatures. The bottom word displays properly typeset "curly quotes" as well as the *fi* ligature.

Changes made to Selection Only.

3 quotes changed.
1 dash, dot, or fraction changed.

[OK]

The Smart Punctuation report lists all the changes made in the selected text. You will see the effects of the curly quotes if you use a serif typeface like Times or Garamond.

To replace punctuation marks in selected text, first select the text with the Type tool before displaying the Smart Punctuation dialog box.

Let me explain...

Let me explain...

Figure 16.18. The three periods in the upper phrase have been converted to properly typeset ellipsis in the bottom phrase.

ROWS & COLUMNS

The Rows & Columns command will distribute all the text in linked objects into a specified number of rows and/or columns. Use the various fields in the Rows & Columns dialog box to change the flow of text within the rows and columns, as well as to adjust the height, width, and gutter space between rows and columns. You also have the option of creating guides between the rows and columns.

EXERCISE F

1. Choose File/New. Choose File/Place. Navigate to the Unit 16 folder on the CD-ROM and highlight the *Congreve2.txt* file. Click on Place (Macintosh) or Open (Windows). It appears on the page selected and in its own text rectangle.

2. Use the Font menu or the Character palette to assign the entire text block a typeface in any size. Use the Type tool to select a few words and assign them a different typeface.

3. Choose Type/Find Font to display the Find Font dialog box. Click a font in the Current Font List that you want to change (Figure 16.19). Use the Font List to select the source of the new document. Choose System to display every font loaded in your system and available to Illustrator. Deselect any kinds of fonts in the bottom check boxes to narrow the search.

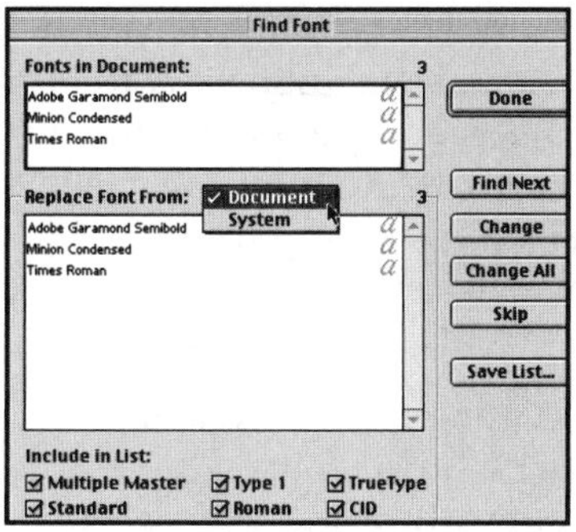

Figure 16.19. Use the Find Font dialog box to change typefaces in an illustration. The *a* icon at the right side of the Replace Font From field indicates a Type 1 font.

4. Click on a font in the Fonts in Document list. Choose Find Next and click on a font in the Replace Font From list. Click on Change All to change every instance of the selected font in the Font List field to the selected font in the Replacement field.

5. Click to select the second font in the Current Font List, select a replacement font, and click on Change All. When you have finished, click on Done to return to the document.

6. Choose Type/Find Change to display the Find/Change dialog box (Figure 16.20). Type *circumstance* in the Find what field. Press the Tab key and type *fact* in the Change to field. Check the Whole Word check box so Illustrator won't find a word like *circumstantial*. Select the Wrap Around option so Illustrator will check from the insertion point and then wrap around the text to the end of the document and then from the start of the text block. Click Find Next. Click Change/Find. A beep tells you that there are no more occurrences of *circumstance*. Click on Done to return to the document, which now displays the new word.

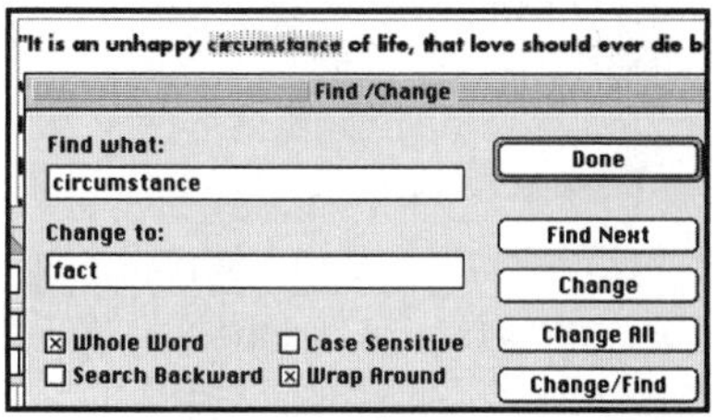

Figure 16.20. Use the Find/Change dialog box to change text singly and globally in a document.

Click this button in the Check Spelling dialog box to add a word or phrase to your custom dictionary.

7. Choose Type/Check Spelling to display the Check Spelling dialog box. The words connected by three dots are listed as misspelled. Click on Skip. You'll fix this later. Illustrator highlights *tis*. Click on Add to List. Click on Edit List to display the Learned Word dialog box. Select *tis* and click Remove to remove it from the custom dictionary.

FYI

To display the Rows & Columns dialog box, the text block must first be selected with the Selection tool.

FYI

To select the entire text block with the text tool, click anywhere in the text block and choose Edit/Select All. Or, triple-click on the text block to select all the text.

Text Flow:

The start of the line indicates the start of the text flow.

Selection Tool

8. The next highlighted word is *yuth* and Illustrator displays suggested corrections. The first, highlighted suggestion is correct, so click on Change All to change all occurrences of the misspelled word to the correctly spelled word. Continue to spell-check the document and click on Done when you have finished to return to the document.

9. Select the entire text block with any type tool, not with the Selection tool. Choose Type/Smart Punctuation to display the Smart Punctuation dialog box. Click to select Smart Quotes and Ellipses. Check the Report Results check box and click on OK. The report is displayed indicating that the single quote and double quotes were changed (to curly quotes) and the three dots were changed to a true ellipse.

10. Use the Selection tool to select the text block. Change the type size to 24 points. Choose File/Preferences/Units & Undo and select points as the unit of measure. Select the text block with the Selection tool.

11. Choose Type/Rows & Columns to display the Rows & Columns dialog box. Make sure the Preview check box is selected so you can see the changes applied without exiting the dialog box (Figure 16.21).

Rows & Columns		
Rows	**Columns**	
Number: 1	Number: 1	OK
Height: 648 pt	Width: 468 pt	Cancel
Gutter: 12 pt	Gutter: 12 pt	
Total: 648 pt	Total: 468 pt	☒ Preview
Options		
Text Flow:	☐ Add Guides	

Figure 16.21. Specify the number of rows and columns and the text flow within them in the Rows & Columns dialog box. If you select the Add Guides option, guidelines in the current stroke color will be added to the illustration. You can always select the guides and change their stroke color and stroke weight.

12. Type 2 in the Columns field or click once on the Up Arrow next to the Columns field. The text block splits in half with 12 points between the columns. Click on OK. Your screen should resemble Figure 16.22.

13. To change the direction of the text flow from left to right to up and down, make sure the text block is still selected. Then choose Type/Rows & Columns again. Click on the different icons in the Text Flow field to change the direction of the text flow. Click on OK to return to the document (Figure 16.22).

14. Close this file. Don't save your changes.

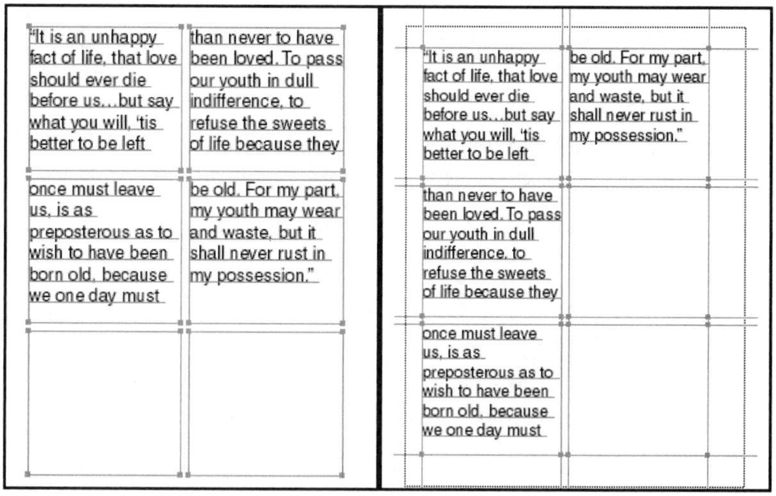

| "It is an unhappy fact of life, that love should ever die before us…but say what you will, 'tis better to be left | than never to have been loved. To pass our youth in dull indifference, to refuse the sweets of life because they |
| once must leave us, is as preposterous as to wish to have been born old, because we one day must | be old. For my part, my youth may wear and waste, but it shall never rust in my possession." |

"It is an unhappy fact of life, that love should ever die before us…but say what you will, 'tis better to be left	be old. For my part, my youth may wear and waste, but it shall never rust in my possession."
than never to have been loved. To pass our youth in dull indifference, to refuse the sweets of life because they	
once must leave us, is as preposterous as to wish to have been born old, because we one day must	

Figure 16.22. The default text flow is from the first row in the first column to the second row in the second column (left). Change the text flow so that it flows from one column to another. Guides have been added (right).

REVIEW

In this unit you learned that:

1. Type attributes are applied from the Character palette.

2. Leading is the vertical space between lines of type and is measured in points.

3. Kerning is adding or deleting space between two characters.

4. Tracking is adding or deleting space between two or more selected characters.

5. The Baseline Shift values in the Character palette move text above (positive value) and below (negative value) the baseline.

6. Type can be scaled horizontally from the Character palette.

7. Paragraph alignment, indents, spacing, and hyphenation options are specified in the Paragraph palette.

8. Word and character spacing can be increased or decreased when Show Options is selected from the Paragraph Palette menu.

9. Tab positions are set and edited in the Tab Ruler palette.

10. Hidden characters, such as spaces between words, paragraph returns, and tabs, can be displayed with the Show Hidden Characters command.

11. To find and replace text in a file, use the Find/Change command. To find and replace fonts, use the Find Font command.

12. The Check Spelling command finds and corrects misspelled words.

13. Use the options in the Smart Punctuation dialog box to properly typeset documents.

14. The Rows & Columns command distributes text in linked objects into a specified number of rows and/or columns.

UNIT 17
Automating with Actions

OVERVIEW

In this unit you will learn how to:
record multiple commands as a single action
use the Actions palette
save and load actions
edit, duplicate, and play actions

TERMS

action
command parameter
Modal Control
set

HOW IT WORKS

A recorded action duplicated the original two blocks and then moved the four blocks onto a patterned background. A Modal Control was inserted which allowed the colors to be changed before the action was completed.

AUTOMATING WITH ACTIONS

Many tasks, especially repetitive tasks, can be automated using the Actions palette (Figure 17.1). By grouping multiple commands into a single action, you can execute complicated processes with a single keystroke. For example, you could create an action that draws an object, colors it, transforms it, and duplicates it. This might take as many as ten different keystrokes or commands, but once all the actions are recorded, they can be played back by selecting the action and clicking the Play Action button on the Actions palette.

Version 7

There is no Actions palette in version 7.

Does this look familiar?

if you have used the Actions palette in Photoshop, then you're ahead of the game, because the Actions palette in Illustrator functions in almost the same ways.

Who's in charge here?

The Actions palette is a hierarchy of commands. **Sets** contain actions. **Actions** contain commands. **Commands** contain parameters. **Parameters** contain values. Clicking on an item's triangle displays the next level in the hierarchy.

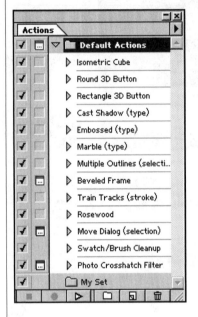

Figure 17.1. The Actions palette displays two sets, Default Actions and My Set. The Default Actions set contains thirteen actions that can be applied to type and to artwork.

EDITING ACTIONS

You can always add commands to an action by selecting the command after which you want to add commands and recording more commands. Any commands you record after another command become part of the original action. For example, you could decide to add a paint command after moving an object or add a selection command after a command that creates multiple objects. Just because you stop recording an action doesn't mean that you can't add commands to that action.

Actions and the commands within those actions can be rearranged to alter their order of execution. You can also edit an action or command's name, color, and function key.

RECORDING ACTIONS

Almost anything you can do in Illustrator can be recorded. The painting tools and their options, view commands, and preferences cannot be recorded. You can, however, use the Insert Menu item command to add many of these commands to an action. For example, choosing a view option from the View menu cannot be recorded while you are recording the action, but you can go back and insert a view option once the action is completed. When you play that action, the view option you selected will be activated.

ACTIONS PALETTE

The Actions palette is used to record, play, edit, and delete actions. Sets, or groups of related actions, are stored in the Actions palette. You can save, load, and replace action sets.

SETS

Sets are groups of different actions saved in a separate folder in the Actions palette. The Default Actions set that ships with Illustrator contains many prerecorded actions. Unless you create a new set, any actions you record will be saved in the Default Actions folder. You might create one set of actions for type and another set for printing commands. The Type set could contain actions that affect text attributes; the Printing set might contain actions with commands that affect printing, such as printing composites or separations and/or selecting different printers. Click the triangle next to a set to display the actions in that set (Figure 17.2).

Click the New Set icon to display the New Set dialog box where you assign a name to the new set.

Option/Alt-click the New Set button to create a new set named Untitled Set-1 without displaying the New Set dialog box.

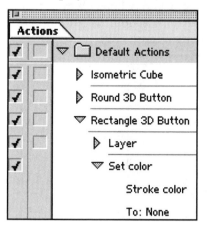

Figure 17.2. *Default Actions* is a set; *Rectangle 3D Button* is an action; *Layer* is a command executed by the *Rectangle 3D* action; *Set color* is another command in the *Rectangle 3D* action; *Stroke color* is a parameter of the *Set color* command.

Create new action

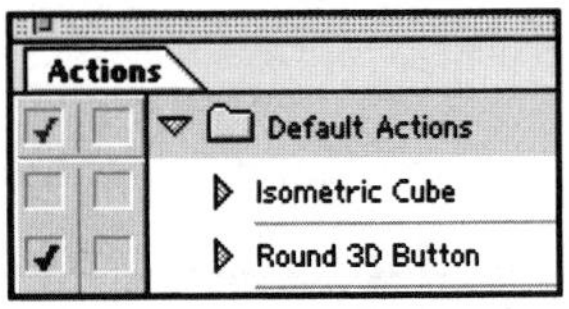

The checkmark next to the *Round 3D Button* action indicates that it is an active action. The Isometric Cube action is not active. Because one or more actions in the Default Actions set has been made inactive, a red check mark appears next to that set's name.

Because a Modal Control has been set, the Move dialog box will appear when the action gets to that command.

ACTIONS

An *action* is a series of recorded commands executed when the action is played. For example, an action can contain commands to duplicate, move, and deselect an object. Click the triangle next to an action to display the commands in that action, and click the triangle next to the command to view the command parameters. (Figure 17.2).

COMMANDS

Every action contains a list of commands, which when executed will create or edit artwork. Commands such as drawing objects, applying color, and transforming objects are executed in the order in which they are recorded.

COMMAND PARAMETERS

Parameters are values used by commands to create or edit artwork. For example, the Move command moves a selection a specific distance to the right or left, up or down. That distance value is a command parameter. The Rectangle tool draw a rectangle with a certain height and width. Those size values are the command's parameters.

VIEWING MODES

Figures 17.1 and 17.2 display sets and actions in List mode. In this mode, sets can be expanded to display actions, actions can be expanded to display individual commands, and commands can be expanded to display their recorded values—all by clicking on the triangle next to the set, action, or command. Button mode, in contrast, displays only the name of the action. Choose Button mode from the Actions palette menu to display actions in Button mode. Choose it again to return to List mode (Figure 17.3).

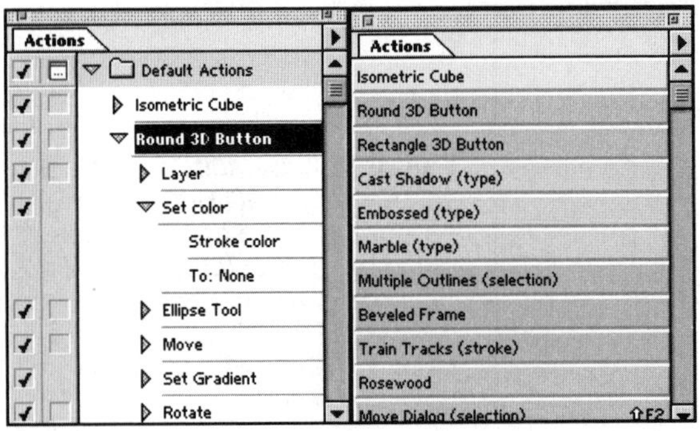

Figure 17.3. The Actions palette in List mode (left) and Button mode (right). In List mode the sets, actions, commands, and values are displayed. In Button mode, only the actions appear. The Actions palette does not display any of the command icons at the bottom of the palette in Button mode.

PALETTE COMMANDS

Icons to start and stop recording actions, to play actions, and to create new sets and new actions appear at the bottom of the Actions palette. The Trash icon is used to delete actions and sets. Many more commands for creating and editing actions are also available from the Actions palette menu (Figure 17.4).

Macintosh Keystrokes

⌘-N File/New

Windows Keystrokes

Ctrl-N File/New

New Action...
New Set...
Duplicate
Delete
Play

Start Recording
Record Again...
Insert Menu Item...
Insert Stop...
Insert Select Path
Select Object...

Action Options...
Playback Options...

Clear Actions
Reset Actions
Load Actions...
Replace Actions...
Save Actions...

Button Mode

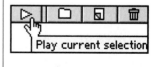

Play current selection

Stop playing/recording

Figure 17.4. The Actions palette menu contains not only the same commands available from the icons at the bottom of the palette, but also commands to control how the actions are recorded and displayed.

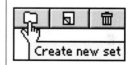

Create new set

EXERCISE A

1. In a new document (File/New), display the Actions palette (Window/Show Actions). Click the New Set icon at the bottom of the Actions palette to display the New Set dialog box.

2. Type *Filter Set* in the Set Name field. Click on OK. The new set appears in the Actions palette below the Default Actions set.

3. Click the New Action button at the bottom of the Actions palette to display the New Action dialog box. Type *Funky Flower* in the Name field. Use the Set pull-down menu to select *Filter Set*. Choose a Function key and color for the action and click on Record (Figure 17.5). From now on, almost anything you do will be recorded as part of the *Funky Flower* action.

Create new action

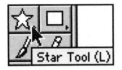
Star Tool (L)

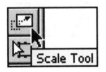
Scale Tool

Selection Tool (V)

Stop playing/recording

Click the Stop Recording button to stop recording and create the action.

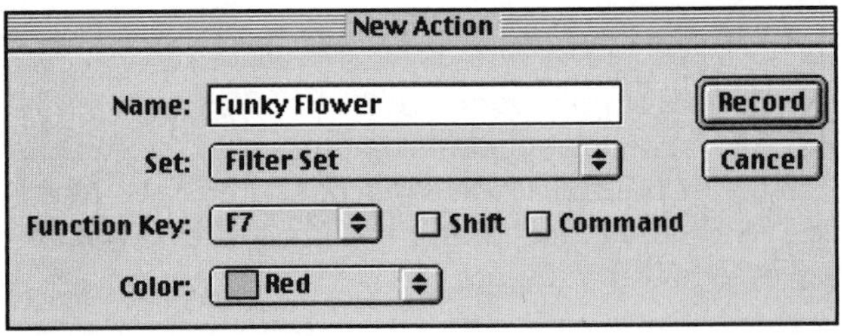

Figure 17.5. The New Action dialog box appears when you click the New Action button or select New Action from the Action palette menu.

4. Use the Star tool to draw a star. Assign it a fill and stroke. Choose Filter/Distort/Punk & Bloat. Click the Preview button. Move the slider to the right to about 90% and click OK.

5. With the art still selected, double-click on the Scale tool. Type 120 in the Uniform field and *click on Copy*. Use the Selection tool to move the copy away from the original. Assign the copy a different fill and stroke.

6. Click the Stop Recording button at the bottom of the Actions palette to stop recording and create the action. Your screen should resemble Figure 17.6.

Figure 17.6. The *Funky Flower* action in the *Filter Set* creates two objects with different fills and strokes. All the recorded commands used to create the action are visible in List mode.

7. Choose Edit/Select All (Command/Ctrl-A) and delete the objects.

8. Click on the *Funky Flower* action in the Actions palette to select it. Click on the Play Action button at the bottom of the Actions palette and watch Illustrator recreate the two objects.

9. Close this file (Command/Ctrl-W). Don't save your changes.

EXERCISE B

1. In a new document (File/New), display the Actions palette (Window/Show Actions).

2. Use the Pen tool to draw a straight vertical line about 4 inches long. Select it with the Selection tool so that both endpoints are selected.

3. Click the New Action button at the bottom of the Actions palette or choose New Action from the Actions palette menu. Type *Arrowheads* in the Name field. Select Filter Set from the Set pull-down menu. Choose a function key and color for the button and click on Record.

4. With the line selected, choose Filter/Stylize/Add Arrowheads. Select an arrowhead for the start of the arrow, choose Start from the Arrowhead at pull-down menu, and click on OK.

5. Choose Filter/Stylize/Add Arrowheads again or press Command/Option-E (Macintosh) or Ctrl-Alt-E (Windows) to display the Add Arrowheads dialog box. Select an arrowhead for the end of the line.

6. With the arrowheads at the start and end of the line, choose Edit/Select All (Command/Ctrl-A). Choose Object/Group (Command/Ctrl-G) to group the line with its arrowheads.

7. Select the Selection tool, click on the line with the arrowheads, and start dragging, pressing the Shift and Option/Alt keys once you start dragging. The Shift key constrains the copy to the same horizontal axis as the original, and the Option/Alt key creates a duplicate of the selected art. Release the mouse button, *then* the modifier keys to create the duplicate.

8. Choose Object/Transform/Transform Again (Command/Ctrl-D) twice to create a total of four lines with arrowheads.

9. Click the Stop Recording button on the Actions palette. Your screen should resemble Figure 17.7.

Macintosh Keystrokes

⌘-N File/New
⌘-W File/Close
⌘-Option-E Filter/Reapply
   last filter
⌘-D Object/Transform/
   Transform Again
⌘-G Object/Group

Windows Keystrokes

Ctrl-N File/New
Ctrl-W File/Close
Ctrl-Alt-E Filter/Reapply
   last filter
Ctrl-D Object/Transform/
   Transform Again
Ctrl-G Object/Group

Pen Tool

Create new action

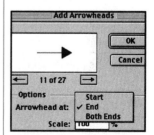

Select arrowhead options in the Add Arrowheads dialog box.

Stop playing/recording

Macintosh Keystrokes

⌘-A Edit/Select All
⌘-W File/Close

Windows Keystrokes

Ctrl-A Edit/Select All
Ctrl-W File/Close

Pen Tool

Selection Tool (V)

Play current selection

Recording paths

The Actions palette can't record drawing paths with the Pen tool, so you have to draw the path you want to incorporate into an action, select it, and use the Insert Selected Path command. When the action is played back, the entire inserted path will be reproduced.

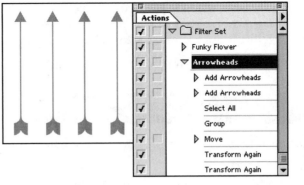

Figure 17.7.
The Arrow-heads action creates three additional lines with arrow-heads from the original selected line.

10. Choose Edit/Select All (Command/Ctrl-A) and press the Delete/Backspace key to delete the lines.

11. Use the Pen tool to draw another vertical line. Select it with the Selection tool.

12. Click to select the *Arrowheads* action in the Actions palette. Click the Play Action button on the Actions palette to play back the action.

13. Save this file (File/Save As) as *Arrows.ai* as an Illustrator file in your Projects folder.

14. Close the file (Command/Ctrl-W).

SAVING AND LOADING ACTIONS

By default, any actions you create and do not manually save are saved in the Preferences folder in the System folder (Macintosh) or in the Adobe Illustrator folder (Windows). If the Preferences file is removed, or if you open the Illustrator file on another computer using that computer's Preferences file, those actions created with the Illustrator file will not appear. To save actions for use at a later date, save the set containing the actions with the Save Actions command from the Actions palette menu.

To load saved actions into the Actions palette of the current file, use the Load Actions command from the Actions palette menu. This command does not replace actions currently available in the palette, but adds the loaded actions to the existing list of actions.

DELETING ACTIONS, COMMANDS, AND SETS

To delete any action, set, or command: (1) drag it to the Trash icon on the Actions palette; or (2) select the action, command, or set you want to delete and click the Trash button on the Actions palette; or (3) select the action, command, or set you want to delete and choose Delete from the Actions palette menu. Dragging an item to the Trash button does not display the alert.

INSERTING MODAL CONTROLS

Sometimes you will want to input a value in a dialog box or perform a task that cannot be recorded each time you play an action. To do this, insert a Modal Control, or breakpoint, in the action after you have recorded it.

INSERTING MENU ITEMS

Some menu selections cannot be automatically recorded and must be inserted manually. Use the Insert Menu Item command from the Actions palette to access that menu item when a recorded action is being played.

SELECTING OBJECTS

In a complex drawing where you want the action to operate on a specific object, name the object, so the action will know exactly to which object commands should be applied. Once you name the object in the Attributes palette, that name is entered in the Actions palette and Illustrator will select the object and apply the action commands.

EXERCISE C

1. Open the *Arrows.ai* file you created in the last exercise or open the *Arrows.ai* file in the Unit 17 folder on the CD-ROM. Display the Actions palette (Window/Show Actions). If you did not move the Preferences file, the Arrowheads action will appear in your Actions palette.

2. Click on the *Arrowheads* action in the Actions palette and click the Delete (Trash) icon in the Actions palette. At the alert, click the Yes button to delete the action.

3. Choose Load Actions from the Actions palette. Navigate to the Unit 17 folder on the CD-ROM and select the *Arrows Actions.aic* file. Click on Select (Macintosh) or Open (Windows) to load the action into the Actions palette. Draw another vertical line and select it with the Selection tool.

The Insert Menu Item option is accessed from the Actions palette menu.

Breakpoints

Because many commands have dialog boxes where you input information, breakpoints, or Modal Controls, are set to stop the action from playing when the dialog box appears. Unless you input values, the action will apply the current values in that dialog box.

Actions icons display *Action* on the thumbnail. Save an action with the .aca suffix (Macintosh) or .aic (Windows).

4. Click the column to the left of the Move action in the Actions palette, the column to the right of the check mark. This displays the Modal Control icon (Figure 17.8). When you play this action, the Move dialog box will appear, letting you input values different from the ones created when you moved the first line.

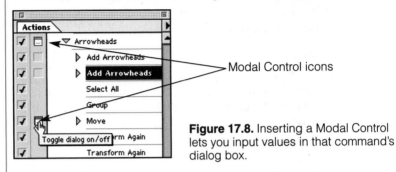

Modal Control icons

Figure 17.8. Inserting a Modal Control lets you input values in that command's dialog box.

FYI

When choosing a command during a recording session, if the command opens a dialog box, clicking OK records the command, but clicking on Cancel does not record the command.

5. Select the Arrowheads action and click the Play Action button on the Actions palette. When the action gets to the Move command, the Move dialog box appears. Type .5 in (or just .5 if you have inches selected as the unit of measure in the Units & Undo Preferences dialog box) in the Horizontal field and .5 in in the Vertical field. Click on Copy (Figure 17.9).

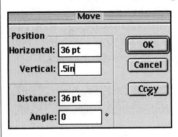

Figure 17.9. The Modal Control lets you type different values for an action based on a command executed with a dialog box.

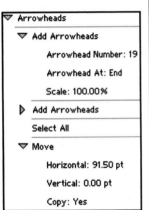

The arrowhead number, location, and size are parameters of the Add Arrowheads command. The horizontal and vertical values and the duplicate (Copy) values are parameters of the Move command.

6. The action is completed, but this time each of the last three lines is positioned a half inch to the right and a half inch above the previous line. Your screen should resemble Figure 17.10. Select the four lines and delete them.

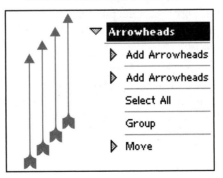

Figure 17.10. The positive numbers entered in the Move dialog box move the copied lines up and to the right.

Unit 17 ★ Automating with Actions

7. Click on the Modal Control icon next to the Move command in the Actions palette to deactivate it. Click on the second Transform Again command in the Actions palette to add other commands under the Transform Again command.

8. Click the Default Colors icon in the Toolbox. Choose Insert Menu Item from the Actions palette menu to display the Insert Menu Item dialog box. Choose Edit/Select All to display the Select All command in the text field. Click on OK. Select All appears as a new command under the Transform Again command.

9. Choose Insert Menu Item again from the Actions palette menu. Choose Object/Path/Offset Path to display Offset Path... in the text field. The ellipse indicates that a dialog box will appear when this command is executed. Click on OK. Offset Path appears as a command under the Select All command.

10. Use the Pen tool to draw another vertical line. Select it with the Selection tool. Click to select the Arrowheads action and click the Play Action button on the Actions palette. Because the Modal Control was removed from the Move command, the action creates the three additional lines on the horizontal axis. When it stops at the Offset Path command, type 6 pt in the Offset Path dialog box and click on OK. The lines display a 6-pt. offset path. Your screen should resemble Figure 17.11. Deselect everything (Command/Ctrl-Shift-A).

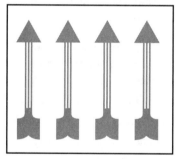

Figure 17.11. The Offset Path command creates a copy of the original path and offsets that copy by the specified distance, in this case 6 points from the original line.

11. Display the Swatches palette. Draw and select a straight line. Click on the Offset Path command in the Actions palette and click the Record button on the Actions palette to begin recording commands after the Offset Path command. Click on a swatch in the Swatches palette that is a different color than the line. Click the Stop Recording button on the Actions palette. *Swatches* should appear as a new command under the Offset Path command. Delete everything on the page.

12. Draw and select another straight line. Click the Arrowheads action in the Actions palette and click the Play Action button.

Macintosh Keystrokes

⌘-A Edit/Select All

Windows Keystrokes

Ctrl-A Edit/Select All

Select a set and choose Save Actions from the Actions palette menu to save all the actions in that set.

Click the Begin Recording button to record actions; click the Stop Recording button to stop recording and create the action.

Macintosh Keystrokes

⌘-W File/Close
⌘-O File/Open
F11 Window/Show
    Attributes
⌘-Shift-A Edit/Deselect All

Windows Keystrokes

Ctrl-W File/Close
Ctrl-O File/Open
F11 Window/Show
    Attributes
Ctrl-Shift-A Edit/Deselect
    All

FYI

An action must be selected (highlighted) to make the Play Action button active.

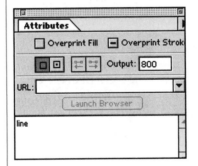

Create new action

Stop playing/recording

13. When the action stops at the Offset Path command, type 8 in the Offset Path dialog box and click on OK. The action is completed with the offset path painted the color you selected. The color is applied to the line's fill or stroke, depending on which icon was active in the Toolbox when you recorded the Swatches command.

14. Close this file. Don't save your changes.

EXERCISE D

1. Open the *Arrows.ai* file you created earlier or open the *Arrows.ai* file in the Unit 17 folder on the CD-ROM (Command/Ctrl-O).

2. Select the third vertical line and display the Attributes palette (Window/Show Attributes). Choose Show Note from the

Figure 17.12. When you choose Show Note from the Attributes palette menu, you can click in the text field and type a name for the selected object.

Attributes palette menu. Click in the text field at the bottom of the palette and type *line* to assign the selected object a name. Choose Hide Note from the palette's menu (Figure 17.12).

3. Select the first line. Click the New Action button in the Actions palette and type *Select Arrow* in the Name field. Click on Record.

4. Choose Object/Transform/Scale. Type 50 in the Uniform field. Select the Scale Line Width option and click on OK.

5. Choose Select Object from the Actions palette menu. Type *line* in the Set Selection dialog box and click on OK. This tells Illustrator to select the object named *line* in the Note field of the Attributes palette.

6. Choose Object/Rotate. Type 90 in the Rotate dialog box. Click on OK.

7. Choose Insert Menu Item from the Actions palette menu.

8. Choose Edit/Deselect All. The command appears in the text field. Click on OK. Click the Stop Recording button on the

Actions palette or choose Stop Recording from the Actions palette menu.

9. Now that the *Select Arrow* action is recorded, play it in the original file. Choose File/Revert. At the alert, click the Revert button to revert to the last saved version of the file.

10. Select the third line and assign it a new fill and stroke color from the Swatches palette. Display the Attributes palette (F11) and type *line* in the text field. Deselect that line.

11. Select the first line. Click to select the *Arrow Select* action in the Actions palette. Click the Play Action button. Your screen should resemble Figure 17.13.

Macintosh Keystrokes
⌘-W File/Close

Windows Keystrokes
Ctrl-W File/Close

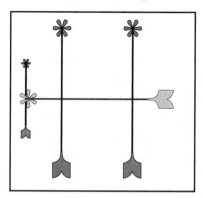

Figure 17.13. The Select Object command selects an object named in the Attributes palette.

FYI
Reverting to a previously saved version of a file deletes any text in the Attributes palette.

12. Click to select the *Select Arrow* set. Choose Save Actions from the Actions palette menu. Save the set as *Select.aic* in your Projects folder.

13. Close this file (Command/Ctrl-W). Don't save your changes.

PLAYING ACTIONS

Thus far you have played a completed recorded action by selecting the action in the Actions palette. You can, however, play only certain commands in an action by selecting that command and clicking the Play Action button. When you do this, the action plays from that point to the end of the action.

STOPPING ACTIONS

If you need to perform a task that cannot be recorded, or if you want a reminder to appear while an action is playing, insert a stop in the action. If you don't select the Allow Continue check box in the Record Stop dialog box, the alert appears and the action stops at that point. You can then do something else and click the Play Action button to continue the action from that point.

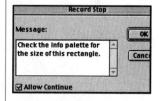

Insert a Record Stop to remind yourself of something. If you click the Allow Continue check box, the action will continue to play once you click OK. Otherwise, the action stops.

Drag a set from the Actions palette to the New Set button on the palette to create a duplicate set.

Tip

To select multiple commands within an action, Shift-click to select adjacent sets, commands, and actions or Command/Ctrl-click to select nonadjacent sets, commands, and actions.

FYI

Option/Alt-dragging an item displays a double line indicating where the duplicate item will be placed.

SLOWING ACTIONS

When trying to get an action to play properly, it's difficult to see where the problem is, because the action plays so quickly. Use the Playback Options to set the playback at a slower speed or to play back at a specified pause rate, so you can watch Illustrator working and see where it's not behaving (Figure 17.14).

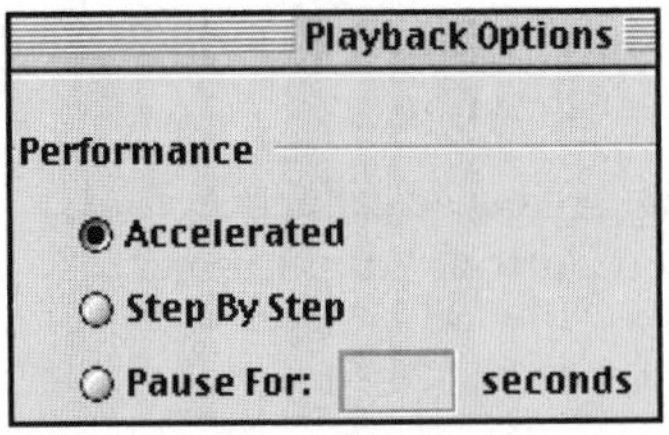

Playback Options

Performance

◉ Accelerated

○ Step By Step

○ Pause For: [   ] seconds

Figure 17.14. The Step By Step option completes each command and redraws the image before going on to the next command in the action. Enter a value in the Pause For field to pause the action between steps.

DUPLICATING ACTIONS

Sometimes it's easier to duplicate an action (or a command or set) and then make changes to the duplicate than to record a complicated action from scratch. To duplicate an action, command, or set, Option/Alt-drag it to a new location in the Actions palette. Once the highlighted line appears, release the mouse button, then the Option/Alt key. You can also select a single set, action, or command, or Shift-select multiple sets, actions, and/or commands and choose Duplicate from the Actions palette menu. The easiest way to duplicate anything in the Actions palette, however, is to drag an action or command to the New Action button on the Actions Palette or drag a set to the New Set button on the palette. The duplicate displays the word *copy* after its name.

EDITING ACTIONS

Just as you can move layers up and down in the Layers palette to change the stacking order in the file, so you can move actions and commands up and down in the Actions palette to change the order in which those actions and commands are executed. New commands can be added to an action, and you can record new commands or new values for commands that display dialog boxes.

DEFAULT ACTIONS

To clear the Actions palette of all the actions, even the Default Actions set, choose Clear Actions from the Actions palette menu. To restore the Default Actions set, choose Reset Actions from the palette's menu. If you click the Append button in the dialog box, Illustrator adds the Default Actions set to the palette without removing any other sets or commands. If you click the Replace button, the Default Action set replaces any other sets or commands in the palette.

DEACTIVATING COMMANDS

To exclude (deactivate) a command from an action, click the check mark next to the command to remove it. Unless a check mark appears next to an action or command, it will not play. To restore the action or command, click the check box again. To include or exclude all the commands in an action or set, click the check box to the left of the action or set.

Macintosh Keystrokes

⌘-N File/New
⌘-A Edit/Select All

Windows Keystrokes

Ctrl-N File/New
Ctrl-A Edit/Select All

EXERCISE E

1. In a new document (File/New), display the Actions palette (Window/ Show Actions) and the Swatches palette. Choose Load Actions from the Actions palette menu. Navigate to the Unit 17 folder on the CD-ROM and highlight the *My Set.aic* file. Click on Select to load that set into the current Actions palette.

2. Select a solid color fill color and no stroke from the Swatches palette. Do this each time before you play the action, otherwise the blocks will be drawn with the current colors.

3. Click on the triangle next to the *My Set* folder (set) to display the *Quilt Pattern* action. Click on the *Quilt Pattern* action and click the Play Action button on the Actions palette. It creates four blocks set on a patterned background. However, there are two problems with this action: It doesn't apply a different color to one of the blocks, and it doesn't position the four blocks properly on the background.

4. Choose Edit/Select All and delete everything.

5. Click on the *Quilt Pattern* action and drag it down onto the New Action button on the Actions palette. It creates a duplicate action named *Quilt Pattern copy*.

6. Choose Playback Options from the Actions palette menu. Type 5 in the Pause For field of the Playback Options dialog box. This tells Illustrator to pause 5 seconds between commands when executing an action (Figure 17.15).

Figure 17.15. Select performance options in the Playback Options dialog box.

Check marks

A check mark in the far left column next to an action or command indicates that the action or command is active and will be executed. You can deselect a check mark by clicking on it for any action you want to make inactive or for a command you wish to exclude from execution when the action is played.

Drag an action onto the New Action button on the Actions palette to duplicate the action.

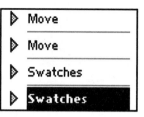

When playing an action at a slow speed, you can watch each command become highlighted as it is executed.

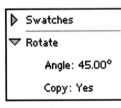

Double-click on an action or set to display its Options dialog box, where you can change its name and options.

---

7. Click the triangle next to the *Quilt Pattern* action to display all its commands. Click the Play Action button. The action proceeds very slowly. Notice that the first problem appears to occur when the duplicate swatches are moved off the page with the second Move command. By recording a new Move command, we can fix this. Choose Edit/Select All and delete everything.

8. Click on the triangle next to each Move command to display the command parameter (Figure 17.16). Drag the first Move command, the one that reads *Copy: No* to the Trash button on the Actions palette to delete it.

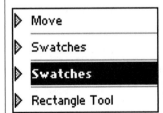

Figure 17.16. The second Move command moves the duplicate blocks too far to the right side of the page.

9. Select the *Quilt Pattern* action and click the Play Action button again. This time the blocks are better positioned on the page, but they are still too far up. Click on the second Swatches command, the one below the Move command, to highlight it (Figure 17.17). You will start recording from this point in the action. Choose Edit/Select All and delete everything.

Figure 17.17. Commands are recorded after the selected (highlighted) command.

Click on the triangle next to an item in the Actions palette to display the next level in the palette's hierarchy.

10. Click the Record button. Choose Edit/Select All. Use the Selection tool and click on any anchor point and drag the four blocks down onto the center of the page. Click the Stop Recording button. Two new commands appear under the Swatches command, a Select All command and another Move command (Figure 17.18).

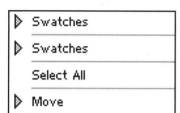

Figure 17.18. Recording after the second Swatches command creates the Select All and Move command.

Macintosh Keystrokes

⌘-A Edit/Select All
⌘-Shift-[Object/Arrange/
    Send to Back

Windows Keystrokes

Ctrl-A Edit/Select All
Ctrl-Shift-[Object/
    Arrange/Send to Back

11. Reset the Toolbox to a colored fill and no stroke. Click the *Quilt Pattern* action again and click the Play Action button. Notice that now the four blocks are positioned correctly.

12. Now that you know where the blocks are, it will be easier to redraw the rectangle from their center outward. Choose Edit/Select All and delete everything.

13. Shift-click the last Rectangle Tool, Swatches, and Send to Back commands in the action. Choose Delete from the Actions palette menu to delete the last three commands in the action, thus making Move the last command in the action (Figure 17.19). Reset the Toolbox to a colored fill and no stroke.

Hurry up!

Use the Playback Options command from the Options palette menu to select another Performance option to speed up the action playback.

Figure 17.19. Shift-click to select multiple adjacent commands.

14. Click the *Quilt Pattern* action and click the Play Action button. When the four blocks appear on the page, click on the last Move command to specify it as the command after which additional commands will be recorded.

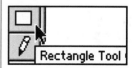

15. Select the Rectangle tool, and press the Option/Alt key to draw a rectangle from the center outward around the four blocks. Use the spacebar to move the rectangle without resizing it. When the rectangle is the right size and in the right position, release the mouse button, *then* release the Option/Alt key.

16. Click the Fill icon in the Toolbox and select a pattern in the Swatches palette.

17. Choose Object/Arrange/Send to Back. Click the Stop Recording button. Your screen should resemble Figure 17.20.

When the Pathfinder/ Exclude filter was applied to the original rectangles, it created a compound path, making the overlapping areas of the rectangles transparent against the background.

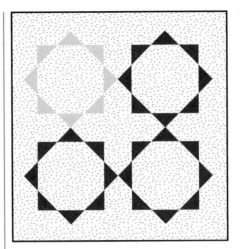

Figure 17.20. The four blocks are properly positioned on the background.

18. The color of the blocks depends on the color you start with. Therefore, to give you the opportunity to recolor the blocks, insert a Stop command without the option of continuing. This lets you select any block and change its fill and/or stroke color. You can then continue to play the rest of the action.

19. Shift-select the two Swatches commands between the Move and Select All commands in the action (Figure 17.21), and drag them to the Trash button on the Actions palette.

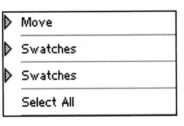

Figure 17.21. By deleting the two Swatches commands and inserting a Stop command, you will be able to change any block's colors.

Because you can't select objects and make color changes during a Stop command, don't allow it to continue playing the action.

20. Select the Move command and choose Insert Stop from the Actions palette menu. Type *Change block color.* in the text field, but do not select the Allow Continue action. You want to stop the action at that point so you can make the color changes.

21. Delete anything on the page. Select a solid fill and no stroke in the Toolbox. Select the *Quilt Pattern* action and click the Play Action button. When the action stops, click OK. Use the Selection tool and click on an empty area of the page to deselect the two blocks. Select any block and change its fill and/or stroke color.

22. When the blocks are properly painted, click the Play Action button in the Actions palette to complete the action (Figure 17.22).

Unit 17 ★ Automating with Actions

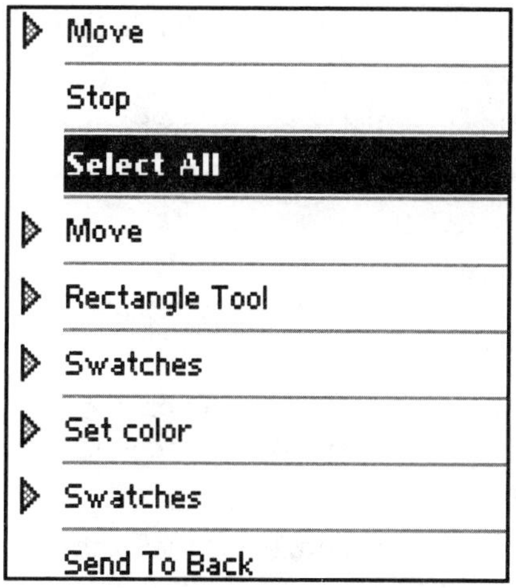

```
┌─────────────────────────────────┐
│ ▷  Move                          │
├─────────────────────────────────┤
│    Stop                          │
├─────────────────────────────────┤
│ ▓▓Select All▓▓                   │
├─────────────────────────────────┤
│ ▷  Move                          │
├─────────────────────────────────┤
│ ▷  Rectangle Tool                │
├─────────────────────────────────┤
│ ▷  Swatches                      │
├─────────────────────────────────┤
│ ▷  Set color                     │
├─────────────────────────────────┤
│ ▷  Swatches                      │
├─────────────────────────────────┤
│    Send To Back                  │
└─────────────────────────────────┘
```

Figure 17.22. After making changes when the action stops, clicking the Play Action button continues the action from the Select All command.

FYI
You cannot create an action unless there is a set into which the action is placed. You cannot save an action unless you save the set containing that action.

23. Select the *My Set* set of actions and choose Save Actions from the Actions palette menu. Navigate to your Projects folder and save the set there. It can now be loaded into any Illustrator document.

24. Close this file (Command/Ctrl-W). Don't save your changes. Because you have saved the action, you can always recreate the file.

REVIEW

In this unit you learned that:

1. The Actions palette is used to record actions, which are multiple commands executed with a single keystroke.

2. Actions can be edited by adding and deleting commands even after an action has been recorded.

3. The Actions palette contains sets of actions. Actions contain commands, which are comprised of parameters. Command parameters have values. Commands, command parameters, and parameter values can all be edited.

4. Sets are groups of different actions saved in a separate folder in the Actions palette.

5. The Actions palette can be viewed in List mode or in Button mode. Actions listed in Button mode display only the name of the action, not any of its recorded values.

6. Paths can be selected and made part of the action using the Insert Selected Path command.

7. Actions created in one document can be saved and loaded into another Illustrator document.

8. When you need to input a value in a dialog box or perform a task that cannot be recorded, insert a Modal Control, (a breakpoint) in the action.

9. To insert menu selections that cannot be automatically recorded, use the Insert Menu Item command to access that menu item when the action is run.

10. To play all the commands in an action, select the action and click the Play Action button on the Actions palette or choose Play from the Actions palette menu.

11. To play only certain commands in an action, select that command and click the Play Action button in the Actions palette.

12. When editing action, slow down the accelerated replay of an action by selecting a different playback speed in the Playback Options dialog box.

13. Change the order in which actions are played by moving the action up or down on the Actions palette.

14. Exclude a command from an action by deselecting the check mark next to that command.

Masks and
Compound Paths

HOW IT WORKS

The fabric image was placed in Illustrator and the type created over it. The type was converted to outlines and made into a compound path so the mask would appear behind every "text character" path. The fabric image and compound path were selected and the Make Masks command applied to the selected objects. This displays only the parts of the image that can be revealed in the mask "window."

MASKING OBJECTS

A *mask* is an object that restricts your view of an object underneath. It is analogous to a clipping path. You can only use one object to mask another object at one time; grouped objects don't mask other objects. Only the part of the object directly underneath the masking object is visible, and only in the shape of the masking object. You can use any object as a mask for any other object, but the masking object should be smaller than the object it masks (Figure 18.1).

mask

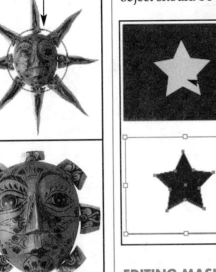

The circle (mask) is placed over the art (masked object). When the Make Masks command is applied, only the area beneath the circle is displayed.

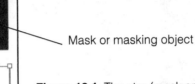

Masked object

Mask or masking object

Figure 18.1. The star (mask or masking object) is placed on top of the rectangle (masked object). When both objects are selected and the Make Masks command is applied, the yellow star loses its fill and stroke and becomes transparent against the masked object (rectangle).

EDITING MASKS

Once the mask is created, after you deselect the masked and masking objects, you can edit either the masked or masking objects independently of the other, including moving, resizing, rotating, and skewing. You can apply any kind of fill to a masked object—solid, gradient, or pattern—as well as a solid or pattern stroke.

When you make an object a mask for another object, its fill and stroke colors both become transparent. However, you can reapply a stroke color to the masking object. You also can reapply a fill color to the masking object, but that color will be visible only when the masking object isn't covering part or all of the masked object.

LOCKING AND UNLOCKING MASKS

Illustrator allows you to lock and unlock masks, so that both the masking object and the object masked can be manipulated as one object. Once masks are locked, both the mask and masked objects can be resized, rotated, or skewed in the same way. You can manipulate parts of the masking object with the Direct Selection tool; the masked object remains locked. To manipulate either the masking or the masked object, unlock the mask.

Unit 18 ★ Masks and Compound Paths

Macintosh Keystrokes

⌘-O File/Open
⌘-7 Object/Masks/Make
⌘-Shift-A Edit/Deselect All
F10 Window/Show Stroke

Windows Keystrokes

Ctrl-O File/Open
Ctrl-7 Object/Masks/Make
Ctrl-Shift-A Edit/Deselect
   All
F10 Window/Show Stroke

1. Open the *Mask.ai* file in the Unit 18 folder on the CD-ROM (File/Open). It displays a rectangle filled with a spiral pattern. Display the Swatches palette and Stroke palette (F10).

2. Select the Star tool (behind the Ellipse tool) and draw a star over the rectangle. Assign the star fill and stroke colors.

3. Use the Selection tool to Shift-select both the box and the star. With both selected, choose Object/Masks/Make. The star (mask) displays only that part of the rectangle that can fit inside its path (Figure 18.2). Deselect everything (Command/Ctrl-Shift-A).

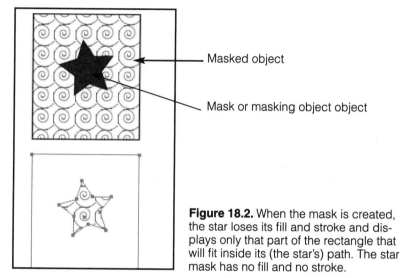

Masked object

Mask or masking object object

Star Tool (L)

Selection Tool (V)

Figure 18.2. When the mask is created, the star loses its fill and stroke and displays only that part of the rectangle that will fit inside its (the star's) path. The star mask has no fill and no stroke.

4. Use the Direct Selection tool and click on the star's edge. Select the Stroke icon on the Color palette and apply a dark stroke color. Use the Stroke palette and assign the star (mask) a stroke a weight of 3 points.

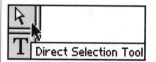

Direct Selection Tool

5. With the star (mask) still selected, click on the Fill icon in the Color palette and click on a yellow color in the Swatches palette (Figure 18.3).

Figure 18.3. The mask (star) is selected with the Direct Selection tool and assigned a fill and stroke color.

Macintosh Keystrokes

⌘-Y View/Artwork/Preview
⌘-W File/Close

Windows Keystrokes

Ctrl-Y View/Artwork/
   Preview
Ctrl-W File/Close

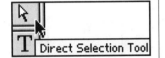

Release Mask command

To release a mask, first select the mask, then choose Object/Masks/Release.

6. Drag the star around and notice how it displays different spirals, depending on where you move it over the masked object (rectangle).

7. Choose View/Artwork (Command/Ctrl-Y) and use the Direct Selection tool to select the masked object (rectangle) (Figure 18.4). Return to Preview view.

Figure 18.4. It's easier to select the masked object (rectangle) in Artwork view.

8. With the rectangle selected and the Fill icon active, apply a gradient fill to the masked object (rectangle). Drag the star (mask) around on the new masked object (rectangle) and notice how it displays different colors of the gradient depending on where the star is positioned.

9. Shift-select the rectangle and the star. This is easier to do in Artwork view. Choose Object/Masks/Lock. Double-click on the Scale tool, type 50 in the Uniform field, and click on OK. Both the star (mask) and rectangle (masked object) are resized.

10. Choose Object/Masks/Unlock, and use the Selection tool to move the star independently of the box.

11. Close this file (File/Close). Don't save your changes.

RELEASING MASKS

Masks can be released, which turns the single mask back into the two original objects, the masked object and the masking object. However, the masking object (top object) does not resume its original paint attributes. Rather, it remains unfilled and unstroked as a result of the earlier Make Masks command.

MASKS AND TEXT PATHS

If you create text on a path and want to mask out the area behind the text path, you will have to create two paths, one for the text and one for the mask—you cannot use a text path as a mask (masking object). When doing this kind of masking, it is important that all the elements in the artwork appear on different layers so you can select and edit them easily.

Unit 18 ★ Masks and Compound Paths

Macintosh Keystrokes

⌘-N File/New
F7 Window/Show Layers

Windows Keystrokes

Ctrl-N File/New
F7 Window/Show Layers

1. Create a new document (File/New). Display the Layers palette (F7). Choose File/Place and navigate to the Unit 18 folder on the CD-ROM. Highlight the *Sunfl.tif* file and click on Place. The raster image appears in the center of the page. You will create a text path around the center of the flower and then mask out the rest of the flower.

2. Click on the New Layer icon in the Layers palette twice to create Layers 2 and 3, with Layer 3 the topmost layer.

3. Double-click on Layer 3 and type *type* in the Name field. Click on OK. Double-click on Layer 2 and type *mask* in the Name field. Click on OK (Figure 18.5).

Image info

Sunflower, by Joseph Dai

Figure 18.5. The raster image appears on Layer 1 and the two new layers have been named.

4. On the *mask* layer, use the Ellipse tool, and press the Option-Shift keys (Macintosh) or Alt-Shift keys (Windows) while dragging from the center of the flower to draw a circle from the center outward. Don't worry about the circle's fill and stroke. It will disappear later.

5. With the circle still selected, press the Option/Alt key and drag the colored selection square on the right side of the *mask* layer up to the *type* layer. This action does three things: (1) It duplicates the selection (the circle). (2) It places the duplicate on the new layer. (3) It selects the new layer, in this case the *type* layer (Figure 18.6).

FYI

Pressing the Option/Alt key, when moving a Selection Square on the Layers palette, duplicates the selected artwork as well a moving it to a new layer.

Macintosh Keystrokes

⌘-7 Object/Masks/Make
⌘-T Type/Character

Windows Keystrokes

Ctrl-7 Object/Masks/Make
Ctrl-T Type/Character

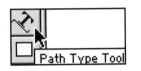

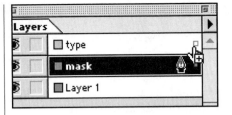

Figure 18.6. Press the Option/Alt key to duplicate a selection while moving it to a new layer.

6. On the *type* layer, select the Path Type tool, click on the circle path, and type a few words (Figure 18.7).

FYI

Locking the type layer when selecting the circle on the mask layer ensures that you are selecting the mask (circle), not the circle text path.

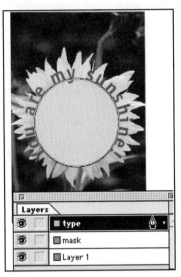

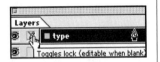

Click on the Locked Layer icon to unlock the layer and make it editable.

Figure 18.7. Type is created on the path moved to the *type* layer. Use the Paragraph palette to center align the type on the path.

7. Click in the second column next to the *type* layer to lock it. Click on the *mask* layer to select it and use the Selection tool to Shift-select both the circle on the *mask* layer and the flower image in Layer 1.

8. Choose Object/Masks/Make. Only the area enclosed by the circle (mask) appears, with the type running around the type path. Unlock the *type* layer by clicking on the Locked Layer icon in the Layers palette. Unless you unlock this layer, you will not be able to edit the type on that layer.

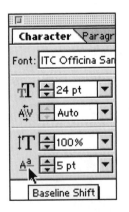

Assign a positive number in the Baseline Shift field to move selected text above the text path.

9. Display the Character palette and choose Show Options from the palette menu (Command/Ctrl-T). Select any type tool and triple-click on the text to select the entire line of text. Specify a positive number in the Baseline Shift field of the Character palette to move the text above the type path. Apply tracking values to move the type evenly around the type path. Your screen should resemble Figure 18.8.

Figure 18.8. The type is moved above the type path and tracked.

Macintosh Keystrokes

⌘-A Edit/Select All
⌘-Option-7 Object/
    Masks/Release
⌘-Z Edit/Undo
⌘-W File/Close

Windows Keystrokes

Ctrl-A Edit/Select All
Ctrl-Alt-7 Object/
    Masks/Release
Ctrl-Z Edit/Undo
Ctrl-W File/Close

10. Choose Edit/Select All (Command/Ctrl-A). Choose Object/ Masks/Release. The entire flower image appears with the text running around the text path.

11. Choose Edit/Undo (Command/Ctrl-Z) to restore the mask.

12. Close this file (Command/Ctrl-W). Don't save your changes.

COMPOUND PATHS

A compound path consists of two or more overlapping paths that have been combined so as to make the paths transparent against the page where they overlap. A compound path is a "window" through which other objects on the page are visible. The fill color disappears in the area of intersection and any underlying colors or patterns show through. If the two objects don't overlap, no change is apparent when the Compound Path command is applied.

COMPOUND PATHS AND GROUPS

When compound paths are applied to two objects, those objects become grouped and take on the color of the backmost selected object. When selected with the Selection tool, these grouped objects can be edited as if one object. If selected with the Direct Selection tool, each object can be edited separately, even after switching back to the Selection tool, as long as that object remains the only object selected.

REVERSING PATH DIRECTION

Reversing the direction of compound paths in two or more overlapping objects determines whether the overlapping portions of the objects are transparent. When you first create compound paths among objects, the path of every other object is reversed. You can use the Reverse Path Direction buttons in the Attributes palette to turn reverse direction on or off. At least one of the two objects with com-

When the text character *B* was converted to outlines, Illustrator automatically combined the outline of the character and the two counters (holes) into a single compound path, thus making the counters transparent against the page.

Select a Reverse Path Direction option from the Attributes palette to change the flow of the selected path from clockwise to counterclockwise or vice versa. The sub-path must be selected with the Direct Selection tool.

Macintosh Keystrokes

⌘-N File/New
⌘-8 Object/Compound
    Paths/Make
⌘-K File/Preferences/
    General
⌘-W File/Close

Windows Keystrokes

Ctrl-N File/New
Ctrl-8 Object/Compound
    Paths/Make
Ctrl-K File/Preferences/
    General
Ctrl-W File/Close

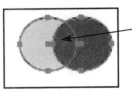

pound paths should have Reverse Direction Path On, while the other should not, for the background to show through. If both are on or off, they have the same path direction and the effect disappears.

EXERCISE C

1. In a new file (File/New), create a large rectangle and two smaller objects. Make sure you are in Preview mode. Drag one of the small objects over the other small object so that the two objects overlap. Select both small objects with the Selection tool (Figure 18.9).

overlapping area

Figure 18.9. The overlapping area will become transparent when the Compound Paths command is applied.

2. Choose Object/Compound Paths/Make. The two objects are grouped into one object and display the color of the backmost object. You should see the background of the page showing where the two objects overlap.

3. Use the Selection tool to drag the compound path on top of the rectangle. Notice that the overlapping area of the smaller objects is transparent against the rectangle (Figure 18.10).

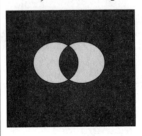

Figure 18.10. The overlapping area is transparent against the rectangle's color.

4. Choose File/Preferences/General (Command/Ctrl-K) and make sure the Use Area Select option is checked. Choose the Direct Selection tool and click on one of the objects in the compound path. Drag it around on top of the rectangle and notice that wherever it overlaps the other object, that overlap is transparent against the rectangle.

5. Close this file. Don't save your changes.

PATHFINDER PALETTE

The Pathfinder palette (Window/Show Pathfinder) contains several tools to combine single paths, many times overlapping paths, into more complex paths. Paths can be merged together, subtracted from one another, and dissected into discrete segments—all in the name of art!

To use any of the Pathfinder tools, select the object or objects you wish to modify, then click on the appropriate tool icon. Like most palettes in Illustrator, the Pathfinder palette has several options, accessible by clicking on the arrow in the top right corner of the palette.

MAKING COMPOUND PATHS WITH PATHFINDER TOOLS

Several Pathfinder commands use compound paths to achieve the desired effect. With commands that combine several objects, the paint style of the topmost object in a stack of objects will be applied to all objects affected. The Hard Mix and Soft Mix commands allow you to choose how colors in the stack mix. You can use Pathfinder commands on objects with a variety of paint styles, except gradient mesh fills. Figure 18.11 displays the effects of the Unite, Intersect, and Exclude filters.

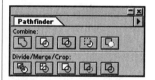

Version 7

In version 7 the Pathfinder filters are accessed from the Object menu.

Unless you select Show Options from the Pathfinder menu, only the filters that combine, divide, merge, and crop objects are available.

Figure 18.11. The rectangle and circle in the top row were combined into one object with the Unite command. The text on the circle in the second row fits the contours of the circle using the Intersect command. The circle in the bottom row excludes any overlapping area, making it transparent against the page.

FYI

The Pathfinder filters work best on filled but unstroked closed paths. You can use these commands on open paths, but you may not like the results.

UNITE

The Unite command combines several overlapping objects into a new single object. This new, combined object takes on the paint style of the topmost object of the group.

INTERSECT

The Intersect command traces the outline of the overlapping shapes of the selected objects and "clips away" all parts of the object that do not overlap, leaving one object with the paint style of the topmost object of the group. If you want to display the clipped object, select it and paste it in back before applying the Intersect command.

EXCLUDE

The Exclude command does the opposite of the Intersect command, by analyzing the intersections of two or more objects and deleting any areas where two objects intersect. This command acts like the Compound Paths command, in that all the objects are grouped but can be manipulated separately with the Direct Selection tool. All the objects take on the color of the foremost object in the stack.

MINUS FRONT AND MINUS BACK

The Minus Front command is similar to Exclude, except that it subtracts the frontmost object entirely, including the intersection with objects in back, leaving a hole in the shape of the overlap.

The Minus Back command subtracts the backmost object from objects in front, leaving gaps in the shape of the intersection. Both Minus Front and Minus Back will give different results based on the stacking order of the objects selected (Figure 18.12).

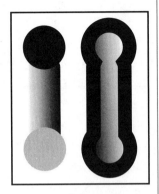

The three objects on the left (round-cornered rectangle and two circles) were joined using the Pathfinder Unite command. The resulting single path was then stroked.

Figure 18.12. The entire star in the top row is subtracted from the square, even in the nonoverlapping areas, by the Minus Front command. In the second row, the Minus Back command subtracts the backmost object (square) wherever the paths intersect.

Unit 18 ★ Masks and Compound Paths

DIVIDE

The Divide command splits two or more overlapping objects into separate paths wherever those shapes overlap. This is often an easier and more accurate way to separate overlapping objects without using the Scissors tool (Figure 18.13). The Divide command does not change the paint attributes of any of the overlapping objects when it divides them.

TRIM

The Trim command removes any part of a filled object that is hidden behind another object. It removes strokes and doesn't merge objects with the same color (Figure 18.13).

MERGE

The Merge command operates on objects with the same fill color, uniting them as does the Unite command. If the overlapping objects have different fill colors, like objects are united and the other objects are trimmed (Figure 18.13).

WARNING!

You cannot use the Pathfinder commands on objects created with the Gradient Mesh tool.

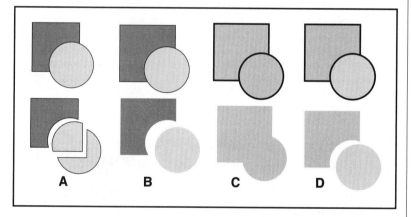

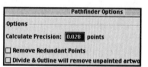

The Pathfinder Options dialog box is available from the Pathfinder menu. It's a good idea to select the two options that remove extra anchor points and unpainted artwork.

Figure 18.13. When the Divide command was applied to the square and circle on the left, the two objects were divided into three separate paths where the two objects overlapped (A). When the square and circle (B) were trimmed with the Trim command, the area of the square behind the circle was removed. Because the square and circle (C) contain the same fill color, the Merge command united them. The square and circle in D have different fills, so the Merge command trimmed them.

CROP

The Crop command removes any objects not directly beneath the frontmost object. Like a mask, the Crop command allows only objects directly beneath the frontmost object (mask) to be displayed; unlike a mask, which only *hides* the unrevealed objects, the Crop command *deletes* them (Figure 18.14).

Macintosh Keystrokes

⌘-N FIle/New
⌘-D Object/Transform/
   Repeat Transform

Windows Keystrokes

Ctrl-N File/New
Ctrl-D Object/Transform/
   Repeat Transform

OUTLINE

The Outline command converts any object into paths, with no fill or stroke. Where any path segments overlap, the lines are divided. The segments can be moved individually with the Group Selection tool and edited with the Direct Selection tool (Figure 18.14).

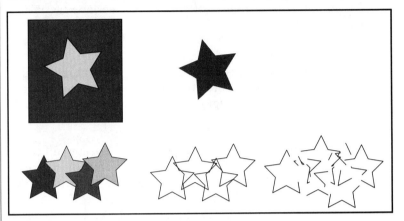

Figure 18.14. When the Crop command was applied to the star and rectangle (top), the star became a mask against the rectangle, and anything not revealed by the star (mask) was deleted. The overlapping stars (below left) were selected and the Outline command applied (center). This stripped all the fill and stroke colors from the stars (stroke applied for visibility only), and converted the shapes to outlines. Any intersecting lines were divided and can be edited individually (right).

FYI

The Outline command is useful when preparing artwork that needs a trap for overprinting objects. Trapping is used to prevent misregistration when the paper moves over the printing plates on press.

Version 7

The Pathfinder filters are located under the Object menu in version 7.

EXERCISE D

1. In a new file (File/New), draw two overlapping circles with different fill colors, but the same stroke color.

2. Select both objects with the Selection tool and press the Option/Alt key while dragging down to clone the circles. Choose Object/Transform/Repeat Transform to create a third set of circles (Figure 18.15).

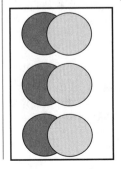

Figure 18.15. Select the first set of overlapping circles and clone them twice to create three sets.

3. Display the Pathfinder palette (Window/Show Pathfinder). Select the first pair of objects and click on the Unite button. The two circles are merged and display the fill color of the front-most object.

4. Select the next pair and use the Intersect command. Only the overlapping areas remain; everything else is deleted.

5. Select the third set of circles and assign them the same fill color. Click on the Merge command and notice that the paths are merged because they are the same fill color. Choose Edit/Undo to restore the circles.

6. With the circles still selected, click the Trim button. Use the Group Selection tool and click on an empty area of the page to deselect everything. Click and drag (don't release the mouse button) the right side of the circle away and notice that the overlapping area was trimmed away.

7. With the next pair, select the Rectangle tool and draw a box that covers most but not all of the first two objects. Next, select all three objects and apply the Crop command. Only those parts of the circles covered by the rectangle appear; everything else has been cropped away.

8. Close this file (File/Close). Don't save your changes.

REVIEW

In this unit you learned that:

1. You can use an object as a "window" to display an object underneath it by making it a mask.

2. The "window" object is called a *mask* or *masking object*, and whatever it displays beneath or behind it is called a *masked object*.

3. You can only use one object to mask another object.

4. You can lock and unlock masks, and edit the masked and masking objects independently of each other.

5. A mask can be stroked and filled.

6. Two or more objects can be made into a compound path that is transparent against the page or against any background.

7. You can reverse the direction of a compound path, which will turn off the transparency effect.

Macintosh Keystrokes

⌘-Z Edit/Undo
⌘-W File/Close

Windows Keystrokes

Ctrl-Z Edit/Undo
Ctrl-W File/Close

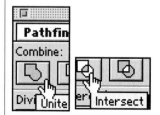

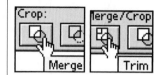

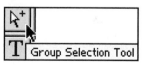

FYI

To use the Group Selection tool on a grouped object where you want to move a single object, click and drag without releasing the mouse button. If you release the mouse button and click to drag, you will select the second object in the group.

8. The Pathfinder palette contains tools that allow you to combine, divide, and manipulate objects.

9. The Unite command combines overlapping objects into a single object.

10. The Intersect command deletes all but the intersecting areas of two objects.

11. The Exclude command eliminates the overlapping areas of two objects.

12. Minus Front uses the front object to cut away the intersection with the back object. The Minus Back command uses the back object to cut away the intersection with the front object.

13. The Divide command splits two intersecting objects into separate shapes.

14. The Trim command removes any parts of a filled object hidden by another object.

15. The Merge command combines objects with the same fill color.

16. The Crop command uses an object to cut away all but the visible areas of other objects behind it.

17. The Outline command deletes all but the paths of intersecting objects.

UNIT 19
Raster Images

OVERVIEW

In this unit you will learn how to:
differentiate between vector art and bitmap art
rasterize vector art
use the Pen and Ink filters
create, modify, and save hatch styles and
    hatch settings
use the Object Mosaic filter
link and embed images in an Illustrator file

TERMS

bitmap art
embedded image
filter
hatch (hatch style)
hatch settings (hatch effects)
linked image
plug-ins
raster image
vector art

HOW IT WORKS

A rectangle was filled with the Swash Hatch and the Grass Hatch Effect was applied in the Hatch Effects dialog box. One hatch element was selected; then, using the Select/Same Paint Style command, all the hatch elements filled and stroked with black were selected and repainted with a Pantone spot color.

VECTOR ART AND BITMAP IMAGES

Adobe Illustrator creates vector art, that is, objects comprised of independent lines and shapes. Each object is generated by a mathematical algorithm which, when printed to a PostScript device, will retain its size and shape without becoming distorted. Adobe Photoshop, in contrast, creates bitmap images comprised of pixels arranged on a grid. The size of the grid and the number of pixels per inch determine the level of detail in the printed image. Enlarging a bitmap image by more than about 10% frequently results in distortion.

These vector filters can be applied to Illustrator (vector) art. The arrows after each filter indicate that there are more options for that filter selection.

RASTER ART

Raster art is another name for bitmap art. When an image is scanned, it is converted to pixels. The scanner maps these pixels line by line, much like an image is drawn or rasterized on a computer monitor or television screen. Each pixel, or bitmap, has a color value that can be edited in a bitmap program such as Photoshop or with bitmap filters in Illustrator.

Continuous tone images such as photographs are bitmap images and can display gradual gradations of color and shades. However, because bitmap images represent a fixed number of pixels, they can appear jagged (pixelated) and lose detail when they are enlarged on screen or printed at a higher resolution than provided for by the scanning process.

RASTERIZE COMMAND

The Rasterize command converts Illustrator's vector objects into bitmap images. This allows you to apply any of the bitmap filters in Illustrator to the image, but you can no longer use the vector tools to modify the new bitmap image. For example, if you rasterize a rectangle, you can use the transformation tools to scale, rotate, shear, and reflect it, but you cannot select anchor points to edit it, and you cannot use the Blend tool, Pathfinder commands, or any of the color application tools to change its color characteristics.

These bitmap filters can be applied to bitmap (rasterized) art, such as placed bitmap images or Illustrator artwork that has been rasterized.

PLUG-IN FILTERS

Filters are small programs called *plug-ins* that work within Illustrator to accomplish a particular task. Some tasks are pure grunt work, such as converting all the colors in the document to process colors, and some, like the Photo Crosshatch filter, can convert a rasterized image into a hatched ink pen image.

VECTOR FILTERS

The first set of filters under the Filter menu can be applied only to vector artwork such as Illustrator objects. It is these filters that let you specify color options for the artwork as well as change the artwork itself.

BITMAP FILTERS

The filters in the last panel are bitmap filters. In fact, they're Photoshop filters, and can be applied only to raster art. To apply these bitmap filters to Illustrator (vector) art, that art must first be rasterized, that is, converted to pixels (Figure 19.1).

Figure 19.1. The TIFF image placed in the Illustrator document is raster art created with pixels when it was scanned into Photoshop. The scissors is vector art created with Illustrator's drawing tools.

Macintosh Keystrokes

⌘-N File/new

Windows Keystrokes

Ctrl-N File/New

Image info

Photograph by Tracey Attlee

The Plug-ins folder, which contains the Illustrator Filters and Photoshop Filters folders, is located in the Adobe Illustrator 8.0 folder on the hard drive.

EXERCISE A

1. In a new document (File/New), choose File/Place. Navigate to the Unit 19 folder on the CD-ROM and highlight the *Joy.tif* file. Click on Place (Macintosh) or Open (Windows). When the image appears, use the Selection tool to move it to the top of the page. This is a raster image and can only be manipulated with the transformation tools.

2. With the image selected, pull down the Filter menu and notice that none of the Distort filters or first set of Stylize filters are available, because these filters work only on vector art.

3. Click on the photograph to select it. Choose Filter/Artistic/Paint Daubs. Use the Brush Size and Sharpness sliders to apply the filter. Notice how increasing and decreasing these values affect the image preview. Select different brushes to change the effect. When you are satisfied, click on OK (Figure 19.2).

4. Use the Star tool to draw a star. Assign it different fill and stroke colors.

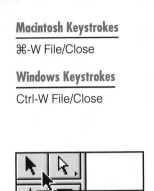

Figure 19.2. The Paint Daubs bitmap filter is applied to the bitmap image. Changing any of the values or selecting a different Brush Type in the Paint Daubs dialog box increases or decreases the filter's effect.

Resolution info

In the Rasterize Options dialog box, select Screen for any kind of monitor output, Medium for laser printer output, or High for imagesetter output.

5. With the star still selected, pull down the Filter menu and notice that none of the raster filters in the lower panel of the Filter menu are available, because the star is vector art and cannot be edited with raster filters.

6. Choose Filter/Distort/Punk & Bloat. Click the Preview button to select it and use the slider to distort the star. Click on OK.

7. Use the Selection tool while pressing the Option/Alt key and drag to create a duplicate star. With the duplicate selected, choose Object/Rasterize to display the Rasterize dialog box (Figure 19.3).

Waiting?

If you rasterize an image to a resolution higher than the screen resolution (72 ppi), the Anti-Alias function can take a long time to rasterize. Also, text characters and thin lines may appear blurred.

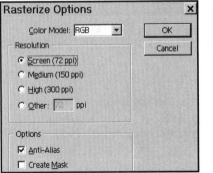

Figure 19.3. Select a format for the conversion from vector to raster art from the Color Model menu in the Rasterize dialog box.

8. Select RGB from the Color Model menu and click the Screen option in the Resolution field.

9. Select the Anti-Alias option to smooth the jagged edges of the new, pixelated image. Click on OK. Notice the jagged edges of the rasterized image (Figure 19.4). You can now apply any of the bitmap filters to this rasterized art.

10. Close this file. Don't save your changes.

Select the Create Mask option in the Rasterize Options dialog box to keep the bitmap image's background transparent (left).

Figure 19.4. The image on the right was rasterized and displays pixilation ("jaggies") where the curves should be smooth as in the vector image on the left.

Drop Shadows

The Drop Shadow filter (Filter/Stylize/Drop Shadow) does not work on raster images. To set a drop shadow, select the vector object and apply the filter, typing the desired amount in the X Offset and Y Offset fields. Typing a negative number applies the drop shadow to the top and left sides of the object instead of to the right and bottom sides.

PEN AND INK FILTERS

The Hatch Effects filter texturizes the vector image as if it were drawn with an ink pen where the crossed lines (hatches) define the image. A good example of ink pen drawings is the series of authors' pictures in the Barnes & Noble stores. These drawings are created with pen and ink, with the density of the ink and width of the pen strokes generating light and shadow areas.

The Photo Crosshatch filter creates the same effect on bitmap photographic images by converting the image into a series of hatched layers, making it appear to have been sketched by an ink pen.

The Photo Crosshatch filter is accessed from the Pen and Ink filter under the Filter menu. This filter is available only when a bitmap image is selected.

HATCH EFFECTS FILTER

The Hatch Effects filter creates patterns that look like hand-dipped brush strokes. If you have ever used an old-fashioned nibbed pen and crosshatched to create the illusion of different tonal ranges with only black ink, you have a good idea of what this filter does.

Using this filter takes a great deal of memory because of the many shapes needed to create the effects. Thus, it is always wise to apply this filter as the last step in an illustration or on a copy of the file.

A hatch or *hatch style* has several options or hatch settings associated with it. Some of these hatch settings come with Illustrator 8.0. You can also create your own hatch settings, and save and load them in different documents.

Version 7

In version 7 there is only the Ink Pen filter. There is no Photo Crosshatch or Object Mosaic filter.

Macintosh Keystrokes

⌘-N File/New
⌘-W File/Close

Windows Keystrokes

Ctrl-N File/New
Ctrl-W File/Close

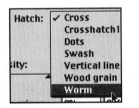

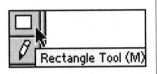

Select a hatch style from the Hatch pull-down menu.

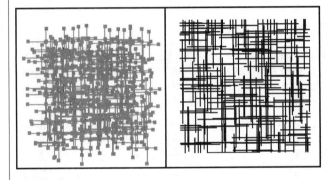

If you select Match Object's Color, the hatch fill is changed to the selection's fill. Don't select this option if the selection is filled with a pattern.

EXERCISE B

1. In a new file (File/New), draw a rectangle and keep it selected. Choose Filter/Pen and Ink/Hatch Effects to display the Hatch Effects dialog box. This overwhelming dialog box offers unlimited possibilities for creating hatch style patterns.

2. Click to select the Preview button on the right side of the dialog box so that you can see how your selections in the dialog box affect the selected rectangle in the preview window above the Preview check box.

3. Use the Settings pull-down menu on the right side of the dialog box to select *Cross texture 1 medium*. A plaid-like design appears in the Preview window. Use the Density slider on the upper left side of the dialog box to make it lighter by decreasing the number of hatch elements. The hatch style appears lighter in the Preview dialog box. Click on OK.

4. When you return to the page, the rectangle appears filled with the selected hatch objects. Illustrator uses the object, in this case the rectangle, as a mask to display only that part of the hatch pattern that fits inside the boundaries of the object (Figure 19.5).

Figure 19.5. When you first create the hatch, it appears selected on the page. Deselecting or choosing View/Hide Edges displays the hatch masked by the object.

5. Draw another rectangle and fill it with red. Choose Filter/Pen and Ink/Hatch Effects and use the Hatch pull-down menu to select *Worm* as the design for the Hatch style. Choose Keep Object's Fill Color to retain the fill color of the selected object (red). Click on OK. Your screen should resemble Figure 19.6.

6. Close this file. Don't save your changes.

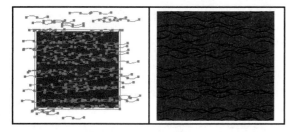

Figure 19.6. Select the Keep Object's Fill Color option in the Hatch Effects dialog box to make the hatch lines display against that color.

HATCH EFFECTS OPTIONS

You can customize the size, density, angle, and scale of the hatch marks, depending on the options selected in the Hatch Effects dialog box. Use the Preview window (press the Tab key to update the Preview) to see how the hatch will look and continue to make selections until you are satisfied.

DISPERSION

Dispersion refers to the way the hatch pattern is spread out or spaced inside a selected object. The higher the Dispersion value specified with the Dispersion sliders, the less space between the hatch marks.

THICKNESS

The Thickness slider adjusts the stroke weight of the individual hatch elements in a range from 10% to 1000%. If the selected object is not stroked, this option is dimmed or unavailable.

ROTATION

The Rotation option (dial or text box) lets you set the angle at which those hatch elements are applied, in ranges from -180° to +180°.

SCALE

Use the Scale pop-up menu to adjust the size of the individual hatch elements from 10% to 1000%.

OTHER VARIABLES

The Linear option increases the effect progressively. Choose Reflect to vary the effect from the center of the object outward. The Constant option creates the same effect evenly across the shape, and the Symmetric option varies the effect proportionately and evenly. This is a good option to select when applying hatches to round or cylindrical shapes. Select a Fade option to specify how the hatch will fade across the object. You can also let Illustrator apply the Hatch effect by selecting the Random option.

Speed demon!

If you find Illustrator running slowly when using the Ink Pen filter, turn off the Preview option in the Hatch Effects dialog box.

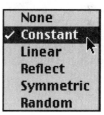

The Constant option creates the same effect evenly across the object.

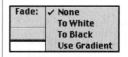

Select None from the Fade menu for no fade, To White to fade the hatch to white, and To Black to fade the hatch to black. If the object is filled with a gradient, select Use Gradient to set the fade's direction and colors.

Unit 19 ★ Raster Images

CREATING AND SAVING HATCHES

Hatches have two properties, style and settings. A *hatch style* is created from Illustrator artwork and is specified as a new hatch from the Pen and Ink menu, where it appears under the Hatch menu in the Hatch Effects dialog box. *Hatch settings* are the effects applied to a particular hatch style in the Hatch Effects dialog box (Figure 19.7).

Hatch:	✓ Cross	Hatch Effect:	crossed threads ✓ Crosshatch heavy
	Crosshatch1		Crosshatch light
	Dots	Hatch:	Crosshatch mediu
	My Line Hatch		Dashed lines
ity:	Swash		Fiberglass heavy
	Vertical lines		Fiberglass light
	Wood grain	Density:	Fiberglass mediun
rsion:	Worm		Grass
			Grass Hatch

Figure 19.7. The Hatch menu (left) displays the default hatch patterns and the new hatch, *My Line Hatch*, which was created from Illustrator art and saved using the New Hatch command under the Pen and Ink menu. The Hatch Effect menu (right) displays the default effects and a new *Grass* effect created in the Hatch Effects dialog box.

The hatch, *My Line Hatch*, is a hatch style. Fiberglass heavy is its hatch setting.

You can create and save hatches as well as modify existing hatch patterns. This allows you to reload them and use them in other Illustrator files. To save a hatch, create it in the Hatch Effects dialog box, and specify it as a new hatch. Or, create a new hatch from your own artwork and specify it as a new hatch from the Pen and Ink menu under the Filter menu. When you use the Library Save As command, all the hatches in the current document are saved to a separate file, not just the hatches you create.

▶ Hatch Effects...
▶ Photo Crosshatch...
New Hatch...
▶ Library Open...
▶ Library Save As...

Use the Library commands under the Pen and Ink filter to save and open hatch libraries.

EXERCISE C

1. In a new file (File/New), draw a circle and keep it selected. Choose Filter/Pen and Ink/Hatch Effects display the Hatch Effects dialog box. Click the Reset button to restore the filter's default values. Select the Preview option in the lower right corner of the dialog box.

2. Select a hatch effect from the Hatch Effect menu and a hatch from the Hatch menu. Select Constant from the menu to the right of the Dispersion sliders and watch the Preview window to see how your selections affect the art.

3. Type a value in the Rotation field or use the rotation dial to change the angle along which to apply the effect.

4. Choose Reflect from the Dispersion pop-up menu to vary the hatch pattern from the center of the selected object outward. Choose Symmetric to vary the hatch pattern proportionately and evenly. Choose Random to apply the effect irregularly around the object.

5. Click on the New button and type a name for the new hatch pattern. It appears in the Hatch Effects menu, where it can be applied to any object in this document (Figure 19.8).

Hatch Effects			
Hatch Effect: [Grass ⬍]	[New...]	[Delete]	[OK]
Hatch: [Swash ⬍]	☐ Match Object's Color		[Cancel]
	☐ Keep Object's Fill Color		
Density: [45%]			[Update]
			[Reset]
Dispersion: [0%] [97%] [Random ⬍]			
Thickness: [ ] [ ] [None ⬍]			
Scale: [30%] [450%] [Random ⬍]			
Rotation: [90°] [-90°] [Random ⬍]			☑ Preview
Fade: [None ⬍]			

Figure 19.8. The grass hatch effect appears in the Hatch Effect menu.

```
  None
  Constant
✓ Linear
  Reflect
  Symmetric
  Random
```

Selecting a Linear value for the Dispersion option creates the hatch effect progressively across the object.

```
  None
  Constant
  Linear
  Reflect
  Symmetric
✓ Random
```

The Random option applies the hatch irregularly, with no obvious order or direction, across the object.

6. Click on OK to return to the document. Draw another object and then press Command-Option-E (Macintosh) or Ctrl-Alt-E (Windows) to display the Hatch Effects dialog box. The hatch effect you just created and saved appears in the Hatch Effects menu. Click on OK.

7. Use the Pen tool or any of the drawing tools to draw a small design. Select it and choose Filter/Pen and Ink/New Hatch. Click on New in the New Hatch dialog box, type a name for the hatch in the text field, and click OK twice to return to the document. You have created a hatch style to which you can apply different settings from the Hatch Effects dialog box.

8. Choose Filter/Pen and Ink/Library Save As. Type a name for the hatch set and save the set in your Projects folder. You can

Density

This value adjusts the number of hatch elements that are applied to the image in a range from 5–10 points.

Dispersion Noise

This value controls the amount of space between the hatch elements in a range from 0–300%. The image on the left has a Dispersion Noise value of 10%; the image on the right a value of 200%.

now use the Library Open command from the Pen and Ink menu to load the hatch set into any Illustrator document.

9. Continue to draw objects and apply different hatch effects until you are comfortable with this filter. Get to know the effects you can achieve with it, because using hatch patterns will often save you much tedious drawing.

10. Close this file. Don't save your changes.

PHOTO CROSSHATCH FILTER

The Photo Crosshatch filter does for bitmap images what the Pen and Ink filter does for vector art: It converts a continuous tone image such as a photograph—or any rasterized image—into a hatched ink pen image.

The Photo Crosshatch filter achieves this effect by layering the hatch layers, with each layer representing a different lightness value found in the original image. The darkest part of the image will have the most hatch layers and the lightest parts the fewest layers.

OBJECT MOSAIC FILTER

The Object Mosaic filter works only on bitmap images and on images that have been rasterized in Illustrator. It gathers pixels with a similar color value and clusters them into individual tiles, much as an artist would do when creating a tiled mosaic wall or floor.

EXERCISE D

1. In a new document (File/New), choose File/Place. Navigate to the Unit 19 folder on the CD-ROM and select the *Gardenia.tif* file. Click on Place. The image appears selected on the page.

2. Choose Filter/Pen and Ink/Photo Crosshatch to display the Photo Crosshatch dialog box.

3. Use the Hatch Layers arrows to select 4 or type 4 in the text field. This tells Illustrator to create 4 layers of hatches with its own distribution of lightness values between 0 and 255. Specifying 4 hatch layers creates Hatch Layer 1 with lightness values ranging from 0–64, which is very dark; Hatch Layer 2 has lightness values ranging from 0 to 128, or twice the range of Hatch Layer 1; Hatch Layer 3 has lightness values from 0–192; and Hatch Layer 4 has lightness values from 0 to 255, the full spectrum.

4. The Photo Crosshatch dialog box (Figure 19.9) displays a histogram, a graphic representation of the dark and light areas of the image, and provides sliders for adjusting those values.

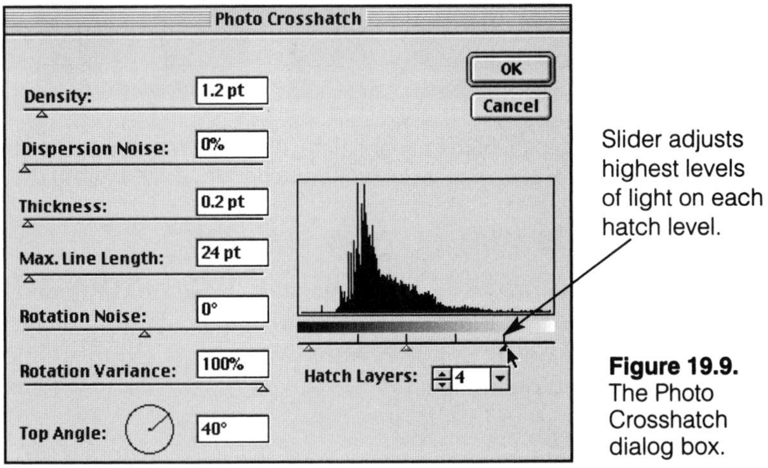

Slider adjusts highest levels of light on each hatch level.

Figure 19.9.
The Photo Crosshatch dialog box.

Macintosh Keystrokes

⌘-W File/Close
⌘-Z Edit/Undo

Windows Keystrokes

Ctrl-W File/Close
Ctrl-Z Edit/Undo

Thickness

This value controls the weight of the stroked hatch elements in a range from 1–10 points. If the object is unstroked, this option is unavailable (dimmed).

5. Drag the middle slider to the right to lighten the threshold levels on each hatch layer. If you drag it to the left, you will darken the layer.

6. Drag the rightmost slider to to the right to adjust the highest levels of light on each level. Drag the leftmost slider to the right to adjust the darkest levels of light on each layer. By moving all three sliders to the right, you will create a light hatch effect.

7. Leave the sliders on the left side of the dialog box at their default values and click on OK. The image appears with the crosshatch effect.

8. Choose Edit/Undo to undo the filter. With the image still selected, choose Filter/Create/Object Mosaic to display the Object Mosaic dialog box. Type 15 in the Width and Height text boxes in the Number of Tiles field.

9. To create the effect of grouting between the tiles, type 1 or 2 in the Width and Height text boxes of the Tile Spacing field. Select Gray in the Result area to have the result appear as a grayscale image. If you select the Delete Raster option, the original bitmap image is deleted, leaving only the mosaic image. This will create a grid effect because the underlying pixels are removed. Don't select this option for now. Click on OK. The raster image is transformed into a mosaic tile (Figure 19.10).

10. Close this file. Don't save your changes.

Max. Line Length

This value determines the maximum length of any hatch element in a range from 5–999 points.

Rotation values

The **Rotation Noise** is a random rotation of objects within the hatch layers. The **Rotation Variance** sets the amount that each layer is rotated from the previous layer. Top Angle sets the angle of rotation for the topmost hatch layer.

Figure 19.10. The original bitmap image (left), with the Photo Crosshatch filter applied (center), and with the Object Mosaic filter applied (right).

Image info

Gardenia, by Joseph Dai.

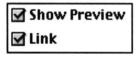

When you choose the Place command, the Link option is available.

FYI

When an image is placed in Illustrator with the Link option selected, only a low-resolution screen version of the image is placed in the file. When the file is printed, Illustrator follows the link back to the original, high-resolution image and prints that version of the image.

LINKED AND EMBEDDED IMAGES

When you place an image in Illustrator with the Place command, you have to ensure that Illustrator will be able to access that image when printing the document. There are two ways to do this: link the image or embed the image.

LINKING IMAGES

The Link option in the Place dialog box is selected by default. A linked image remains independent of the Illustrator file, but Illustrator establishes a connection, or link, to that image wherever it is, on a hard drive, external drive, floppy disk, or network server. When the document is printed, Illustrator follows the link back to the image and prints the image from its original location at its actual resolution. Furthermore, when linked files are modified in their original applications, such as Photoshop, the Illustrator image is automatically updated to reflect the editing.

EMBEDDING IMAGES

If you deselect the Link option when placing an image in the Illustrator document, the image is embedded in the Illustrator document. This gives you a larger file than if the image is linked to the original file. The advantage of embedding the image is that if the file is saved as an Illustrator EPS file with the Embed Placed Images option selected and then is imported into another application such as QuarkXPress, the image is available to XPress and will print without any problems. If the image is linked, applications other than Illustrator must be able to access the file by following Illustrator's link.

LINKS PALETTE

The Links palette is used to identify, select, monitor, and update placed images that are linked to external files. Once you place a linked image in an Illustrator document, it appears in the Links palette and is available for editing.

EXERCISE E

1. In a new document (File/New), choose File/Place. Navigate to the Unit 19 folder on the CD-ROM and highlight the *Mosaic.tif* file. Notice that the Link option is selected in the Place dialog box. Click on Place (Macintosh) or Open (Windows) to place the file as a linked image.

2. Display the Links palette (Window/Show Links). The Links palette displays a thumbnail of the placed image. Double-click on the thumbnail to display the Link Information dialog box, which gives you the current information on the image. Any transformational changes you make to the image will be reflected in this dialog box.

3. Click on the Edit Original button at the bottom of the Links palette. If you have Photoshop or any other bitmap application on your hard drive, the image will open in that program. Make any change to the image and save the image. When you return to Illustrator, an alert appears telling you that the linked image has been modified and asking if you want to update the link in the Illustrator document. Click Yes. The linked image is updated to reflect the changes you made.

4. Choose File/Place. Highlight the *Wood.tif* file in the Unit 19 folder on the CD-ROM, and click on Place (Macintosh) or Open (Windows). The image is placed in the file. Use the Selection tool to move it so you can see both images. The Links palette updates to display thumbnails of both images (Figure 19.11).

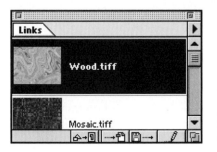

Figure 19.11. The Links palette automatically updates when a new image is placed in the document.

5. Select the *Wood.tif* image and double-click on the Scale tool. Type 50 in the Uniform field and click on OK.

6. Double-click on the *Wood.tif* link in the Links palette to display the Link Information dialog box. Notice that the Transform field displays the scaling information.

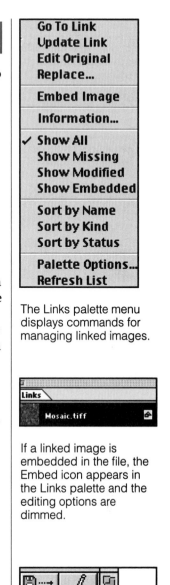

The Links palette menu displays commands for managing linked images.

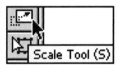

If a linked image is embedded in the file, the Embed icon appears in the Links palette and the editing options are dimmed.

7. Choose Show Missing from the Links palette menu. The Links palette clears, indicating that all the images are properly linked and available for printing.

8. Close this file. Don't save your changes.

REVIEW

In this unit you learned that:

1. Raster, or bitmap, art is a series of pixels mapped line by line when the image is scanned. Raster art cannot be scaled up without losing image detail.

2. Vector art is created with mathematical algorithms and can be resized and reshaped without losing detail.

3. Illustrator's vector filters can be applied only to vector art. Raster filters can be applied to raster art or to vector art that has been rasterized with the Rasterize command.

4. The Hatch Effects filter texturizes a vector image as if it had been drawn with an ink pen. The Crosshatch filter applies the same effect to raster art.

5. A hatch such as Wood Grain can have different effects such as dashed lines or swirls. Custom hatches can be created and edited.

6. The Hatch Effects options include dispersion, thickness, rotation, scale, and other variables.

7. Hatch settings are the effects applied to a particular hatch style and can be edited.

8. Custom hatches can be saved and loaded into other Illustrator documents.

9. The Object Mosaic filter turns raster art into clusters of pixels.

10. Placed images can be linked to the high-resolution image while a low-resolution preview image appears in the Illustrator document. Illustrator must be able to access the high-resolution image when the file is printed.

11. Deselecting the Link option when placing images embeds the high-resolution image in the document, where it is available to other applications when the Illustrator EPS file is imported into a document.

12. The Links palette identifies, monitors, and updates all placed images in a document.

UNIT 20
Illustrator and Other Applications

OVERVIEW

In this unit you will learn how to:
export text
save files in Acrobat PDF format
save files in Illustrator and Illustrator
EPS format
export artwork for print and Internet
move artwork between Illustrator and
Photoshop
import Illustrator art into QuarkXPress
create clipping paths

TERMS

clipping path
GIF
JPEG
PDF
Save
Save a Copy
Save As

HOW IT WORKS

The paint tubes started life as a single Art brush dragged out of the Brushes palette, where it became Illustrator art. The art was duplicated, colored, and arranged in rows using the Repeat Transform command. The file was saved as an Illustrator EPS file and opened in Photoshop at a resolution of 300 pixels per inch as a grayscale file. In Photoshop, filters were applied to the background, and the file was saved as a TIFF file and imported into the QuarkXPress 4.0 document.

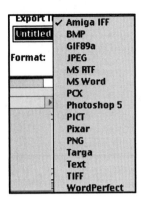

Illustrator 8's export file formats include many graphics and word-processing plug-ins.

Save this document as:

Art.ai

Format: Illustrator

Illustrator files can be saved in one of three file formats.

It's free!

Acrobat Reader is usually on every application CD distributed by Adobe. It is also available on Adobe's Web site.

Save as type: | Amiga IFF
Amiga IFF
BMP
Enhanced Meta-File
GIF89a
JPEG
PCX
Photoshop 5
Pixar
PNG
Targa

The Windows export file formats include the BMP format.

"PLAYS WELL WITH OTHERS"

One of the reasons Adobe Illustrator is so popular is that its files can be exported or saved in a variety of formats for print and Internet production. Version 8 ships with more than a dozen export formats that allow you to open Illustrator files in other graphics and word-processing applications on Macintosh and Windows platforms. Illustrator files can also be saved in Acrobat PDF format for use on the Internet, or as EPS files which can be imported into page layout programs, as well as in native Illustrator format.

The Export and Save As commands apply to the entire Illustrator file. You can also export selected parts of Illustrator artwork using the Clipboard and the drag-and-drop feature. For example, you can select anything in an Illustrator file and drag it into a Photoshop document, where it will appear on a new layer, or drag a selection into a Microsoft Office file.

EXPORTING TEXT

Any type created as point type, type on a path, or as area type can be exported as a text file that can be opened in most word processors (Figure 20.1). You will, however, lose any formatting applied in Illustrator, such as typeface and type style.

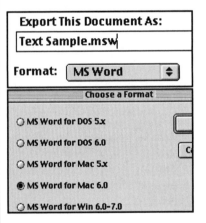

Figure 20.1. Exporting selected text as a Microsoft Word file displays a general format option in the Export dialog box (top) and specific options in the Choose a Format dialog box (below).

SAVING FILES IN ACROBAT PDF FORMAT

Saving a file as a PDF (Portable Document Format) file makes it accessible to anyone with a copy of Acrobat Reader. PDF files retain the font and color attributes of the Illustrator file. Selecting the PDF format gives you three options for how Illustrator prepares that PDF file.

PRESS READY

The Press Ready option should be selected if the document will be used for professional print publishing. Select this option to ensure that all the fonts are embedded and that the JPEG images are saved at their maximum quality. Because all images are saved at their maximum image quality and all fonts are embedded in the document, file size tends to be high.

PRINT QUALITY

Select this option if you will be printing the PDF document to a laser or ink jet printer or to a color copier. The CMYK information is included and all the fonts are embedded, but images are not saved with their high-resolution options. Print Quality gives you excellent image quality without the inflated file size.

WEB READY

If the PDF document will be posted on the Internet, select this option, as it gives you the smallest file size. Images are converted to RGB color and saved at 72 ppi (pixels per inch). Fonts are not embedded unless you manually select that option.

SAVING FILES

Illustrator provides three options for saving files: the Save, Save As, and Save a Copy commands. Only the Save command automatically overwrites the previously saved file without giving you a chance to abort the save, so select this option or press the keyboard shortcut keys [Command-S (Macintosh) or Ctrl-S (Windows)] with caution.

When saving files with the Save As or Save a Copy command, you have the option of saving the file in native Illustrator format, as an Illustrator EPS file, or in Acrobat PDF format.

SAVE

The Save command saves the document under its current name at its current location and file format. For example, if you saved a file as *Flowers.ai* as an Illustrator file in your Projects folder, choosing Save from the file menu saves that file as *Flowers.ai* as an Illustrator file in your Projects folder, overwriting the previously saved file.

SAVE AS

To change the name, location, or file type of any file, select Save As from the File menu. This option does not overwrite the existing file unless you select Replace should you be saving the file with exactly the same name as an existing file.

The PDF Format dialog box is where you specify whether the PDF document will be used for printing or for Internet distribution.

Shortcut

To save *all* open documents with their current names, to their current locations, and in their current formats, press the Option/Alt key and choose File/Save.

Web color

Because Illustrator defaults to CMYK color mode, select the RGB color model from the Color palette's menu. This is the correct color mode for Web work.

SAVE A COPY

The most versatile of the save commands, Save a Copy, saves an identical copy of the file with the *Copy* extension added to the file name. This command leaves the original document untouched.

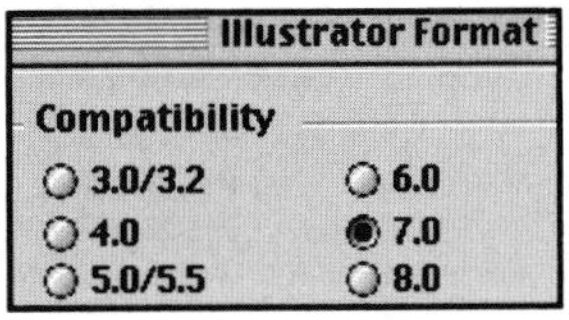

SAVING IN ILLUSTRATOR FORMAT

When saving a file in Illustrator format, you will most likely select the 8.0 option in the Illustrator Format dialog box. If you save the version 8 file in an earlier version of Illustrator, you may lose some of version 8's features. For example, saving an Illustrator 8 file that contains a mesh object as an Illustrator 7 file will display the mesh object as a non-editable object filled with the mesh gradient. You will not be able to change the color attributes of that object, only transform it with the transformation tools.

SAVING IN ILLUSTRATOR EPS FORMAT

This is the most versatile format for Illustrator files, as it can be read by almost every major graphics and text program on the market. EPS files preserve all the graphic elements as well as RGB and CMYK color attributes. And because the format is *Illustrator* EPS, the EPS document remains an Illustrator file and can be opened and edited in Illustrator.

When saving a file in Illustrator EPS format, the EPS Format dialog box lets you select options for compatibility with earlier versions of Illustrator, as well as Preview and other options for the document (Figure 20.2).

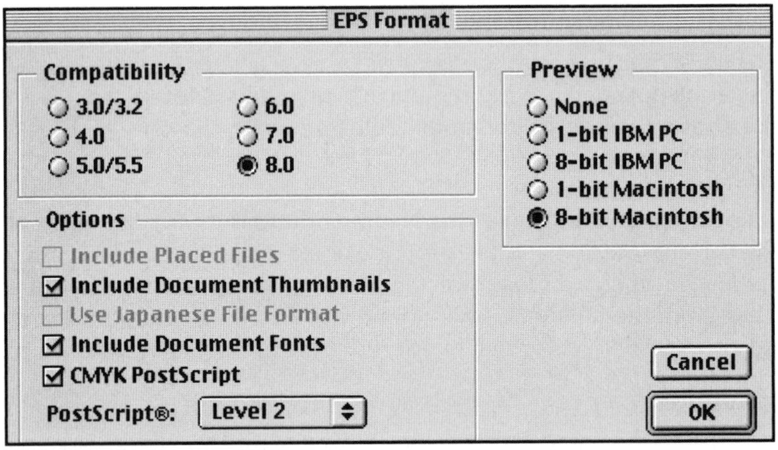

Selecting an earlier version of Illustrator when saving a file in native Illustrator format may limit the features preserved in the file.

When a file is saved in Illustrator EPS format, it remains an Illustrator file.

Figure 20.2. Select EPS options for the Illustrator EPS file in the EPS format dialog box.

Select a thumbnail preview option in the Preview field for either Macintosh or Windows files. Selecting 1-bit previews displays the file in black and white, whereas the 8-bit preview displays the file in color. Select the Include Placed files option if you have placed images in the Illustrator file and you want to embed the image files, in the document. The Include Document Thumbnails option displays a thumbnail image of the EPS artwork in the Open dialog box of most applications or in the QuarkXPress Get Picture dialog box.

If you select Include Document Font, Illustrator will save any fonts used in the document with that file. This means that if the file is opened on a computer where the font is not installed, the Illustrator file will display the font properly. This option increases file size, but ensures that the document will display the correct fonts, not substitute fonts.

EXPORTING ARTWORK

Unless you are going to use Illustrator artwork in Adobe Photoshop, you must save or export the file in a format that other applications can read. Illustrator comes with many export modules that let you export the file in a variety of formats. Some of these formats are designed specifically for Illustrator files that will be used on the Internet; others are more appropriate for Illustrator files that will be used in other applications.

INTERNET EXPORT FILES

The two major graphic file formats used on the Internet are the JPEG and GIF89a formats, and Illustrator 8 contains export modules for both formats. The JPEG (Joint Photographic Experts Group) format is a lossy compression format that reduces a file's size by eliminating what it considers to be unnecessary data. It usually produces smaller files than GIF files and can be imported into other applications as well as by Internet-specific programs such as Adobe PageMill.

JPEG

The JPEG export option is the best one to use when exporting Illustrator documents that will be used in Web pages, especially when those files contain gradients and placed photographic images. It allows you to specify image quality, resolution, and a compression level for the file (Figure 20.3). To specify the desired image quality, do one of three things: (1) enter a value between 0 and 10 in the Quality field; (2) select an option from the Quality pull-down menu; or (3) drag the slider to the left to export the image with less quality but as a smaller file, or drag it to the right to export a high-quality image with a larger file size.

When Include Document Thumbnails is selected, a thumbnail preview of the document appears in Illustrator's Open dialog box if Show Preview is checked.

Specify the image quality of a JPEG file in the Image field of the JPEG Options dialog box.

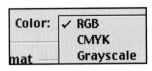

Select the RGB option for a JPEG image to be used on the Internet. The CMYK and Grayscale options are for print images.

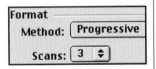

The Progressive JPEG format requires more RAM for viewing and is not supported by all Web browsers.

Imagemaps

The **Client-side (.html)** option saves the image for use in a Web page creation application such as Adobe PageMill. It saves two files, a .jpg file and an .html file that contains the HTML linking information. Both files must be saved in the same location to be read properly by the Web page creation application or by the Web browser. The **Server-side (.map)** option saves the artwork to be loaded on a Web server.

Figure 20.3. The JPEG Options dialog box lets you specify options for an Illustrator file that will be used on a Web page.

In the Format field, select Baseline Optimized to optimize the color quality of the image or the Progressive option to save the file as a progressive JPEG, which displays the image gradually as it is downloaded from a Web browser.

In the Resolution field, select Screen to export the image at 72 dpi, Medium to export it at 150 dpi, and High to export it at 300 dpi. You can also enter another resolution level in the Custom field.

Select the Anti-Alias option to smooth the edges of the artwork and Imagemap to save the Illustrator artwork as an imagemap if you are linking objects in the artwork to URLs in the Attributes palette (Figure 20.4).

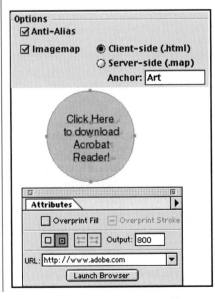

Figure 20.4. When you link objects to a URL in the Attributes palette (bottom), the Imagemap option in the JPEG Options dialog box (top) will save the Illustrator artwork as an imagemap.

Unit 20 ★ Illustrator and Other Applications

GIF89a

Export a file in GIF89a format for Web use when it contains large areas of flat color rather than continuous tone images such as placed photographic images. The GIF89a Options dialog box lets you select a color palette for the Web image, among other options (Figure 20.5).

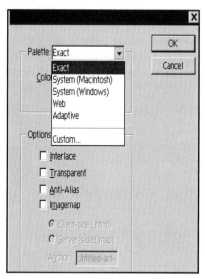

Figure 20.5. The GIF89a Options dialog box is where you specify a color palette and other options for an Illustrator file that will be used on a Web page.

The Color pull-down menu contains several palette options. The Exact palette uses the exact same colors as those used in the image, thus avoiding any dithering, which can distort the image. The Macintosh and System 8-bit palette options create a color table using the colors in the computer's operating system.

The Web palette is a cross-platform 8-bit color palette (256 colors) that is your best choice if you are displaying more than one image on a page. This palette ensures that all the images are composed of the same colors on any platform.

The Adaptive palette uses a representative sample of colors in the image. When selecting this option, select the smallest number of colors that keep the most detail in the image.

The last four options in the GIF89a Options dialog box affect the way the image displays. The Interlace option displays the image with the "Venetian blind" effect as it downloads from the browser. Select Transparent to let Illustrator decide which areas should be transparent in the Web browser. Always select Anti-Alias to smooth the edges of the artwork, although this can distort type set at small sizes. If you have linked objects in the document to URLs in the Attributes palette, select the Imagemap option.

Dithering

When an image is dithered, colors are mixed to approximate the colors that were removed from the image when a limited color palette such as a System or Web palette could not supply that color.

Select the Halftone Dithering option to keep moiré patterns to a minimum by dithering the image.

System palettes

Selecting a System palette can cause surprising results when an image is displayed on an 8-bit monitor that is using a different system palette.

The Adaptive color palette option lets you reduce the number of colors in an image, thus reducing file size.

Because the Button file contains a link to a URL that will be accessed by the Web page creation program, the Anchor option displays the file's name.

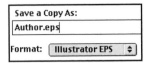

Saving a file in Illustrator EPS format lets you import it into many other applications.

When you save a file in Acrobat PDF format, Illustrator creates a PDF icon for the file instead of the standard Illustrator icon.

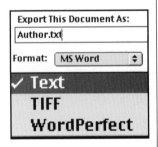

Export text in a word processor or text format.

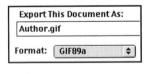

Exporting a file in GIF89a format makes it available to Web page creation programs and text-to-html conversion programs.

1. Open the *Author.ai* file in the Unit 20 folder on the CD-ROM.

2. Choose File/Save a Copy and navigate to your Projects folder. Type *Author.eps* in the name field and choose Illustrator EPS from the Format menu in the Save As dialog box. In the EPS Format dialog box, select 8.0 in the Compatibility field and 8-bit IBM PC or 8-bit Macintosh in the Preview field. Because this document contains text, select the Include Document Fonts option. Select the Include Document Thumbnails option to see a thumbnail of the image in Illustrator's Open dialog box. Click on OK.

3. Choose File/Save a Copy again. Type *Author.pdf* in the name field and select Acrobat PDF from the Format menu. In the PDF Format dialog box, select Web Ready from the PDF Options Set. Select the Embed All Fonts option in the Fonts In PDF field and RGB from the Color Conversion field. Select Acrobat 3.0 from the Compatibility menu and click on OK.

4. Use the Selection tool to select the large text block on the left side of the file. Choose File/Export. Type *Author.txt* in the name field and select a word-processing format or the Text option from the Format menu. Click on Save.

5. Choose File/Export. Type *Author.gif* in the name field and choose GIF89a from the Format menu. In the GIF89a Options dialog box, select Web from the Palette menu. Select the Interlace, Transparent, and Anti-Alias options from the Options field. Click on OK.

6. Don't quit out of Illustrator, but go to your Projects folder where you saved the *Author.pdf* file. Double-click on the Acrobat PDF icon to launch Acrobat Reader 3.0 and view the Illustrator document as an Acrobat PDF file (Figure 20.6). If you don't have Acrobat 3.0 or later installed on your hard drive, you will get an alert and will not be able to view the file.

Figure 20.6. The Illustrator file saved as an Acrobat PDF file can be viewed in Acrobat Reader.

7. If you have Adobe PageMill installed, double-click on the *author.html* file in the Unit 20 folder on the CD-ROM to display the file in PageMill. If you have Netscape Navigator or Microsoft Explorer installed, launch those programs and choose File/Open File in Netscape to display the file (Figure 20.7).

Figure 20.7. The Illustrator file saved as an html file can be viewed with a Web browser.

Notice that because you selected the Transparency option in the GIF89a Options dialog box, the nonpainted areas of the Illustrator file appear transparent against the browser page.

8. Close the Illustrator file.

ILLUSTRATOR AND PHOTOSHOP

There are three ways to travel between Illustrator and Photoshop, depending on what you want to do with the artwork. The grownup way is to export Illustrator artwork to Photoshop, versions 4 and 5, which lets you open the file in Photoshop and work with it, just as if you had created it in Photoshop. When you export an Illustrator file to Photoshop, you have the option of saving the Illustrator layers as Photoshop layers, which makes it easy to select and edit the image in Photoshop.

Another way to get Illustrator artwork into Photoshop is to use the Copy and Paste commands. Copy selected artwork to the Clipboard and paste it into Photoshop as bitmap art.

DRAG-COPYING OBJECTS

For the command-impaired, just drag the selected artwork from the Illustrator document onto the Photoshop document where it is placed on the selected layer. Pressing the Shift key before releasing the mouse button positions the selection in the center of the Photoshop image.

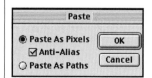

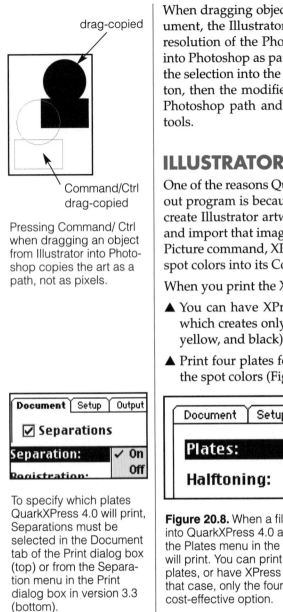

drag-copied

Command/Ctrl
drag-copied

Pressing Command/Ctrl when dragging an object from Illustrator into Photoshop copies the art as a path, not as pixels.

Document | Setup | Output

☑ **Separations**

Separation: | ✓ On
            | Off
Registration:

To specify which plates QuarkXPress 4.0 will print, Separations must be selected in the Document tab of the Print dialog box (top) or from the Separation menu in the Print dialog box in version 3.3 (bottom).

When dragging objects from Illustrator onto a Photoshop 4/5 document, the Illustrator object is converted to a bitmap image at the resolution of the Photoshop document. To drag and drop artwork into Photoshop as paths, press the Command/Ctrl key as you drag the selection into the Photoshop document. Release the mouse button, then the modifier key. The Illustrator object is converted to a Photoshop path and can be edited with any of Photoshop's pen tools.

ILLUSTRATOR AND QUARKXPRESS

One of the reasons QuarkXPress has become the foremost page layout program is because it handles color images so well. When you create Illustrator artwork with either process colors or spot colors, and import that image into a QuarkXPress picture box with the Get Picture command, XPress reads the color information and loads the spot colors into its Colors palette.

When you print the XPress file, you have the following options:

▲ You can have XPress convert the spot colors to process colors, which creates only the four process color plates (cyan, magenta, yellow, and black), or

▲ Print four plates for the process colors and additional plates for the spot colors (Figure 20.8).

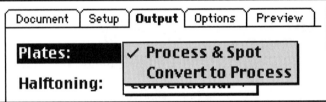

Document | Setup | **Output** | Options | Preview

Plates: | ✓ **Process & Spot**
        | **Convert to Process**

Halftoning:

Figure 20.8. When a file containing process and spot colors is imported into QuarkXPress 4.0 and Separations is selected in the Document tab, the Plates menu in the Output dialog box lets you specify which plates will print. You can print the four process color plates and any spot color plates, or have XPress convert all the spot colors to process colors. In that case, only the four process color plates will print. This is the most cost-effective option.

EXERCISE B

Note: Do this exercise only if you have access to Photoshop 4/5 and QuarkXPress 3/4.

1. Open the *Balloons.ai* file in the Unit 20 folder on the CD-ROM. It contains objects colored with both process and spot colors. The green balloon is a spot color.

2. Choose File/Save a Copy. Type *Balloons.eps* in the name field and select Illustrator EPS from the Format field. Select the Illustrator 8 and Include Document Thumbnails options in the EPS Format dialog box. Click on OK.

3. Launch QuarkXPress and create a new document. Draw a picture box and choose File/Get Picture. Double-click on the *Balloons.eps* file to import it into the picture box.

4. Display the Colors palette (View/Show Colors). The green spot color is listed with its CMYK percentages (Figure 20.9).

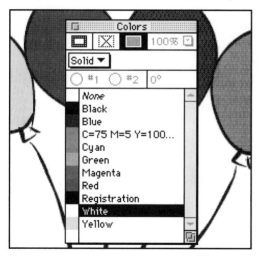

Figure 20.9. The Colors palette in the QuarkXPress document displays the green spot color with its CMYK equivalents.

| Name: |
| C=75 M=5 Y=100 |
| Model: CMYK |
| ☑ Process Separation |

In QuarkXPress 3, you must select the Process Separation check box in the Edit Colors dialog box to separate spot colors imported with an Illustrator EPS document.

Version 7

In version 7 a spot color's CMYK values do not appear in the Quark XPress Colors palette. Only the spot color's Swatch Name is displayed in the Colors palette.

5. Choose File/Print. Select the Separations check box in the Document tab of version 4.0 or in the Print dialog box of earlier versions. Click the Output tab and use the Plates menu to select Convert to Process from the Plates pull-down menu. If you have a color printer available, make the other necessary selections and print the file. You should get four pages, one for each of the process color plates.

6. Close the XPress file without saving any changes.

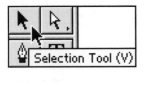

Selection Tool (V)

Create new layer

Select the balloon and drag its Selection Square from Layer 1 to the appropriate layer on the Layers palette.

Delete selected layers

Export This Document As:

Balloons.psd

Format: | **Photoshop 5** |

Use the .psd suffix (Photoshop document) when naming a file that will be opened in Photoshop.

Version 7

You cannot export an Illustrator version 7 file to Photoshop 5. If you export it to Photoshop 4 and open it in Photoshop 4 or 5, you will not have separate layers because Illustrator 7 does not include a Write Layers option..

7. In the *Balloons.ai* file, display the Layers palette. Select the yellow balloon with the Selection tool and Option/Alt-click on the New Layer icon in the Layers palette. Type *Yellow balloon* in the Name field and click on OK. Drag the Selection Square on Layer 1 up to the *Yellow balloon* layer to move the artwork to that layer.

8. Repeat to create separate layers for the red, purple, and green balloons. Be sure to move each selected balloon to its correct layer.

9. Create a new layer named *Text*. Type a few words on the *Text* layer.

10. Select Layer 1 and click the Delete icon on the Layers palette or select Delete "Layer 1" from the Layers palette menu. Your screen should resemble Figure 20.10.

Figure 20.10. The Illustrator file contains layers that will be saved with the file and will be available when the file is opened in Photoshop.

11. Choose File/Export. Type *Balloons.psd* in the name field. Choose Photoshop 5 from the Format menu and click on OK to display the Photoshop Options dialog box. Choose RGB from the Color Model menu and Screen from the Resolution options. Select the Anti-Alias option, and most importantly, the Write Layers option, so that the layers created in the Illustrator file will be converted to Photoshop layers. Click on OK to export the file (Figure 20.11).

Unit 20 ★ Illustrator and Other Applications

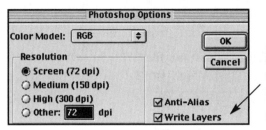

Figure 20.11. Select the Write Layers option in the Photoshop Options dialog box to convert Illustrator layers to Photoshop layers.

12. Launch Photoshop and display the Layers palette (Window/ Show Layers). Choose File/Open and open the *Balloons.psd* file. It appears with all its layers. However, if you choose Image/Image Size, you will notice that the image has been rasterized to only 72 pixels per inch, suitable for screen display but not for print.

13. Click on the Eye icon in the left column of Photoshop's Layers palette to turn layers on and off and hide and display the individual balloons (Figure 20.12).

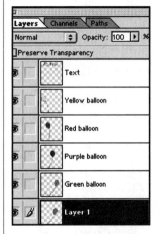

Figure 20.12. When Write Layers is selected in the Photoshop Options dialog box, the Illustrator layers are converted to Photoshop layers. The text layer, however, is not an editable text layer, even in Photoshop 5 which supports editable text layers.

When an object is drag-copied from Illustrator to Photoshop, it appears on a new layer.

14. With both the Illustrator and Photoshop files open, resize the windows so that they are both visible. In Illustrator, make sure all the layers are visible and use the Selection tool to drag one of the balloons onto the Photoshop document, where it appears on a new layer, Layer 1.

15. In Photoshop, choose File/Open. Open the *Balloons.eps* file in the Unit 20 folder on the CD-ROM. The Rasterize Generic EPS Format dialog box appears. Select the values in Figure 20.13 if you have enough memory installed. If not, type 72 in the Resolution field, RGB from the Mode menu, and click on OK. The Image appears, but the Layers palette displays only one layer,

The branch in the Photoshop image on the left was clipped out of the background and placed in Illustrator, where it was placed in front of a rectangle filled with an Illustrator pattern (right).

Layer 1. You cannot have both a high-resolution image and editable layers when you open an Illustrator file in Photoshop.

16. Close the Photoshop and Illustrator files without saving changes. Don't quit out of either program.

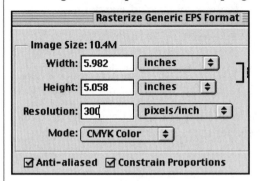

Figure 20.13. When you open an EPS file in Photoshop, you can specify the image size and resolution.

CLIPPING PATHS

A Photoshop file frequently contains pixels that you want to isolate and bring into Illustrator without displaying the whole image. To "clip" just selected pixels from an image, save only those pixels as a clipping path in Photoshop. When you place that image in Illustrator, it will *place* the entire image, but it will *display* only the pixels in the clipping path.

EXERCISE C

1. In Photoshop, open the *Leaf.tif* file. Display the Paths palette (Window/Show Paths). Choose Select/Load Selection and load the selection in Alpha Channel 1. The selected leaf appears in the image.

2. The Paths palette displays *Leaf path*. Select that path by clicking on its name in the Paths palette. Choose Clipping Path from the Paths palette menu to display the Clipping Path dialog box. Make sure that *Leaf path* is selected in the Path menu. Leave the Flatness field empty. Click on OK (Figure 20.14).

Flatness

Leaving this value blank specifies that the path will print following the path exactly. The lower the value, the more precise the printed path. If you have trouble printing a file with a clipping path, resave the file using a Flatness value between 1 and 5.

Figure 20.14. Select the path to clip in the Clipping Path dialog box.

3. Choose File/Save a Copy. Save the file as *Leaf.eps* and choose Photoshop EPS from the Format menu. Leave the EPS Options values at their defaults and click on Save. If you are using Photoshop 4, a dialog box appears where you must specify the clipping path to be saved with the file (Figure 20.15). Be sure to select *Leaf path*.

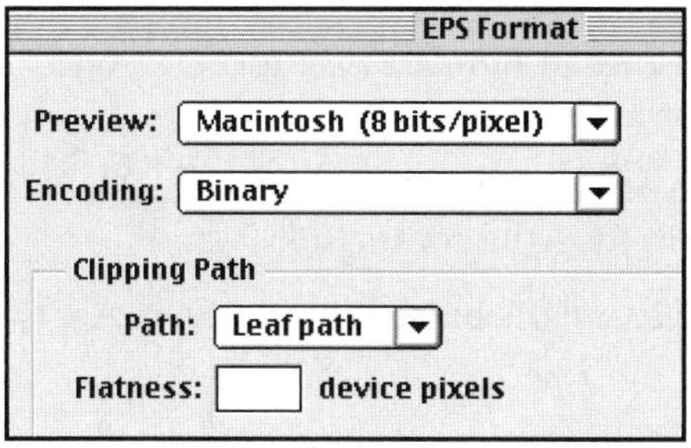

EPS Format

Preview: [Macintosh (8 bits/pixel) ▼]

Encoding: [Binary ▼]

Clipping Path

Path: [Leaf path ▼]

Flatness: [ ] device pixels

Figure 20.15. The EPS Format dialog box for Photoshop 4 requires that you select a clipping path before saving the file.

4. In Illustrator, create a new file. Choose File/Place. Navigate to the *Leaf.eps* file and click on Place (Macintosh) or Open (Windows). Only the leaf is displayed because the rest of the pixels in the image were clipped out in Photoshop. This image can be transformed, but it cannot be edited or colored with any of Illustrator's tools. But when placed in front of an Illustrator object, it will be transparent against that object (Figure 20.16).

5. Close all Photoshop and Illustrator files without saving any changes.

Save a copy in:

Leaf.eps

Format: [Photoshop EPS]

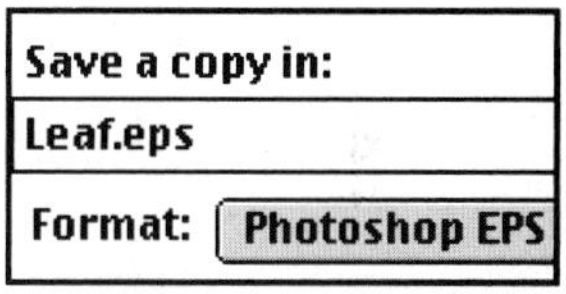

In Photoshop, using the Save a Copy option lets you save an unflattened file in EPS format and preserves the clipping path.

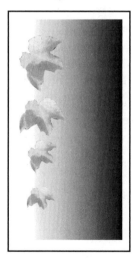

Figure 20.16. The original clipped leaf on the left was duplicated, rotated, and styled with the Glass filter from the Filter/Distort menu.

REVIEW

In this unit you learned that:

1. Any kind of text can be exported as text or in specific word-processor formats.

2. When exporting Illustrator files in Acrobat PDF format, you make selections for print or Internet distribution.

3. Files can be saved with the same name, at the same location, and in the same format with the Save command.

4. Files can be saved with different attributes with the Save As command.

5. Files saved in Illustrator EPS format can be imported into almost any other program.

6. The JPEG and GIF89a export formats are the most appropriate for Web-based documents.

7. JPEG files are more suitable for exporting Illustrator files with placed images, as well as gradients and blends.

8. GIF files are better for files with large areas of flat color.

9. Illustrator artwork can be exported in Photoshop format, copied from Illustrator and pasted into a Photoshop document, or drag-copied onto a Photoshop document.

10. When Illustrator art is saved in Illustrator EPS format and imported into a QuarkXPress picture box, any spot colors in the Illustrator file are added to the XPress Colors palette, and process colors will be separated when printing the XPress file.

11. Selected areas of a Photoshop file can be specified as a clipping path and placed in an Illustrator file, where only the clipped pixels will appear.

Face, Joon Y Lee

UNIT 21
Printing

OVERVIEW

In this unit you will learn how to:
print color separations
print color composites
print gradients and gradient mesh objects to
   avoid banding
trap overlapping colors

TERMS

banding
choke trap
color separating
composite
separations
spread trap
trapping

HOW IT WORKS

The face and hair were drawn with the various drawing tools and filled with solid
colors and gradients.

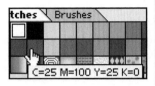

This process color is produced by combining 25% cyan, from the cyan plate, 100% magenta from the magenta plate, 25% yellow from the yellow plate, and no black from the black plate.

Selection

Info: [Linked Images]

Linked Images:

Macintosh HD:Graphics:JPEG Files:ALMON
Type: RGB
Bits per Pixel: 24
Channels: 3
Size: 860K, 551 by 533 pixels
Dimensions: 132.24 by 127.92 points
Resolution: 299.999 by 300 pixels per inch

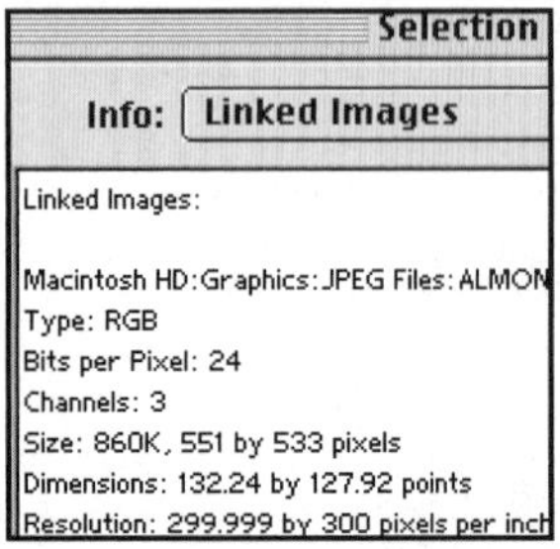

The Linked Images dialog box indicates that Illustrator can access the linked image, because it is on the hard drive.

PRINTING IN COLOR

Color comes in two flavors, process color and spot color. With process color, artwork is separated into four plates: one for cyan, one for magenta, one for yellow, and another for black. When these four plates are inked with the appropriate color and printed in register—that is, each plate prints *directly* on top of the other—the four process colors will combine in the percentages necessary to reproduce all the colors in the original artwork. This is how continuous tone images, such as photographs, are printed.

Even if you are printing separations, you will still want to see what the artwork will look like when the plates are combined *before* the four process color plates reproduce the image. To see all the colors in a document, print a composite, ideally to a high-end proofing machine, but more likely to a black-and-white laser printer or to a color ink jet printer.

DOCUMENT INFO/SELECTION INFO

Before printing anything, use the Document Info dialog box (Figure 21.1) to view information about your document and ensure that the document can access everything it needs to print properly. If you have an object selected, the Selection Info command appears instead of Document Info.

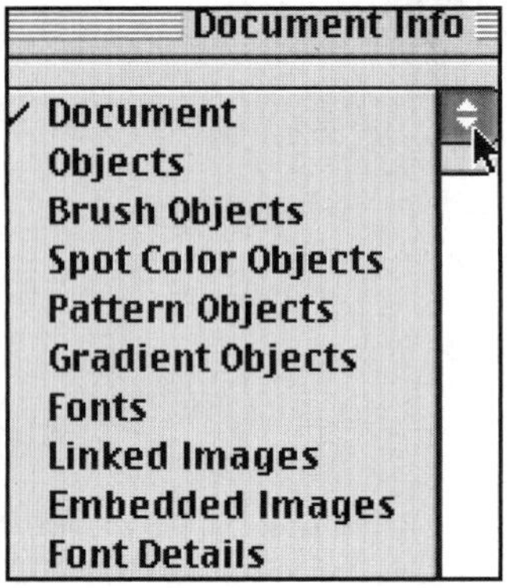

Document Info

✓ **Document**
Objects
Brush Objects
Spot Color Objects
Pattern Objects
Gradient Objects
Fonts
Linked Images
Embedded Images
Font Details

Figure 21.1. The Document Info dialog box lists information about selected objects or about all the objects in the file.

Use the pull-down menu to select the different elements of the document. You want to be especially sure that any fonts used in the file are available to the printer, as well as any linked images. If you have embedded an image, then you don't have to worry about Illustrator following the link to print the image. But if you selected the Link option in the Place dialog box when you placed an image, you should check the Linked Images field and make sure that the image is available on some drive for Illustrator to access it.

To print a black-and-white or color composite of Illustrator artwork, follow the instructions below for your computer platform.

MACINTOSH PRINTING OPTIONS

1. Go to the Chooser and select the printer—it *is* turned on, isn't it?

2. Choose File/Document Setup. Click the Page Setup dialog box.

3. Select the options you want—these will vary depending on the printer you selected—but choose a page orientation (Portrait is vertical; Landscape is horizontal) and type a scaling value if you want to reduce or enlarge the printed artwork. Click OK.

4. Choose File/Print. In the Print dialog box, use the pull-down menu to select Adobe Illustrator 8.0 to display Illustrator's printing options (Figure 21.2).

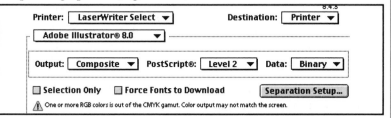

Figure 21.2. The Illustrator printing dialog box provides information about the file as well as printing options.

5. If a gamut alarm appears indicating that an RGB color will not print properly, click Cancel to return to the document. Choose Filter/Colors/Convert to CMYK. This filter converts the screen colors (red, green, and blue) to printing colors (cyan, magenta, yellow, and black).

6. Choose File/Print and select the Adobe Illustrator option again. The warning is no longer displayed. Make sure that Composite is selected from the Output menu so that only one page will print.

7. Choose File/Print and select Color Matching from the menu. Choose Color/Grayscale if you are printing to either a color printer or to a black-and-white printer.

8. Choose General from the menu and type the number of pages you want to print. Click on Print to print the document.

WINDOWS PRINTING OPTIONS

1. Choose Start/Settings/Printers from the Taskbar. Choose File/Document Setup and choose a printer from the Print Setup dialog box.

Tile Imageable Areas

Select this option to sub-divide the page into multiple pages (tiles) that display different parts of the image. This is a useful option for oversized pages.

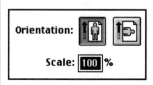

In the Page Setup dialog box (Macintosh), choose either Portrait (left) or Landscape (right) orientation. To reduce or enlarge the printed artwork, type a value less than or greater than 100 in the Scale field.

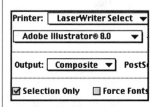

Choose Selection Only to print just the selected objects in the document. For example, if you want to proof just the text, select only the text objects before choosing the Print command.

Macintosh Keystrokes

⌘-O File/Open
⌘-P File/Print

Windows Keystrokes

Ctrl-O File/Open
Ctrl-P File/Print

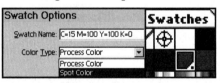

Choose Color/Grayscale to print in color or to print colors as grays instead of as solid black and white.

WINDOWS WARNING!

Any changes you make in the Properties dialog box at the desktop level affect how documents will print in all applications, not just in Illustrator.

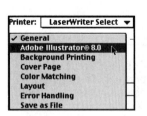

Use the menu in the Mac OS Print dialog box to access the Adobe Illustrator printing options.

2. In Illustrator, choose File/Document Setup. Click Print Setup and click Properties. Click the Paper tab. Choose a size from the Paper pop-up menu and select Portrait (vertical) or Landscape (horizontal) orientation.

3. Choose Color/Grayscale to print colors in shades of gray on a black-and-white printer. Choose the specific options for a color printer.

4. Type the number of copies you want to print and click OK.

EXERCISE A

1. Open the *Distort.ai* file in your Projects folder or navigate to the Unit 12 folder on the CD-ROM and select the file there (File/Open). Display the Swatches palette. Make sure the Fill icon is the active icon in the Toolbox.

2. Because this file will be printed as a composite (instead of being separated into the cyan, magenta, yellow, and black plates), the single color should be converted to a spot color. This way, if you ever decided to print this file to a commercial printer, only two plates would print, the black plate and the color plate. Select one of the distorted stars to display its fill and stroke colors in the Toolbox. Notice that the fill color is outlined in the Swatches palette. If it doesn't have a dot in the corner, it is a process color.

3. To convert the process color to a spot color, double-click on the swatch to display the Swatch Options dialog box. Use the Color Type menu to select Spot Color (Figure 21.3). Click on OK. The swatch now displays a dot in the corner, indicating that it is a spot color and will print on one plate instead of separating onto four plates. Deselect everything.

Figure 21.3. Use the Swatch Options dialog box to convert colors. The dot on the swatch indicates that it is a spot color.

4. Make sure the printer is turned on. Choose File/Document Info, and use the menus to check for fonts, linked images (there should be none), and spot colors (there should be one). Click on Done.

5. Choose File/Document Setup. Click Page Setup (Macintosh) or Properties (Windows). Select the appropriate options and click OK. Press Return/Enter. Choose File/Print (Command/Ctrl-P).

Choose Adobe Illustrator 8.0 (Macintosh). Choose Color Matching and select Color/Grayscale.

6. Choose General (Macintosh). Enter the desired number of copies and click Print (Macintosh) or OK (Windows) to print the file as composite artwork.

7. Close this file (Command/Ctrl-W). Save the changes, because they include all your printing options.

PRINTING COLOR SEPARATIONS

The first—and most important—rule of color printing is to talk to the printer about how to prepare your files. Only the printer knows how the press settings and software options must be synchronized to achieve optimum printing results.

The process of dividing an image into two or more colors is called *color separating*. The films from which the printing plates are created are called the *separations*. It is the separations, or film, that control the color fidelity of the final printed product.

PRINTING GRADIENTS AND MESH OBJECTS

If the artwork contains a gradient that contains process colors, that file will be separated and printed on the four CMYK plates. If the gradient blends from tints of the same spot color, however, that spot color will be separated on a single spot color plate.

If the gradient mesh object is composed of different tints of the same spot color, it will print on a single spot color plate. However, if different colors have been applied to the mesh object, the file will be separated on the four CMYK plates.

TRAPPING

Trapping is a method of compensating for gaps that appear when overlapping colors are printed on a printing press. Because presses shift, even slightly, gaps can appear when one color is printed on top of another color. By creating a small area of overlap, this gap between overlapping colors can be eliminated (Figure 21.4).

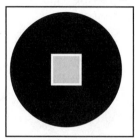

Figure 21.4. Notice the white paper showing through the gap between the black circle and the yellow square. Trapping will eliminate this gap.

Because the radial gradient object (left) and the gradient mesh object (right) were created with tints of the same spot color, that spot color will print on only one plate.

Page Size

The Page Size you select in the Separation Setup dialog box must match the Paper Size you select in Page Setup. Otherwise, output may be clipped.

FYI

You will not see the need for trapping or the effects of trapping on the screen or on laser printout, only on a high-resolution proof and, of course, in the final output.

Saving Document Info

Click the Save button in the Document Info dialog box to save the information in a text file that you and the printer can refer to. It's especially helpful to have a list of all the fonts in a document before printing.

If you linked or embedded an image in the Illustrator document, the Links palette will give you all the information you need to print the image properly.

Version 7

The Trap filter in version 7 is under the Object/ Pathfinder menu.

Double value

Double the assigned stroke value for a trap because Illustrator centers the stroke on the path. A 2-point stroke applied to a path results in 1 point of color on each side of the path.

SPREAD TRAPS AND CHOKE TRAPS

There are two kinds of traps, a spread trap and a choke trap. A spread trap extends or spreads the lighter object over the darker background. In Figure 21.4 a spread trap would be used to spread (extend) the yellow square (object) over the black circle (background).

A choke trap extends the lighter background color behind the darker foreground object (Figure 21.5). Regardless of the kind of stroke you apply, the foreground object overprints the background, creating a combination of the two colors where the object and background overlap.

Figure 21.5. A choke trap is used here to spread the lighter yellow background behind the darker object (circle).

TRAP COMMAND

The Trap command in the Pathfinder palette traps two objects, allowing you to set a Thickness value for the stroke and a percentage of the Height/Width field to specify the trap on horizontal lines as a percentage of the trap of vertical lines. By specifying different horizontal and vertical trap values, you can compensate for paper stretching on-press.

Before using the Trap command, talk to your printer about which values you should use. Every press is different and you will be applying different values for each press you work with.

EXERCISE B

1. In a new file (File/New), display the Pathfinder, Stroke, Attributes, and Swatches palettes. Use the drawing tools to draw a purple rectangle and a yellow circle. Make sure both colors are process colors. Move the circle (object) on top of the rectangle (background). Select both the circle and the rectangle and Option/Alt-drag to create a copy of the objects. You will work with the copy later. Save the file (File/Save As) in your Projects folder as *Trap Practice.ai*.

2. Select the lighter object (circle) and drag the Fill icon from the Toolbox to the bottom of the Swatches palette. Then apply that same yellow color as a stroke to the selected circle.

3. Assume that the printer told you to apply a 1-point trap. You should double that value for a trap in Illustrator, so make the stroke weight 2 points. Type 2 in the Weight field.

4. In the Attributes palette, select the Overprint Stroke option. This will blend the 1 point overlapping the background into the background, thus eliminating any gap between the objects (Figure 21.6). This is called a spread trap because the trap spreads out of the lighter object onto the darker background.

Select the Overprint Stroke option in the Attributes palette to cause the stroke to print over the darker background.

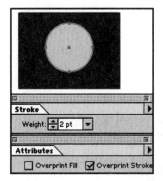

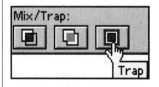

Figure 21.6. Apply a 2-point yellow stroke to the lighter foreground object (circle) and overprint it to create a 1-point trap that extends into the darker background.

5. Use the Selection tool to select the duplicate circle and rectangle. Make sure both objects are selected. Choose Show Options from the Pathfinder palette's menu. Click the Trap button, the last button in the last row, to display the Pathfinder Trap dialog box.

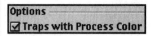

Select this option in the Pathfinder Trap dialog box to convert the custom (spot) colors to process colors.

6. Type 2 in the Thickness field. Leave the other values at their defaults and click on OK. Ordinarily, you would input the values your printer gives you. Illustrator creates a trap on the selected objects.

7. Choose File/Separation Setup. Select a PPD (PostScript Printer Description) file by clicking on the Open PPD button on the right side of the dialog box. Navigate to the Adobe Illustrator 8.0 folder on the hard drive, open the Utilities folder, open the Sample PPDs folder, and open the General PPD.

Click on this button to navigate to the folder with the printer description file for the printer you are using.

8. In the Options field, decide which layers to separate. In this case, select All Layers.

9. Notice that each separation is labeled with the color name that Illustrator assigned it. If the color displays a printer icon to the left of its name, that color will separate (Figure 21.7). Click on OK to return to the document.

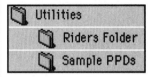

Sample PPDs are in the Utilities folder in the Adobe Illustrator folder.

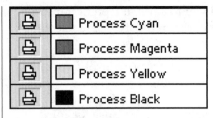

		Process Cyan
		Process Magenta
		Process Yellow
		Process Black

Figure 21.7. A printer icon next to a color specifies that a separation will be created for that color. Here, only four plates will print.

10. Choose File/Print. Select the Adobe Illustrator 8.0 option and use the Output menu to select Separate (Figure 21.8). Click on Print to print four pages, one for each plate.

11. Close this file. Don't save your changes.

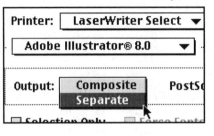

Process Magenta
Process Yellow
Process Black
Bubble Gum Pink

req.: 60 lpi Angle: 75

☑ Convert to Process

Select this option in the Separation Setup dialog box to separate individual spot colors as process colors. Click the printer icon next to the spot color to change the icon to the CMYK icon.

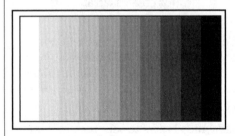

Printer: **LaserWriter Select** ▼

Adobe Illustrator® 8.0 ▼

Output: **Composite** **Separate** PostS

☐ Selection Only ☐ Force Fonts

Figure 21.8. You must select the Separate option to print the file on four separate plates. If you don't, the file will print as a composite.

TROUBLESHOOTING

Documents that contain gradients, gradient mesh objects, and color blends are sometimes difficult to print, especially if you have all of these objects in one document. When they do print, they frequently display *banding*, discrete bands of color where the color makes an abrupt transition from one shade to the next (Figure 21.9).

Figure 21.9. This grayscale blend displays banding where one shade of gray transitions into the next shade.

AVOID BANDING

To avoid problems with banding, use a blend, preferably a short blend, that changes at least 50% between two or more process colors. The higher the transition value, the smoother the blend. Any blend or gradient longer than 7.5 inches can cause you problems when printing.

Another way to avoid banding is to use lighter colors or make dark blends and short gradients. You're most likely to have printing problems when blending very dark colors to white.

LINESCREEN VALUES

Always use the appropriate line screen that retains all 256 levels of gray as another way to avoid banding. A higher linescreen decreases the levels of gray available to the printer. For example, if you are printing to an imagesetter at a resolution of 2400 dots per inch (dpi), using a line screen higher than 150 will result in fewer shades of gray and increase the possibility of banding. If you are printing to a laser printer with an output of 300 dpi, use a linescreen of 19. Use a linescreen of 38 when printing to a 600 dpi laser printer.

CROP MARKS

Crop marks specify where the printed page is trimmed and should be applied to artwork printed on an imagesetter. You can use Illustrator's Crop Marks command under the Object menu or you can create your own.

PRINTING OPTIONS

If you have trouble printing gradients, blends, and mesh objects, especially if you are printing to a PostScript Level 1 printer or even to a PostScript Level 2 printer, select the Compatible Gradient and Gradient Mesh Printing options in the Document Setup dialog box under the File menu. The optimum setup for printing gradient mesh objects is to use a printer or imagesetter running PostScript Level 3. Otherwise, Illustrator converts a gradient mesh object to a bitmap image when printing to an older PostScript Level 1 printer or to a JPEG image when printing to a Level 2 printer or imagesetter.

SERVICE BUREAU SECRET

Service bureaus and printers often save the Illustrator file as an Illustrator EPS file and import it into a QuarkXPress document instead of printing it directly from Illustrator. This allows them to take advantage of Quark's excellent—and far less complicated—color printing controls, but it also means that the EPS file must be trapped in Illustrator before it is imported into a Quark document.

Although you can't trap an Illustrator document in XPress, you can trap the EPS image to a background color in XPress by creating a trap stroke around the artwork (in Illustrator) that will spread into or be choked by the background color of the XPress picture box. As with all trapping in *any* application, talk to your printer—first!

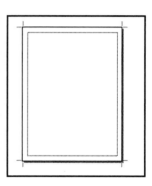

The crop marks appear on the corners of the page, indicating where the paper will be cut.

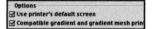

Select the Compatible gradient and gradient mesh printing option in the Document Setup dialog box only if you're having trouble printing gradient mesh objects.

1. Process color artwork is separated into the four process colors (cyan, magenta, yellow, and black), with each color printed on a separate plate.

2. Spot color is a single-ink color printed on one plate.

3. Continuous tone images, such as photographs, are printed as process colors.

4. When printing color separations, check with the printer before inputting values in the Separation Setup dialog box.

5. Gradients and gradient mesh objects will print as process colors if they contain process colors.

6. Gradients that blend from tints of the same spot color will be separated on a single spot color plate.

7. Trapping is a method of compensating for misregistration on press when one color overprints another color.

8. A spread trap extends the lighter object over the darker background.

9. A choke trap extends the lighter background behind the darker foreground object.

10. Banding is the appearance of discrete bands of color when one color in a blend, gradient, or gradient mesh makes a sharp transition into another color.

11. Avoid banding problems by using short blends and lighter colors in blends and gradients.

GLOSSARY

Action—a series of recorded commands that, when played back, are automatically executed.

Align—position objects horizontally and vertically in relation to their topmost, bottommost, or center points.

Anchor point—a point at the beginning and end of a segment. When the segment is selected, anchor points are visible. Anchor points appear hollow when deselected and filled when selected.

Anti-alias—when rasterizing artwork, this option smooths the jagged edges around the bitmap image.

Area (rectangle) type—type created inside, and therefore bounded by, an open or closed path; type created inside the boundary of a rectangle created by dragging the Type tool.

Arrange—position objects in front or behind other objects in the stacking order on a selected layer.

Art brush—a single art object specified as a brush in the Brushes palette that is stretched across an open or closed path with every stroke of the Paintbrush tool.

Artwork view (mode)—displays the art in only its path outlines without any fill or stroke attributes.

Auto Trace Tolerance—value from 0 to 10 that defines the number of pixels the Auto Trace tool traces or skips on a template. A value of 0 tells the Auto Trace tool to trace every pixel in the template. The higher the Auto Trace Tolerance value, the smoother the line to be traced or to be drawn with the Pencil tool.

Average command—reshapes open and/or closed paths by realigning their endpoints or any of their anchor points. Anchor points are not joined, just realigned on the horizontal or vertical axis, or on both axes.

Backmost object—the last painted object in the stacking order on any layer; any object to which the Arrange/Send to Back command is applied. See **stacking order**.

Banding—the appearance of discrete bands of colors in gradients, gradient mesh objects, or color blends.

Baseline—an imaginary line on which type sits. The baseline is displayed when type is selected with any of the selection tools, or when you click on the type tool used to create the text immediately after creating it.

Baseline shift—moving selected text characters above or below the **baseline**.

Bevel Join—where two connected endpoints appear to be slit diagonally across.

Bitmap art (raster art)—created in paint and image-editing programs such as Photoshop and Painter; use a grid of small squares, called pixels, to represent the image. This is the preferred format for continuous tone images, such as photographs.

Blend—multiple progression of shapes and/or colors between two open or two closed paths. Objects in a blend are evenly distributed between the two paths in a specified number of steps, at a specified distance, or in a combination of these to create a smooth color transition. When only colors are blended, the result is a **gradient fill**.

Blend object—any object selected with the Blend tool or to which the Make Blends command is applied.

Blend path—an editable straight path created between two blended objects.

Bounding Box—rectangular box around an object selected with the Selection tool. Drag any of the eight handles to resize the box or select the Free Transform tool to rotate the object outside any of the handles.

Bounding Rectangle—the rectangle surrounding artwork designated as a pattern tile.

Butt Cap—creates stroked lines with squared ends.

Calligraphic brush—creates paths or strokes paths with a brush that resemble strokes drawn with the angled point of a calligraphy pen; strokes are drawn along the center of the path with half the stroke width on either side of the path.

Cap—stroke attributes for lines: **Butt Cap** creates lines with squared ends; **Round Cap** strokes lines with semicircular ends; and **Projecting Cap** strokes lines with squared ends that extend half the line width beyond the end of the line.

Center point—a point at the center of an object created with a rectangle or ellipse tool. Use the center point to drag an object to align an object with other art elements. The center point can be made visible or invisible via the Attributes palette, but cannot be deleted.

Choke trap—where the the lighter background "squeezes" itself under the darker object that overlaps the background.

Clipboard—an area of memory reserved for holding anything that is copied or cut with the Copy and Cut commands. Once artwork or text is cut or copied, the new artwork or text overwrites the existing artwork or text on the Clipboard.

Clipping path—selected pixels saved as a clipping path in Photoshop. When the image is placed as an EPS image in Illustrator, only the pixels saved as a clipping path in Photoshop are displayed.

Closed path—a group of connected segments or **shape**.

CMYK sliders—on the Color palette, used to adjust the cyan, magenta, yellow, and black percentages of the active process color.

Color separations—a printing option that produces a separate page or printing plate

for each of the four process colors, and for any specified spot colors, as opposed to printing a **composite**.

Color Stop—a square below the gradient bar indicating the point at which a gradient changes from one color to the next. When selected, its "roof" turns black, indicating that its color, and therefore the gradient color, can be changed.

Command parameter—any value recorded in an action that affects how a command is executed. For example, the size of an object or its degree of rotation is a command parameter.

Composite—a printing option that prints a document as one full page instead of printing **color separations**.

Compound paths—two or more overlapping paths painted, filled, and/or stroked that are transparent against the page where those paths overlap.

Constrain—when drawing with the Rectangle or Ellipse tool, creates a square or circle; when drawing with the Pen tool, creates a straight horizontal line or a line at a 45° angle; when rotating, constrains the angle of rotation to 45°.

Continuous curve—curves connected by smooth points.

Copy—command that places the selected text or artwork on the **Clipboard** without removing it from the document. Anything copied can be pasted back into the document.

Corner point—created (1) by clicking without dragging with the Pen tool to establish the corner between two straight segments of a path; (2) clicking a smooth point with the Convert Direction Point tool. Used to connect **noncontinuous curves**.

Custom color—a single, premixed color such as a Pantone or Trumatch color with a particular name or number and specified as a spot color. Custom **spot colors** print on separate plates.

Cut—to delete a selection from the artwork. Cut objects, text or art, are placed on the

Clipboard and can be pasted back into the document. See **Paste**.

Dash/Gap fields—in the Stroke palette, where you input values that determine the size of the dashed line in the Dash field and the space between the dashes in the Gap field.

Default Colors icon—in the Toolbox, displays the default fill and stroke colors, a white fill and black stroke.

Default settings—settings contained in the Preferences file that determine which palettes are displayed and which command settings are active when you launch Illustrator. Each time you quit Illustrator, the position of the palettes and certain command settings are recorded in that Preferences file.

Direct Selection tool—used to select individual segments and anchor points on a path; designated in the Toolbox by a white arrow.

Direction handles—appear when a segment connected to a smooth point is selected with the Direct Selection tool, or when a **smooth point** is selected. Drag a handle to reshape the segment.

Direction point—appears at the top of a direction handle and is used to drag the direction handle.

Discretionary hyphen—manually inserted between text characters, which disappears if the text flow changes and the hyphenated word will fit on the line. Created by clicking where you want to insert the hyphen and pressing Command-Shift-hyphen (Macintosh) or Ctrl-Shift-hyphen (Windows) when any text tool is active.

Distribute—positions objects along the horizontal or vertical axis or evenly distributes the space between objects horizontally or vertically.

Embedded image—an image placed at its current resolution in an Illustrator document and which becomes part of the file, as opposed to a linked image, which places only a screen version of the image.

Encapsulated PostScript (EPS)—file format combining the PostScript page description language with a low-resolution preview image; required format for importing Illustrator artwork into many other applications, such as PageMaker and QuarkXPress.

Endpoints—anchor points at the beginning and end of an open path.

Fill—paint attributes applied to an open or closed path.

Filter—a plug-in application used for applying special effects to both vector and raster art in Illustrator.

Flatten Artwork—command that merges all the visible layers into the bottommost layer and deletes any hidden layers.

Font family—the complete set of characters in one style for a specific typeface. Helvetica, with all its special upper- and lower-case characters, is a font family; Helvetica Bold is a style of Helvetica.

Frontmost object—the most recently painted object in the **stacking order** on any layer; any object to which the Arrange/Bring to Front command is applied.

GIF (Graphics Interchange Format)—a non-lossy export image compression format appropriate for images created with large areas of flat color that are used on Web pages.

Gradient fill—a graduated linear or radial blend between two or more colors. The Gradient tool is used to modify the direction and/or the starting and ending point of a gradient fill across single or multiple objects.

Gradient slider—on the Gradient palette, displays Color Stops and Midpoint diamonds used to apply and edit the colors in a gradient.

Group—two or more combined objects that can be moved, painted, and transformed as one unit.

Group Selection tool—used for selecting a group of objects by clicking on any object in the group to select the first object; click again to select the rest of the objects in the group; click again to select another entire group of objects in the illustration. Designated by a white arrow and + in the Toolbox.

Guide object—a guide created from an object by using the Make Guide command. Guide objects have no fill or stroke attributes.

Hatch settings (hatch effects)—the options associated with a particular hatch.

Hatch style—the vector art used by the Pen & Ink filter to fill a selected object.

Include Placed Files—option in the Save As dialog box. When selected, placed images are embedded in the Illustrator document and are available for preview and printing in other applications such as PageMaker, Photoshop, and QuarkXPress.

Join command—connects two endpoints of two different paths.

JPEG (Joint Photographic Experts Group)—a lossy export compression format suitable for continuous tone images such as photographs.

Kerning—adding and/or deleting space between two text characters. A positive number in the Kerning field of the Character palette increases space between characters; a negative number reduces space.

Layer—a specified level in the artwork that allows objects on that layer to be displayed, edited, locked, and printed.

Leading—the vertical white space between lines of type. Leading is measured in points from one **baseline** to the baseline of the line of type above or below it in a paragraph.

Letter spacing—the space between text characters in a selected paragraph, measured as a percent of the width of a space in that type size. Justified text defaults to 100% minimum, 100% desired, and 200% maximum. At 100%, no additional space is added between words.

Ligatures—The *ff, fi,* or *fl* letters combined into a single character such as *ff, fi,* or *fl.*

Line—a straight or curve segment between two endpoints; an **open path**.

Linked image—image placed as a screen version in the Illustrator document and linked to the high-resolution version of the image, which it accesses when the file is printed.

Lock/Unlock—Object menu command or Layers palette option that prevents objects and/or layers from being selected and edited.

Mask (masking object)—an object placed over other artwork like a stencil and that prevents any objects not overlapping it from being previewed or printed. Any object covered by the mask (masked object) will preview and print. The mask is always the frontmost object in the **stacking order**.

Masked object—any object covered by a mask. Masked objects can be previewed and will print.

Merge Layers—combines the contents of all selected layers into the topmost layer on the Layers palette. Objects on that single layer retain their stacking order from the original layers.

Mesh lines—crisscross lines that appear on a mesh object. Where those mesh lines cross, **mesh points** are created.

Mesh object—any object on which the Gradient Mesh tool has been used or to which the Create Gradient Mesh command has been applied. A gradient mesh object displays mesh lines connected by mesh points to which different colors can be applied.

Mesh point—diamond-shaped anchor points connecting **mesh lines** and used to hold color, thus creating a gradient mesh.

Mesh segment—the area enclosed by four mesh points.

Midpoint diamond—in the Gradient palette, indicates where two adjacent colors are of equal intensity.

Miter Join—when two connected endpoints on a stroked line meet in a corner.

Miter Limit—a value that determines when the corner's join angle changes from mitered/pointed to a beveled squared-off join. The default Miter Limit of 4 specifies that when the length of the point reaches four times the weight of the stroke, Illustrator changes from a miter join to a bevel join. A Miter Limit of 1 creates a bevel join.

Modal Control—a breakpoint in an action which stops the action and displays a dialog box where you enter command parameters.

Modifier keys—used in conjunction with clicking and dragging to execute commands. For example, pressing the Option/Alt modifier key while dragging an object creates a duplicate of that object. Likewise, pressing the Shift modifier key while dragging with the Rectangle tool creates a square.

Noncontinuous curve—curve created by adding a corner point to change the direction of a curve.

None button—in the Toolbox and on the Color palette, removes any fill or stroke from the selected object.

Object—a line or shape that can be isolated and manipulated independently of other objects in the illustration. Objects can be artwork and text blocks.

Open path—a path with two endpoints. An open path does not have a segment connecting the first and last segments in the path; any segment or segments existing between two endpoints; a **line**.

Overflow Indicator—a plus sign in the side of a type container or on an open text path, which appears when you create or import more type than will fit on or inside that path.

Paste—command that pastes the contents of the Clipboard as the frontmost object on the page.

Paste in Back—pastes the contents of the Clipboard behind the selected object.

Paste in Front—pastes the contents of the Clipboard in front of the selected object.

Paste Remembers Layers—option on the Layers palette that pastes objects onto the layer from which they were copied. If that original layer was deleted or merged, a layer is created and the objects are pasted onto that new layer.

Path—a single segment or any number of connected segments.

Path pattern—designed to stroke a path using inner and outer corner tiles and applied perpendicular to the path.

Path type—type placed along an open or closed path.

Pathfinder—one of several commands available from the Pathfinder palette, used to merge, split, divide, or trim specific paths in overlapping objects.

Pattern—tile created from artwork used as fill and stroke attributes. Patterns fill and/or stroke paths.

Pattern brush—individual tiles that repeat along a path created by (1) dragging with the Paintbrush tool or (2) being applied as a stroke to a selected path.

PDF (Portable Document Format)—an export format that embeds fonts and graphics; suitable for electronic publishing.

Plug-ins—ancillary software programs that are "plugged-in" to a main program such as Illustrator and add features to the main program. Plug-ins are created by Adobe and other software developers.

Point of Origin—a fixed point on an object from which the transformation occurs. The default is the object's center point.

Point type—type created with the Type tool anywhere on the drawing page; point type is not connected to any path.

Preview view (mode) the artwork's fill and stroke attributes.

Process color—an ink in which the color is based on a percentage of any or all of the four process colors (cyan, magenta, yellow, and black).

Projecting Cap—strokes lines with squared ends that extend half the line width beyond the end of the line. This option makes the line's stroke weight extend equally in all directions around the line.

Raster image—a bitmap image created from pixels on a horizontal and vertical grid in a program such as Photoshop. Continuous tone images such as photographs are bitmap images. When vector art in Illustrator is rasterized, the PostScript lines and curves are converted to pixels.

Reflect—create a mirror image of a selected object or path segment over a specified axis with the Reflect tool.

Revert—goes to the last saved version of the file. Using the Revert command does not give you the option of saving changes.

Rotate—rotate a selected object or path segment a specified number of degrees from a specified point on the object with the Rotate tool.

Round Cap—strokes lines with semicircular ends.

Round Join—where the corner formed by two connected endpoints is rounded.

Ruler guide—nonprinting guide accessed from the horizontal and vertical rulers.

Ruler origin—the zero point at the intersection of the horizontal and vertical rulers; the point from which all measurements are taken.

Save—command that saves the current file with the same name in the same format at the same location as the previously saved file, which it overwrites.

Save a Copy—saves a copy of a file without touching the original file.

Save As—allows you to save a file under another name, at another location, and in another format.

Scale—enlarging or reducing the size of a selected object or path segment from a specified point with the Scale tool.

Scatter brush—brush that places artwork at a specified distance (1) when applied as a stroke to selected paths, or (2) when a path is drawn with the Paintbrush tool.

Segment—a line or curve existing between two anchor points.

Selection tool—used to select a whole path or an entire object by clicking on any point on the path or on any path segment; designated in the Tool palette as a black arrow. When the Selection tool is on an anchor point, a white box appears next to the tool icon. When the Selection tool is on a path segment, a black box appears next to the tool icon.

Separations—color art that is separated into the four process colors (cyan, magenta, yellow, and black). Each of the four process colors separates, or prints, on a separate printing plate.

Set—a folder in the Actions palette used to hold different actions.

Shape—a group of connected segments; a closed path. Because they are closed paths, shapes do not have endpoints.

Shear—skewing or slanting a selected object or path segment horizontally, vertically, or along a specified angle with the Shear tool.

Shift-select—to select an object, press the Shift key and select another object. When Shift-selecting, clicking on a selected object deselects that object.

Skew—slant an object at a specified angle.

Slice—command that cuts overlapping objects in a designated shape, using the selected object as a cookie cutter or stencil to cut through other objects and create discrete shapes, discarding the original selection. This command works only on ungrouped objects.

Smart Guides—nonprinting guidelines that help you create, align, and edit objects in relation to other objects on the page. Smart Guides display tips, such as *center* and *45˚*, to let you know exactly how the object is being created or moved.

Smooth point—anchor point on a straight line between two symmetrical direction handles. Smooth points create a continuous arc and connect curve segments; created by clicking and dragging with the Pen tool or with the Convert Direction Point tool.

Spectrum Bar—on the Color palette, is used to select a CMYK color. The selected process color appears in the Toolbox and Color palette icons and can be converted to a spot color.

Spot color—a custom premixed color printed with one ink of that color. Spot colors print on their own separate plates. See **custom color**.

Spread trap—where the lighter object overlapping a darker background expands into the background.

Stacking order—the order in which objects are drawn, which determines how they are displayed when they overlap. The first object drawn becomes the frontmost object until another object is drawn on top of or overlapping it. That first object then becomes the backmost object in the stacking order and the most recently drawn object becomes the frontmost object in the stacking order.

Stroke—paint attributes applied to the outline of an open or closed path.

Swap Colors icon—in the Toolbox, exchanges the fill and stroke colors.

Template—dimmed bitmapped image which, when placed with the Place command and the Template option selected, appears in the background of the illustration on a separate layer, and can be traced with the Auto Trace tool or with any of the drawing tools. Templates cannot be selected, edited, or printed.

Text object—any type selected with the Selection tool, and which is manipulated or transformed like an art object instead of being edited like text.

Text outlines—created with the Create Outlines command only when the Type 1 or TrueType font is installed for that typeface; converts text characters into compound paths that can be edited and manipulated just like any other graphic object; retains all formatting and paint attributes of the selected type; converts the entire text block, not selected text characters.

Text path—any open or closed path on which type is created using the Path Type tool.

Tint Ramp—on the Color palette, appears when a spot color is selected; displays an Eyedropper to select a tint percentage of the spot color that appears in the Toolbox and Color palette icons; can be saved as an individual spot color swatch.

Tint Slider—on the Color palette, appears when a spot color is selected; is dragged to select a percentage tint of the spot color that appears in the Toolbox and Color palette icons; can be saved as an individual spot color swatch.

Tracing Gap—value from 0 to 2 that defines the number of black pixels the Auto Trace tool will trace. This setting tells the Auto Trace tool to ignore gaps that are equal to or less than the number of pixels you specify. For example, setting the Tracing Gap value to 1 tells the Auto Trace tool to ignore gaps of 1 pixel or less. A value of 0 tells the Auto Trace tool not to skip any black pixels whose corners touch, even when a white pixel exists between them.

Tracking—adding and/or deleting space between all the characters and the space between words in a selected range of text. A positive number in the Tracking field or selected from the Tracking menu on the Character palette adds space; a negative number removes space.

Transform—to move, reflect, rotate, shear, or scale a selected object or group.

Trapping—the process of creating small areas of overlap between overlapping colors to compensate for misregistration on press.

Type container—any closed path in which type is created using the Area Type tool.

Vector art—created by mathematical algorithms using the PostScript page description language. Unlike raster art, vector art can be transformed without losing detail.

Vertical type—flows from top to bottom instead of from left to right.

Word spacing—the space between words in a selected paragraph measured as a percent of the width of a space in that type size. To change the amount of space between words in a line of type, enter minimum, desired, and maximum values in the Word Spacing text boxes. If the text is not justified, only the Desired field is available. For justified type, the default values for word spacing are 100% minimum, 100% desired, and 200% maximum. At 100%, no additional space is added between words.

INDEX

A

Acrobat PDF format, 324–25
  file icon, 330
Actions, 276–93
  command parameters, 278
  commands, 276, 278
  deactivate commands, 289
  default, 288
  delete, 283
  duplicate, 288
  edit, 276, 288
  Options dialog box, 290
  playing, 287
  record new action, 277, 279–80
  saving and loading, 282
  sets, 276, 277
  slowing, 288, 289
  stopping, 287, 292
Actions palette, 277
  check marks, 289
  palette commands, 279
  viewing modes, 278
Adaptive Color palette, 329
Add Anchor Point tool, 134, 135, 136
  blend path, 207, 212
Add Anchor Points command, 136, 137
Add Arrowheads dialog box, 281
Add Space to Fit button, Pattern Brush Options dialog box, 85
Add to Swatches, 67
Align palette, 201
Align to Page option, Blends Option dialog box, 216
Aligning objects, 201
  Smart Guides, 15
Alignment, paragraph, 234–35
Anchor points, 22, 24
  add, 135, 136
  convert, 136

delete, 136
display/hide, 22
moving, 28
selected (solid), 23, 24, 25, 124
selecting, 27, 28
unselected (hollow), 26, 124
Anchor Points option
  Blend tool, 207
  Scribble and Tweak dialog box, 200
Angle field, Gradient palette, 94
Angle value, Brush Options dialog box, 80
Anti-Alias option
  JPEG Options dialog box, 328
  Photoshop Options dialog box, 334
  Rasterize Options dialog box, 312
Appearance menu, Create Gradient Mesh dialog box, 107
Area Select, 13, 20, 27, 72, 250, 302
Area Type cursor, 224, 233
Area type tool, 232–33
Arrange menu, 121, 203
  text wrap, 245
Art brushes, 79, 83–84
  Add Space to Fit option, 85
  Flip buttons, 85
  Options dialog box, 83
Artwork
  duplicating between layers, 147
  exporting, 327
Artwork view, 6, 16
Attributes palette
  Center Point, 115
  Overprint Stroke, 345
  Reverse Path Direction, 301
  Show Note, 286
  URL linking, 328
Auto Hyphenate, 262
Auto Trace Tolerance, 76, 162
Auto Trace tool, 162
Average command, 30–31

B

Banding, 346
   troubleshooting, 346–47
Baseline, 220, 221
   display, 223
   leading, 222
Baseline Shift, 244, 257, 300
Basic shapes, 39–49
   moving, 49
   specify dimensions, 45–49
   tools, 40–49
Begin Recording button, Actions palette, 285
Bitmap filters, 310
   brushes, 79
Blend command, 213
Blend Options dialog box, 207, 208
   Align to Page option, 216
Blend path, 206
Blend tool, 207
Blending objects, 205–17
   delete, 213
   dissimilar paths, 212
   expand, 213
   gradient mesh objects, 206
   open paths, 208–9
   release, 215
   Reverse Spine, 216
   rules, 207
   similar closed paths, 211–12
   stroke, 217
   troubleshooting, 215
Bounding Box, 13
   reset, 184
   resizing text objects, 223, 231
   resizing type containers, 225
   resizing with, 14, 182
   turning on and off, 23
Bounding Rectangle (patterns), 115
Breakpoints (Modal Controls), 283
Bring Forward command, 203
Bring to Front command, 203
Brush libraries, 79, 89
Brush patterns for paths, 118
Brushes
   Art, 79, 83–84
   Calligraphic, 79
   creating, 79–80
   expand, 90

   grayscale, 87
   Options dialog boxes, 80–81
   Pattern, 79, 84–85
   Scatter, 79
   troubleshooting, 79, 82
Brushes palette, 78–79
   adding brushes, 79
   Art, 79, 83–84
   Bitmaps, 79
   Brushes, 78
   Calligraphic, 80–81
   converting to art, 87
   names, 79
   new brushes, 79
   Pattern, 79, 84–85
   removing brush strokes, 87
   Scatter, 81–82
Brushing paths, 78
Button mode, Actions palette, 278

C

Calligraphic brushes, 79, 80–81
Cap options, Stroke palette, 61
CD-ROM, 9
Center point, 24, 35
   display, 42, 115, 180
   moving and deleting, 40
   selecting with Direct Selection tool, 26
Character palette, 221–22, 254
Check marks, Actions palette, 289
Check Spelling, 269, 271
Choke traps, 344
Circles and squares, drawing, 41, 58
Circular type paths, 243–45
Clear command, 24, 86
Clipboard, 86, 142
Clipping paths, 336
Close files, 8
   palettes, 18
Closed paths, reshape, 127
CMYK color, 57
CMYK sliders, moving in tandem, 60
CMYK Spectrum, 58
   gradients, 98
Collapse, palettes, 18
Color. *See also* Colors
   active, 55
   adding to Swatches palette, 58

D

Dashed/dotted lines, Stroke palette, 61, 62
Deactivate
    Blend tool, 207
    commands, Actions palette, 289
    Pen tool, 125, 126
Decay field, Spiral tool, 48
Default Colors icon, 36, 53
Default preferences, 19
Default Swatch library, 65
Default tool values, 40, 43
    actions, 288
Define Pattern command, 112, 117
Delete
    actions, 283
    Color Stop, 103
    colors, 56
    empty text paths, 242
    gradients, 99
    layers, 145
    objects, 12
    pattern, 114
    ruler guides, 167
    swatches, 114
    tabs, 267, 268
Delete Anchor Point tool, 137
Desaturate colors, 60
Deselect All command, 25, 71
    objects, 12, 26
Desired value, Paragraph palette, 265
Diameter value, Calligraphic Brush Options
    dialog box, 80
Dim Image option, Layers palette, 146
Dimensions, specifying for basic shape tools, 45
Direct Selection tool, 12, 26
    black square and white square (cursor), 24, 249
    center point, 26
    dragging selection marquee, 30
    edit pattern, 114
    mesh objects, 106, 109
    moving direction handles, 34
    selecting anchor points, 23, 27, 28, 136
    selecting entire path, 23
    selecting segments, 25, 26, 27
    selecting text paths, 240
    troubleshooting, 185
Direction handles, 34, 128, 135
    move, 132

Direction options, Art Brush Options dialog
    box, 83
Discretionary hyphens, 263
Dispersion, Hatch Effects dialog box, 315
Dispersion Noise, Photo Crosshatch dialog
    box, 318
Display options, palettes, 17
Distort filters, 194
Distribute commands, 202
Dithering, GIF89a Options dialog box, 329
Divide, Pathfinder filter, 305
Document Info, 340
    save, 344
Document Setup dialog box (Macintosh), 342
Drag and drop color, 59
Drag-copying from Illustrator to Photoshop,
    331–32, 335
Drawing, from the center, 41
Drawing area, 5
Duplicate Layer command, 147
Duplicating
    actions, 288
    between layers, 147
    colors, 56
    layers, 145
    objects, 41, 74, 89, 119, 169
    paths, 131
    pattern swatches, 113

E

Edges (selection), hiding, 129
Edit
    actions, 276, 288
    blends, 206
    hidden layers, 151
    masks, 296
    mesh objects, 106, 107, 108
    paths, 131
    patterns, 113
    process color, 58
    text paths, 233, 241
Ellipse tool, 40
    options, 45
    specifying dimensions, 45
Embed icon, Links palette, 321
Embedded images, 163, 320
    Links palette, 344
Endpoints, 29, 47

EPS, saving files, 326–27
Erase tool, 76
Expand command, 90, 103
    blends, 214
    brushes, 90
    mesh objects, 107
Export
    formats, 157, 158, 324, 334
    layers to Photoshop, 157, 334
    text, 324
    word-processor formats, 330
Eyedropper tool, 70, 73
    options, 71
    type attributes, 226–27

F

Fade menu, Hatch Effects dialog box, 315
Fidelity value, Paintbrush tool, 78
Files
    open and close, 8
    save, 8, 325-26
Fill and stroke, 52
    applying, 53
    icons, 14, 58, 213
    multiple objects, 53
    switching, 54, 72
    troubleshooting, 54
Fill paths, 52
Filters
    bitmap, 310, 311, 312
    display last filter, 199
    Distort, 194
    Hard Mix, 73
    Hatch Effects, 313–18
    Pen and Ink, 313–19
    plug-ins, 310
    Punk & Bloat, 195, 199
    Roughen, 195, 199
    Scribble and Tweak, 195–96, 200
    Soft Mix, 73–74
    transformation, 194–201
    vector, 310, 311
    Zig Zag, 196, 200
Find/Change command, text, 269
Find Font command, 269, 271
Fit Headline command, 233
Flatness option, Clipping Path dialog box, 336
Flip buttons, Brush Options dialog box, 85

Flipping type on a path, 242
Fonts
    Create Outlines command, 247
    name, 254
    size, 254
Formats (saved files), Illustrator, 36, 42
Free Transform tool, 181, 186, 189
    reflecting objects, 187
Freehand drawing and painting tools, 75–77

G

General Preferences dialog box, 13, 19
    Bounding Box option, 13
    Keyboard Increments, 173–74
    Paste Remembers Layers option, 142
    transforming patterns, 116
    Use Precise Cursors, 20
Geometric patterns, 116
GIF89a export format, 329–31
Gradient button, Toolbox, 53, 95, 96
Gradient dragging, 95–96
Gradient Mesh
    cursors, 107
    objects, 103, 104, 105
    printing, 343
    tool, 103–105
Gradient Mesh tool, 103–105
    adding mesh lines, 108
Gradient slider, Gradient palette, 100, 101, 102
Gradient tool, 95–96
    creating gradients, 98–99
    selecting, 95
Gradients, 93–109
    add to Swatches palette, 98
    apply color, 101
    apply color from artwork, 102
    custom, 98
    delete, 99
    multi-colored, 100
    printing, 343
    save, 99, 100
    troubleshooting, 101
Grayscale, brushes, 87
Grids, 176–78, 215
    Guides & Grid Preferences, 176, 177
    Snap to Grid, 176
    style, 130, 176

Index

T

Tab Ruler, 267
Tabs, 265–66
    deleting, 267, 268
    troubleshooting, 268
Tearoff palettes, 7, 40, 197
Templates, 155
    icon, 156
    Layer Options, 156
    layers, 163
Text. *See also* Type
    aligning, 234–35
    exporting, 324
    importing, 234
    word processor formats, 330
Text block (object), selecting, 220
    resize/reshape, 240–41
Text containers. *See* type containers
Text layers, Photoshop, 158
Text paths, editing, 233, 241
    masks, 298
    selecting, 240
Text wrap, 245–46
    troubleshooting, 246
Thickness
    Hatch Effects dialog box, 315
    Pathfinder Trap dialog box, 345
    Photo Crosshatch dialog box, 319
Thumbnails, 327, 330
TIFF images, placed in Illustrator, 311
Tile buttons, Pattern Brush Options dialog
    box, 84, 85
Tint Ramp, Color palette, 57, 61
Tint Slider, Color palette, 60, 61, 62
Tints, Colorization option, 87
Tints and Shades, Colorization option, 87
Title bar, 5
    palettes, 17, 18
Tool Tips, 8, 20
Toolbox, 9–10
    basic shape tools, 40–44
    buttons, 53
    Color button, 57
    cycling through tools, 8
    Default Colors icon, 36
    default values for tools, 40
    illustration windows, 7
    keyboard shortcuts, 8

    restore default tools, 44
    selecting tools, 7
    switch fill and stroke colors, 54
Tools
    Area Type, 232–33
    Auto Trace, 162
    Blend, 207
    Direct Selection, 12, 26
    Ellipse, 40
    Erase, 76
    Eyedropper, 70, 73
    Gradient Mesh tool, 103–105
    Gradient tool, 95
    Group Selection, 12–13
    Knife tool, 32
    Paint Bucket, 227
    Paintbrush tool, 77–78
    Path Type, 238
    Pen, 121–37
    Pencil, 75–76
    Polygon, 44
    Rectangle, 41
    Rotate, 84–85
    Scale, 181
    Scissors, 31, 132
    selecting, 7
    selection, 12, 26
    Shear, 189
    Smooth, 76
    Spiral, 44
    Star, 33, 43
Tracing Gap value, 163
Tracing objects, 161–63
    part of a shape, 165–66
Tracking, 256
Transform commands, 186–89
    Transform Again command, 31, 184–97
    Transform Each command, 186–87
Transform palette, 196
Transform Pattern Tiles option, 116
Transformation
    filters, 193–200
    tools, 179–91
Transforming
    objects, 180
    patterns, 116
    point of origin, 180, 181
    type and type containers, 248–49
Transparency, 73
Transparency option, GIF89a Options dialog

Limited Warranty

System Requirements

Macintosh

CPU Type and Speed: Macintosh computer with a 68030 or greater processor (Power Macintosh® recommended)

Operating System: Apple ® System Software version 7.1 or later (7.1.2 or later for Power Macintosh)

Memory: 16 MB of RAM (32 MB recommended)

Hard Drive Space: 20 MB

Graphics: 8-bit (256 colors) or greater display adapter

CD-ROM Speed: 2x or better CD-ROM drive

Windows

CPU Type and Speed: Intel 486 ™, Windows NT (version 3.5.1 or later)

Memory: 16 MB of RAM (32 MB recommended)

Hard Drive Space: 25 MB

Graphics: 8-bit (256-color) or greater display adapter

CD-ROM Speed: 2x or better CD-ROM drive